SHISHIDO SHIHO
SHISHIDO SHIROU

This childhood friend of Youko's is a nympho. When she sees the moon, she transforms into the wolfman Shishido Shirou (male body and all), and that dude is in love with Youko. Her mother is a nympho icon.

CHANGE!!

ACTUALLY FROM THE FUTURE

ACTUALLY A WOLFMAN

KIRYUIN RIN

Came from fifty years in the future to save the world from the clutches of a nympho tyrant. Now she's a refugee who can't return home because she told Asahi (among others) about the future. Asahi's granddaughter.

I am...

KOUMOTO AKANE

HORNED DEVIL

The principal of Asahi's high school *looks* adorable, but she's actually a **millennia-old devil**. The great-great- grandmother of Asahi's homeroom teacher, Koumoto-sensei. Her true weakness is junk food.

ACTUALLY AN ANGEL

SHIROGANE KAREN

The student council president of Asahi's school. She lost her halo to one of the principal's practical jokes and thus became a (self-proclaimed) **fallen angel**. Was a classmate of Shiragami-san's parents.

KOUMOTO AKARI

The teacher in charge of Asahi's class. Although she's a descendant of the principal Akane, she has no demon powers of her own. Formerly a gangster, currently single.

FORMER GANGSTER

THEM

ASAHI'S WORTHLESS FRIENDS

SHIMADA

SAKURADA

OKADA

SEVEN SEAS ENTERTAINMENT PRESENTS

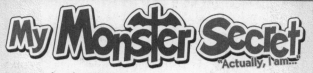

My Monster Secret

"Actually, I am..."

story and art by Eiji Masuda

VOLUME 10

TRANSLATION
Alethea and Athena Nibley

ADAPTATION
Rebecca Scoble

LETTERING AND LAYOUT
Annaliese Christman

LOGO DESIGN
Karis Page

COVER DESIGN
Nicky Lim

PROOFREADER
Shanti Whitesides
Danielle King

ASSISTANT EDITOR
Jenn Grunigen

PRODUCTION ASSISTANT
CK Russell

PRODUCTION MANAGER
Lissa Pattillo

EDITOR IN CHIEF
Adam Arnold

PUBLISHER
Jason DeAngelis

JITSUHA WATASHIHA Volume 10

Originally published in Japan in 2015 by Akita Publishing Co., Ltd.
English translation rights arranged with Akita Publishing Co., Ltd.
through TOHAN CORPORATION, Tokyo.

ISBN: 978-1-626927-24-7

Printed in Canada

First Printing: April 2018

10 9 8 7 6 5 4 3 2 1

READING DIRECTIONS

This book reads from ***right to left***, Japanese style. If this is your first time reading manga, you start reading from the top right panel on each page and take it from there. If you get lost, just follow the numbered diagram here. It may seem backwards at first, but you'll get the hang of it! Have fun!!

1
2
3
4
5
6
7
8
9

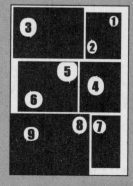

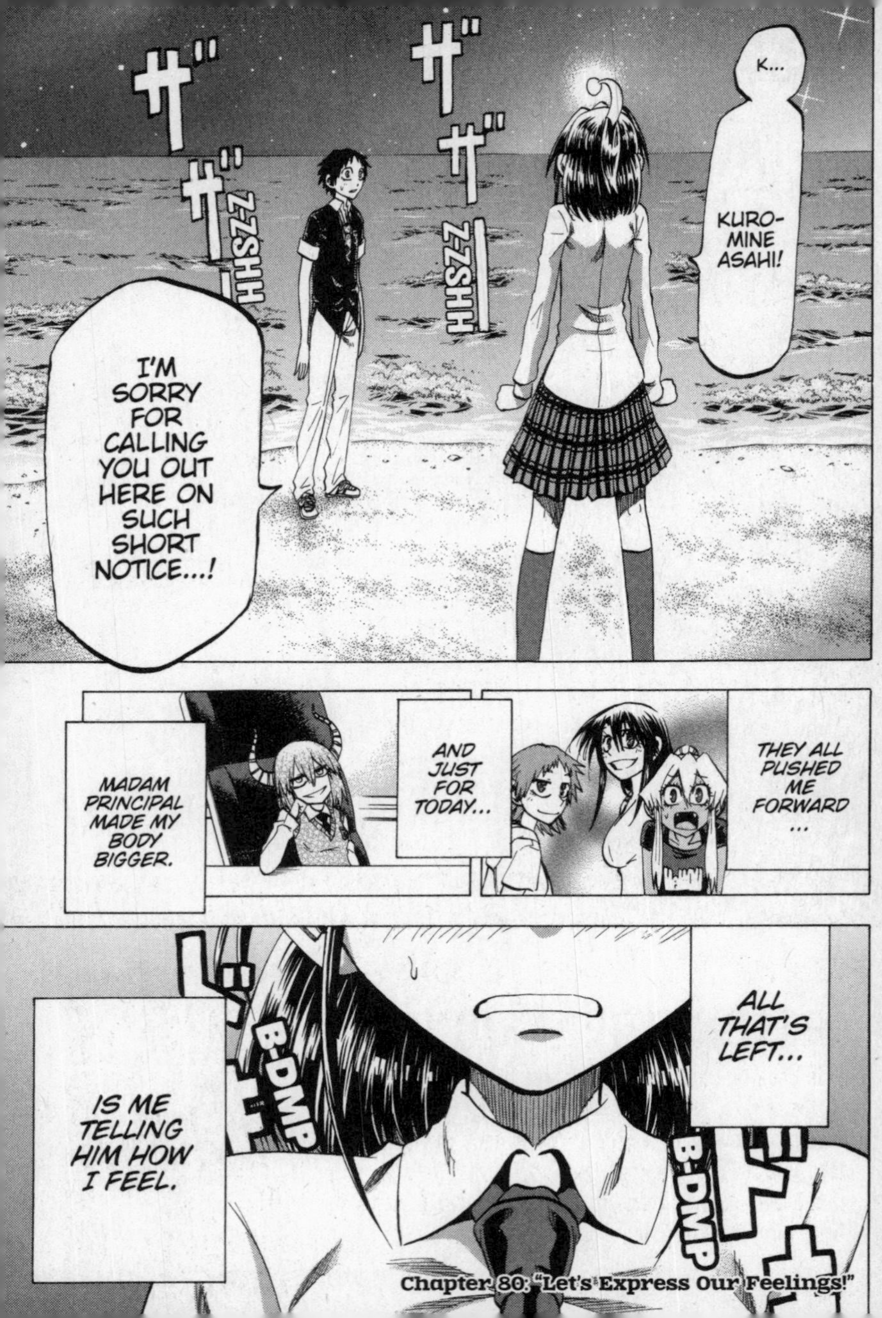
K...
KURO-MINE ASAHI!
Z-ZSHH
Z-ZSHH
I'M SORRY FOR CALLING YOU OUT HERE ON SUCH SHORT NOTICE...!
THEY ALL PUSHED ME FORWARD...
AND JUST FOR TODAY...
MADAM PRINCIPAL MADE MY BODY BIGGER.
ALL THAT'S LEFT...
B-DMP
B-DMP
IS ME TELLING HIM HOW I FEEL.

Chapter 80: “Let's Express Our Feelings!”

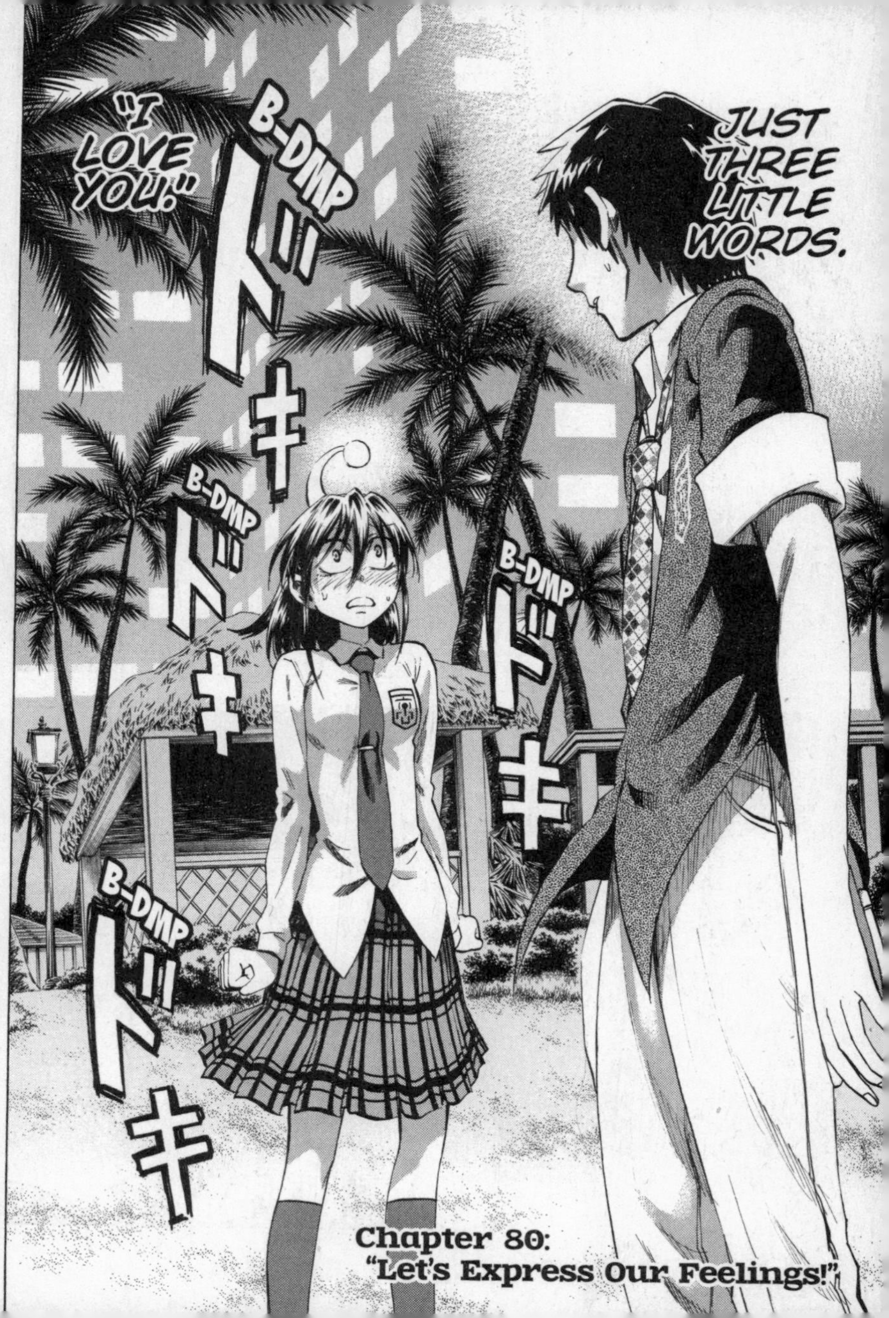
JUST THREE LITTLE WORDS.
"I LOVE YOU."
B-DMP
ドッ
キ
B-DMP
ドッ
キ
B-DMP
ドッ
キ
B-DMP
ドッ
キ
Chapter 80:
"Let's Express Our Feelings!"

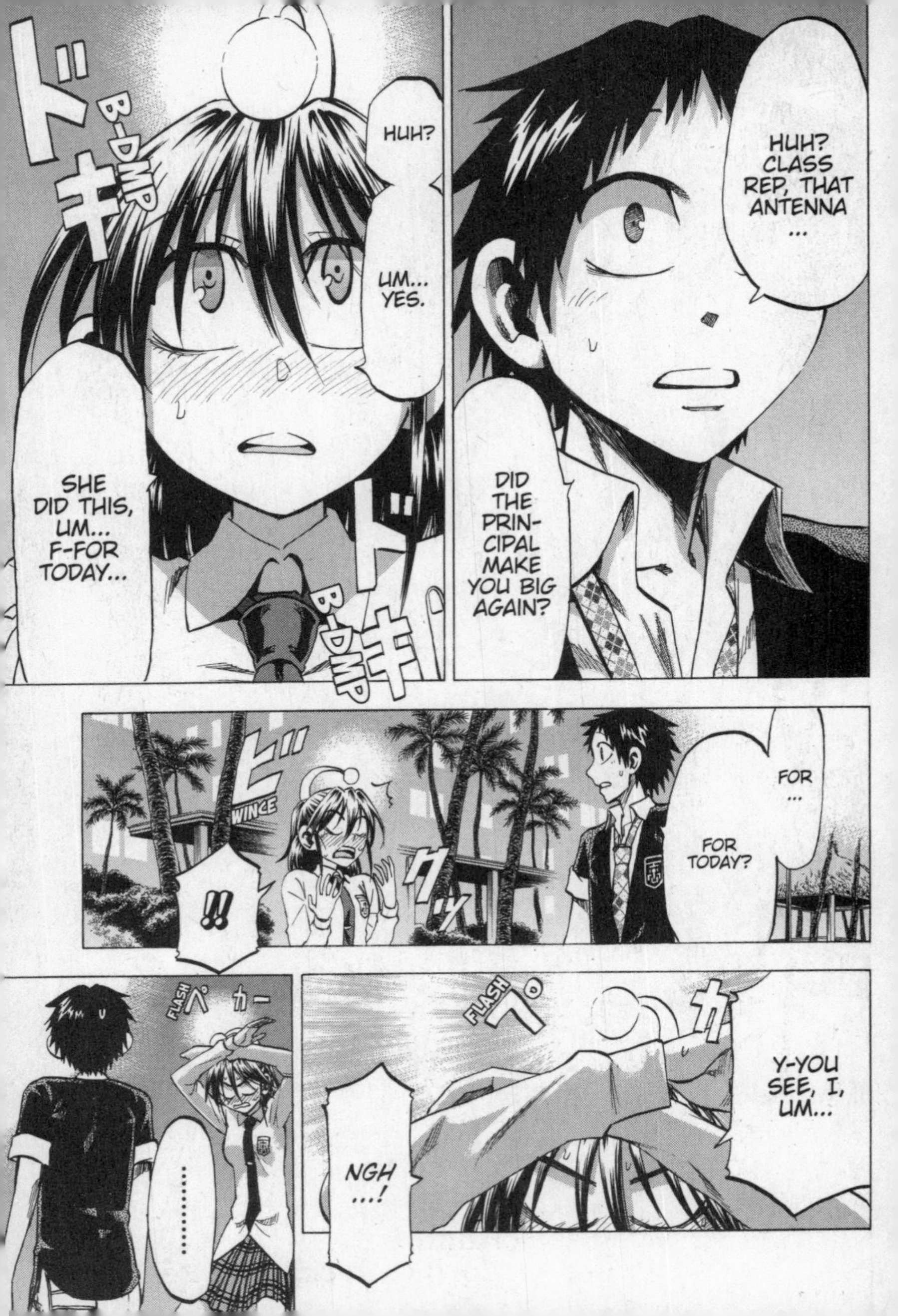
HUH? CLASS REP, THAT ANTENNA ...
DID THE PRIN-CIPAL MAKE YOU BIG AGAIN?
B-DMP
HUH?
UM... YES.
SHE DID THIS, UM... F-FOR TODAY...
B-DMP
FOR ...
FOR TODAY?
WINCE
!!
FLASH
Y-YOU SEE, I, UM...
NGH ...!
FLASH
......

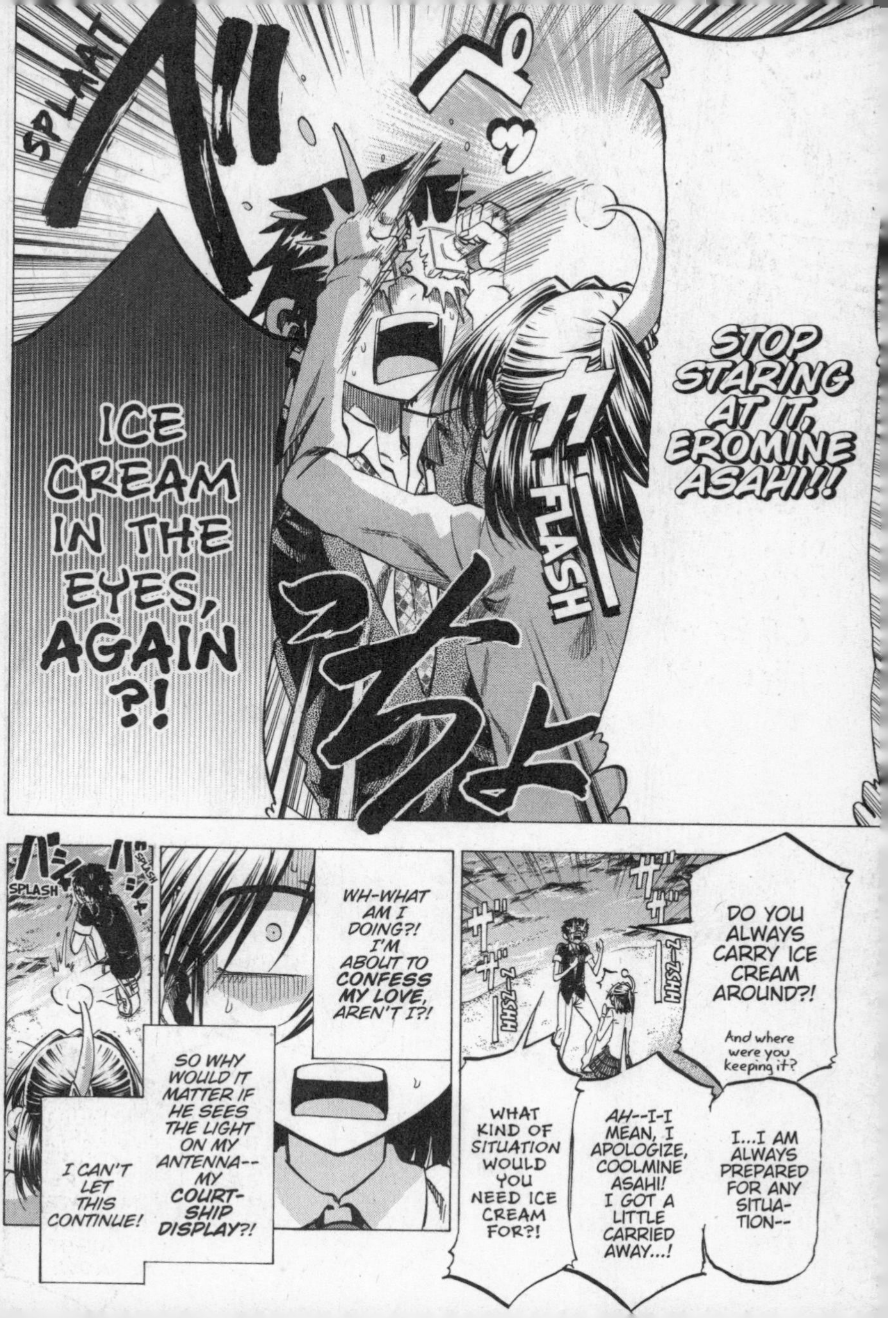

STOP STARING AT IT, EROMINE ASAHI!!
FLASH
SPLAT
ICE CREAM IN THE EYES, AGAIN?!
DO YOU ALWAYS CARRY ICE CREAM AROUND?!
And where were you keeping it?
I...I AM ALWAYS PREPARED FOR ANY SITUATION--
AH--I-I MEAN, I APOLOGIZE, COOLMINE ASAHI! I GOT A LITTLE CARRIED AWAY...!
WHAT KIND OF SITUATION WOULD YOU NEED ICE CREAM FOR?!
WH-WHAT AM I DOING?! I'M ABOUT TO CONFESS MY LOVE, AREN'T I?!
SO WHY WOULD IT MATTER IF HE SEES THE LIGHT ON MY ANTENNA--MY COURTSHIP DISPLAY?!
I CAN'T LET THIS CONTINUE!
SPLASH
SPLASH

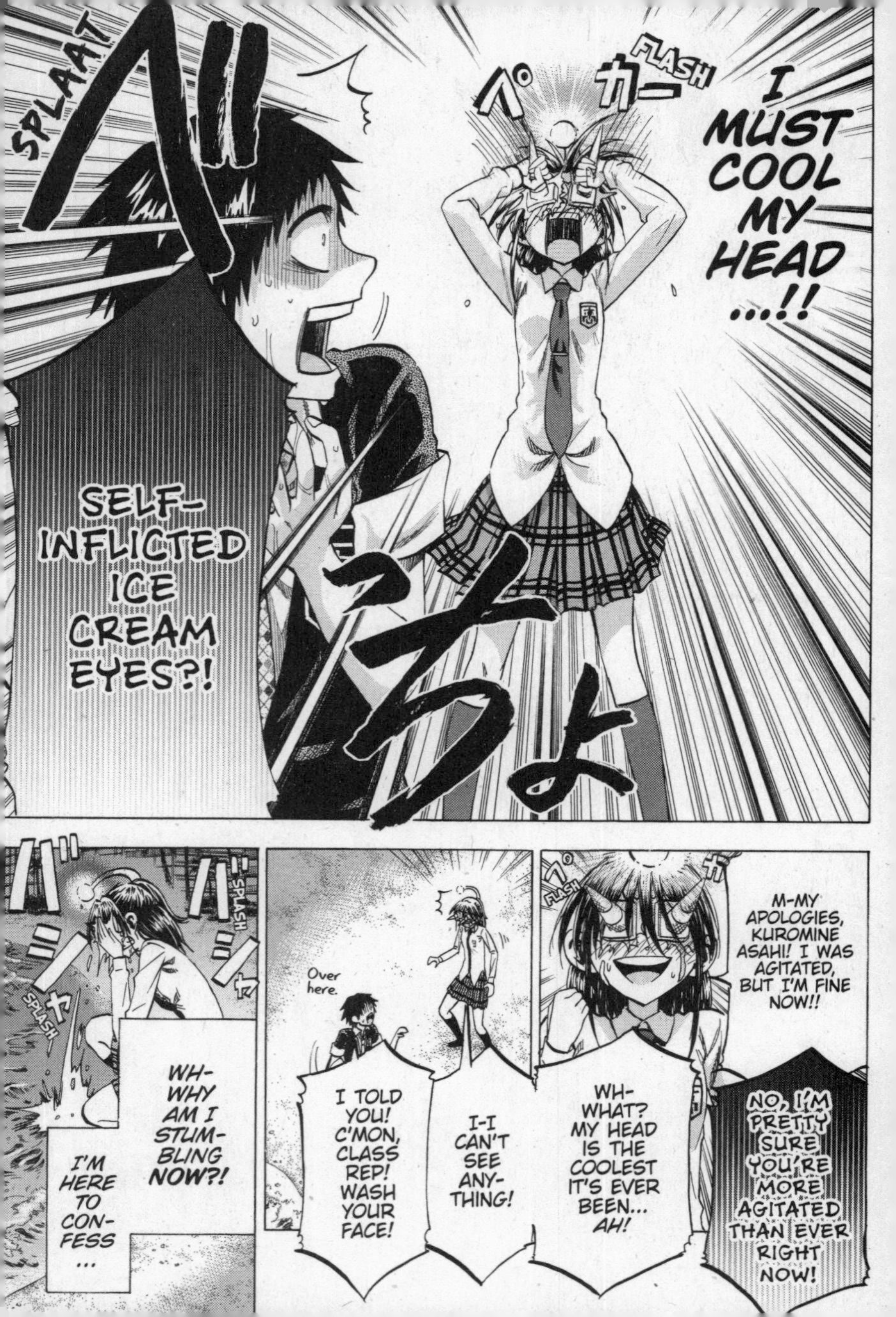
FLASH
I MUST COOL MY HEAD...!!
SPLAAT
SELF-INFLICTED ICE CREAM EYES?!
FLASH
M-MY APOLOGIES, KUROMINE ASAHI! I WAS AGITATED, BUT I'M FINE NOW!!
NO, I'M PRETTY SURE YOU'RE MORE AGITATED THAN EVER RIGHT NOW!
WH-WHAT? MY HEAD IS THE COOLEST IT'S EVER BEEN... AH!
I-I CAN'T SEE ANYTHING!
Over here.
I TOLD YOU! C'MON, CLASS REP! WASH YOUR FACE!
SPLASH
SPLASH
WH-WHY AM I STUMBLING NOW?!
I'M HERE TO CONFESS...

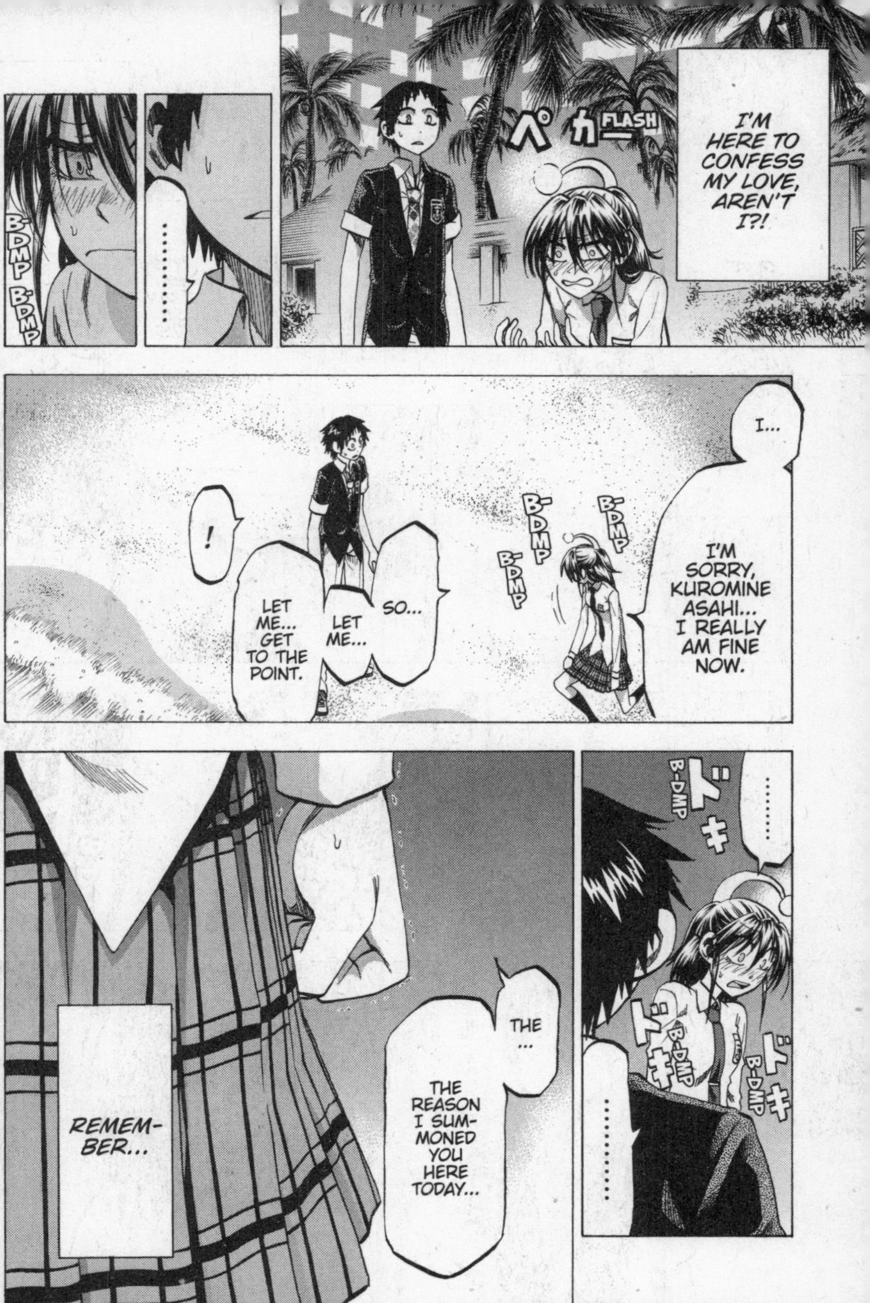
I'M HERE TO CONFESS MY LOVE, AREN'T I?!
FLASH
......
B-DMP B-DMP
I...
I'M SORRY, KUROMINE ASAHI... I REALLY AM FINE NOW.
B-DMP B-DMP B-DMP
SO...
LET ME...
LET ME... GET TO THE POINT.
!
......
B-DMP
B-DMP B-DMP
......
THE ...
THE REASON I SUMMONED YOU HERE TODAY...
REMEMBER...

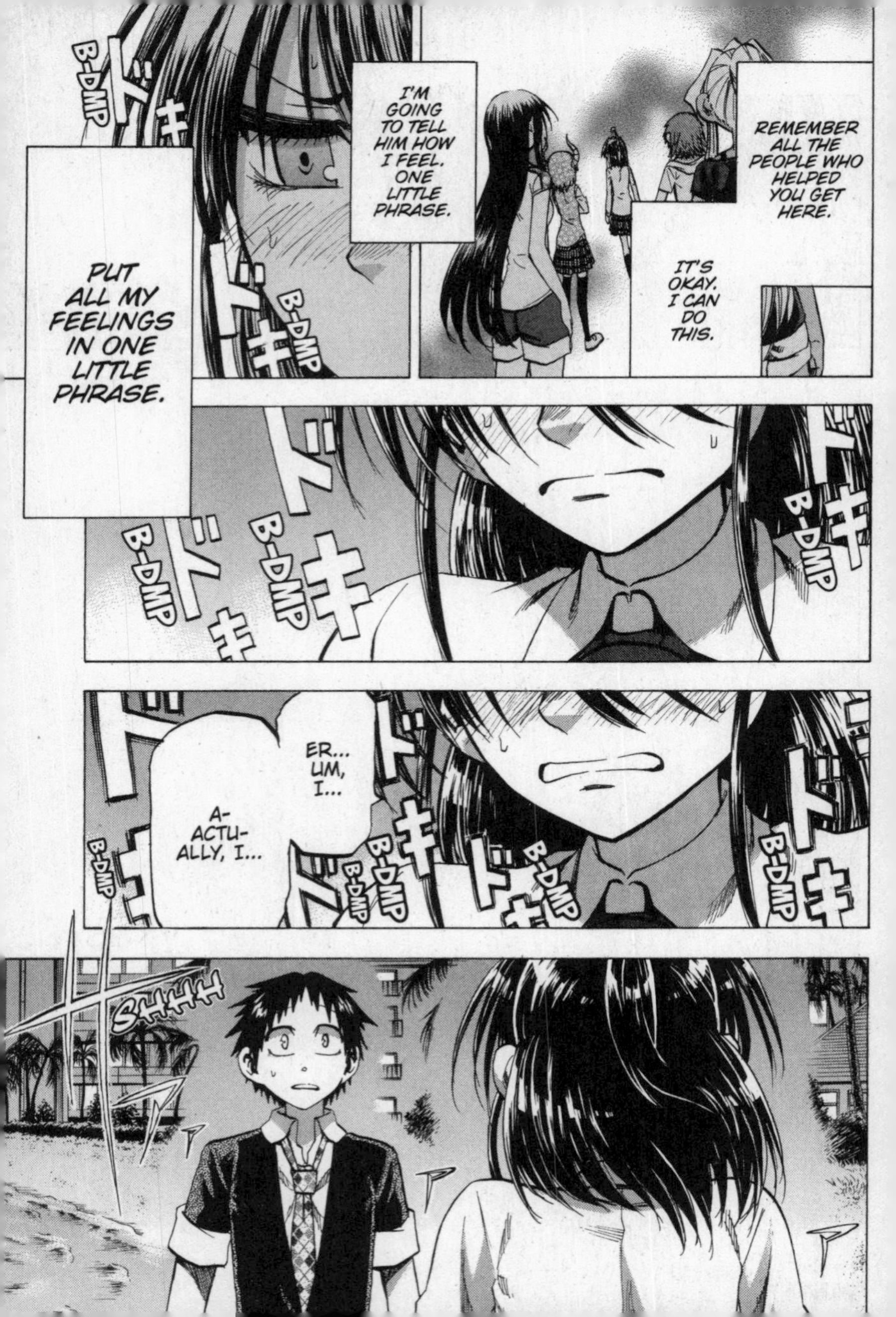
REMEMBER ALL THE PEOPLE WHO HELPED YOU GET HERE.
IT'S OKAY. I CAN DO THIS.
I'M GOING TO TELL HIM HOW I FEEL. ONE LITTLE PHRASE.
B-DMP
B-DMP
PUT ALL MY FEELINGS IN ONE LITTLE PHRASE.
B-DMP
B-DMP
B-DMP
B-DMP
B-DMP
B-DMP
ER... UM, I...
A-ACTUALLY, I...
B-DMP
SHHHH

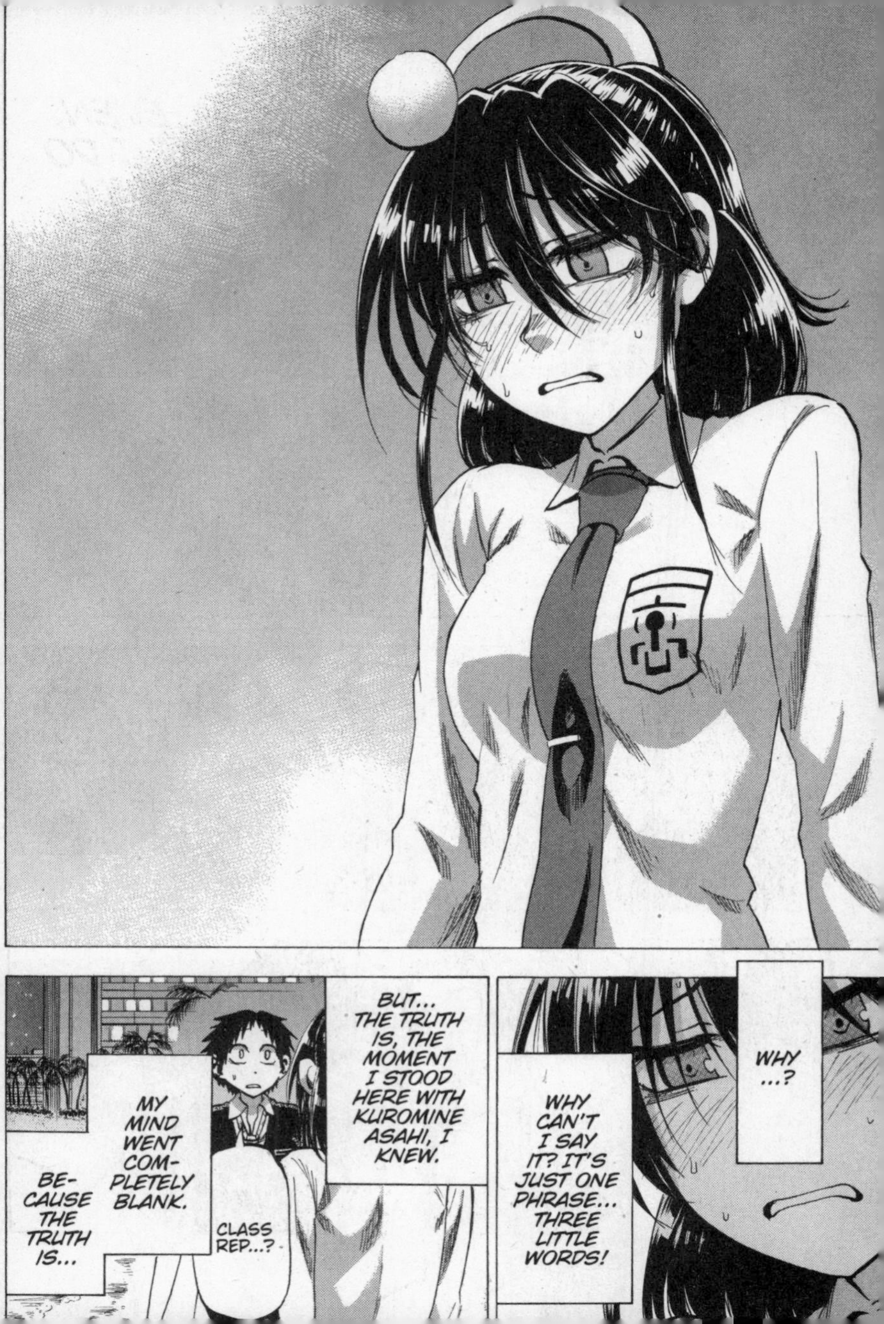
WHY ...?
WHY CAN'T I SAY IT? IT'S JUST ONE PHRASE... THREE LITTLE WORDS!
BUT... THE TRUTH IS, THE MOMENT I STOOD HERE WITH KUROMINE ASAHI, I KNEW.
MY MIND WENT COM-PLETELY BLANK.
BE-CAUSE THE TRUTH IS...
CLASS REP...?

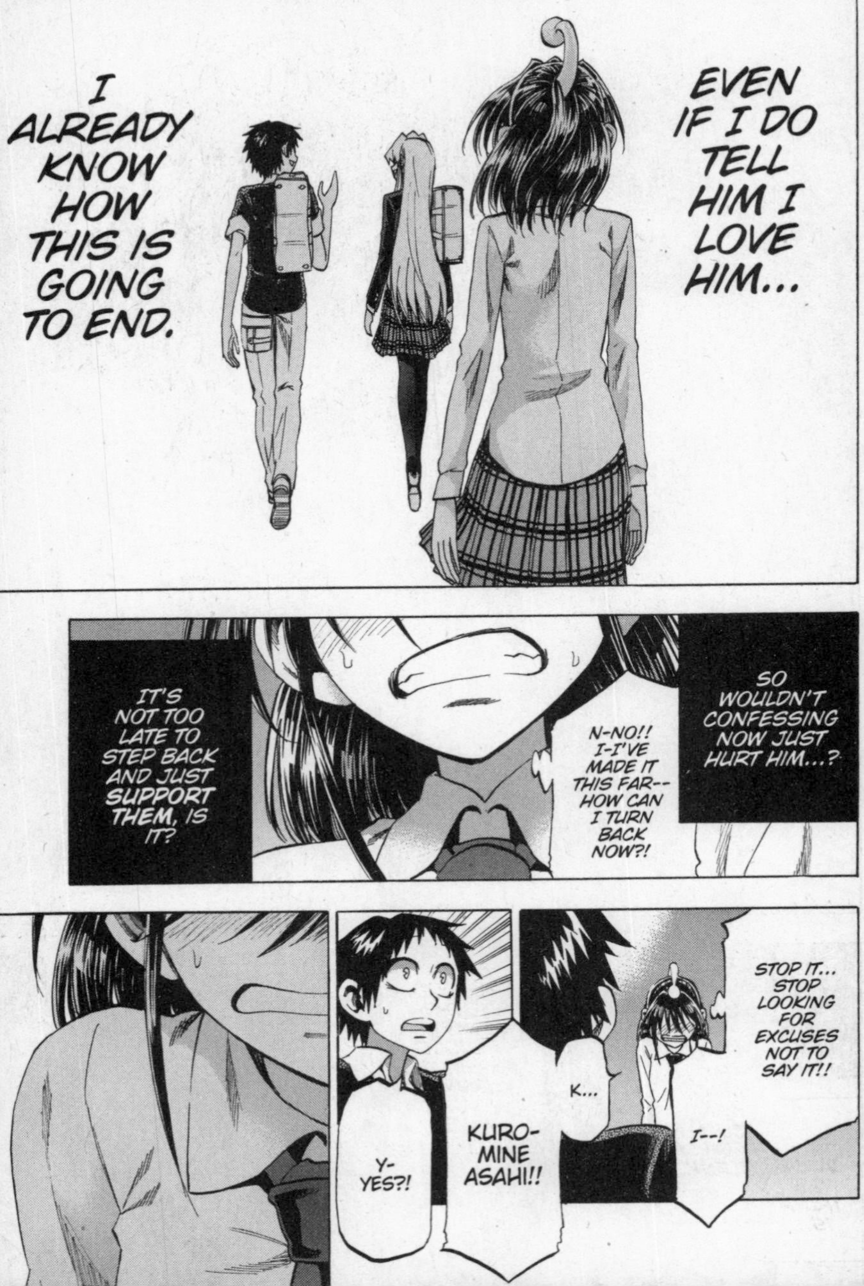
EVEN IF I DO TELL HIM I LOVE HIM...
I ALREADY KNOW HOW THIS IS GOING TO END.
SO WOULDN'T CONFESSING NOW JUST HURT HIM...?
N-NO!! I-I'VE MADE IT THIS FAR-- HOW CAN I TURN BACK NOW?!
IT'S NOT TOO LATE TO STEP BACK AND JUST SUPPORT THEM, IS IT?
STOP IT... STOP LOOKING FOR EXCUSES NOT TO SAY IT!!
I--!
K...
KURO-MINE ASAHI!!
Y- YES?!

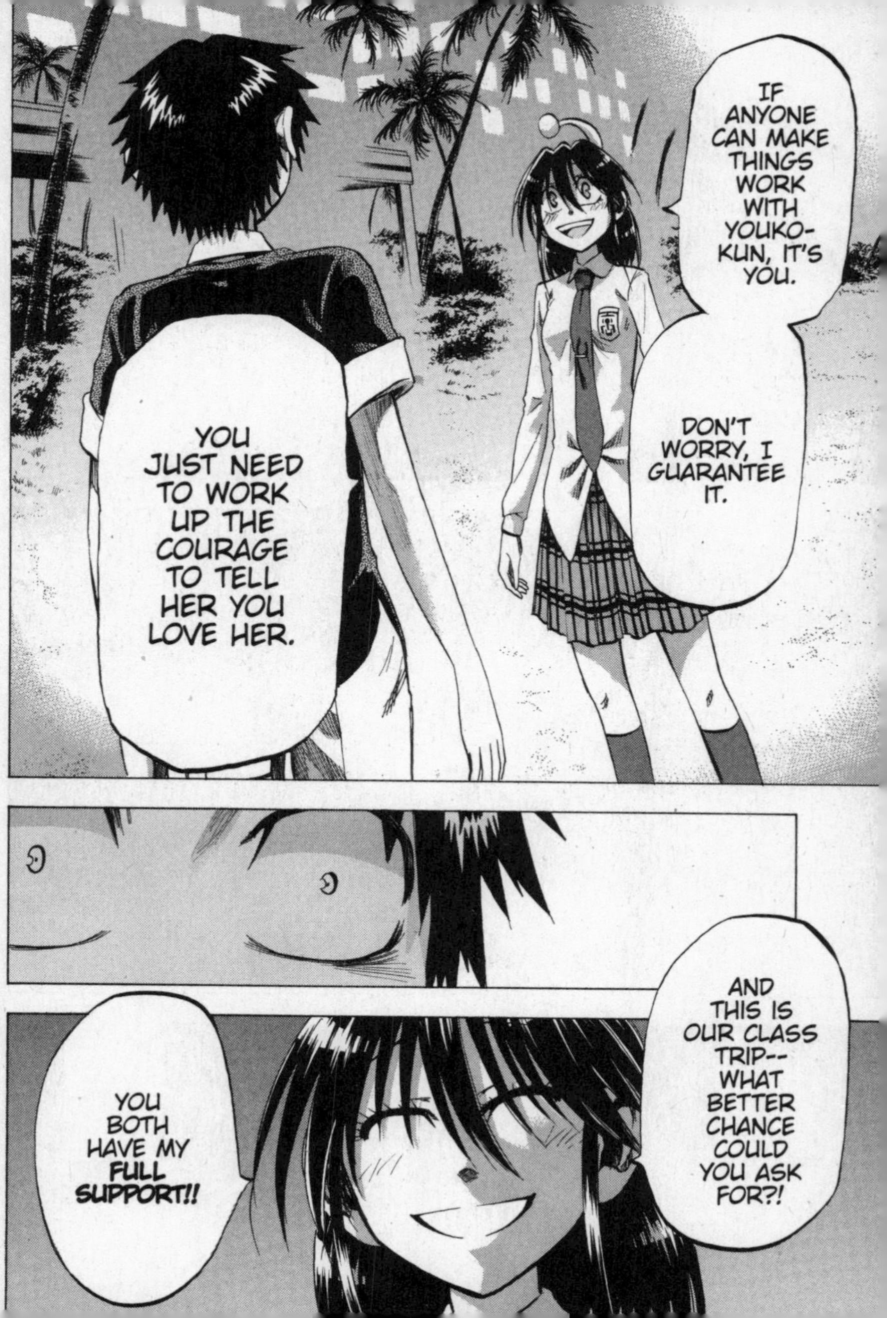
IF ANYONE CAN MAKE THINGS WORK WITH YOUKO-KUN, IT'S YOU.
DON'T WORRY, I GUARANTEE IT.
YOU JUST NEED TO WORK UP THE COURAGE TO TELL HER YOU LOVE HER.
AND THIS IS OUR CLASS TRIP--WHAT BETTER CHANCE COULD YOU ASK FOR?!
YOU BOTH HAVE MY **FULL SUPPORT!!**

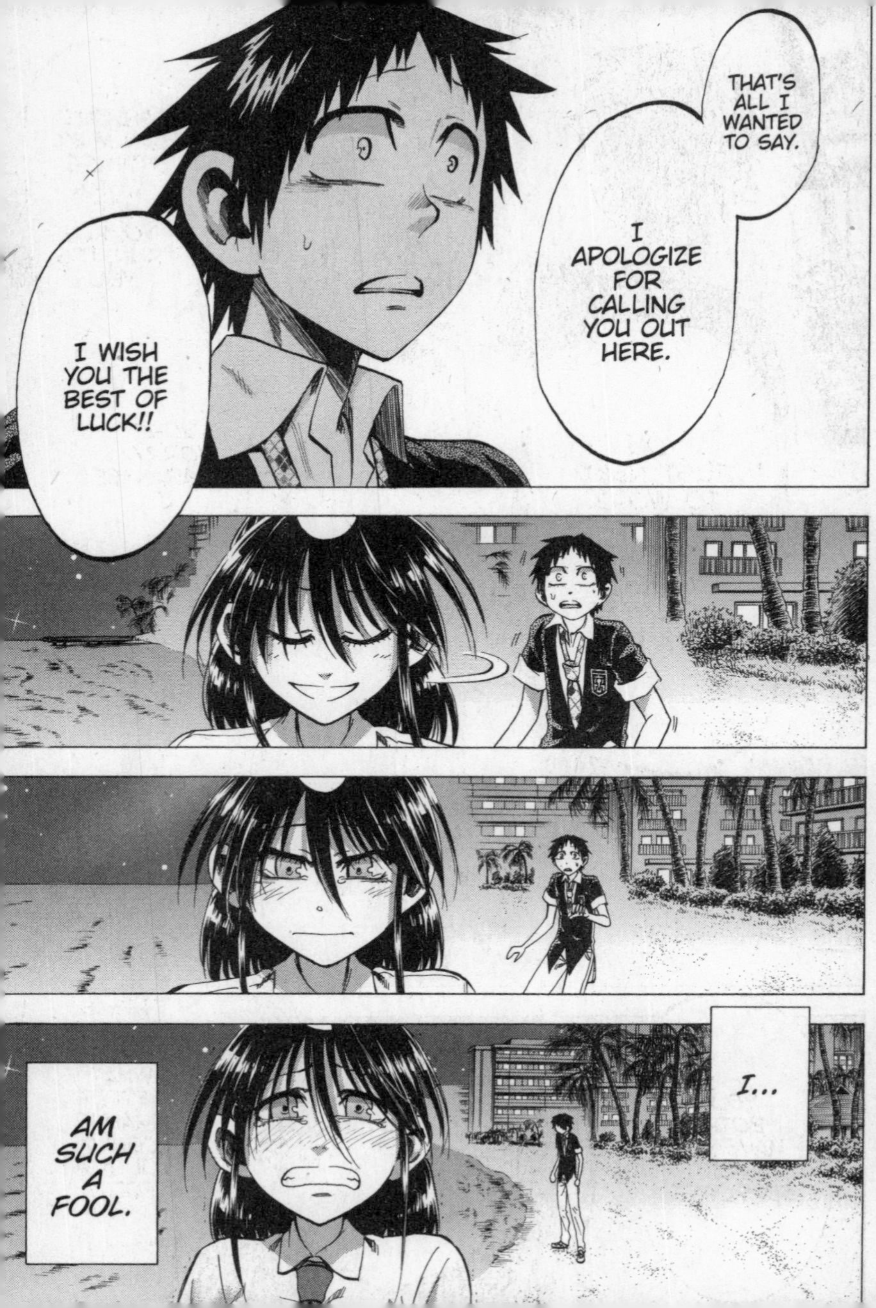
THAT'S ALL I WANTED TO SAY.
I APOLOGIZE FOR CALLING YOU OUT HERE.
I WISH YOU THE BEST OF LUCK!!
I...
AM SUCH A FOOL.

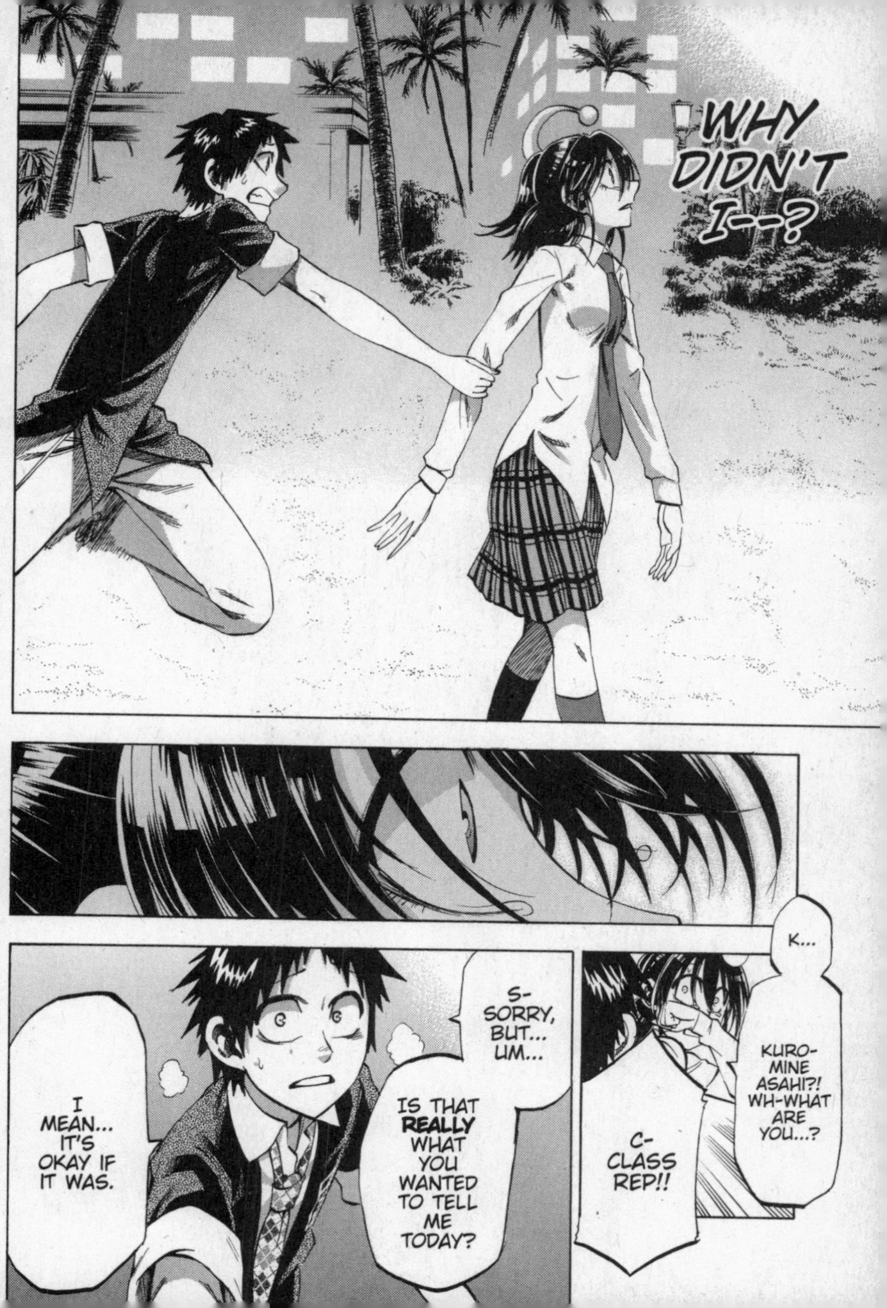
WHY DIDN'T I--?
K...
KURO-MINE ASAHI?! WH-WHAT ARE YOU...?
C-CLASS REP!!
S-SORRY, BUT... UM...
IS THAT **REALLY** WHAT YOU WANTED TO TELL ME TODAY?
I MEAN... IT'S OKAY IF IT WAS.

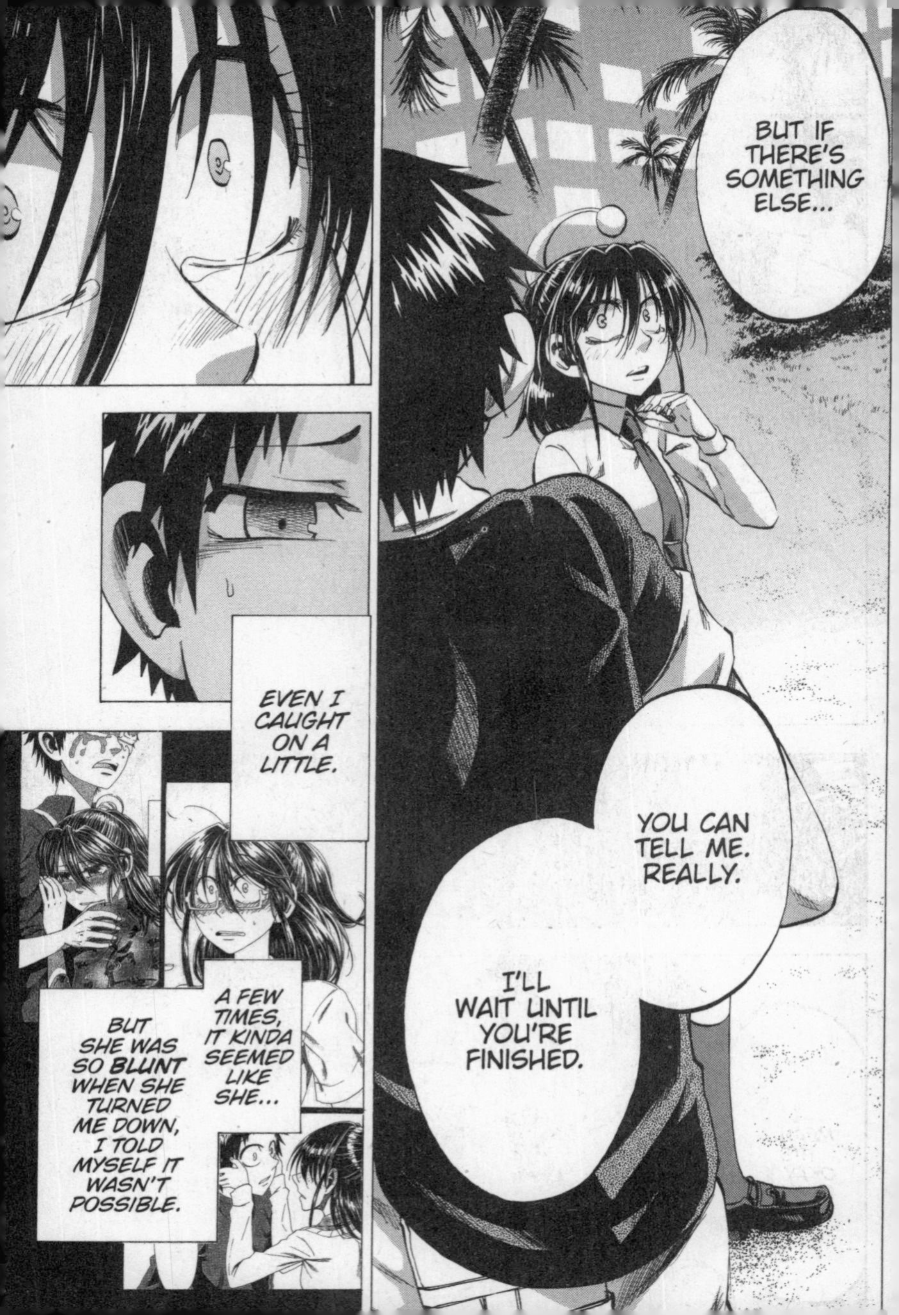
BUT IF THERE'S SOMETHING ELSE...
YOU CAN TELL ME. REALLY.
I'LL WAIT UNTIL YOU'RE FINISHED.
EVEN I CAUGHT ON A LITTLE.
A FEW TIMES, IT KINDA SEEMED LIKE SHE...
BUT SHE WAS SO BLUNT WHEN SHE TURNED ME DOWN, I TOLD MYSELF IT WASN'T POSSIBLE.

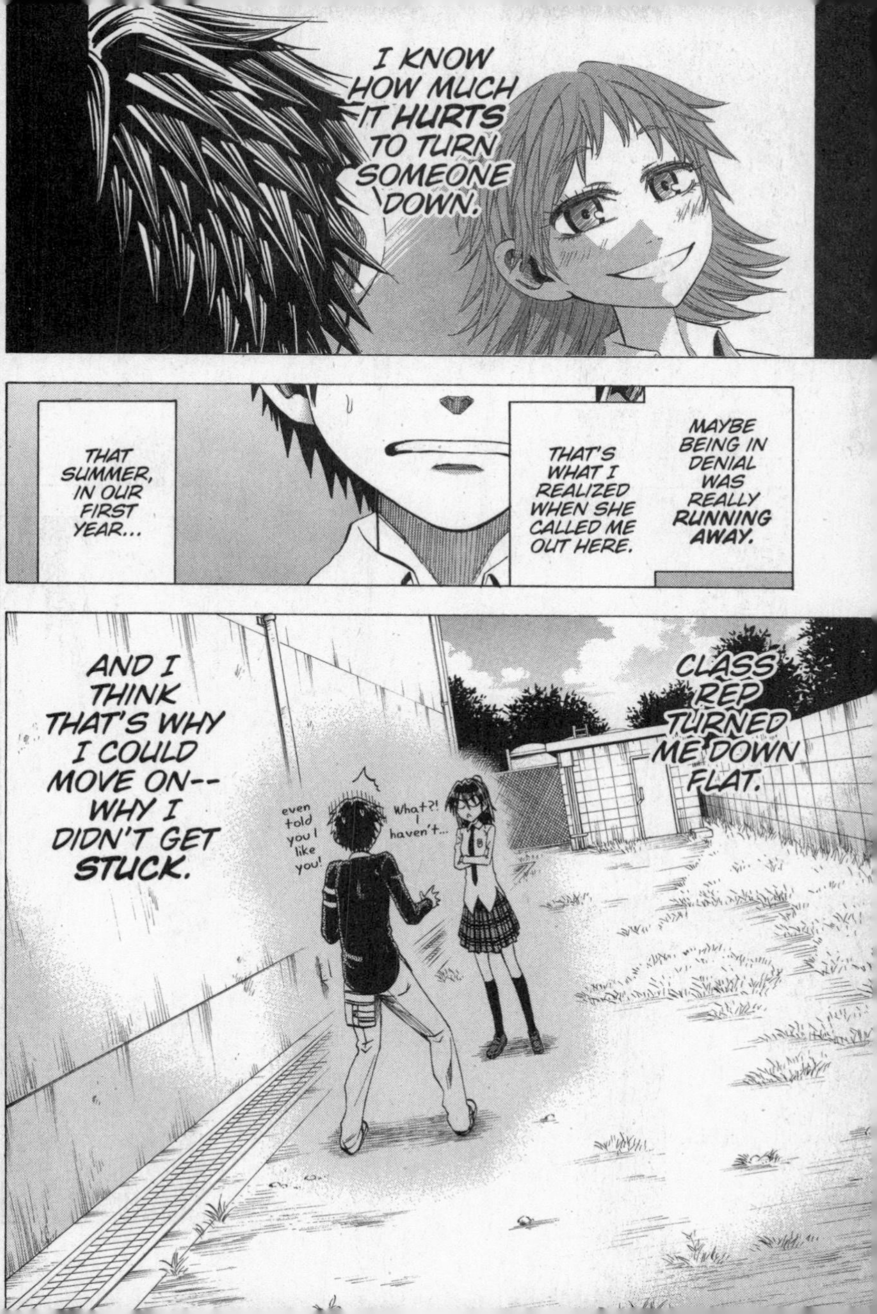
I KNOW HOW MUCH IT HURTS TO TURN SOMEONE DOWN.
MAYBE BEING IN DENIAL WAS REALLY RUNNING AWAY.
THAT'S WHAT I REALIZED WHEN SHE CALLED ME OUT HERE.
THAT SUMMER, IN OUR FIRST YEAR...
CLASS REP TURNED ME DOWN FLAT.
What?! I haven't...
even told you I like you!
AND I THINK THAT'S WHY I COULD MOVE ON-- WHY I DIDN'T GET STUCK.

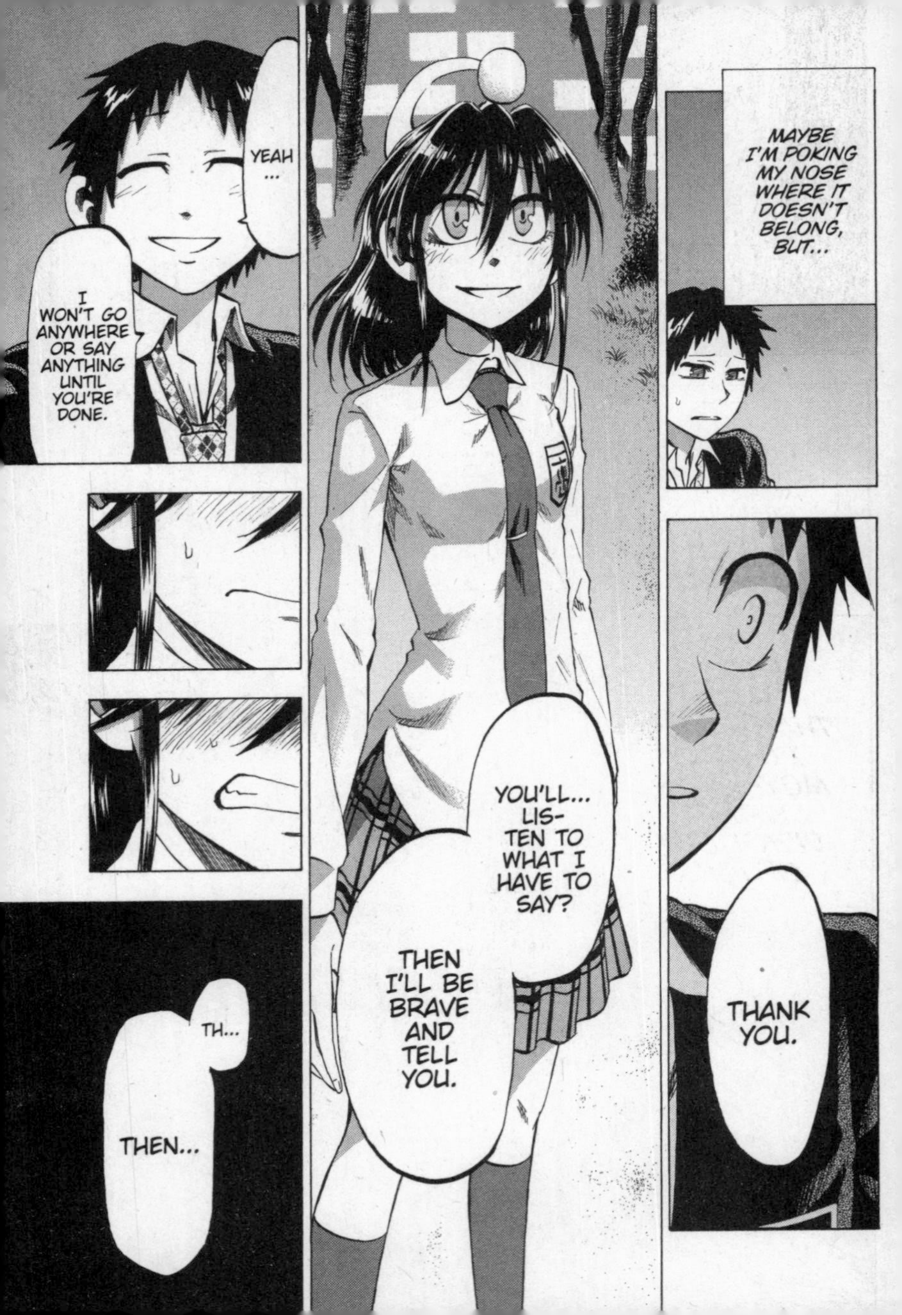
MAYBE I'M POKING MY NOSE WHERE IT DOESN'T BELONG, BUT...
THANK YOU.
YOU'LL... LIS- TEN TO WHAT I HAVE TO SAY?
THEN I'LL BE BRAVE AND TELL YOU.
YEAH ...
I WON'T GO ANYWHERE OR SAY ANYTHING UNTIL YOU'RE DONE.
TH...
THEN...

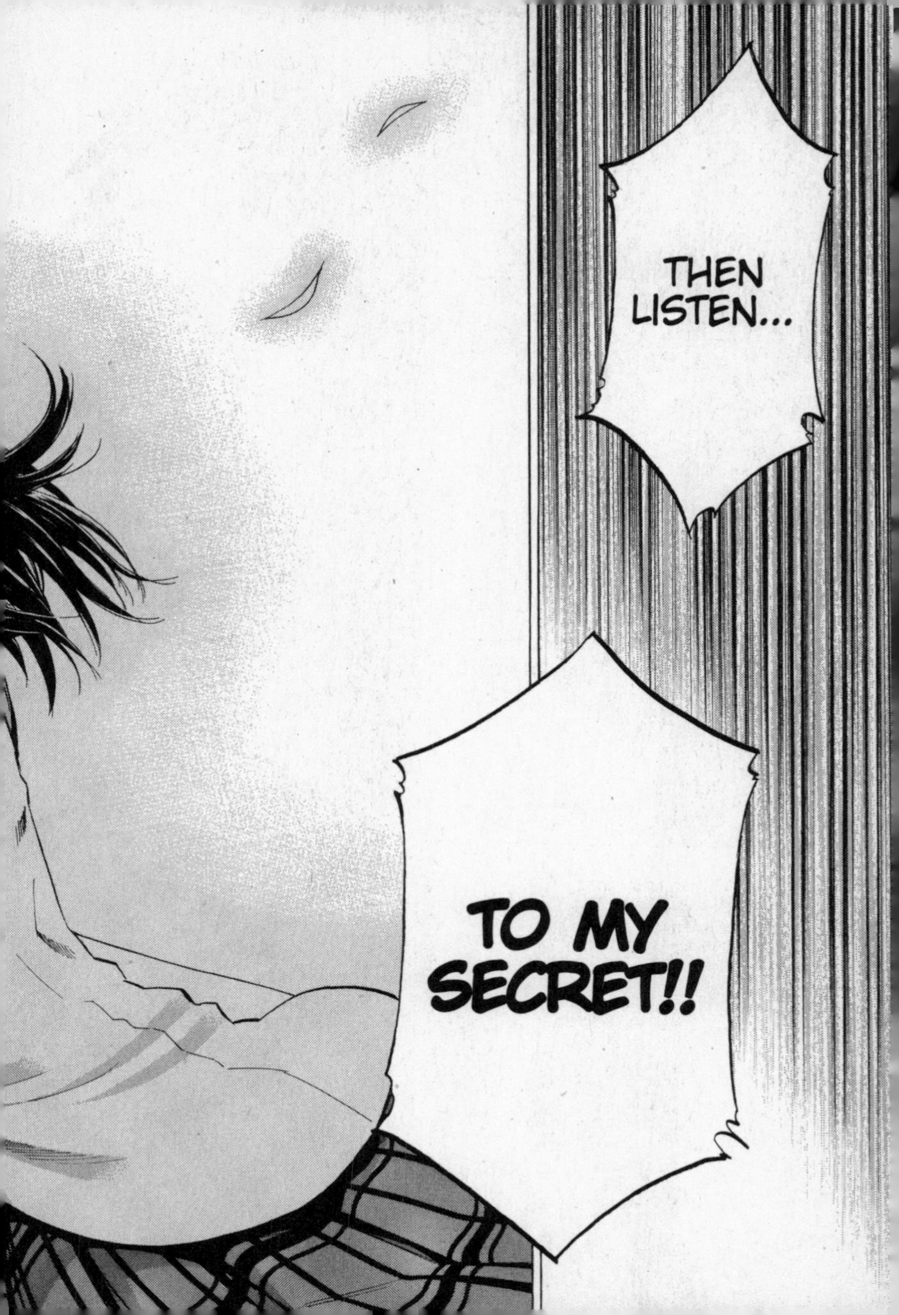
THEN LISTEN...
TO MY SECRET!!

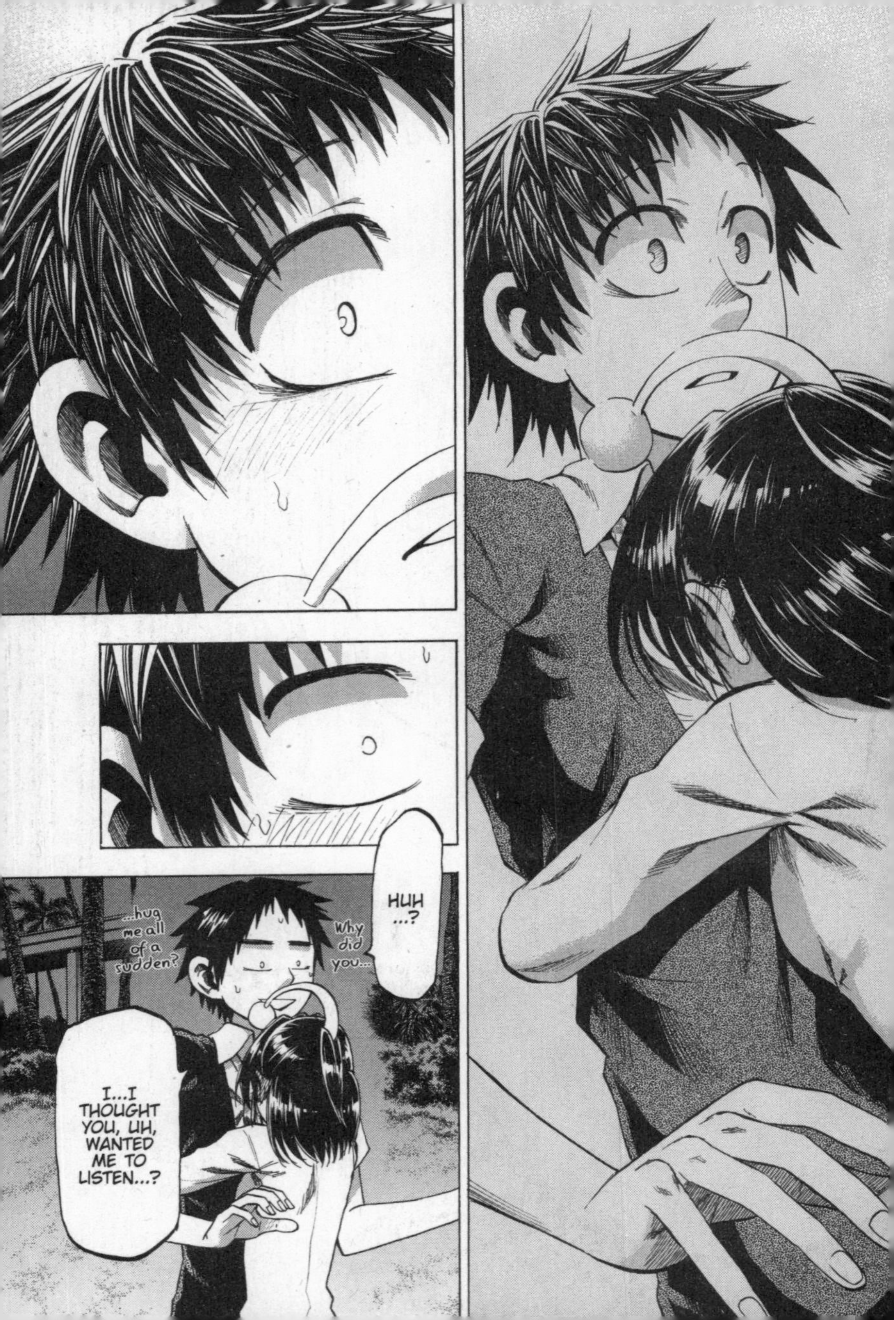
HUH ...?
Why did you...
...hug me all of a sudden?
I...I THOUGHT YOU, UH, WANTED ME TO LISTEN...?

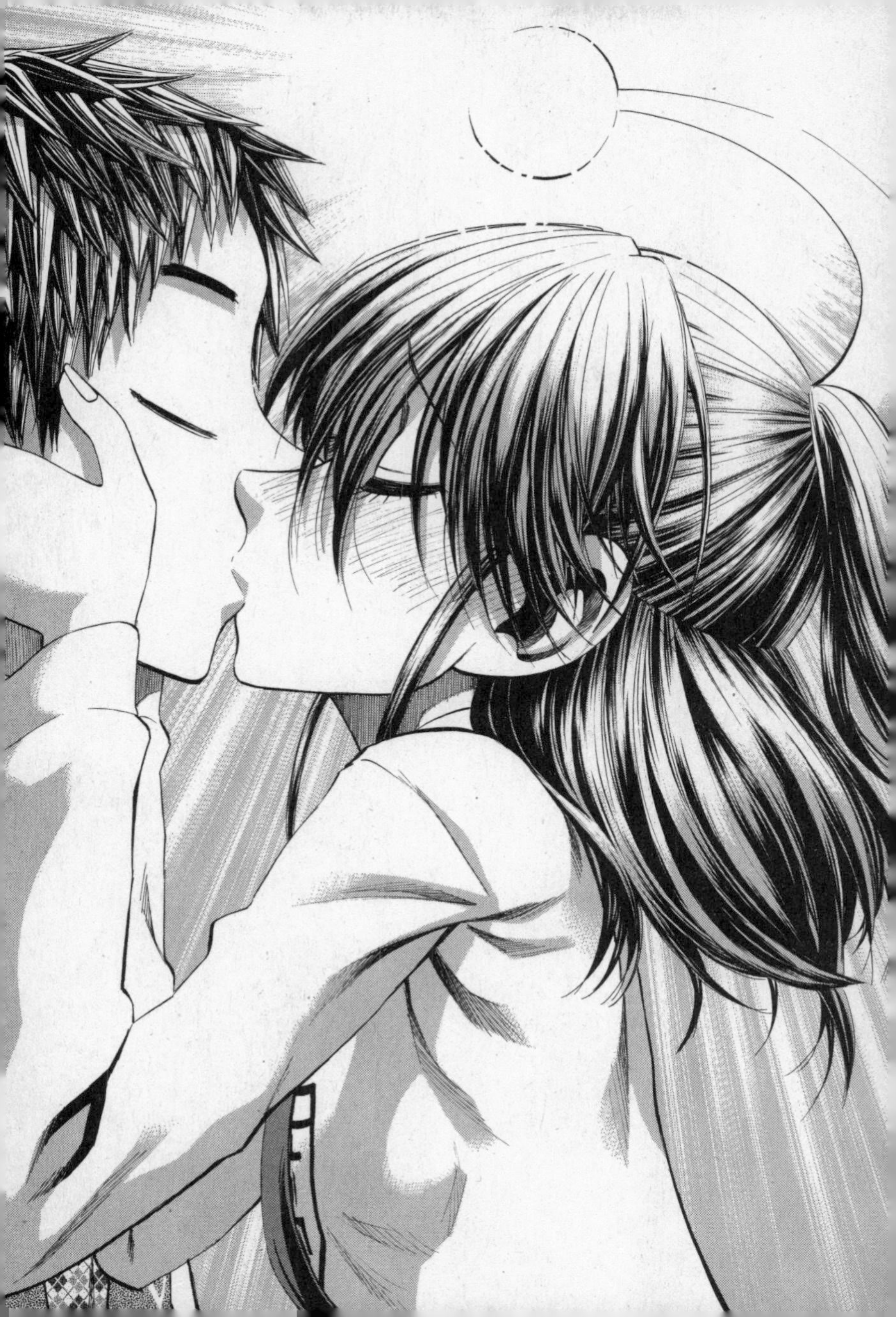

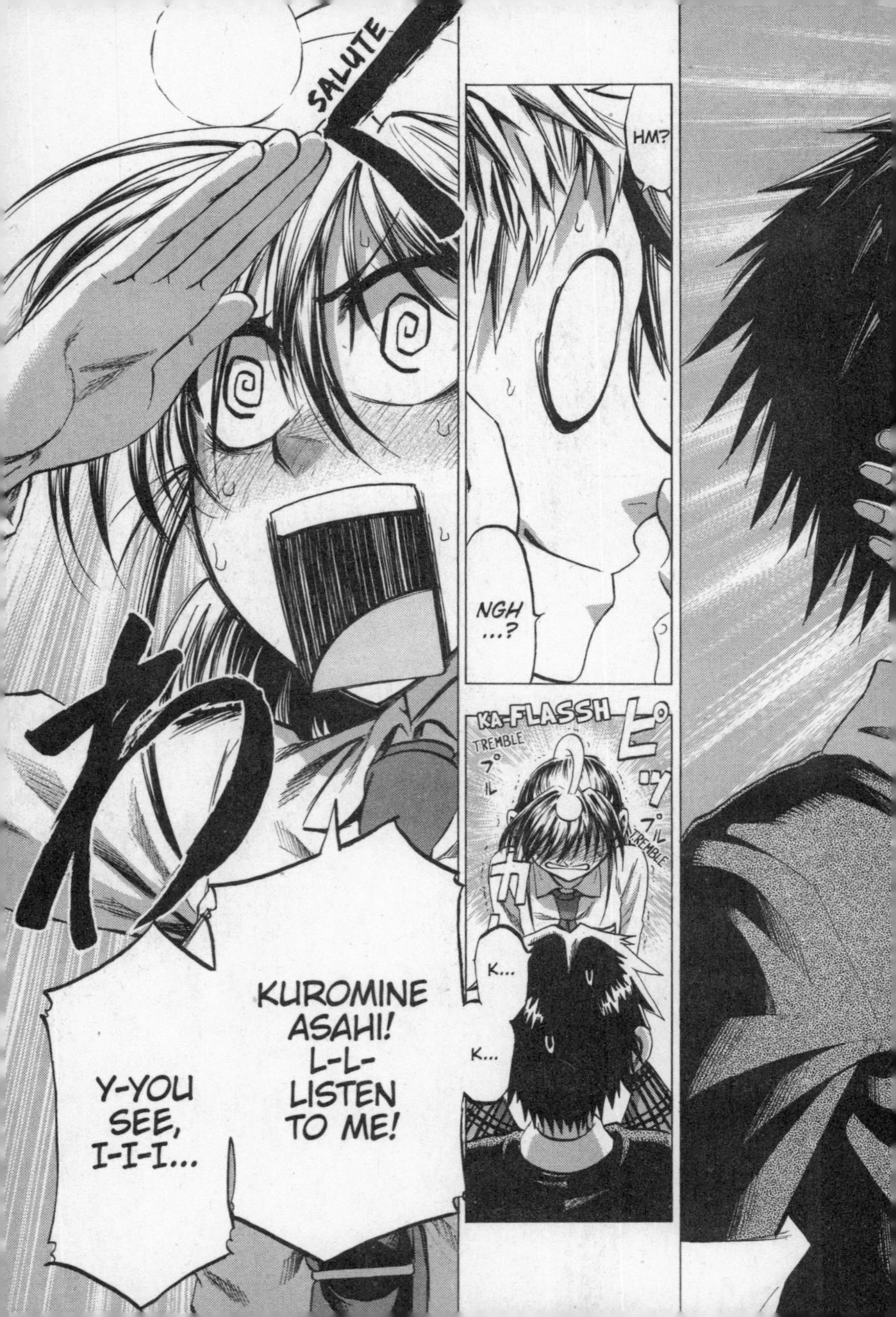
HM?
NGH ...?
KA-FLASSH
TREMBLE
TREMBLE
K...
K...
SALUTE
KUROMINE ASAHI! L-L-LISTEN TO ME!
Y-YOU SEE, I-I-I...

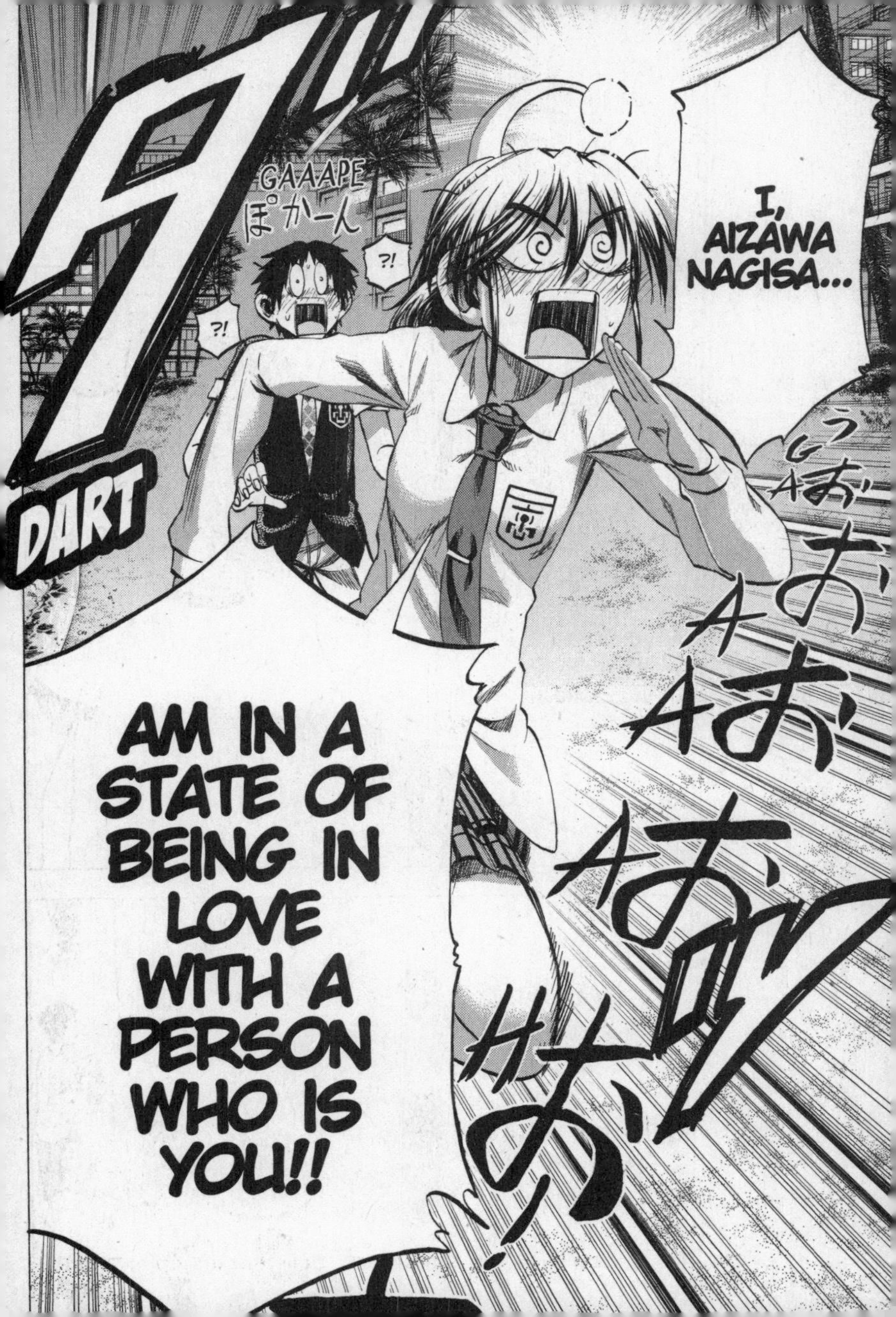
I, AIZAWA NAGISA...
?!
?!
GAAAPE
ぽかーん
DART
AM IN A STATE OF BEING IN LOVE WITH A PERSON WHO IS YOU!!

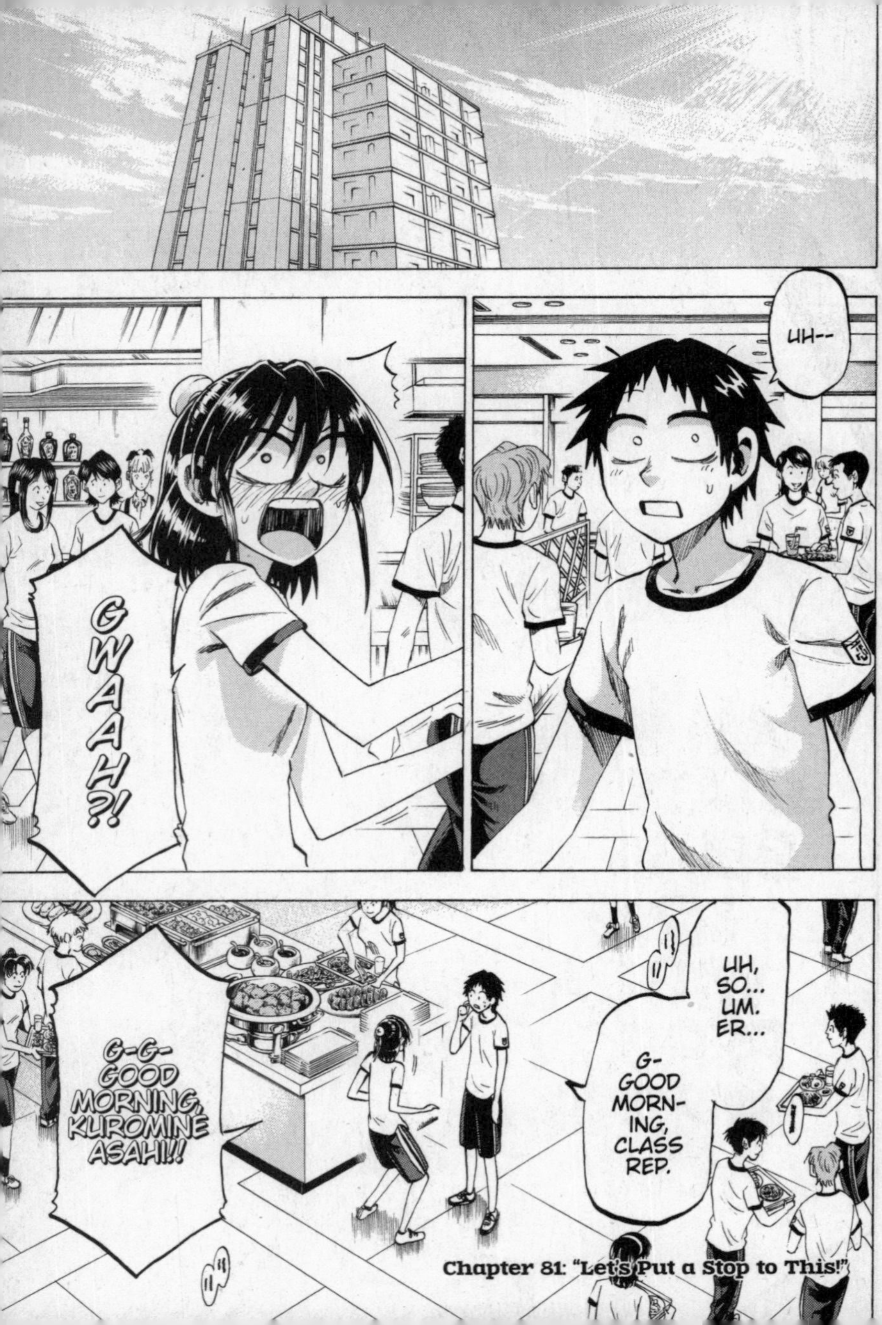
UH--
GWAAAH?!
UH, SO... UM. ER...
G-GOOD MORNING, CLASS REP.
G-G-GOOD MORNING, KUROMINÉ ASAHI!!

Chapter 81: "Let's Put a Stop to This!"

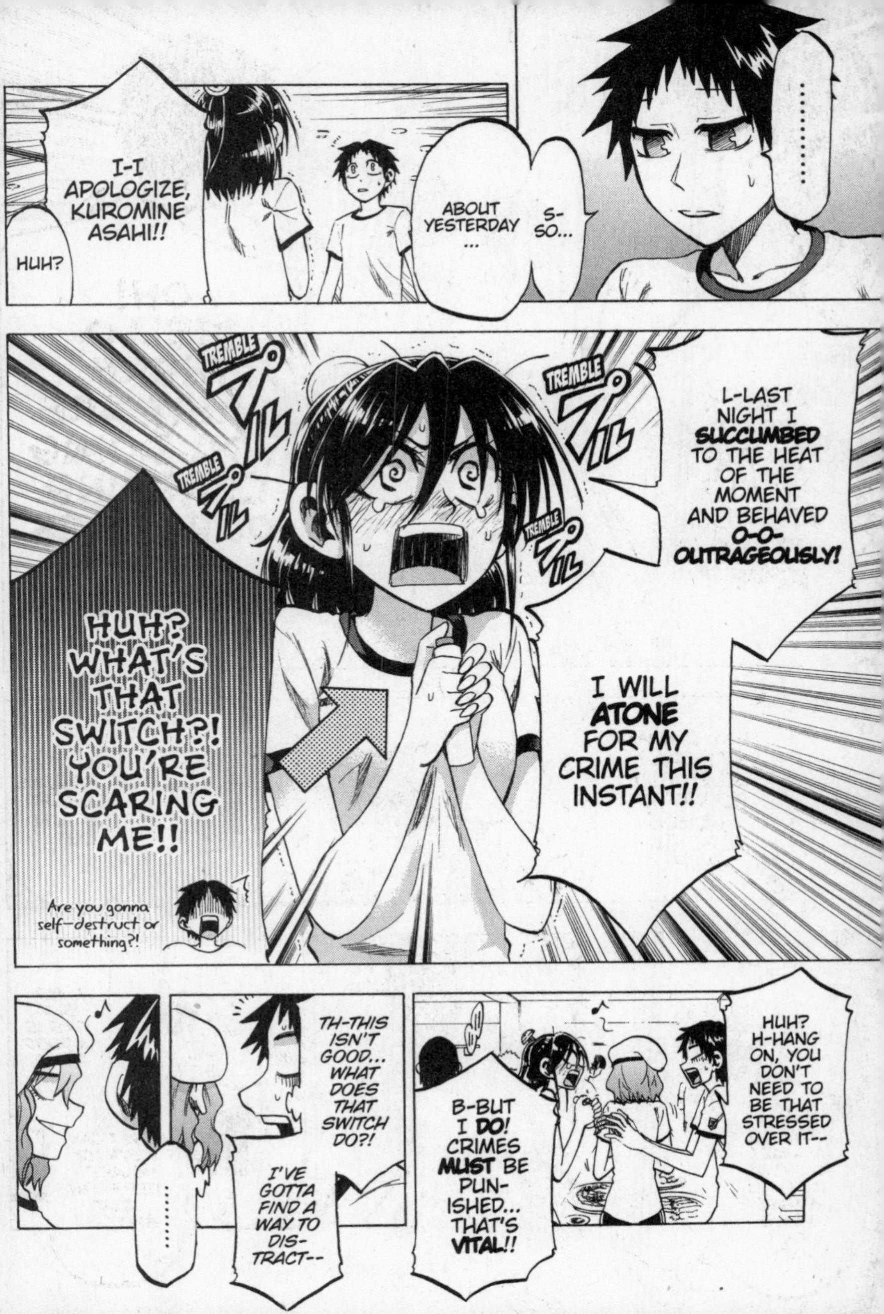
......
S-SO...
ABOUT YESTERDAY ...
I-I APOLOGIZE, KUROMINE ASAHI!!
HUH?
TREMBLE
TREMBLE
L-LAST NIGHT I SUCCUMBED TO THE HEAT OF THE MOMENT AND BEHAVED O-O-OUTRAGEOUSLY!
TREMBLE
TREMBLE
I WILL ATONE FOR MY CRIME THIS INSTANT!!
HUH? WHAT'S THAT SWITCH?! YOU'RE SCARING ME!!
Are you gonna self-destruct or something?!
HUH? H-HANG ON, YOU DON'T NEED TO BE THAT STRESSED OVER IT--
B-BUT I DO! CRIMES MUST BE PUN-ISHED... THAT'S VITAL!!
TH-THIS ISN'T GOOD... WHAT DOES THAT SWITCH DO?!
I'VE GOTTA FIND A WAY TO DIS-TRACT--
......

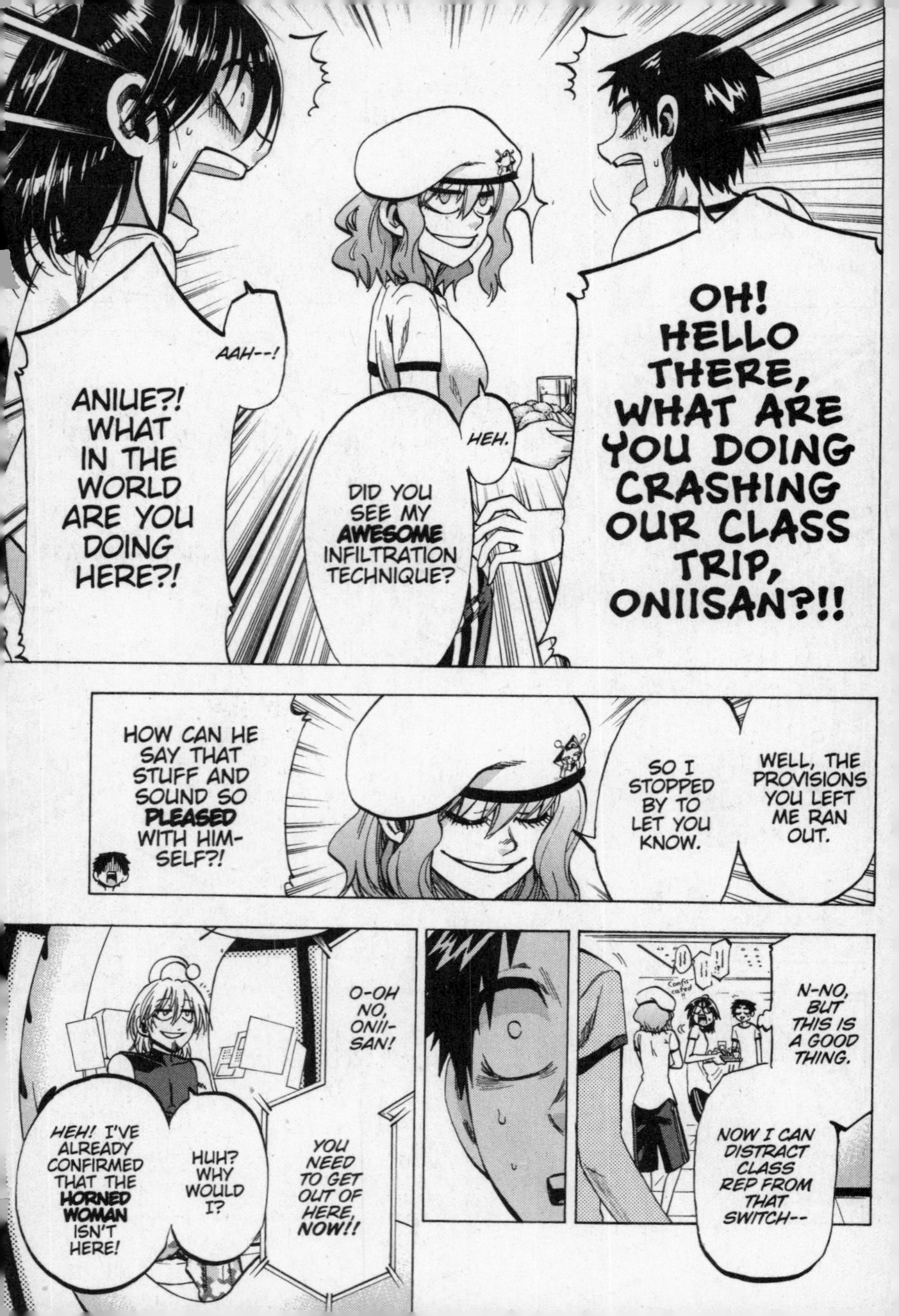
OH! HELLO THERE, WHAT ARE YOU DOING CRASHING OUR CLASS TRIP, ONIISAN?!!
AAH--!
ANIUE?! WHAT IN THE WORLD ARE YOU DOING HERE?!
HEH.
DID YOU SEE MY AWESOME INFILTRATION TECHNIQUE?
WELL, THE PROVISIONS YOU LEFT ME RAN OUT.
SO I STOPPED BY TO LET YOU KNOW.
HOW CAN HE SAY THAT STUFF AND SOUND SO PLEASED WITH HIMSELF?!
N-NO, BUT THIS IS A GOOD THING.
Confiscated!!
NOW I CAN DISTRACT CLASS REP FROM THAT SWITCH--
O-OH NO, ONII-SAN!
YOU NEED TO GET OUT OF HERE, NOW!!
HUH? WHY WOULD I?
HEH! I'VE ALREADY CONFIRMED THAT THE HORNED WOMAN ISN'T HERE!

Chapter 81: "Let's Put a Stop to This!"

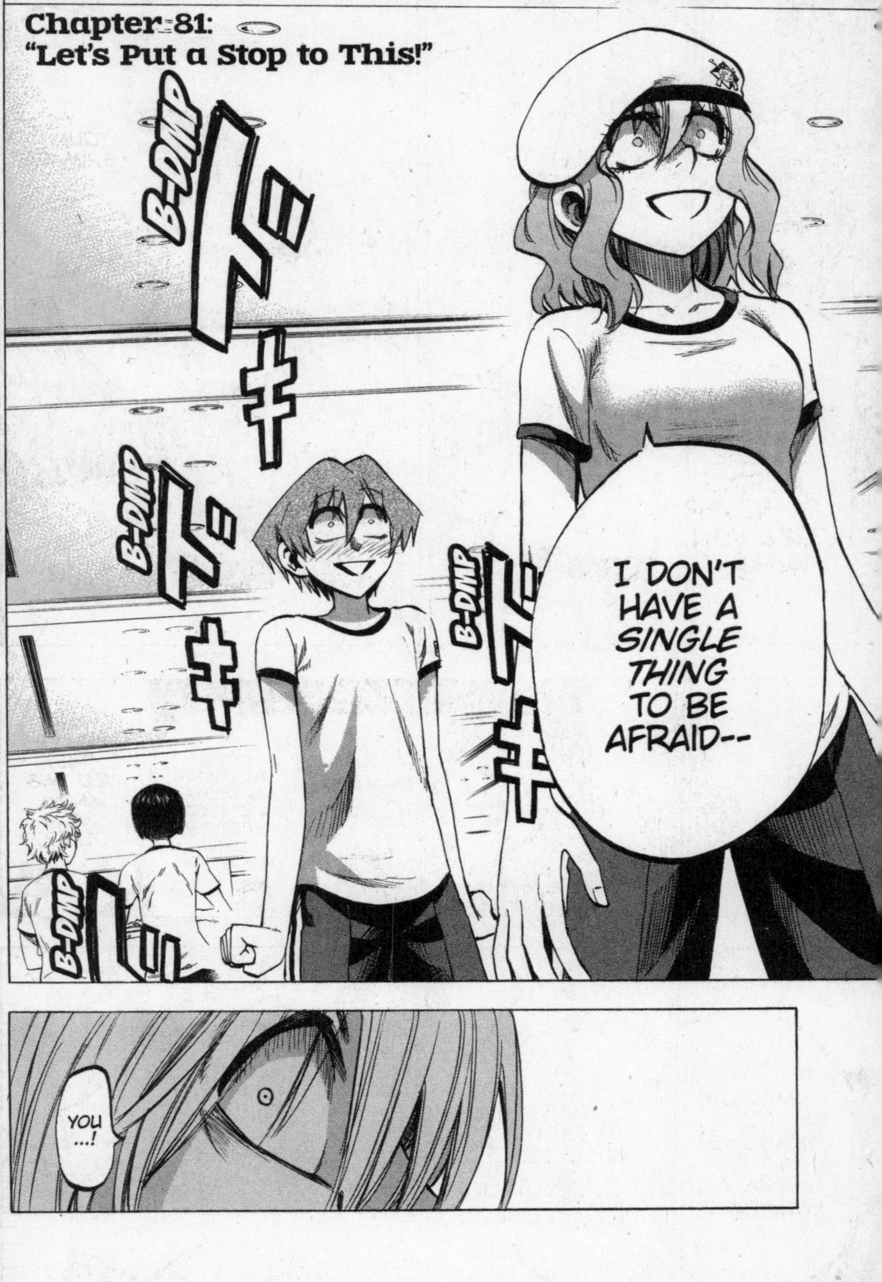
I DON'T HAVE A *SINGLE THING* TO BE AFRAID--
B-DMP
B-DMP
B-DMP
B-DMP
YOU ...!

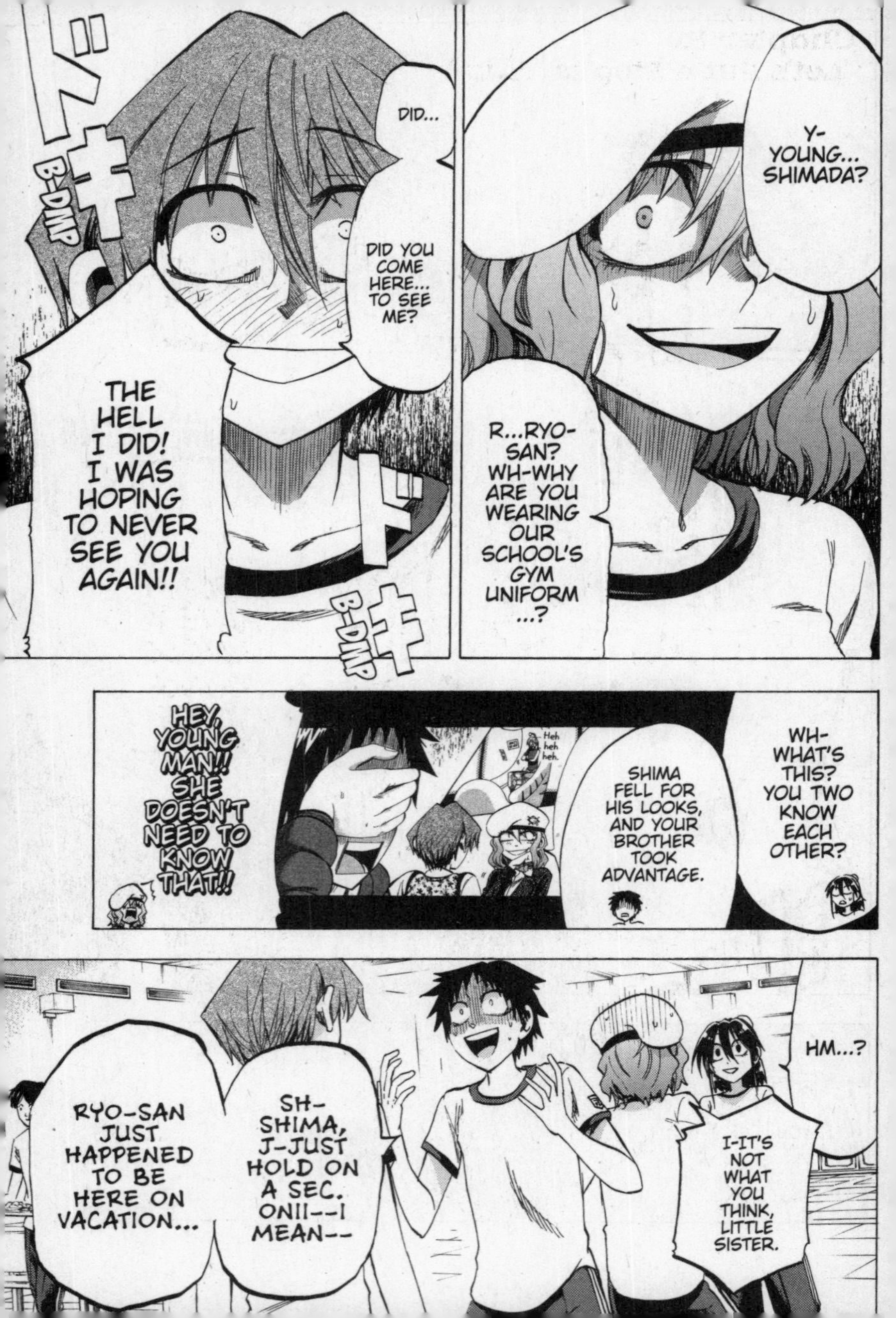
Y-YOUNG... SHIMADA?
R...RYO-SAN? WH-WHY ARE YOU WEARING OUR SCHOOL'S GYM UNIFORM ...?
B-DMP
DID...
DID YOU COME HERE... TO SEE ME?
THE HELL I DID! I WAS HOPING TO NEVER SEE YOU AGAIN!!
B-DMP
WH-WHAT'S THIS? YOU TWO KNOW EACH OTHER?
SHIMA FELL FOR HIS LOOKS, AND YOUR BROTHER TOOK ADVANTAGE.
Heh heh heh.
HEY, YOUNG MAN!! SHE DOESN'T NEED TO KNOW THAT!!
HM...?
I-IT'S NOT WHAT YOU THINK, LITTLE SISTER.
SH-SHIMA, J-JUST HOLD ON A SEC. ONII--I MEAN--
RYO-SAN JUST HAPPENED TO BE HERE ON VACATION...

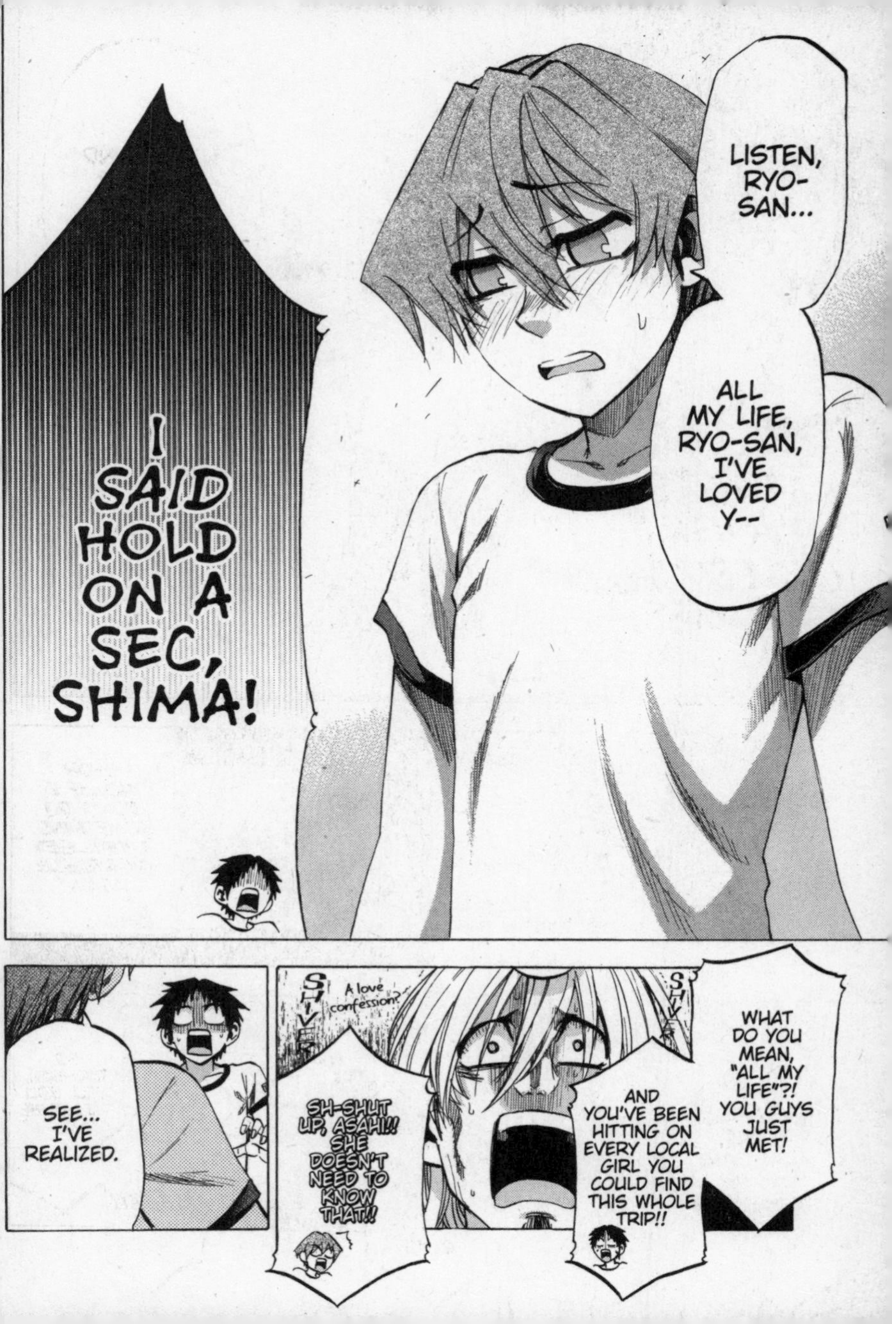
LISTEN, RYO-SAN...
ALL MY LIFE, RYO-SAN, I'VE LOVED Y--
I SAID HOLD ON A SEC, SHIMA!
SHIVER
SHIVER
WHAT DO YOU MEAN, "ALL MY LIFE"?! YOU GUYS JUST MET!
AND YOU'VE BEEN HITTING ON EVERY LOCAL GIRL YOU COULD FIND THIS WHOLE TRIP!!
A love confession?
SH-SHUT UP, ASAHI!! SHE DOESN'T NEED TO KNOW THAT!!
SEE... I'VE REALIZED.

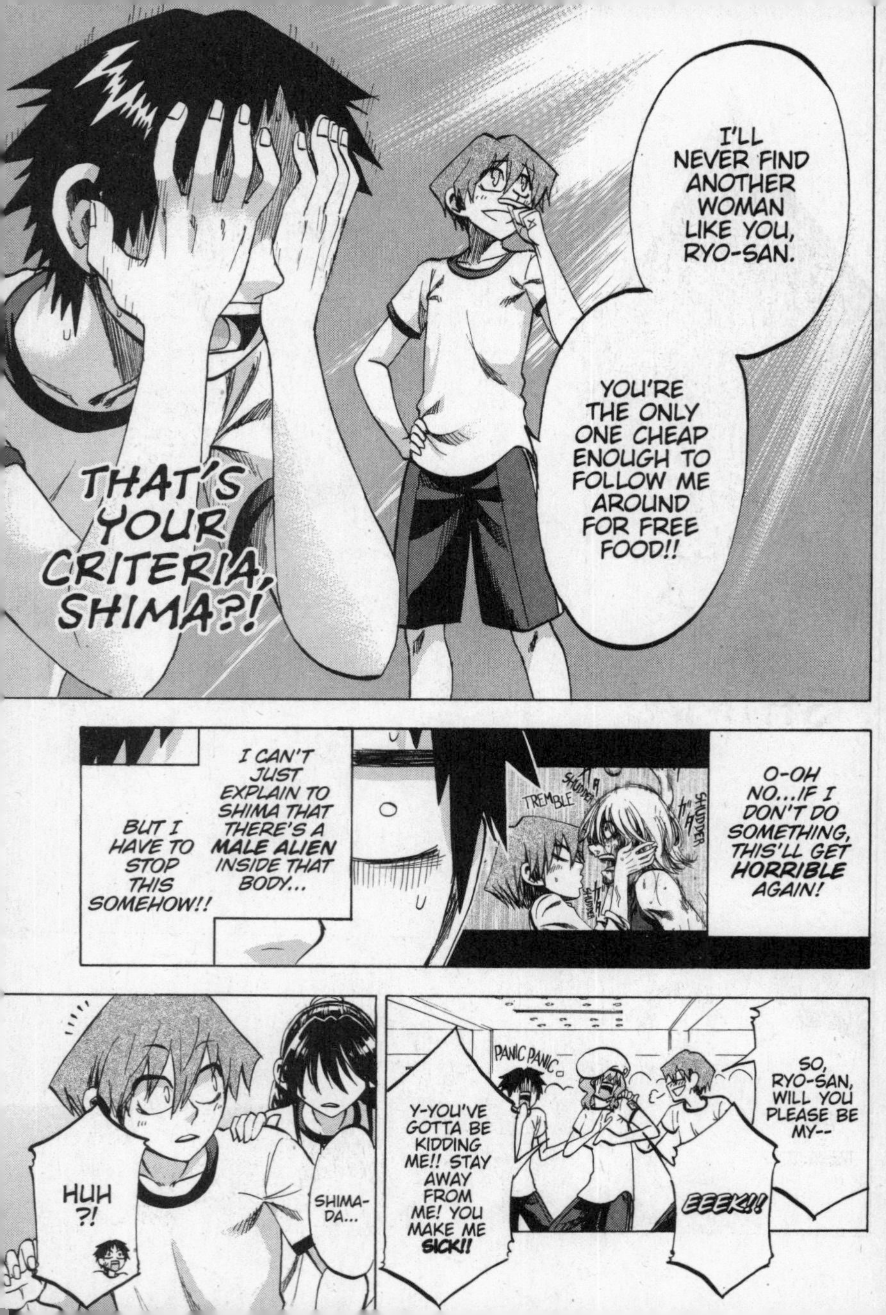
I'LL NEVER FIND ANOTHER WOMAN LIKE YOU, RYO-SAN.
YOU'RE THE ONLY ONE CHEAP ENOUGH TO FOLLOW ME AROUND FOR FREE FOOD!!
THAT'S YOUR CRITERIA, SHIMA?!
O-OH NO...IF I DON'T DO SOMETHING, THIS'LL GET **HORRIBLE** AGAIN!
SHUDDER
SHUDDER
TREMBLE
SHUDDER
I CAN'T JUST EXPLAIN TO SHIMA THAT THERE'S A **MALE ALIEN** INSIDE THAT BODY...
BUT I HAVE TO STOP THIS SOMEHOW!!
SO, RYO-SAN, WILL YOU PLEASE BE MY--
EEEK!!
PANIC PANIC
Y-YOU'VE GOTTA BE KIDDING ME!! STAY AWAY FROM ME! YOU MAKE ME **SICK!!**
SHIMA-DA...
HUH ?!

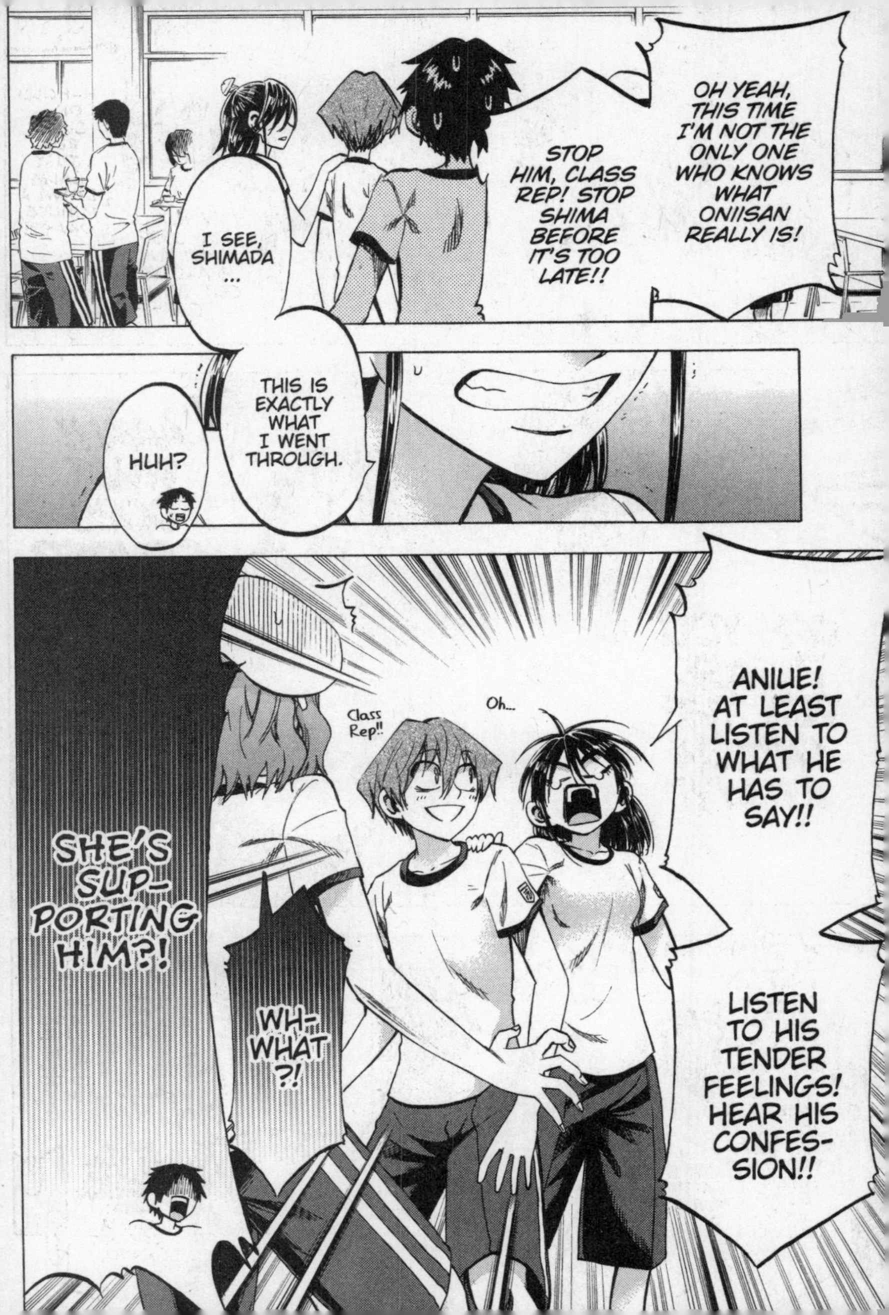

OH YEAH, THIS TIME I'M NOT THE ONLY ONE WHO KNOWS WHAT ONIISAN REALLY IS!
STOP HIM, CLASS REP! STOP SHIMA BEFORE IT'S TOO LATE!!
I SEE, SHIMADA ...
THIS IS EXACTLY WHAT I WENT THROUGH.
HUH?
ANIUE! AT LEAST LISTEN TO WHAT HE HAS TO SAY!!
LISTEN TO HIS TENDER FEELINGS! HEAR HIS CONFESSION!!
Oh...
Class Rep!!
SHE'S SUP-PORTING HIM?!
WH-WHAT?!

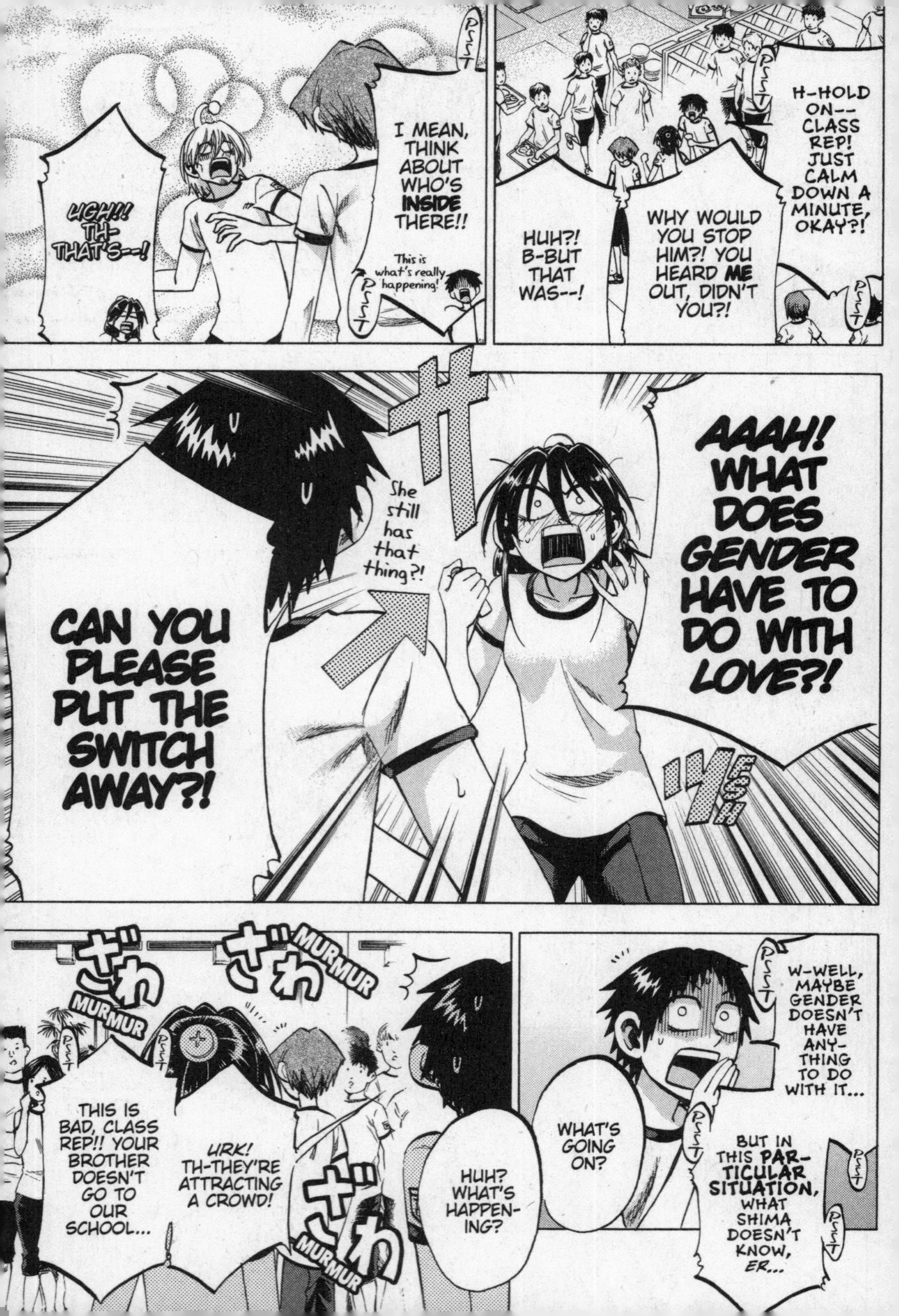
PSST
H-HOLD ON-- CLASS REP! JUST CALM DOWN A MINUTE, OKAY?!
PSST
WHY WOULD YOU STOP HIM?! YOU HEARD ME OUT, DIDN'T YOU?!
HUH?! B-BUT THAT WAS--!
PSST
PSST
I MEAN, THINK ABOUT WHO'S INSIDE THERE!!
This is what's really happening!
PSST
UGH!! TH-THAT'S--!
AAAH! WHAT DOES GENDER HAVE TO DO WITH LOVE?!
She still has that thing?!
CAN YOU PLEASE PUT THE SWITCH AWAY?!
PSST
W-WELL, MAYBE GENDER DOESN'T HAVE ANYTHING TO DO WITH IT...
PSST
PSST
BUT IN THIS PARTICULAR SITUATION, WHAT SHIMA DOESN'T KNOW, ER...
PSST
WHAT'S GOING ON?
ざわ MURMUR
ざわ MURMUR
HUH? WHAT'S HAPPENING?
ざわ MURMUR
URK! TH-THEY'RE ATTRACTING A CROWD!
PSST
PSST
THIS IS BAD, CLASS REP!! YOUR BROTHER DOESN'T GO TO OUR SCHOOL...

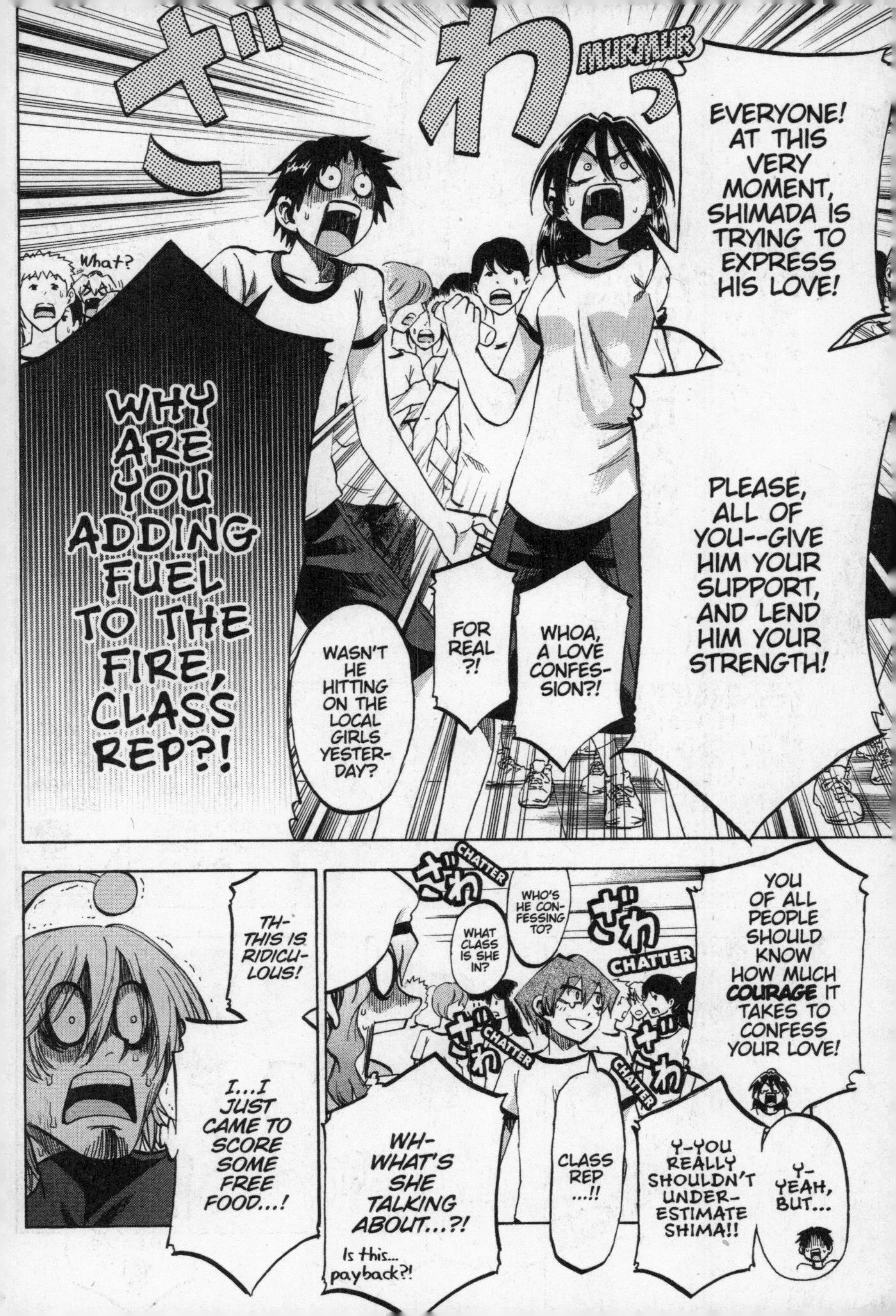
わっ
MURMUR
EVERYONE! AT THIS VERY MOMENT, SHIMADA IS TRYING TO EXPRESS HIS LOVE!
PLEASE, ALL OF YOU--GIVE HIM YOUR SUPPORT, AND LEND HIM YOUR STRENGTH!
WHOA, A LOVE CONFES-SION?!
FOR REAL?!
WASN'T HE HITTING ON THE LOCAL GIRLS YESTER-DAY?
What?
ズ
WHY ARE YOU ADDING FUEL TO THE FIRE, CLASS REP?!
YOU OF ALL PEOPLE SHOULD KNOW HOW MUCH **COURAGE** IT TAKES TO CONFESS YOUR LOVE!
ざわ
CHATTER
WHO'S HE CON-FESSING TO?
ざわ
CHATTER
WHAT CLASS IS SHE IN?
ざわ
CHATTER
ざわ
CHATTER
Y-YEAH, BUT...
Y-YOU REALLY SHOULDN'T UNDER-ESTIMATE SHIMA!!
CLASS REP ...!!
WH-WHAT'S SHE TALKING ABOUT...?!
Is this... payback?!
TH-THIS IS RIDICU-LOUS!
I...I JUST CAME TO SCORE SOME FREE FOOD...!

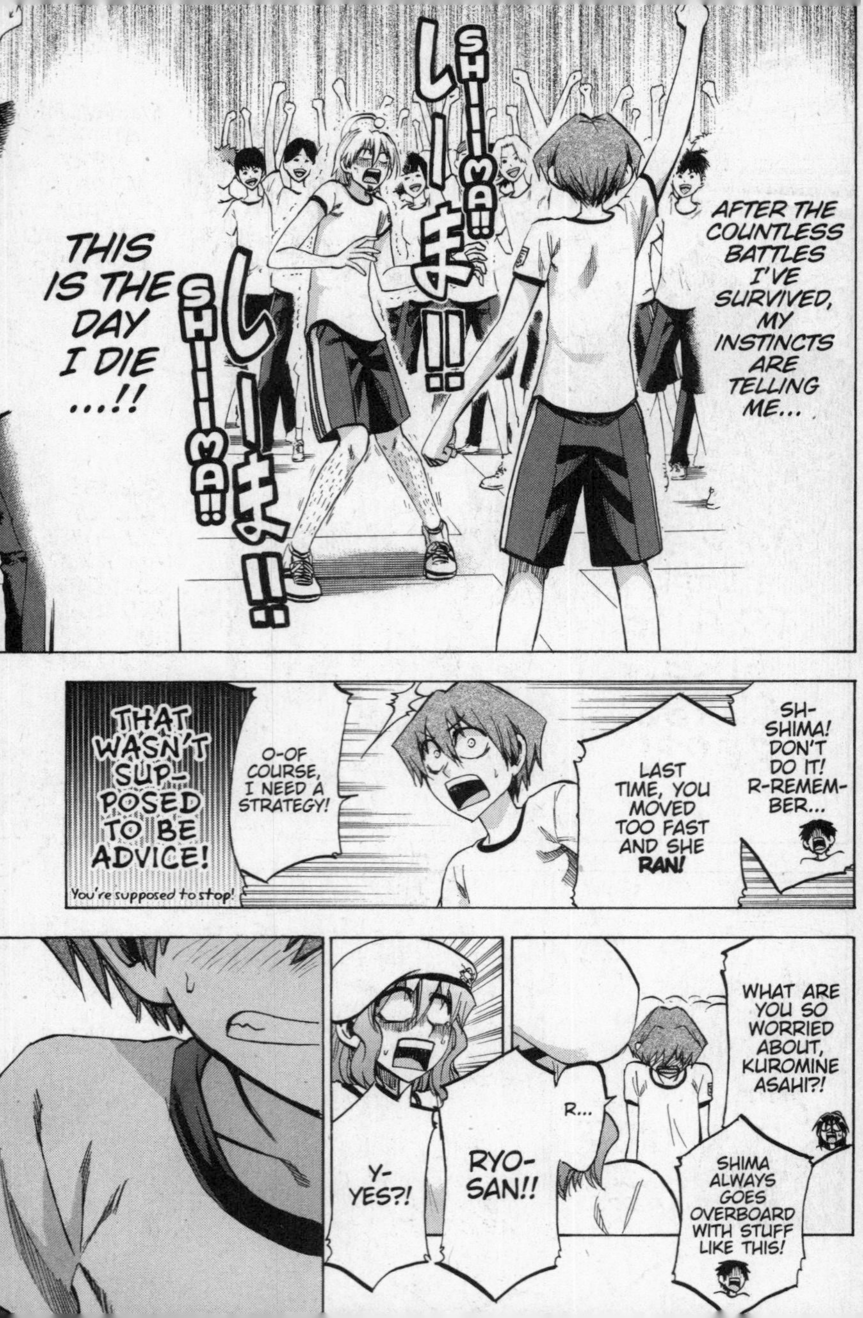

AFTER THE COUNTLESS BATTLES I'VE SURVIVED, MY INSTINCTS ARE TELLING ME...
SHIIIMA!!
しーま!!
SHIIIMA!!
しーま!!
THIS IS THE DAY I DIE...!!
SH-SHIMA! DON'T DO IT! R-REMEMBER...
LAST TIME, YOU MOVED TOO FAST AND SHE RAN!
O-OF COURSE, I NEED A STRATEGY!
THAT WASN'T SUPPOSED TO BE ADVICE!
You're supposed to stop!
WHAT ARE YOU SO WORRIED ABOUT, KUROMINE ASAHI?!
SHIMA ALWAYS GOES OVERBOARD WITH STUFF LIKE THIS!
R...
RYO-SAN!!
Y-YES?!

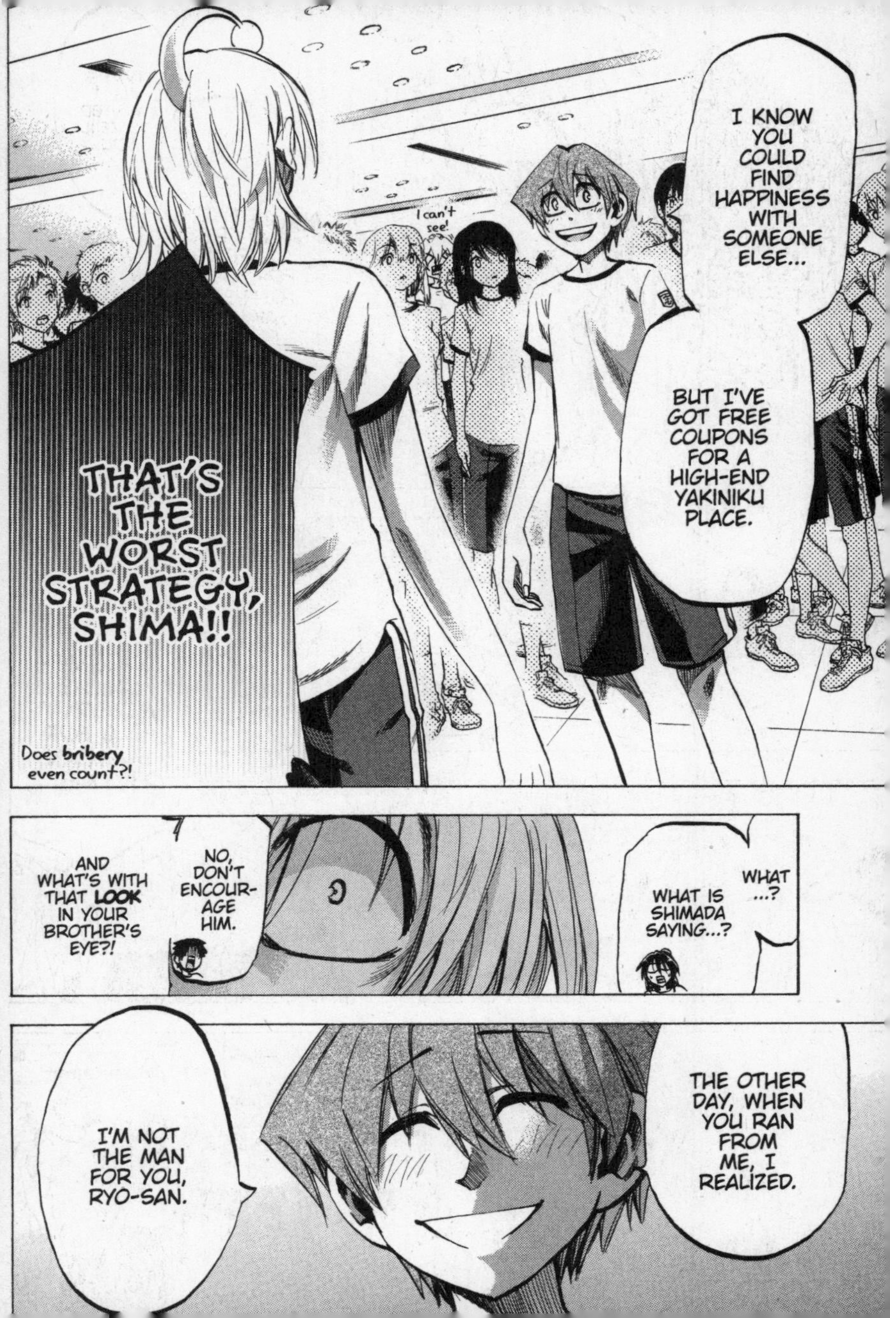
I KNOW YOU COULD FIND HAPPINESS WITH SOMEONE ELSE...
BUT I'VE GOT FREE COUPONS FOR A HIGH-END YAKINIKU PLACE.
I can't see!
THAT'S THE WORST STRATEGY, SHIMA!!
Does bribery even count?!
WHAT ...?
WHAT IS SHIMADA SAYING...?
NO, DON'T ENCOURAGE HIM.
AND WHAT'S WITH THAT LOOK IN YOUR BROTHER'S EYE?!
THE OTHER DAY, WHEN YOU RAN FROM ME, I REALIZED.
I'M NOT THE MAN FOR YOU, RYO-SAN.

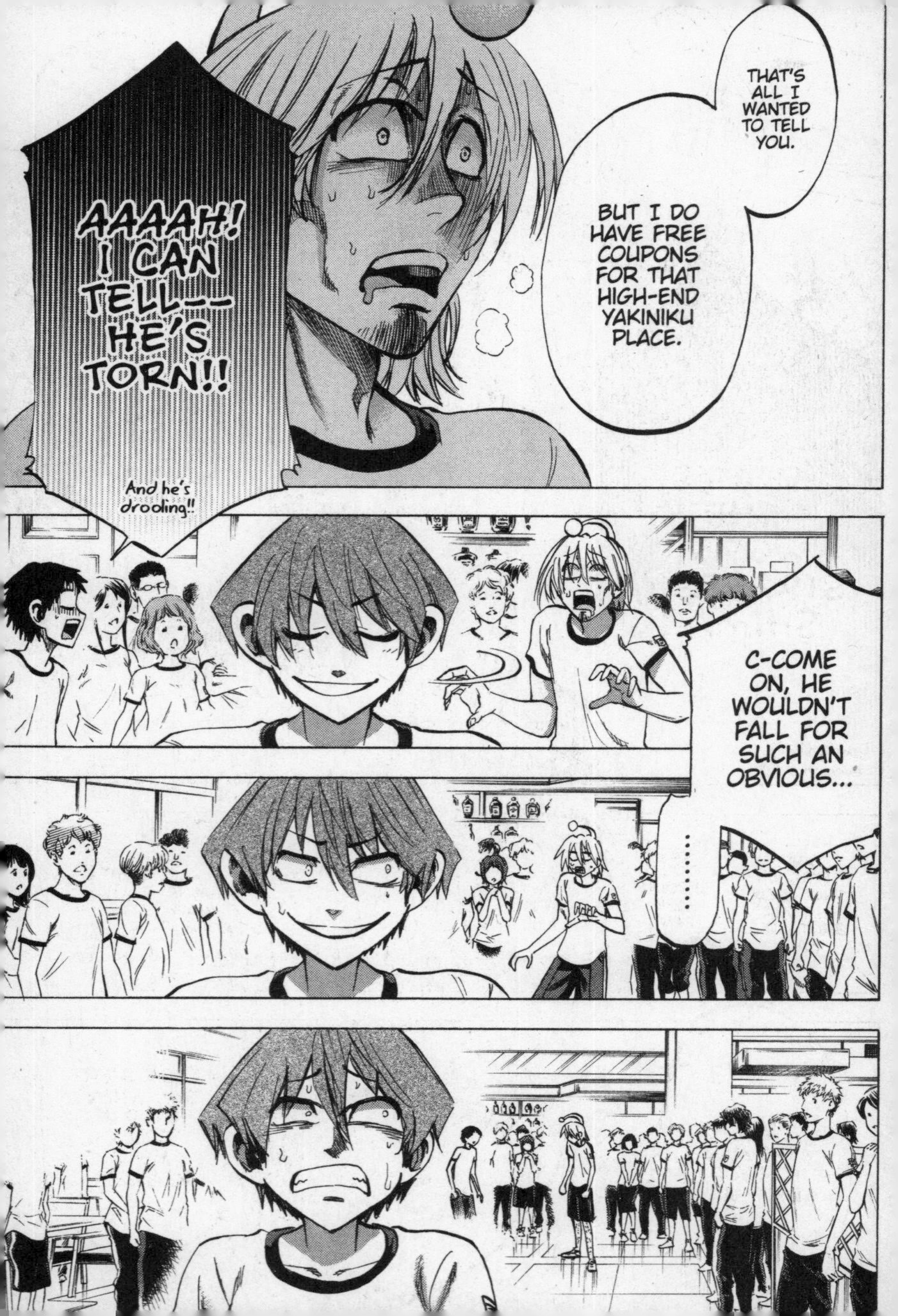
THAT'S ALL I WANTED TO TELL YOU.
BUT I DO HAVE FREE COUPONS FOR THAT HIGH-END YAKINIKU PLACE.
AAAAH! I CAN TELL-- HE'S TORN!!
And he's drooling!!
C-COME ON, HE WOULDN'T FALL FOR SUCH AN OBVIOUS...
......

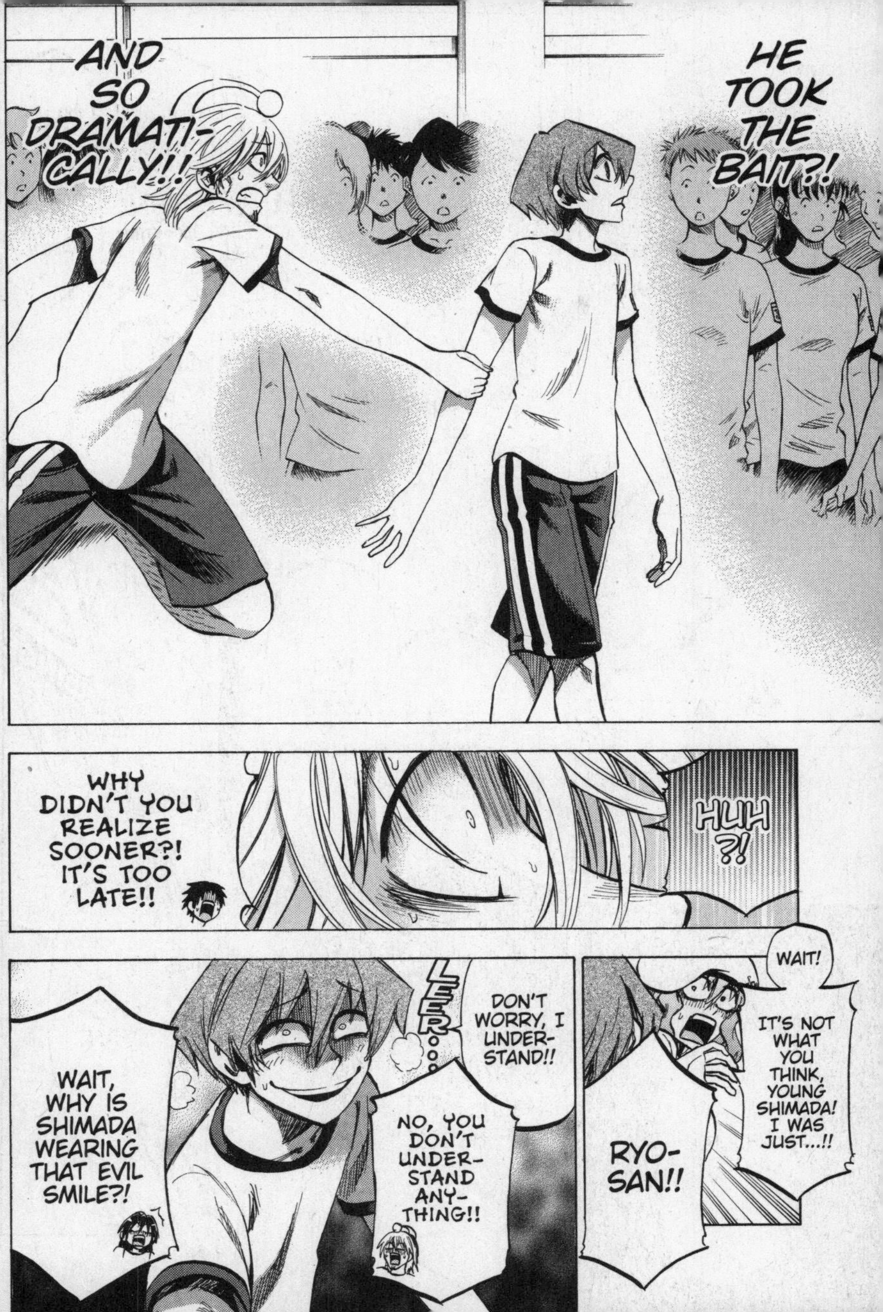
HE TOOK THE BAIT?!
AND SO DRAMATI-CALLY?!!
HUH ?!
WHY DIDN'T YOU REALIZE SOONER?! IT'S TOO LATE!!
WAIT!
IT'S NOT WHAT YOU THINK, YOUNG SHIMADA! I WAS JUST...!!
RYO-SAN!!
LEER...
DON'T WORRY, I UNDER-STAND!!
NO, YOU DON'T UNDER-STAND ANY-THING!!
WAIT, WHY IS SHIMADA WEARING THAT EVIL SMILE?!

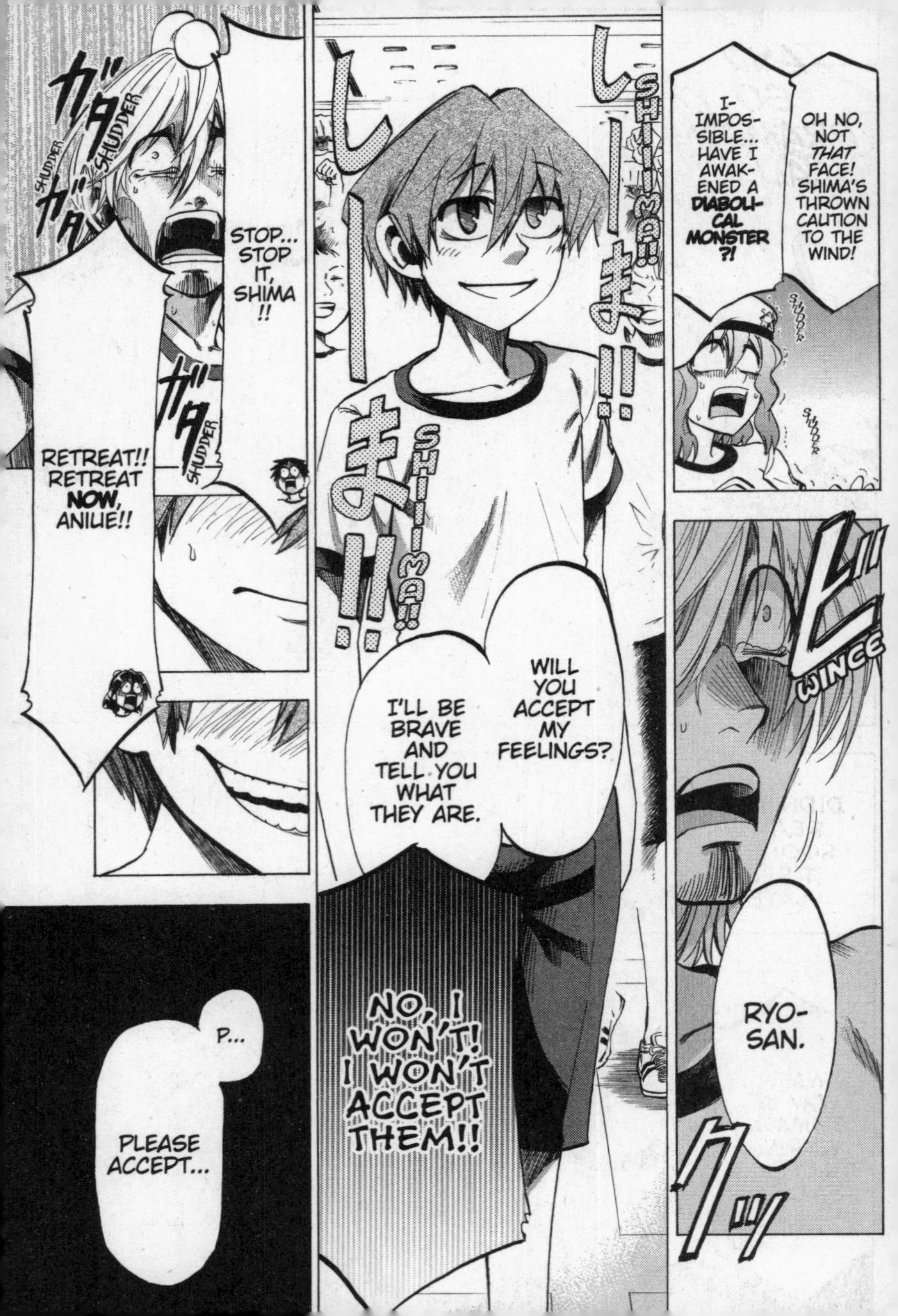
OH NO, NOT THAT FACE! SHIMA'S THROWN CAUTION TO THE WIND!
I-IMPOSSIBLE... HAVE I AWAKENED A DIABOLICAL MONSTER?!
SHUDDER
SHUDDER
WINCE
RYO-SAN.
SHI-I-MA!!
しーまーっ!!
SHI-I-MA!!
しーまーっ!!
WILL YOU ACCEPT MY FEELINGS?
I'LL BE BRAVE AND TELL YOU WHAT THEY ARE.
NO, I WON'T! I WON'T ACCEPT THEM!!
STOP... STOP IT, SHIMA!!
SHUDDER
SHUDDER
SHUDDER
RETREAT!! RETREAT NOW, ANIUE!!
P...
PLEASE ACCEPT...

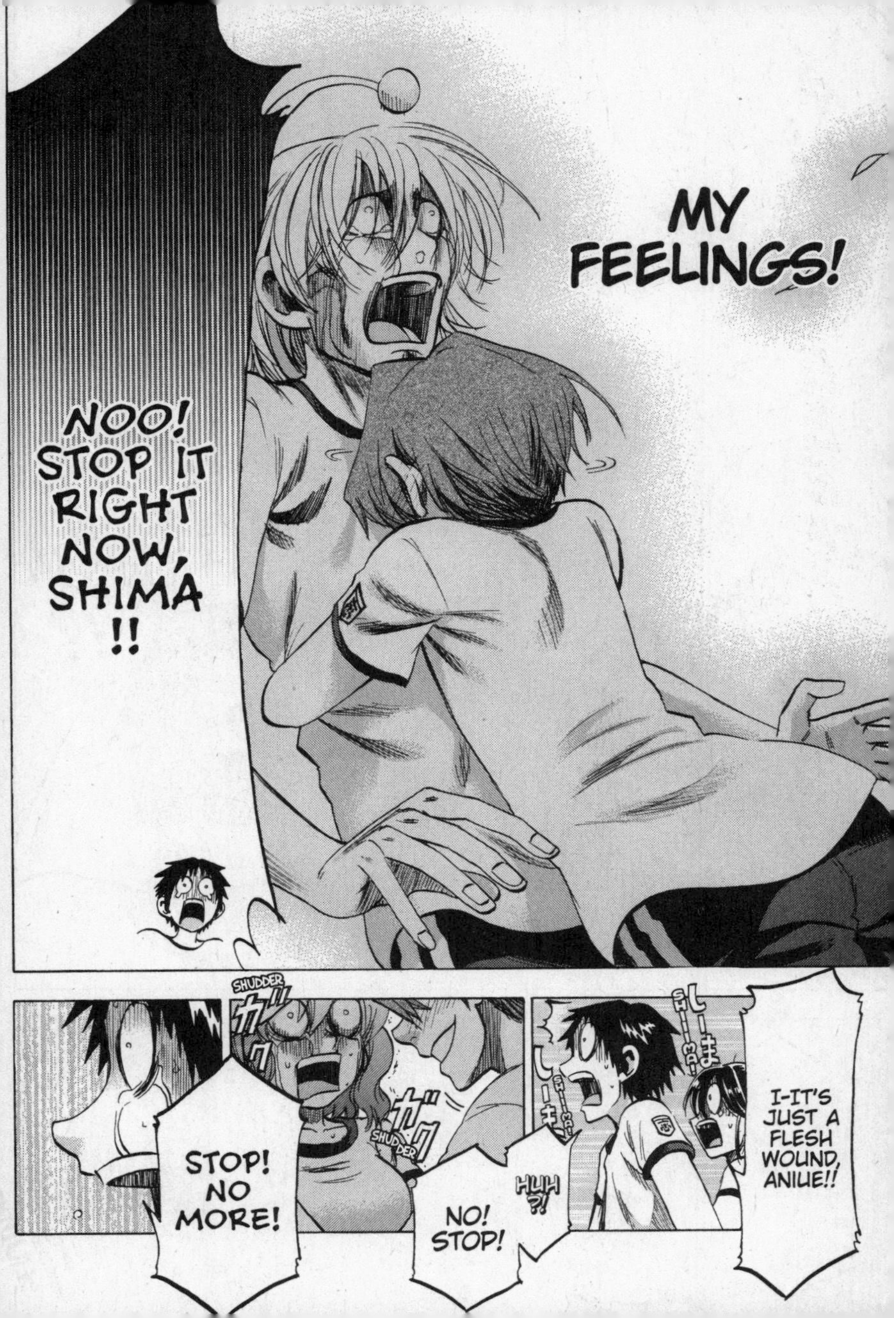
MY FEELINGS!
NOO! STOP IT RIGHT NOW, SHIMA!!
I-IT'S JUST A FLESH WOUND, ANIUE!!
SHI-MA!
SHI-MA!
HUH?!
NO! STOP!
SHUDDER
SHUDDER
STOP! NO MORE!

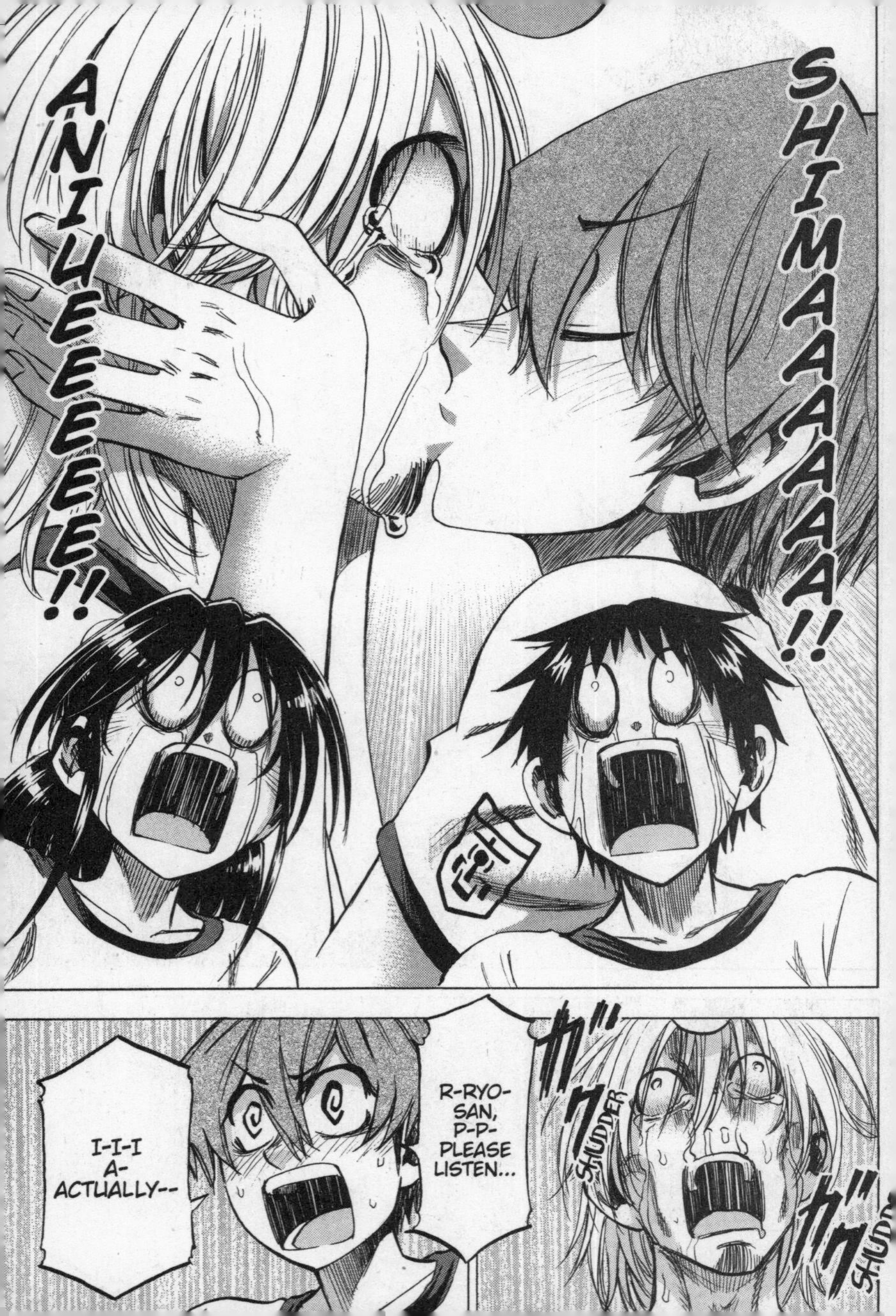
SHIMAAAAAAA!!
ANIUEEEEEE!!
SHUDDER
SHUDD
R-RYO-SAN, P-P-PLEASE LISTEN...
I-I-I A-ACTUALLY--

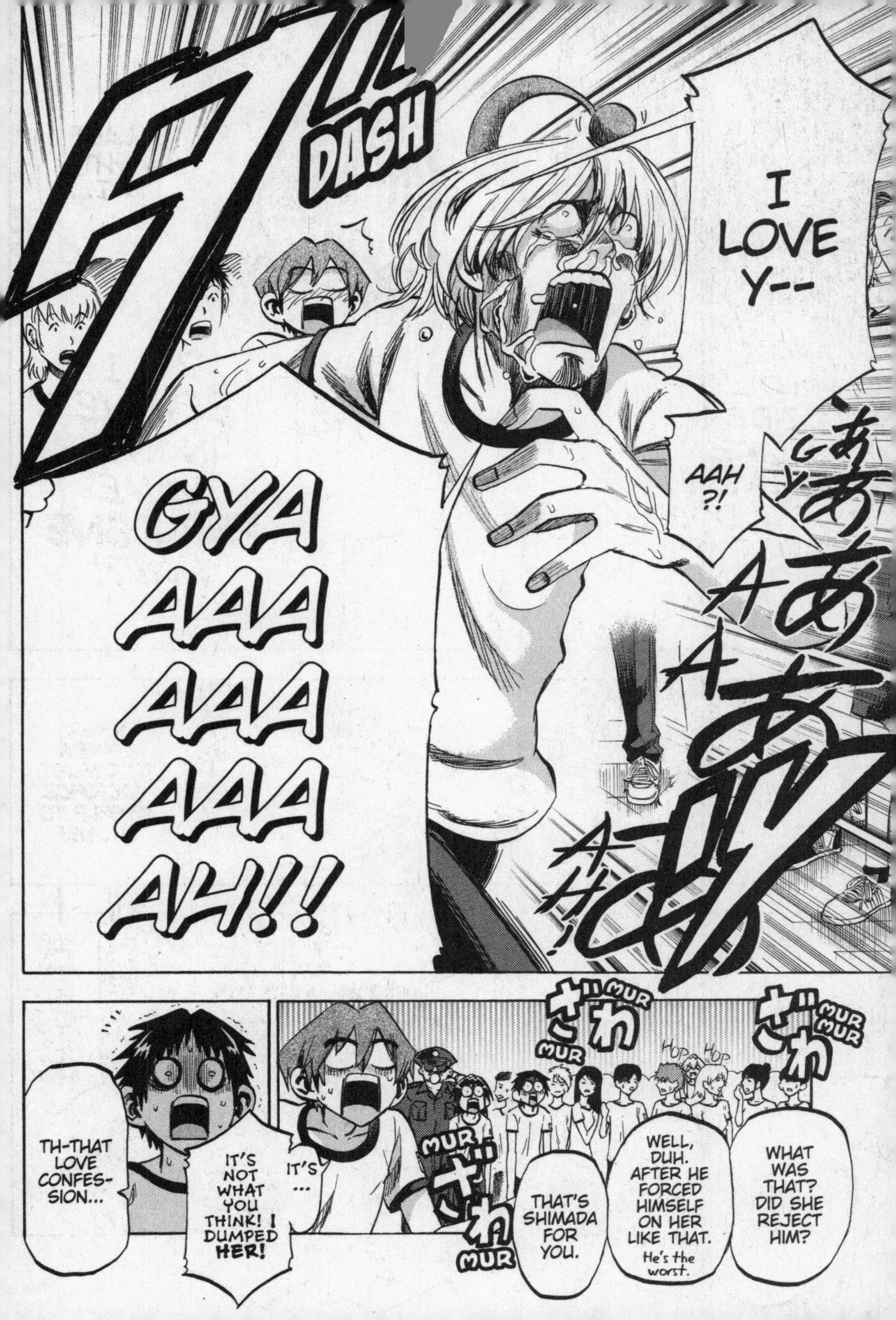
I LOVE Y--
AAH ?!
GYAAAAH!
DASH
GYA AAA AAA AAA AH!!
MUR MUR
MUR MUR
MUR
HOP HOP
WHAT WAS THAT? DID SHE REJECT HIM?
WELL, DUH. AFTER HE FORCED HIMSELF ON HER LIKE THAT.
He's the worst.
THAT'S SHIMADA FOR YOU.
MUR
MUR
IT'S ...
IT'S NOT WHAT YOU THINK! I DUMPED HER!
TH-THAT LOVE CONFES-SION...

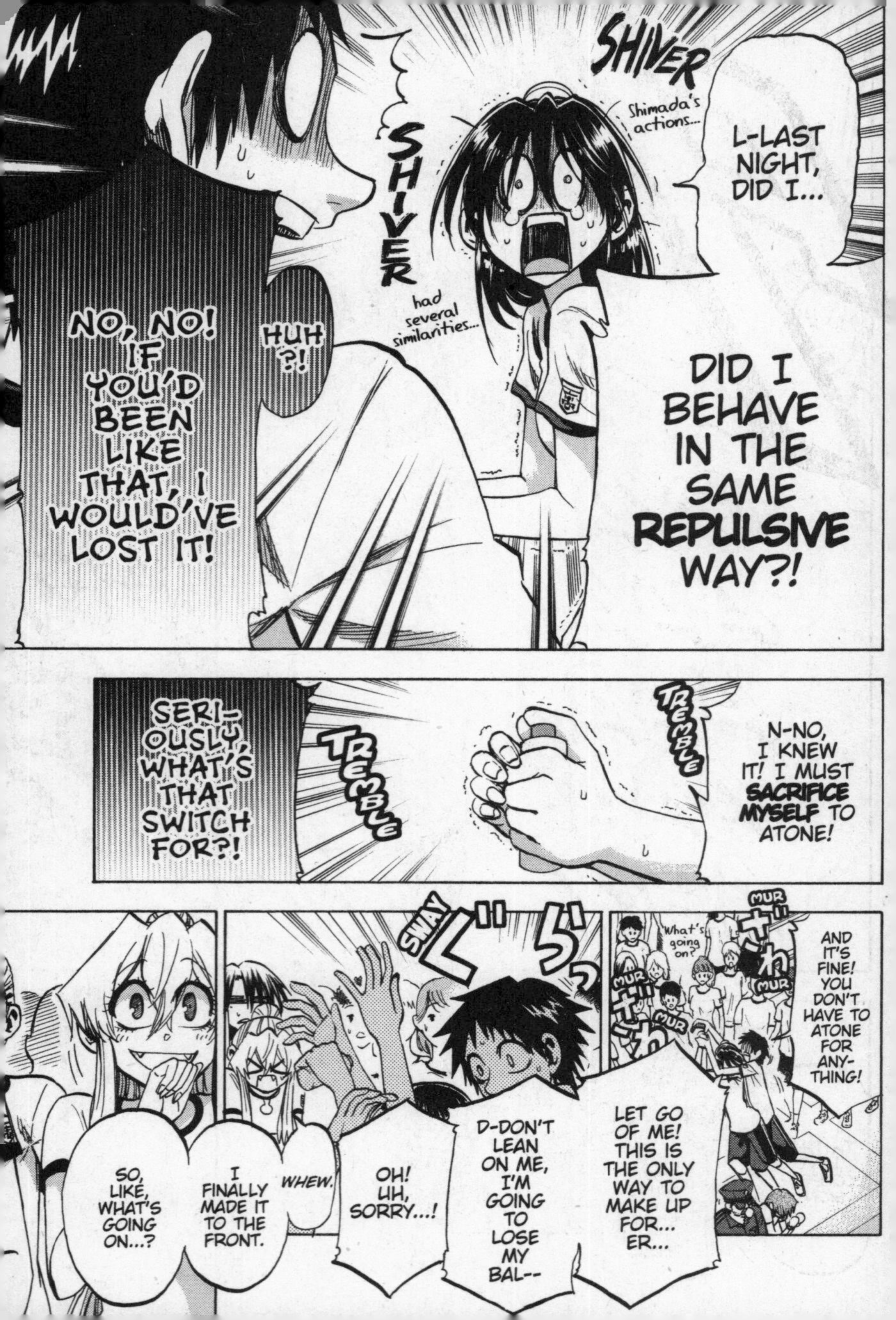
SHIVER
L-LAST NIGHT, DID I...
Shimada's actions...
SHIVER
had several similarities...
DID I BEHAVE IN THE SAME REPULSIVE WAY?!
HUH?!
NO, NO! IF YOU'D BEEN LIKE THAT, I WOULD'VE LOST IT!
N-NO, I KNEW IT! I MUST SACRIFICE MYSELF TO ATONE!
TREMBLE
TREMBLE
SERIOUSLY, WHAT'S THAT SWITCH FOR?!
MUR
What's going on?
MUR
MUR
MUR
AND IT'S FINE! YOU DON'T HAVE TO ATONE FOR ANYTHING!
LET GO OF ME! THIS IS THE ONLY WAY TO MAKE UP FOR... ER...
SWAY ぐらっ
D-DON'T LEAN ON ME, I'M GOING TO LOSE MY BAL--
OH! UH, SORRY...!
WHEW.
I FINALLY MADE IT TO THE FRONT.
SO, LIKE, WHAT'S GOING ON...?

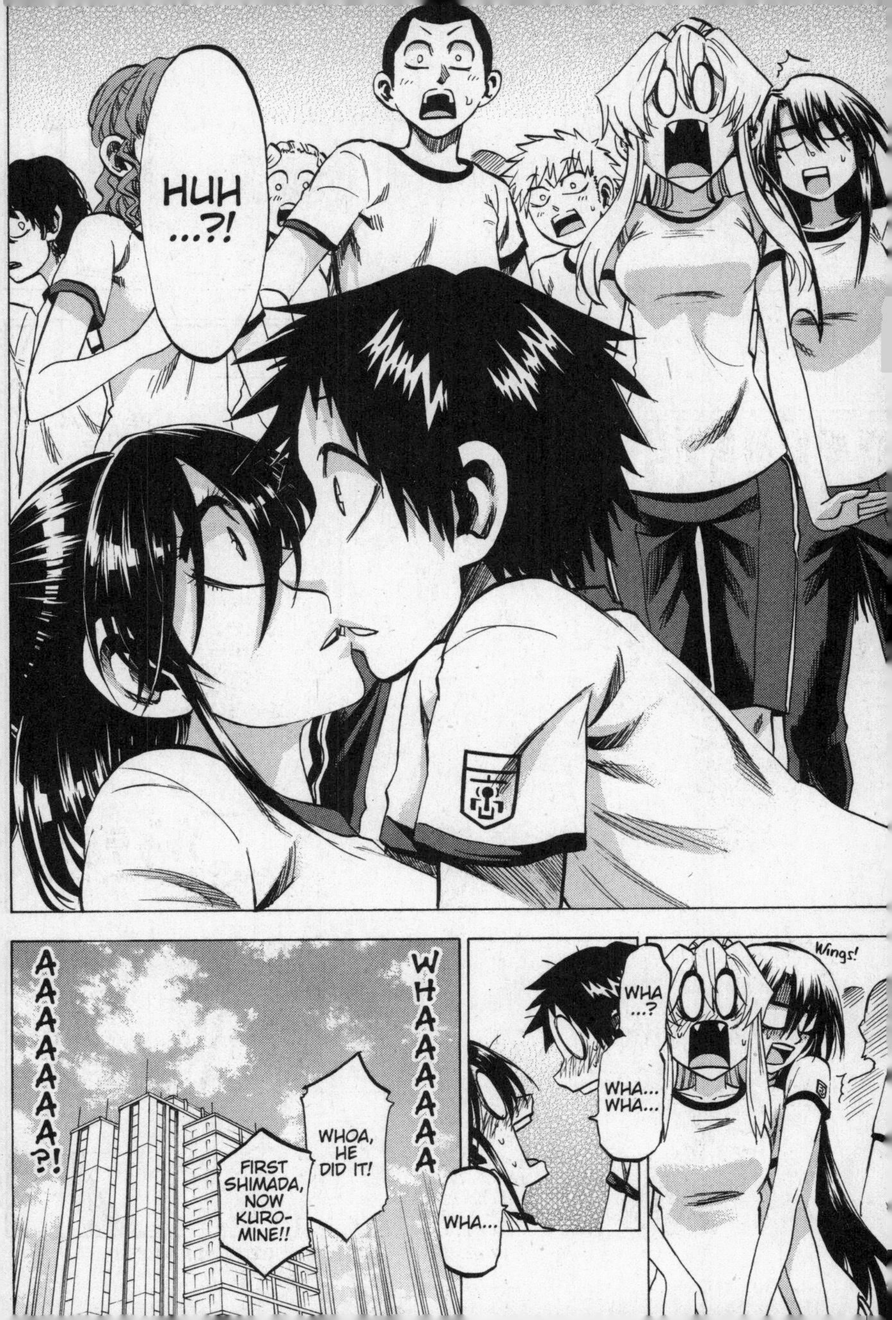
HUH ...?!
Wings!
WHA ...?
WHA... WHA...
WHA...
WHAAAAAAA
WHOA, HE DID IT!
FIRST SHIMADA, NOW KURO-MINE!!
AAAAAAAA?!

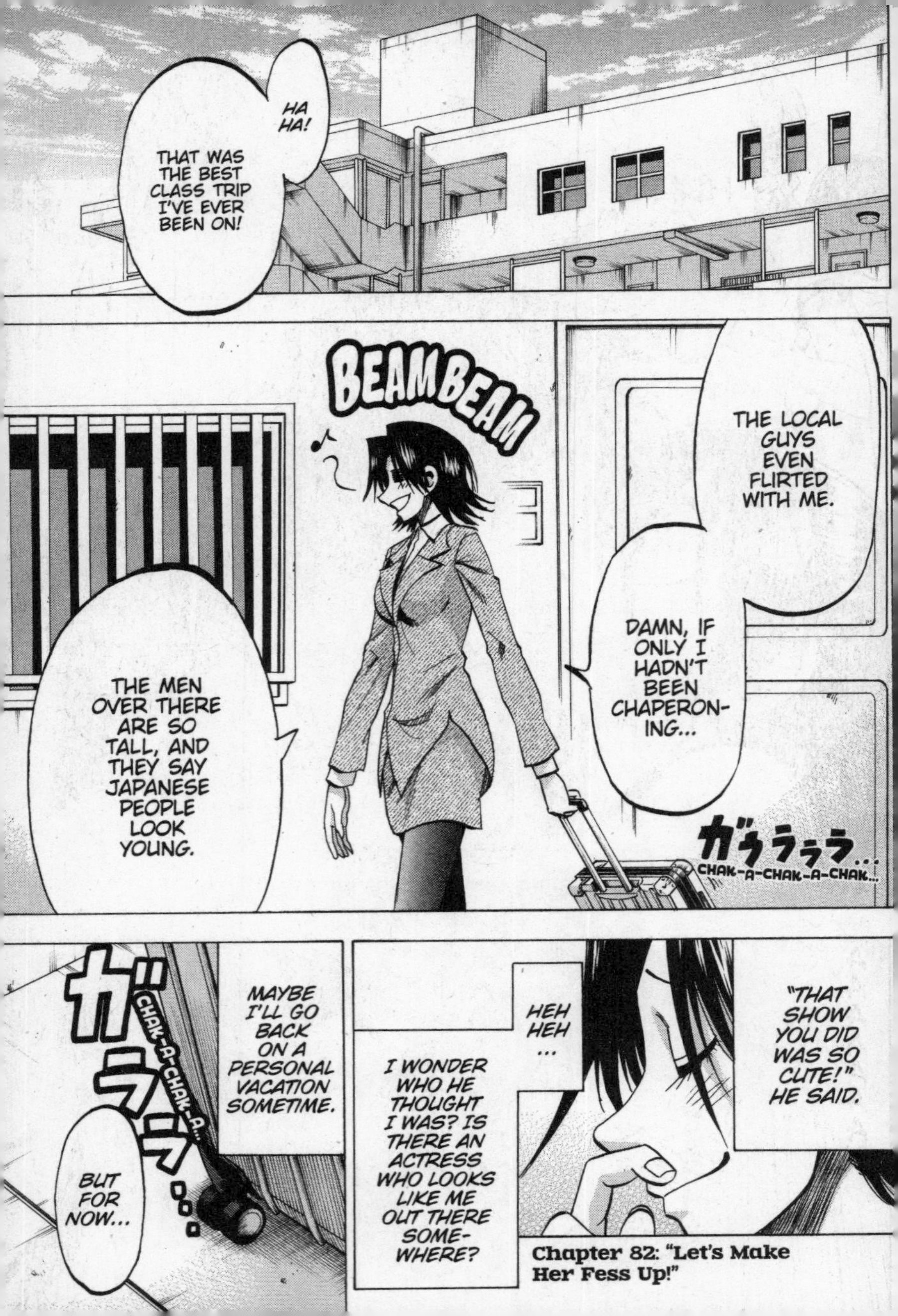
HA HA!
THAT WAS THE BEST CLASS TRIP I'VE EVER BEEN ON!
BEAMBEAM
THE LOCAL GUYS EVEN FLIRTED WITH ME.
DAMN, IF ONLY I HADN'T BEEN CHAPERONING...
THE MEN OVER THERE ARE SO TALL, AND THEY SAY JAPANESE PEOPLE LOOK YOUNG.
ガゥラララ...
CHAK-A-CHAK-A-CHAK...
"THAT SHOW YOU DID WAS SO CUTE!" HE SAID.
HEH HEH ...
I WONDER WHO HE THOUGHT I WAS? IS THERE AN ACTRESS WHO LOOKS LIKE ME OUT THERE SOMEWHERE?
MAYBE I'LL GO BACK ON A PERSONAL VACATION SOMETIME.
ガラララ
CHAK-A-CHAK-A...
BUT FOR NOW...

Chapter 82: "Let's Make Her Fess Up!"

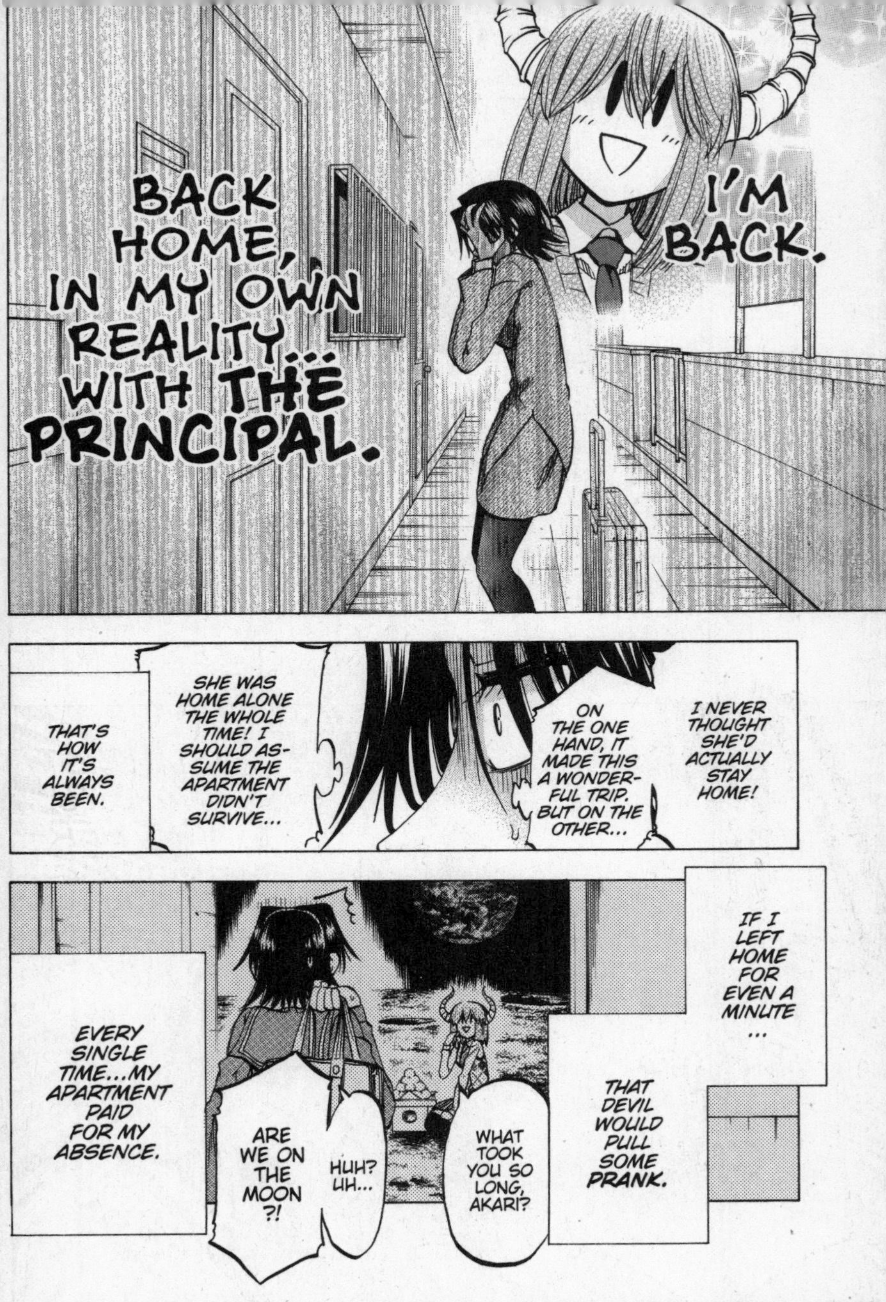
I'M BACK.
BACK HOME, IN MY OWN REALITY... WITH THE PRINCIPAL.
I NEVER THOUGHT SHE'D ACTUALLY STAY HOME!
ON THE ONE HAND, IT MADE THIS A WONDERFUL TRIP. BUT ON THE OTHER...
SHE WAS HOME ALONE THE WHOLE TIME! I SHOULD ASSUME THE APARTMENT DIDN'T SURVIVE...
THAT'S HOW IT'S ALWAYS BEEN.
IF I LEFT HOME FOR EVEN A MINUTE...
THAT DEVIL WOULD PULL SOME PRANK.
WHAT TOOK YOU SO LONG, AKARI?
HUH? UH...
ARE WE ON THE MOON?!
EVERY SINGLE TIME...MY APARTMENT PAID FOR MY ABSENCE.

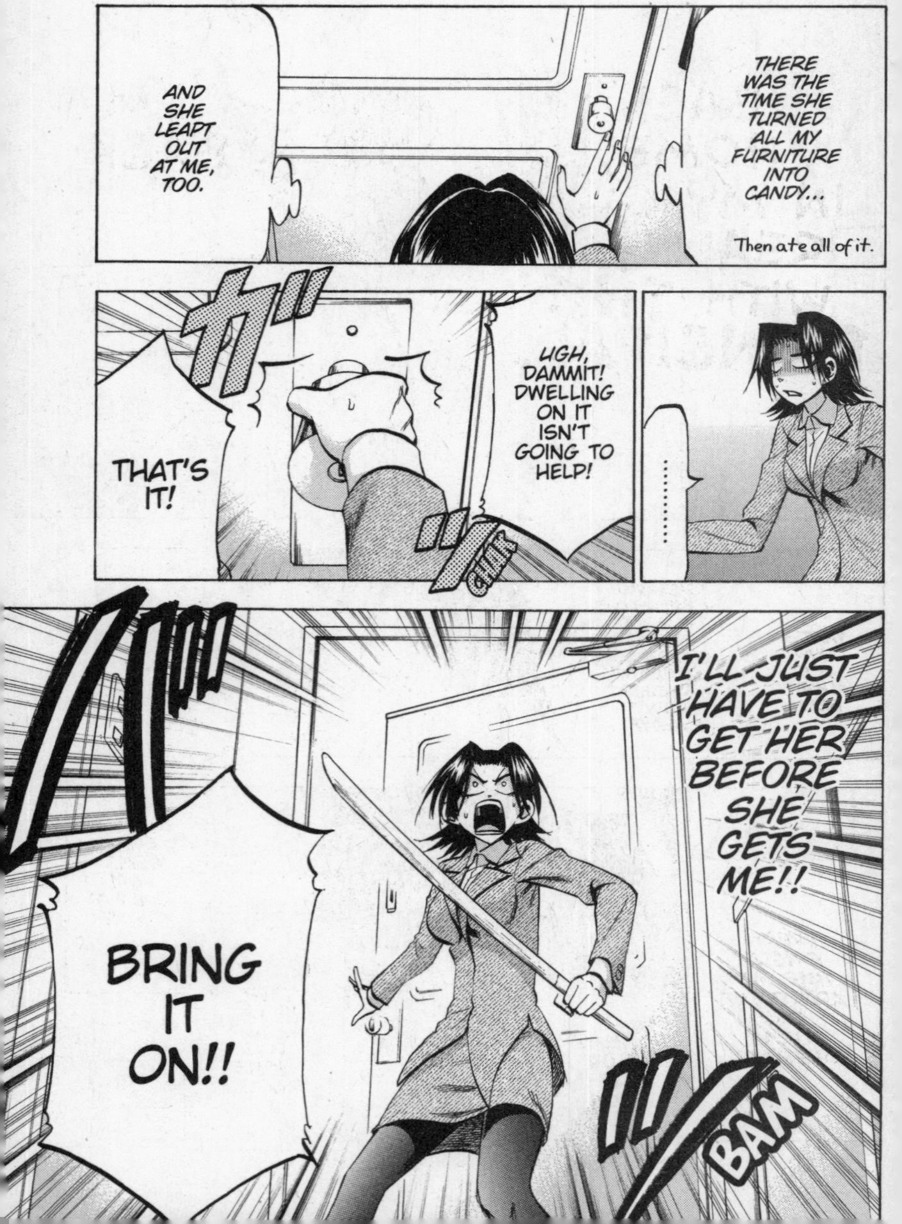
THERE WAS THE TIME SHE TURNED ALL MY FURNITURE INTO CANDY...
Then ate all of it.
AND SHE LEAPT OUT AT ME, TOO.
......
UGH, DAMMIT! DWELLING ON IT ISN'T GOING TO HELP!
ガ
THAT'S IT!
I'LL JUST HAVE TO GET HER BEFORE SHE GETS ME!!
BRING IT ON!!
BAM

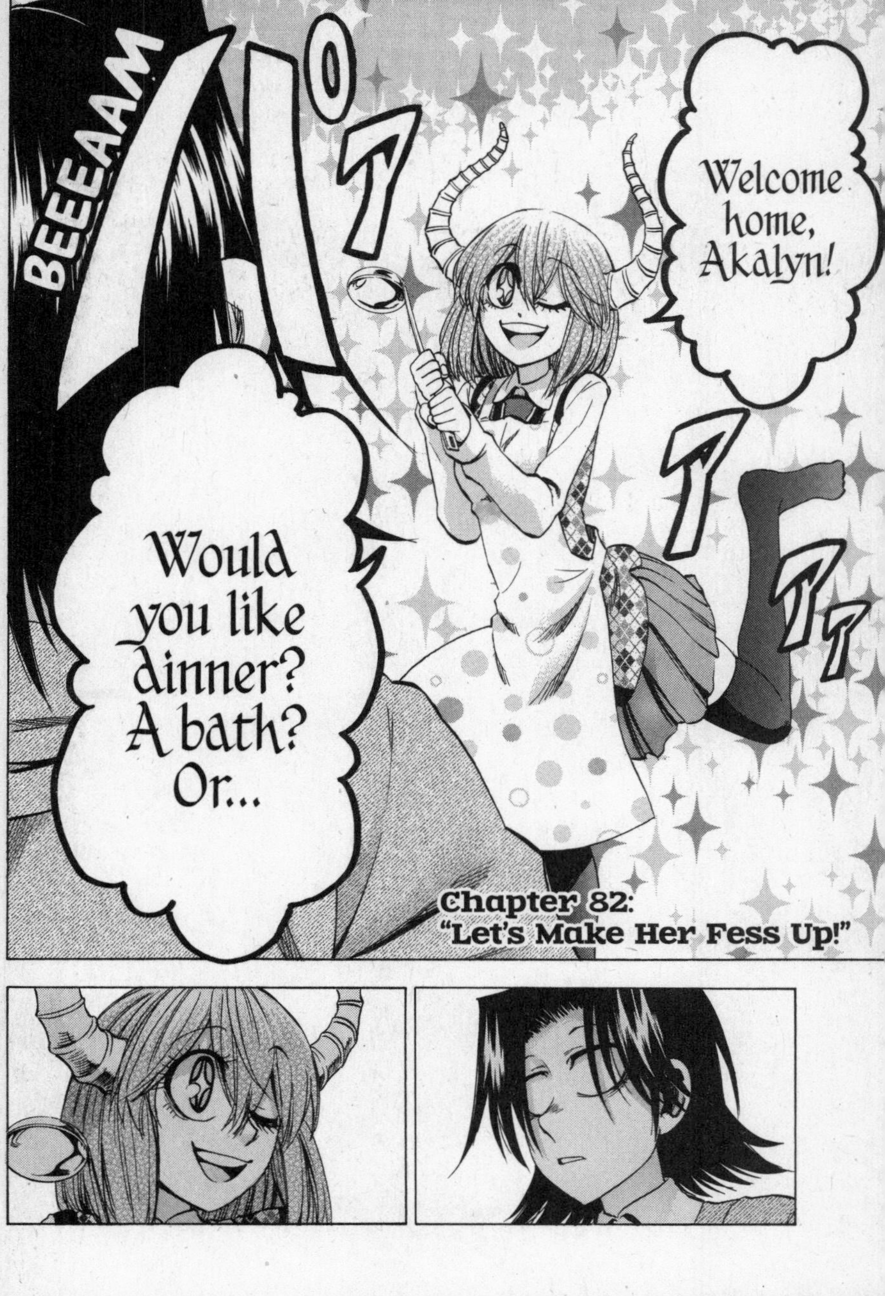
Welcome home, Akalyn!
Would you like dinner? A bath? Or...
BEEEAAM
Chapter 82:
"Let's Make Her Fess Up!"

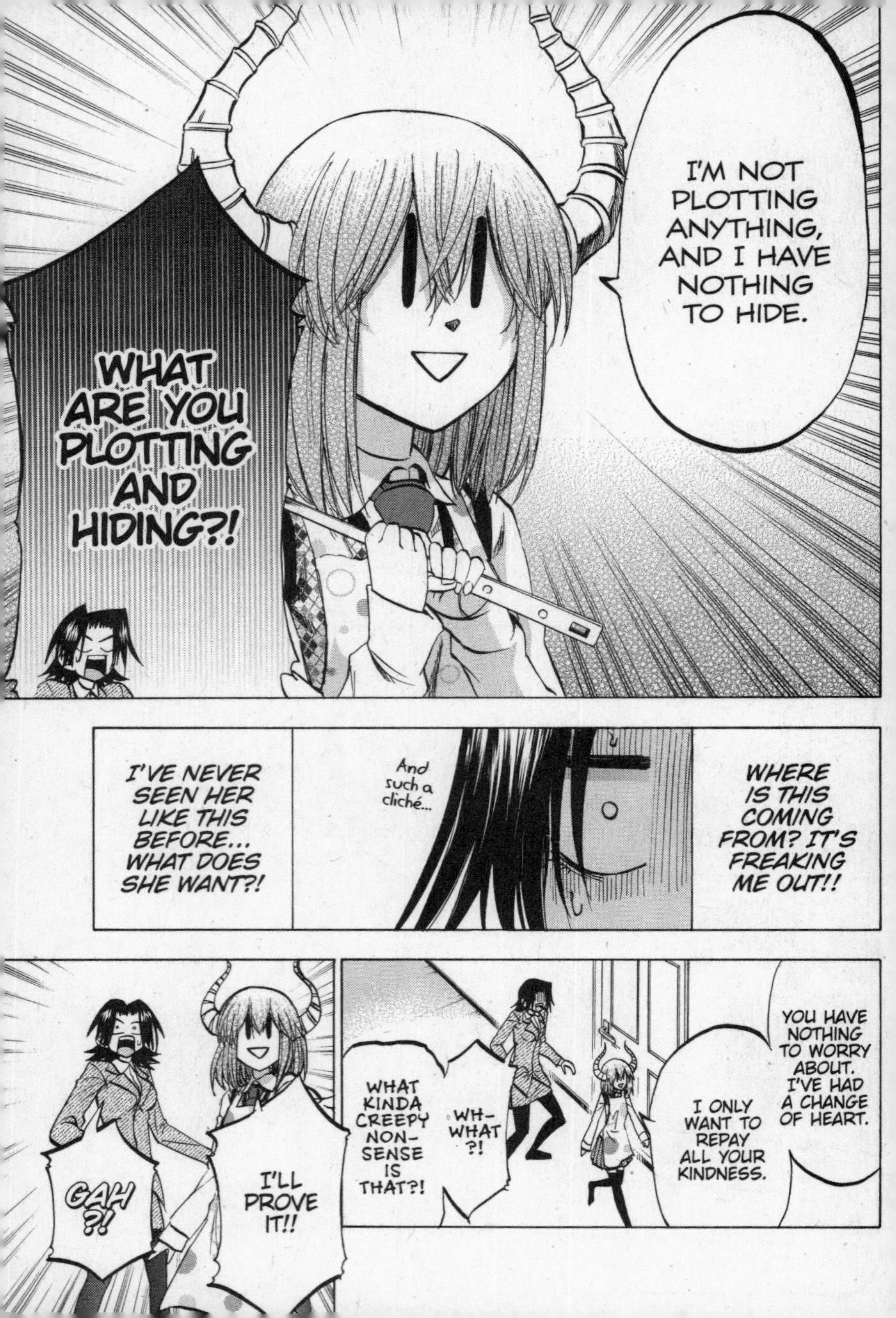
I'M NOT PLOTTING ANYTHING, AND I HAVE NOTHING TO HIDE.
WHAT ARE YOU PLOTTING AND HIDING?!
WHERE IS THIS COMING FROM? IT'S FREAKING ME OUT!!
And such a cliché...
I'VE NEVER SEEN HER LIKE THIS BEFORE... WHAT DOES SHE WANT?!
YOU HAVE NOTHING TO WORRY ABOUT. I'VE HAD A CHANGE OF HEART.
I ONLY WANT TO REPAY ALL YOUR KINDNESS.
WH-WHAT?!
WHAT KINDA CREEPY NON-SENSE IS THAT?!
I'LL PROVE IT!!
GAH?!

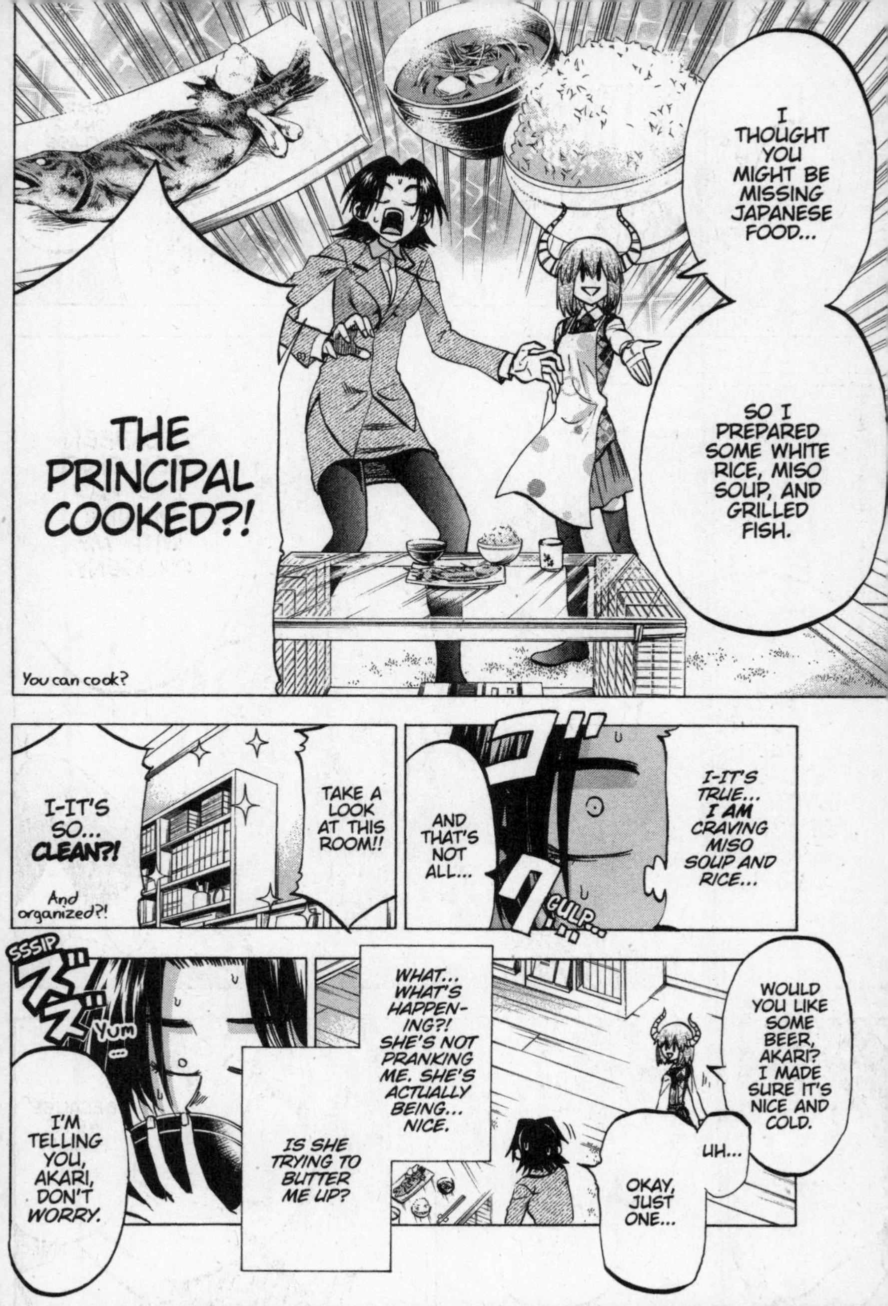

I THOUGHT YOU MIGHT BE MISSING JAPANESE FOOD...
SO I PREPARED SOME WHITE RICE, MISO SOUP, AND GRILLED FISH.
THE PRINCIPAL COOKED?!
You can cook?
I-IT'S TRUE... I AM CRAVING MISO SOUP AND RICE...
AND THAT'S NOT ALL...
GULP...
TAKE A LOOK AT THIS ROOM!!
I-IT'S SO... CLEAN?!
And organized?!
WOULD YOU LIKE SOME BEER, AKARI? I MADE SURE IT'S NICE AND COLD.
UH...
OKAY, JUST ONE...
WHAT... WHAT'S HAPPENING?! SHE'S NOT PRANKING ME. SHE'S ACTUALLY BEING... NICE.
IS SHE TRYING TO BUTTER ME UP?
SSSIP
YUM...
I'M TELLING YOU, AKARI, DON'T WORRY.

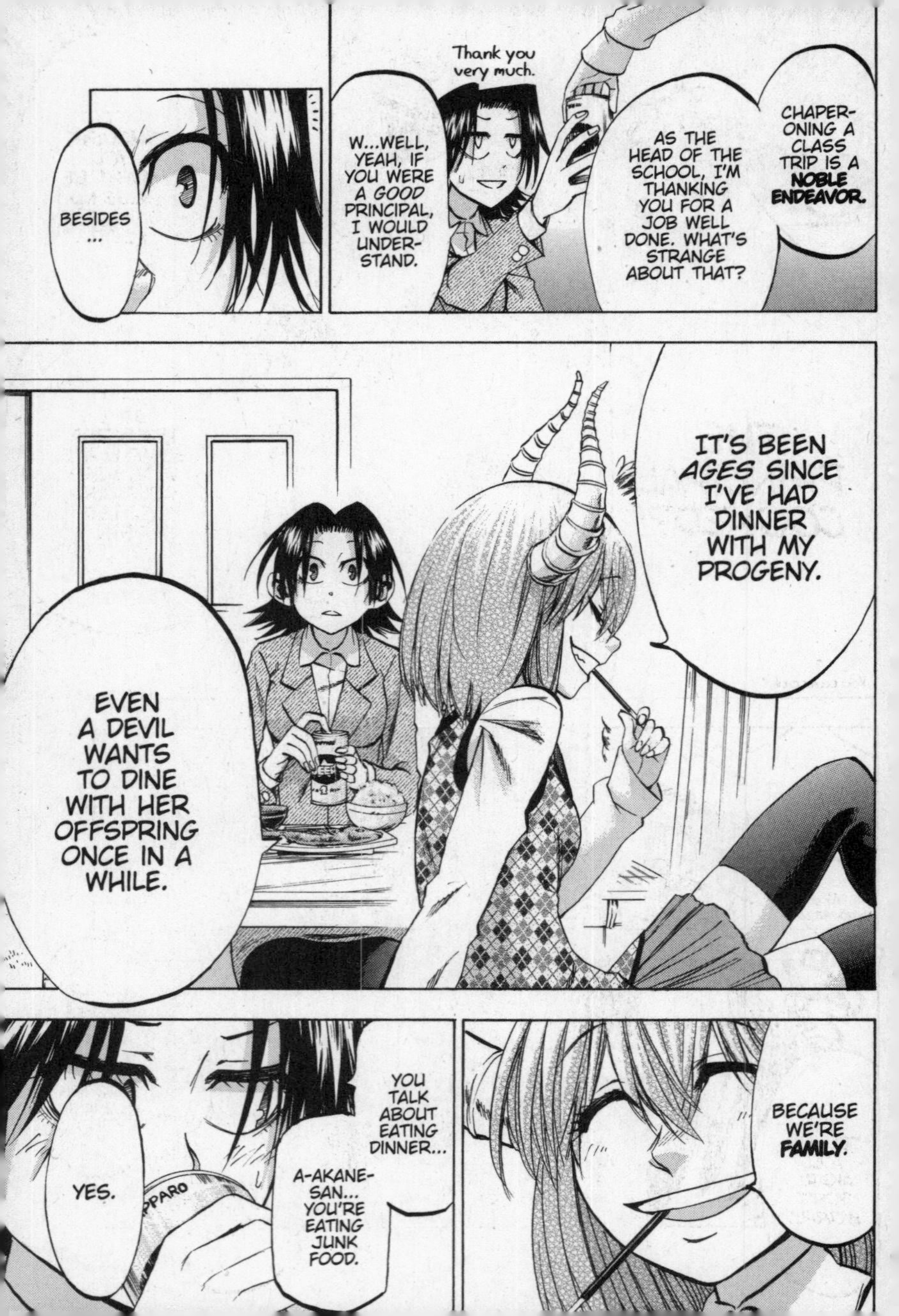
CHAPERONING A CLASS TRIP IS A **NOBLE ENDEAVOR.**
AS THE HEAD OF THE SCHOOL, I'M THANKING YOU FOR A JOB WELL DONE. WHAT'S STRANGE ABOUT THAT?
Thank you very much.
W...WELL, YEAH, IF YOU WERE A *GOOD* PRINCIPAL, I WOULD UNDERSTAND.
BESIDES...
IT'S BEEN *AGES* SINCE I'VE HAD DINNER WITH MY PROGENY.
EVEN A DEVIL WANTS TO DINE WITH HER OFFSPRING ONCE IN A WHILE.
BECAUSE WE'RE **FAMILY.**
YOU TALK ABOUT EATING DINNER...
A-AKANE-SAN... YOU'RE EATING JUNK FOOD.
YES.

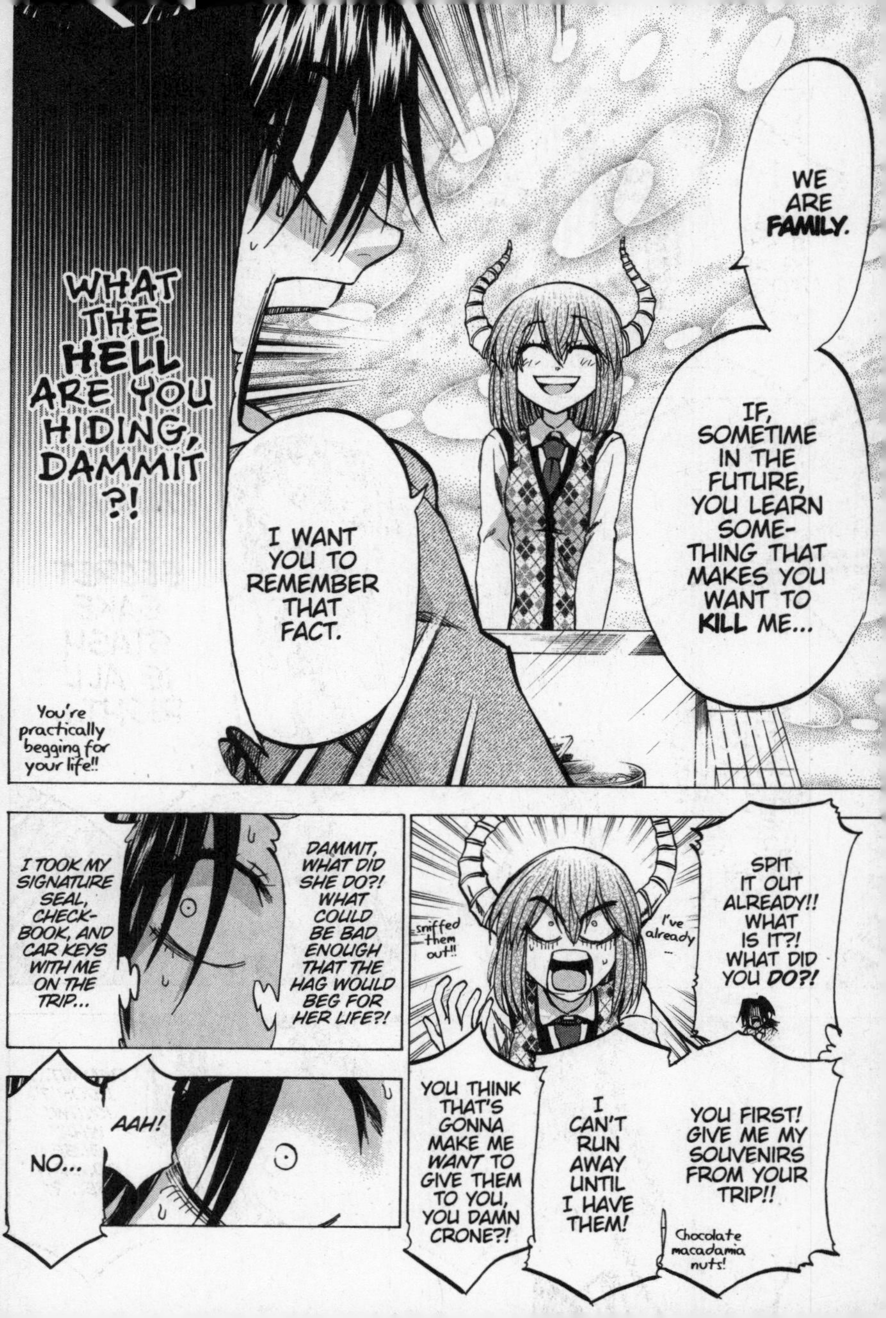
WE ARE FAMILY.
IF, SOMETIME IN THE FUTURE, YOU LEARN SOMETHING THAT MAKES YOU WANT TO KILL ME...
I WANT YOU TO REMEMBER THAT FACT.
WHAT THE HELL ARE YOU HIDING, DAMMIT?!
You're practically begging for your life!!
SPIT IT OUT ALREADY!! WHAT IS IT?! WHAT DID YOU DO?!
I've already...
sniffed them out!!
DAMMIT, WHAT DID SHE DO?! WHAT COULD BE BAD ENOUGH THAT THE HAG WOULD BEG FOR HER LIFE?!
I TOOK MY SIGNATURE SEAL, CHECKBOOK, AND CAR KEYS WITH ME ON THE TRIP...
YOU FIRST! GIVE ME MY SOUVENIRS FROM YOUR TRIP!!
Chocolate macadamia nuts!
I CAN'T RUN AWAY UNTIL I HAVE THEM!
YOU THINK THAT'S GONNA MAKE ME WANT TO GIVE THEM TO YOU, YOU DAMN CRONE?!
AAH!
NO...

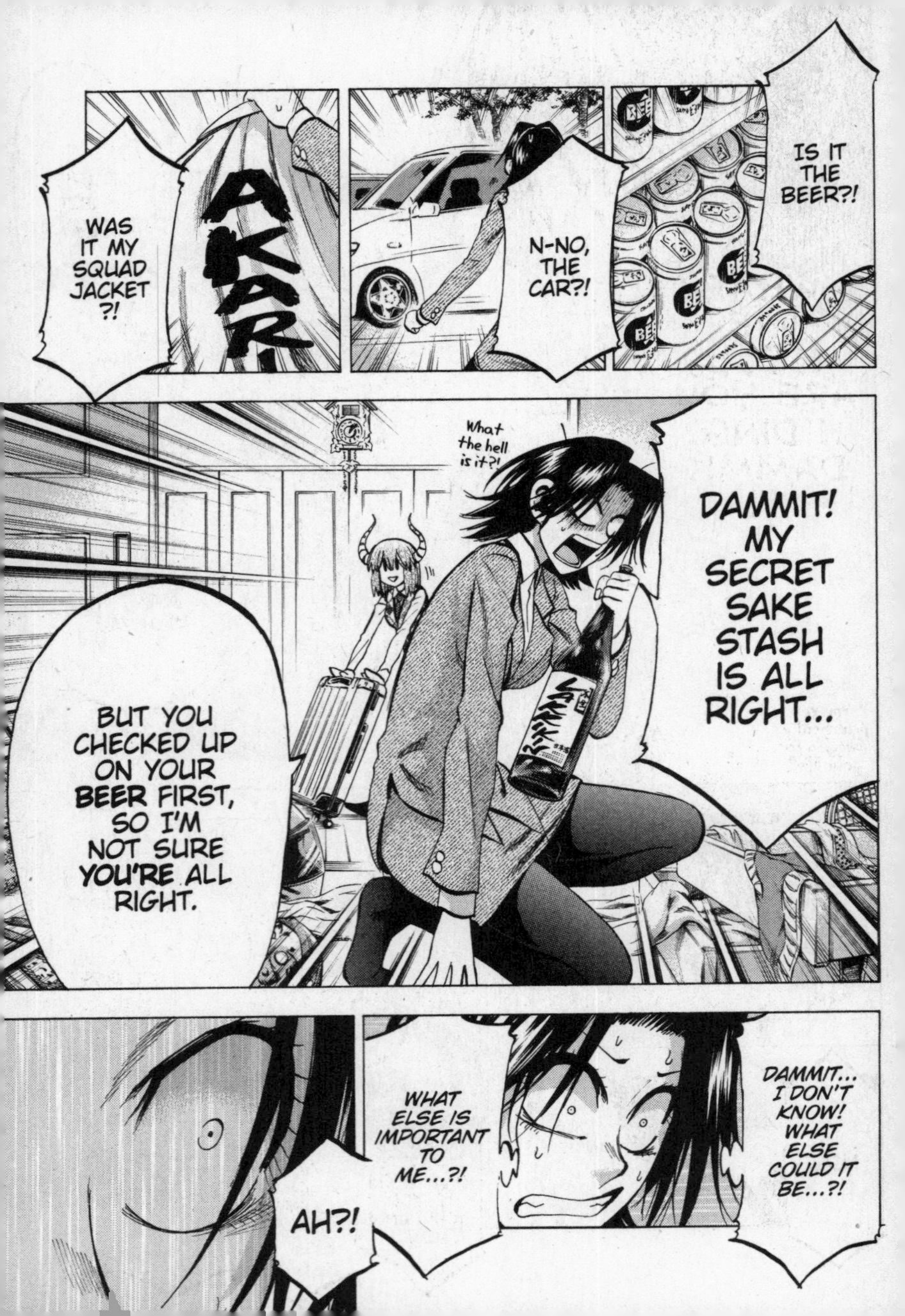
IS IT THE BEER?!
N-NO, THE CAR?!
WAS IT MY SQUAD JACKET ?!
AKARI
What the hell is it?!
DAMMIT! MY SECRET SAKE STASH IS ALL RIGHT...
BUT YOU CHECKED UP ON YOUR BEER FIRST, SO I'M NOT SURE YOU'RE ALL RIGHT.
DAMMIT... I DON'T KNOW! WHAT ELSE COULD IT BE...?!
WHAT ELSE IS IMPORTANT TO ME...?!
AH?!

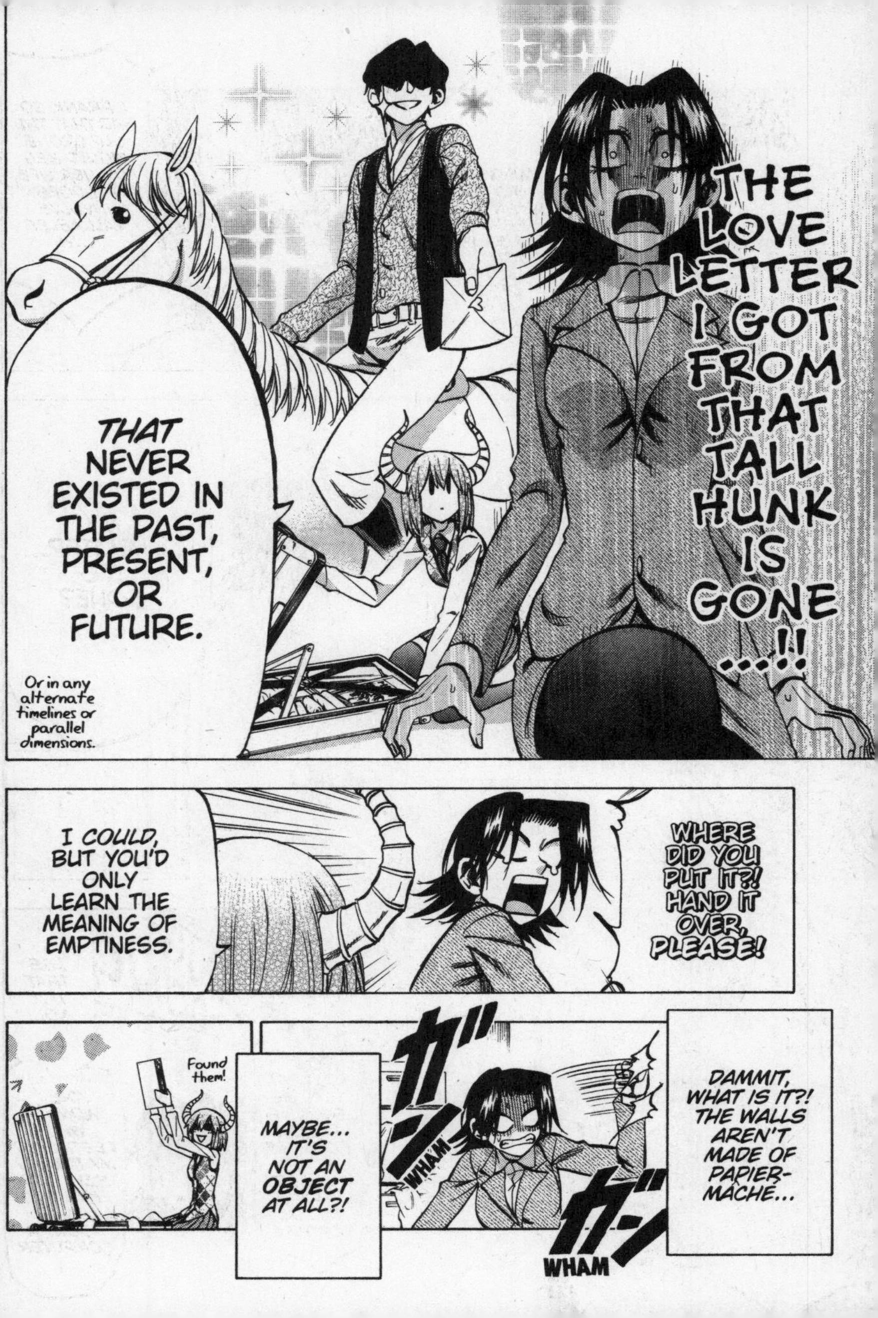
THE LOVE LETTER I GOT FROM THAT TALL HUNK IS GONE ...!!
THAT NEVER EXISTED IN THE PAST, PRESENT, OR FUTURE.
Or in any alternate timelines or parallel dimensions.
WHERE DID YOU PUT IT?! HAND IT OVER, PLEASE!
I COULD, BUT YOU'D ONLY LEARN THE MEANING OF EMPTINESS.
DAMMIT, WHAT IS IT?! THE WALLS AREN'T MADE OF PAPIER-MACHE...
WHAM
WHAM
MAYBE... IT'S NOT AN OBJECT AT ALL?!
Found them!

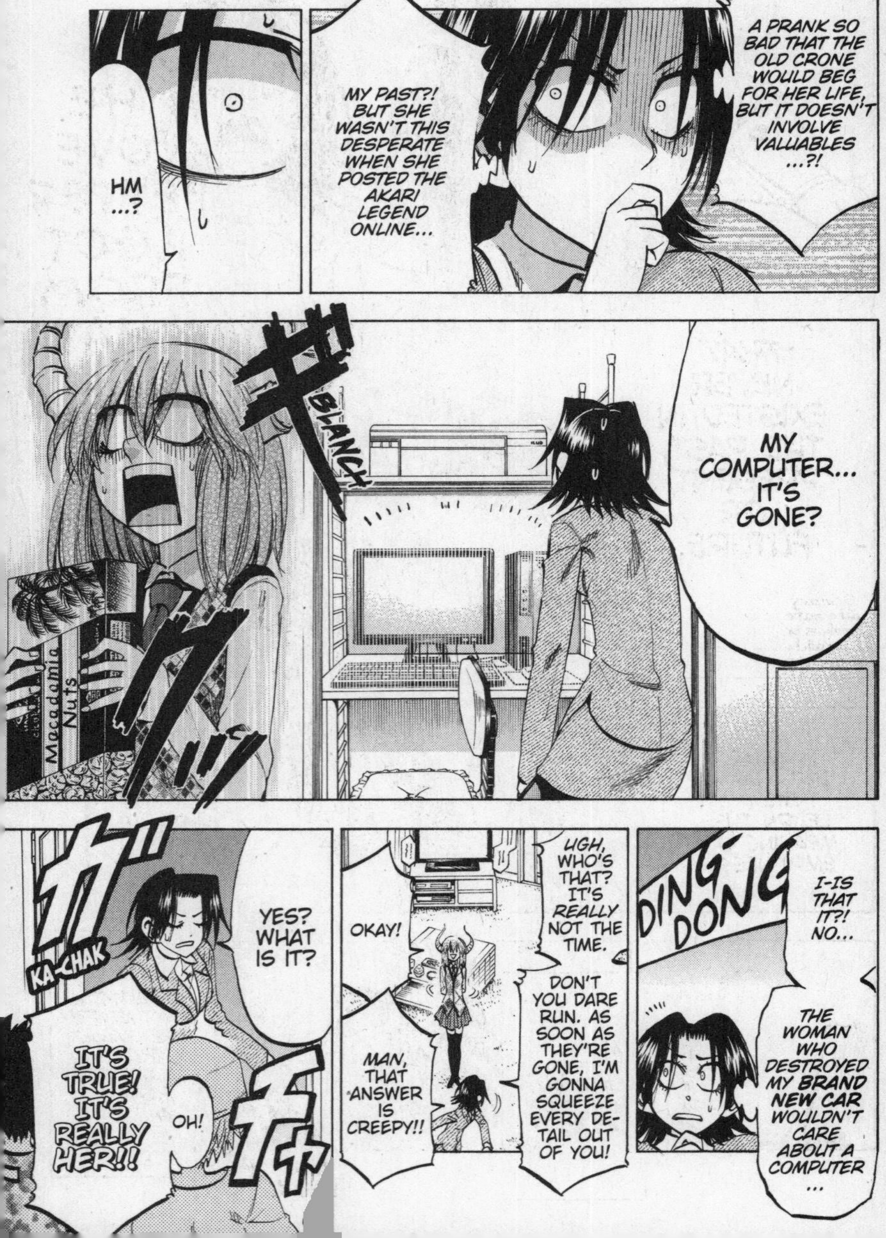
A PRANK SO BAD THAT THE OLD CRONE WOULD BEG FOR HER LIFE, BUT IT DOESN'T INVOLVE VALUABLES ...?!
MY PAST?! BUT SHE WASN'T THIS DESPERATE WHEN SHE POSTED THE AKARI LEGEND ONLINE...
HM ...?
MY COMPUTER... IT'S GONE?
BLANCH
DING-DONG
I-IS THAT IT?! NO...
THE WOMAN WHO DESTROYED MY BRAND NEW CAR WOULDN'T CARE ABOUT A COMPUTER ...
UGH, WHO'S THAT? IT'S REALLY NOT THE TIME.
OKAY!
DON'T YOU DARE RUN. AS SOON AS THEY'RE GONE, I'M GONNA SQUEEZE EVERY DETAIL OUT OF YOU!
MAN, THAT ANSWER IS CREEPY!!
YES? WHAT IS IT?
KA-CHAK
OH!
IT'S TRUE! IT'S REALLY HER!!

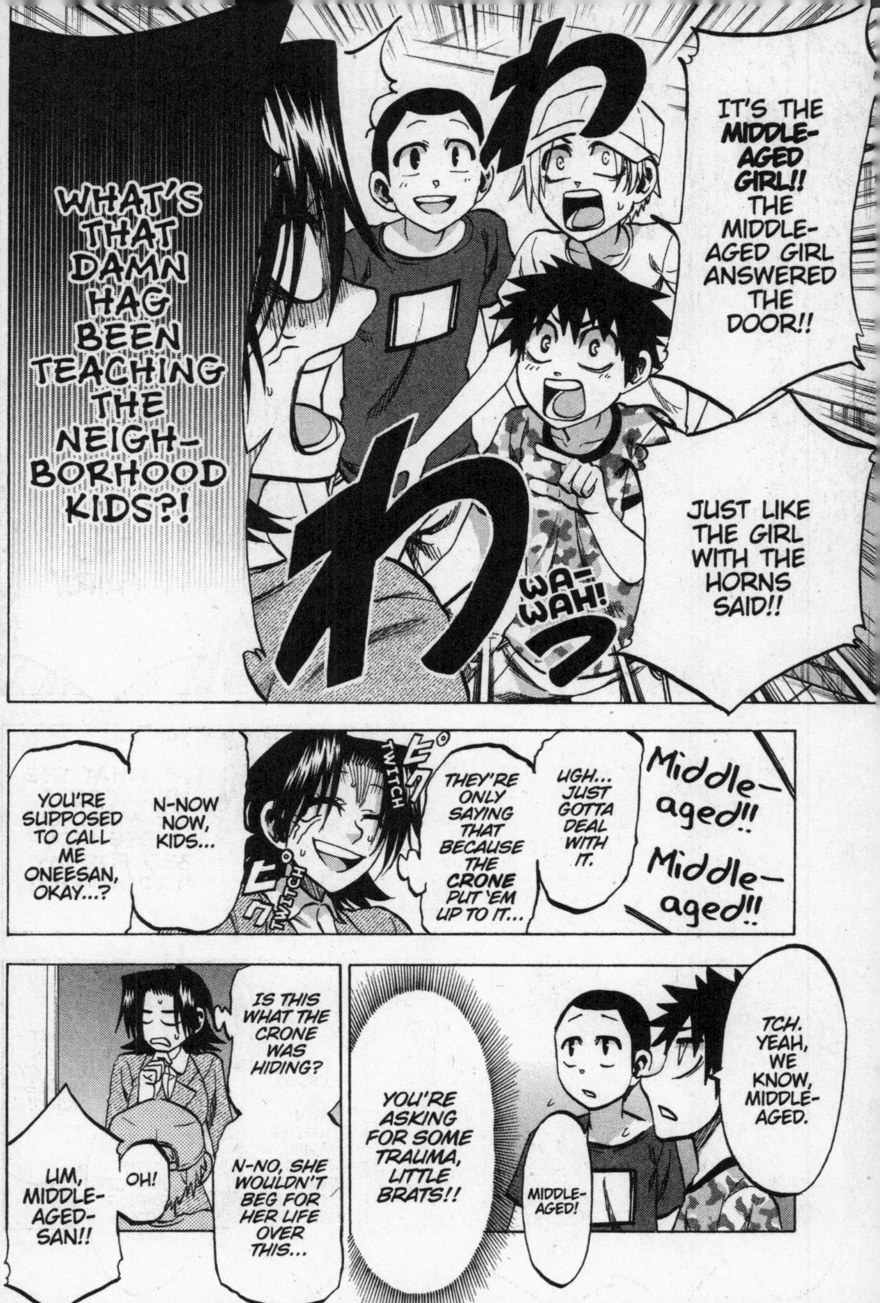
IT'S THE MIDDLE-AGED GIRL!! THE MIDDLE-AGED GIRL ANSWERED THE DOOR!!
JUST LIKE THE GIRL WITH THE HORNS SAID!!
WA-WAH!
WHAT'S THAT DAMN HAG BEEN TEACHING THE NEIGHBORHOOD KIDS?!
Middle-aged!! Middle-aged!!
UGH... JUST GOTTA DEAL WITH IT.
THEY'RE ONLY SAYING THAT BECAUSE THE CRONE PUT 'EM UP TO IT...
TWITCH
TWITCH
N-NOW NOW, KIDS...
YOU'RE SUPPOSED TO CALL ME ONEESAN, OKAY...?
TCH. YEAH, WE KNOW, MIDDLE-AGED.
MIDDLE-AGED!
YOU'RE ASKING FOR SOME TRAUMA, LITTLE BRATS!!
IS THIS WHAT THE CRONE WAS HIDING?
N-NO, SHE WOULDN'T BEG FOR HER LIFE OVER THIS...
OH!
UM, MIDDLE-AGED-SAN!!

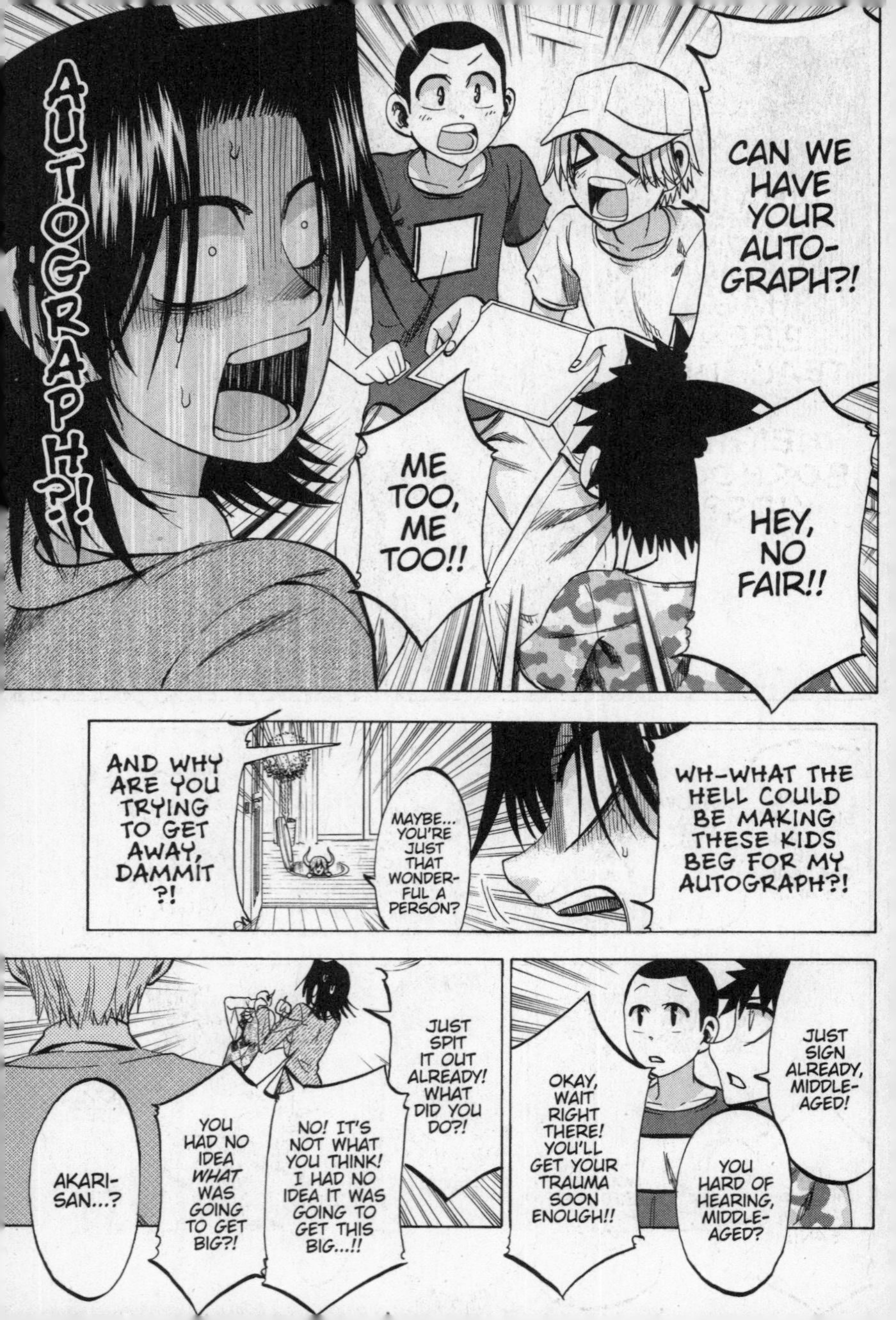
CAN WE HAVE YOUR AUTO-GRAPH?!
HEY, NO FAIR!!
ME TOO, ME TOO!!
AUTOGRAPH?!
WH-WHAT THE HELL COULD BE MAKING THESE KIDS BEG FOR MY AUTOGRAPH?!
MAYBE... YOU'RE JUST THAT WONDER-FUL A PERSON?
AND WHY ARE YOU TRYING TO GET AWAY, DAMMIT ?!
JUST SIGN ALREADY, MIDDLE-AGED!
YOU HARD OF HEARING, MIDDLE-AGED?
OKAY, WAIT RIGHT THERE! YOU'LL GET YOUR TRAUMA SOON ENOUGH!!
JUST SPIT IT OUT ALREADY! WHAT DID YOU DO?!
NO! IT'S NOT WHAT YOU THINK! I HAD NO IDEA IT WAS GOING TO GET THIS BIG...!!
YOU HAD NO IDEA *WHAT* WAS GOING TO GET BIG?!
AKARI-SAN...?

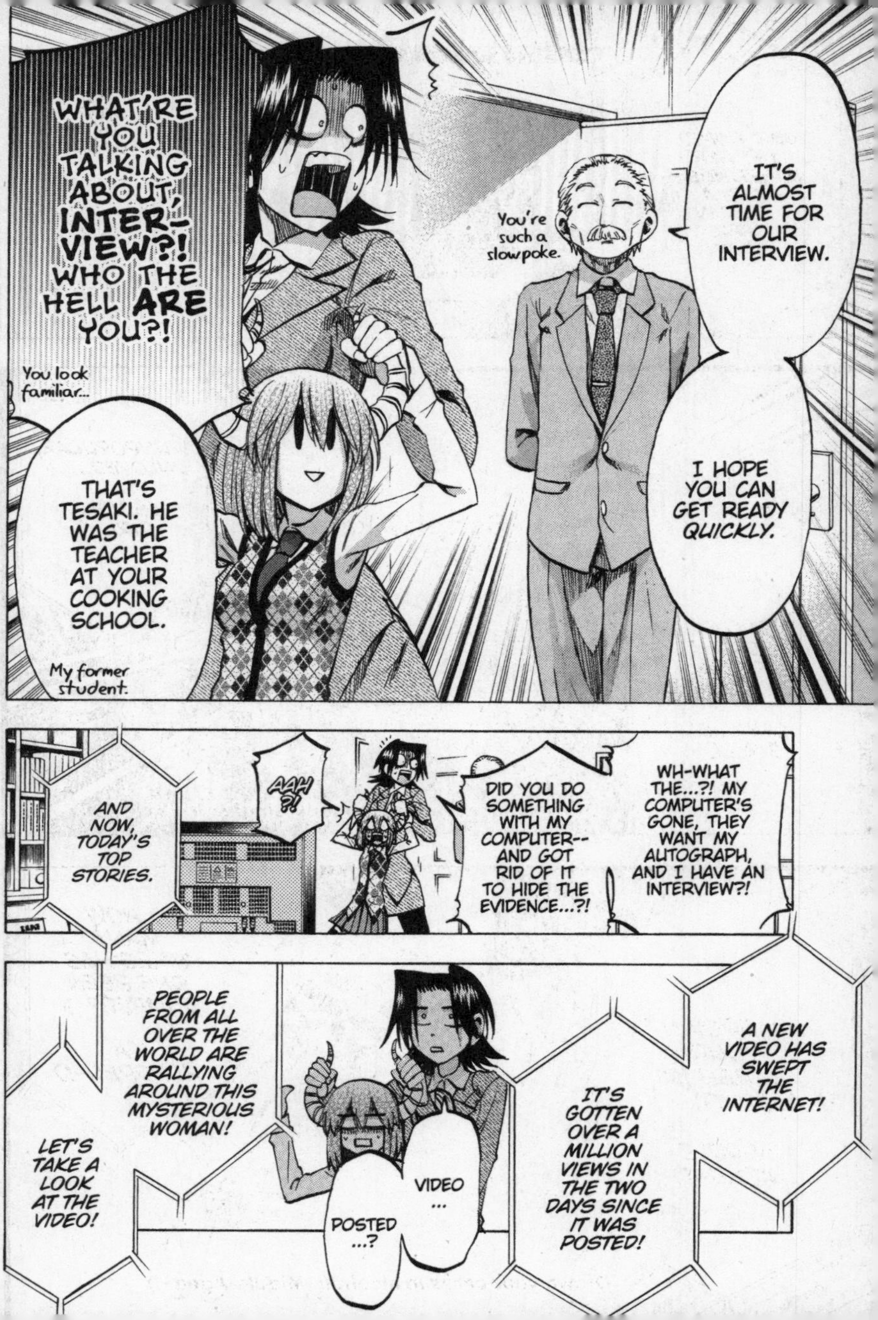
IT'S ALMOST TIME FOR OUR INTERVIEW.
You're such a slowpoke.
I HOPE YOU CAN GET READY QUICKLY.
WHAT'RE YOU TALKING ABOUT, INTERVIEW?! WHO THE HELL ARE YOU?!
You look familiar...
THAT'S TESAKI. HE WAS THE TEACHER AT YOUR COOKING SCHOOL.
My former student.
WH-WHAT THE...?! MY COMPUTER'S GONE, THEY WANT MY AUTOGRAPH, AND I HAVE AN INTERVIEW?!
DID YOU DO SOMETHING WITH MY COMPUTER-- AND GOT RID OF IT TO HIDE THE EVIDENCE...?!
AAH ?!
AND NOW, TODAY'S TOP STORIES.
A NEW VIDEO HAS SWEPT THE INTERNET!
IT'S GOTTEN OVER A MILLION VIEWS IN THE TWO DAYS SINCE IT WAS POSTED!
VIDEO ...
POSTED ...?
PEOPLE FROM ALL OVER THE WORLD ARE RALLYING AROUND THIS MYSTERIOUS WOMAN!
LET'S TAKE A LOOK AT THE VIDEO!

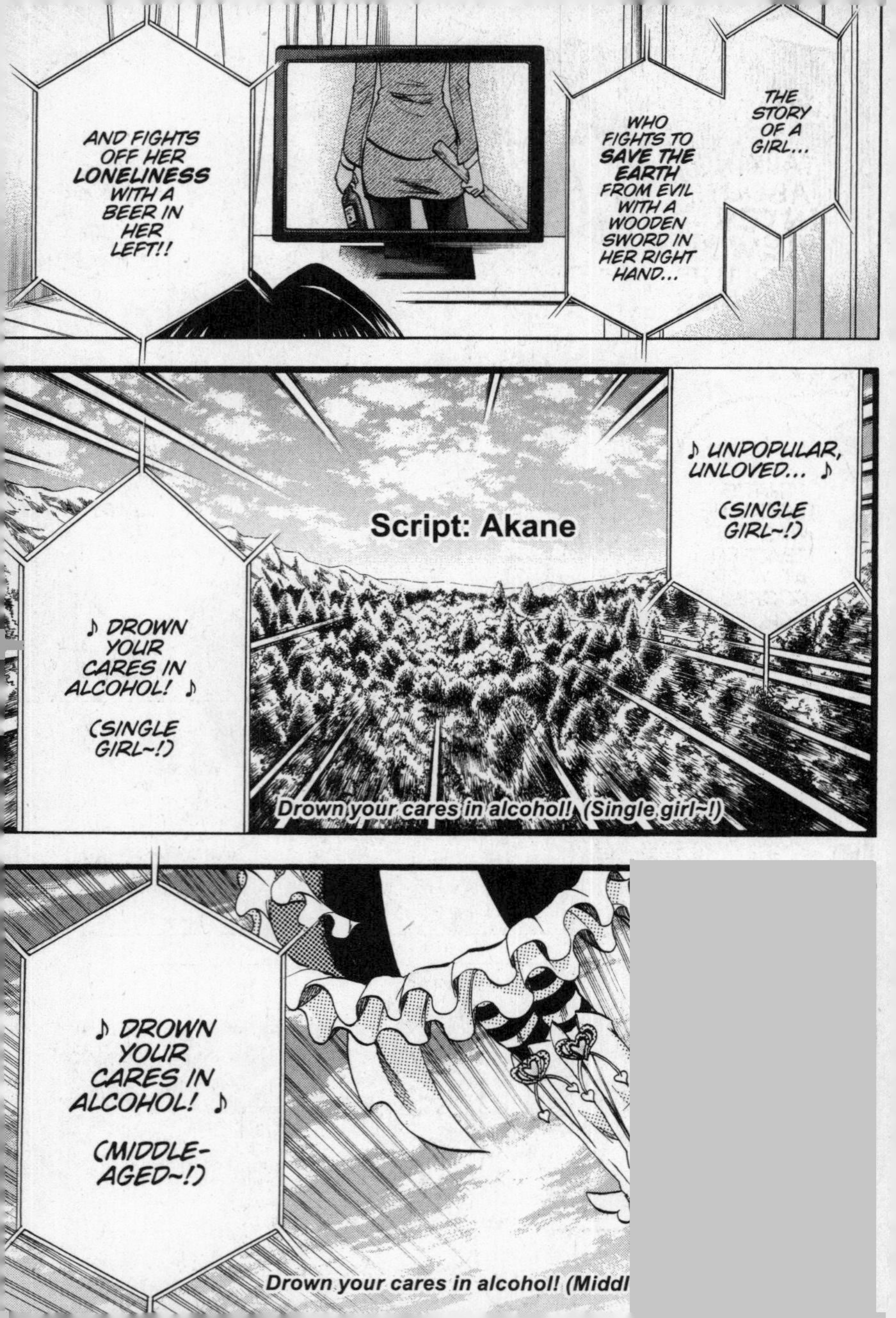
THE STORY OF A GIRL...
WHO FIGHTS TO SAVE THE EARTH FROM EVIL WITH A WOODEN SWORD IN HER RIGHT HAND...
AND FIGHTS OFF HER LONELINESS WITH A BEER IN HER LEFT!!
♪ UNPOPULAR, UNLOVED... ♪
(SINGLE GIRL~!)
Script: Akane
♪ DROWN YOUR CARES IN ALCOHOL! ♪
(SINGLE GIRL~!)
Drown your cares in alcohol! (Single girl~!)
♪ DROWN YOUR CARES IN ALCOHOL! ♪
(MIDDLE-AGED~!)
Drown your cares in alcohol! (Middl

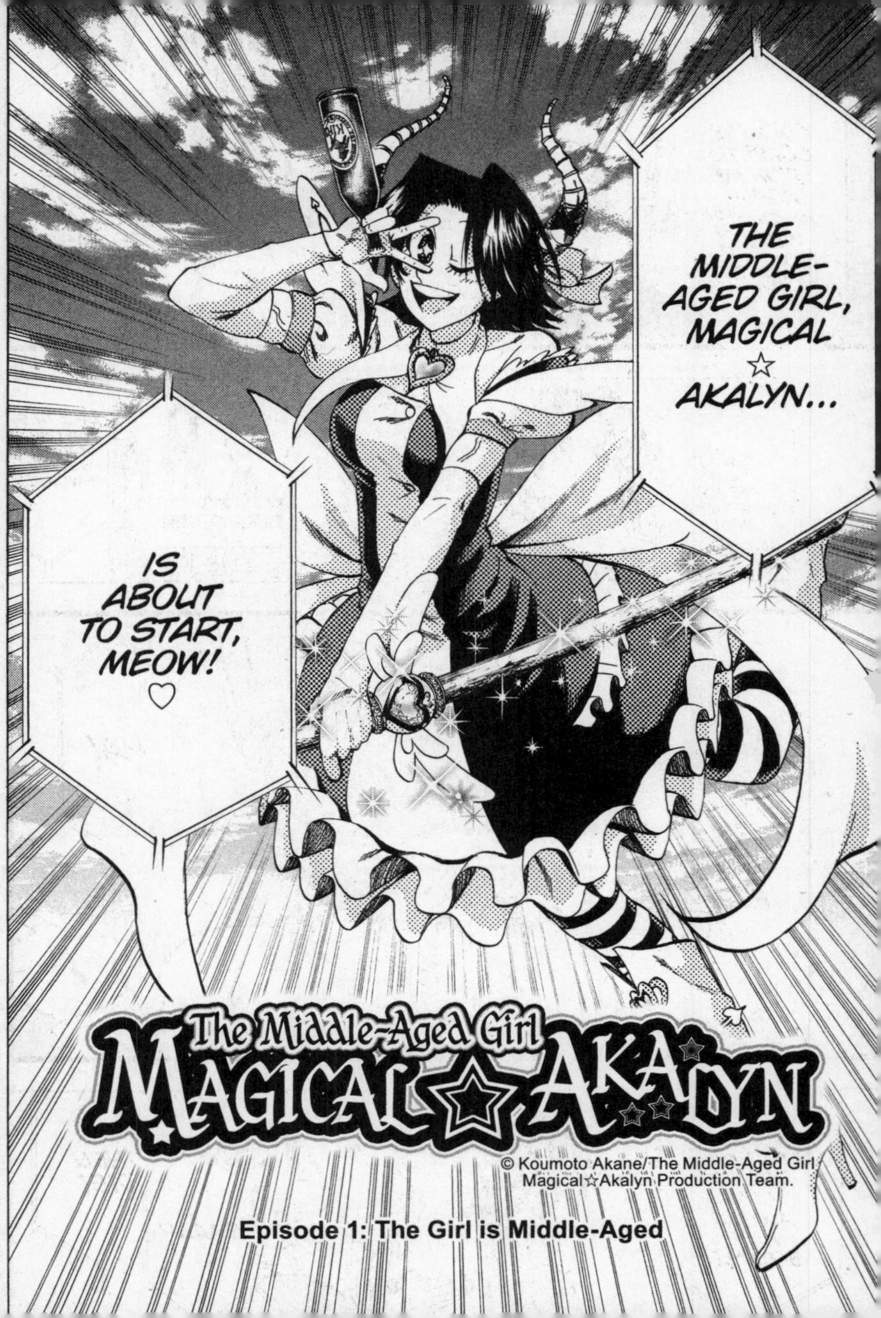
THE MIDDLE-AGED GIRL, MAGICAL ☆ AKALYN...
IS ABOUT TO START, MEOW! ♡
The Middle-Aged Girl
MAGICAL ☆ AKALYN
© Koumoto Akane/The Middle-Aged Girl Magical☆Akalyn Production Team.
Episode 1: The Girl is Middle-Aged

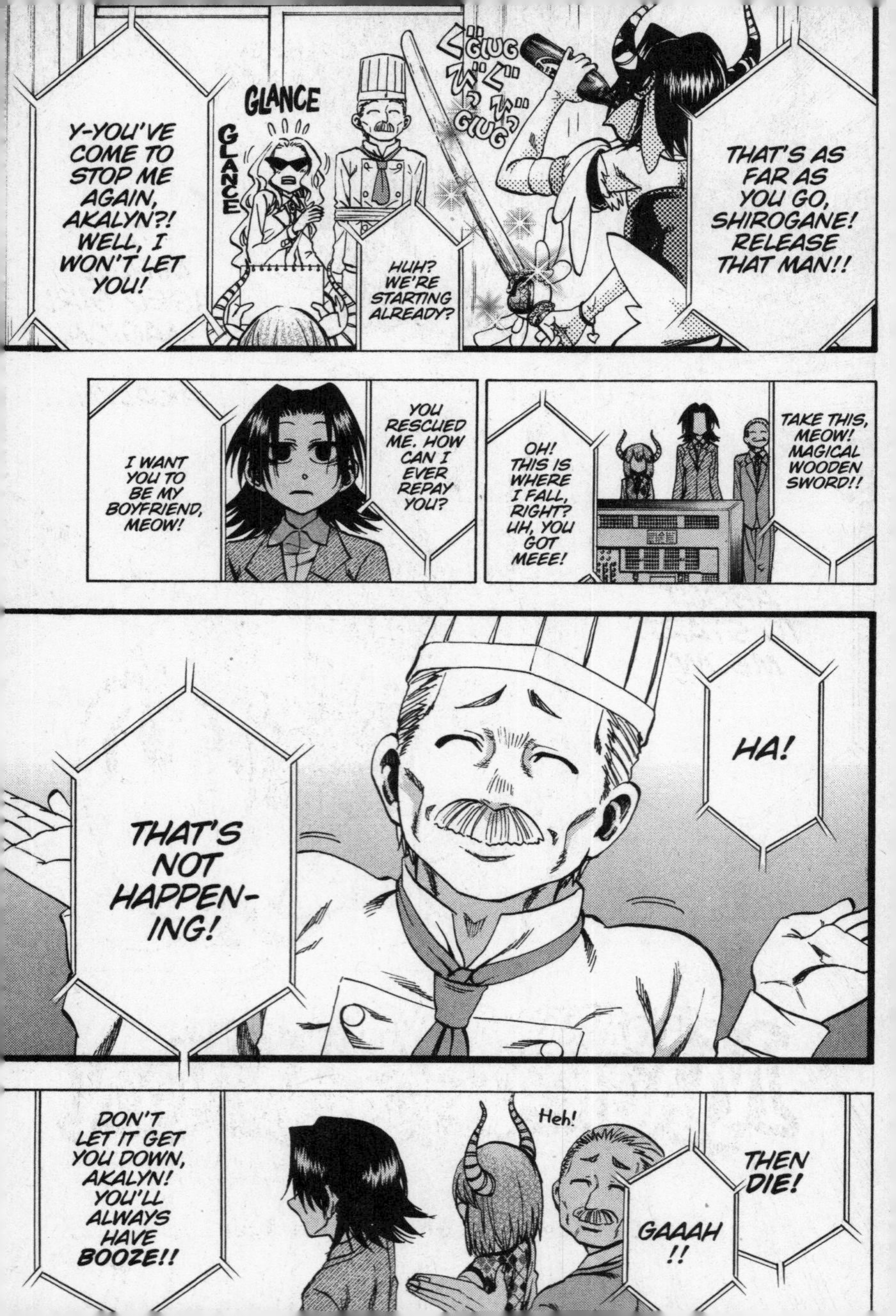
THAT'S AS FAR AS YOU GO, SHIROGANE! RELEASE THAT MAN!!
GLUG
GLUG
HUH? WE'RE STARTING ALREADY?
GLANCE
GLANCE
Y-YOU'VE COME TO STOP ME AGAIN, AKALYN?! WELL, I WON'T LET YOU!
TAKE THIS, MEOW! MAGICAL WOODEN SWORD!!
OH! THIS IS WHERE I FALL, RIGHT? UH, YOU GOT MEEE!
YOU RESCUED ME. HOW CAN I EVER REPAY YOU?
I WANT YOU TO BE MY BOYFRIEND, MEOW!
HA!
THAT'S NOT HAPPEN-ING!
THEN DIE!
Heh!
GAAAH!!
DON'T LET IT GET YOU DOWN, AKALYN! YOU'LL ALWAYS HAVE BOOZE!!

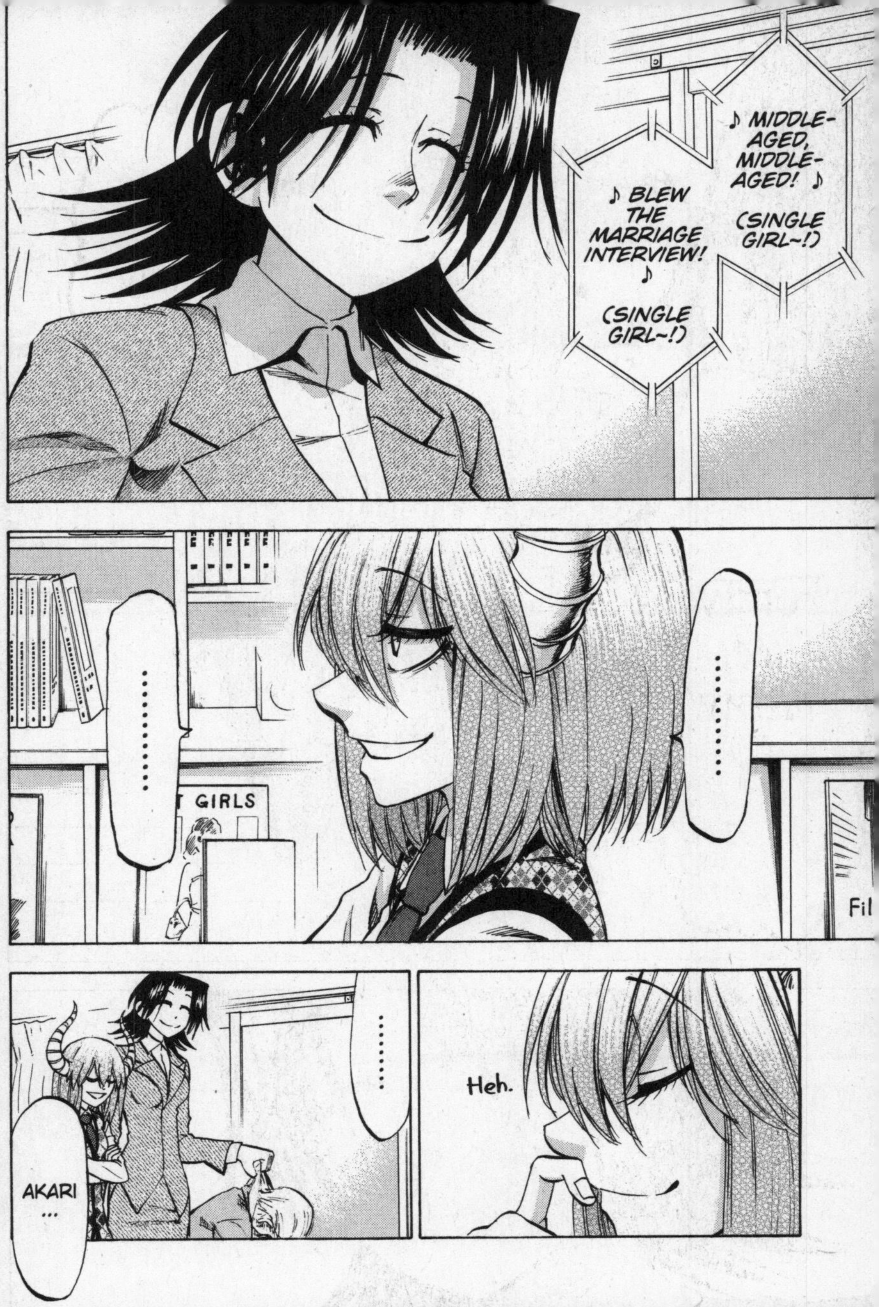
♪ MIDDLE-AGED, MIDDLE-AGED! ♪
(SINGLE GIRL~!)
♪ BLEW THE MARRIAGE INTERVIEW! ♪
(SINGLE GIRL~!)
......
......
GIRLS
Fil
Heh.
......
AKARI ...

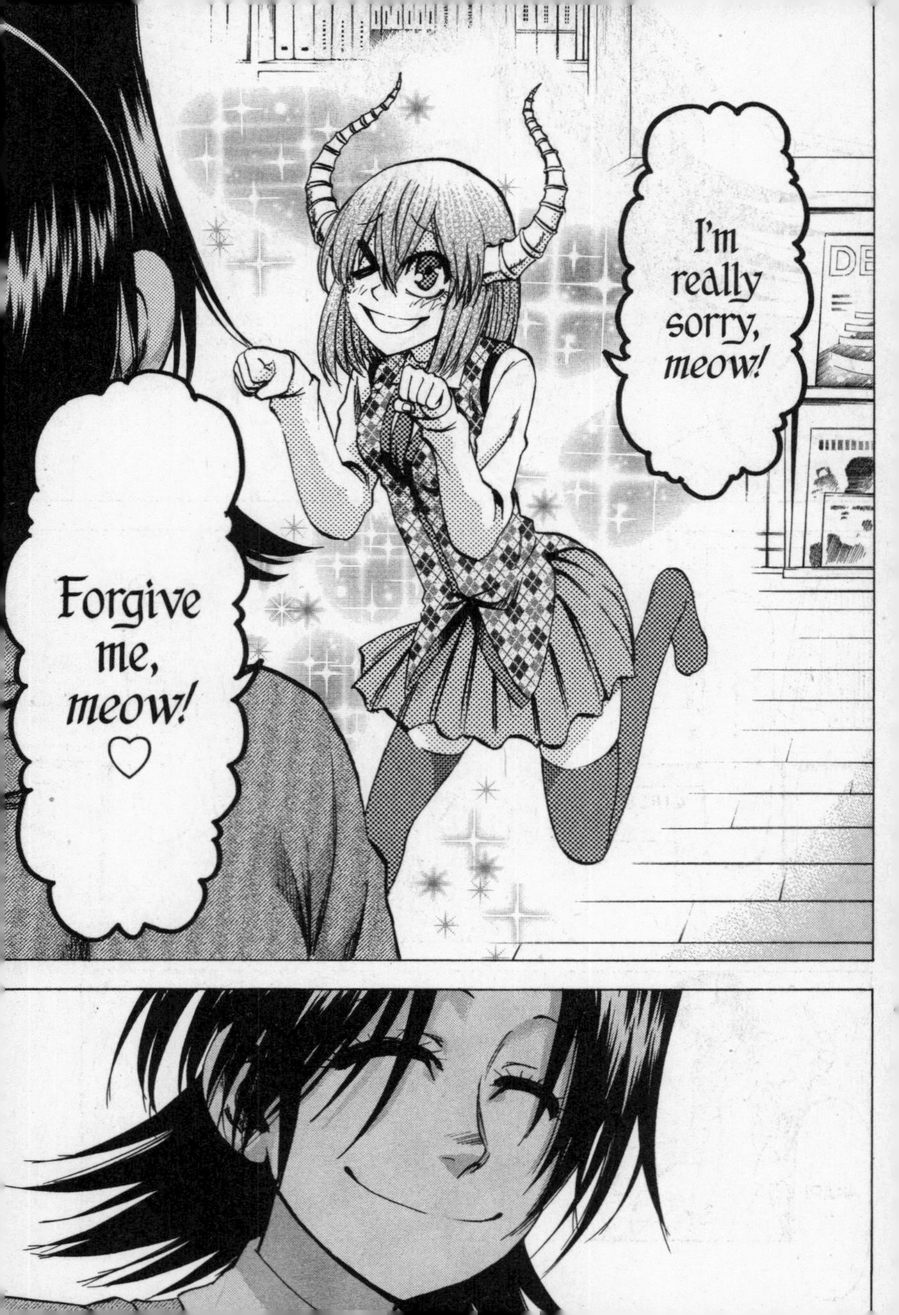
I'm really sorry, meow!
Forgive me, meow! ♡

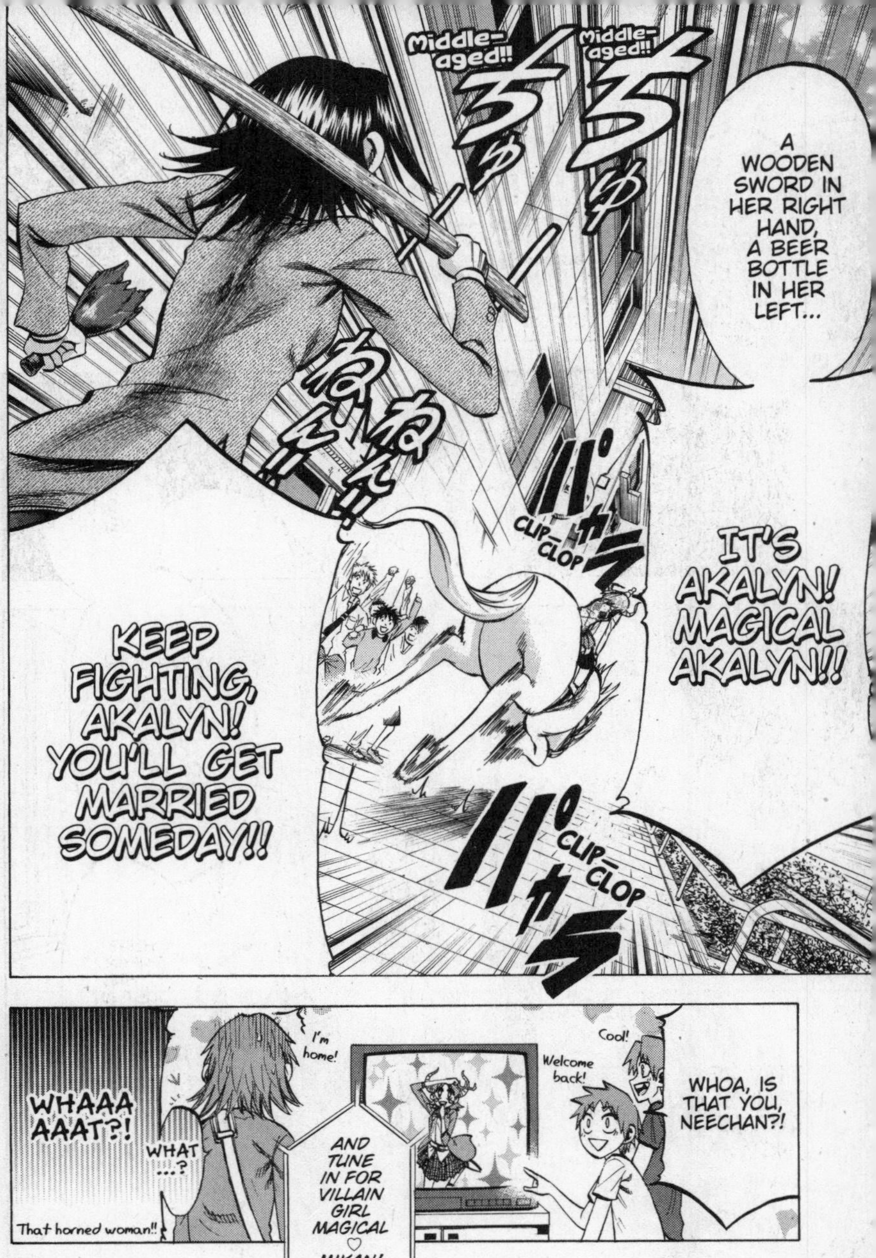

A WOODEN SWORD IN HER RIGHT HAND, A BEER BOTTLE IN HER LEFT...
Middle-aged!!
Middle-aged!!
IT'S AKALYN! MAGICAL AKALYN!!
CLIP-CLOP
KEEP FIGHTING, AKALYN! YOU'LL GET MARRIED SOMEDAY!!
CLIP-CLOP
Cool!
WHOA, IS THAT YOU, NEECHAN?!
Welcome back!
I'm home!
AND TUNE IN FOR VILLAIN GIRL MAGICAL ♡ MIKAN! ☆
WHAAA AAAT?!
WHAT !!!...?
That horned woman!!

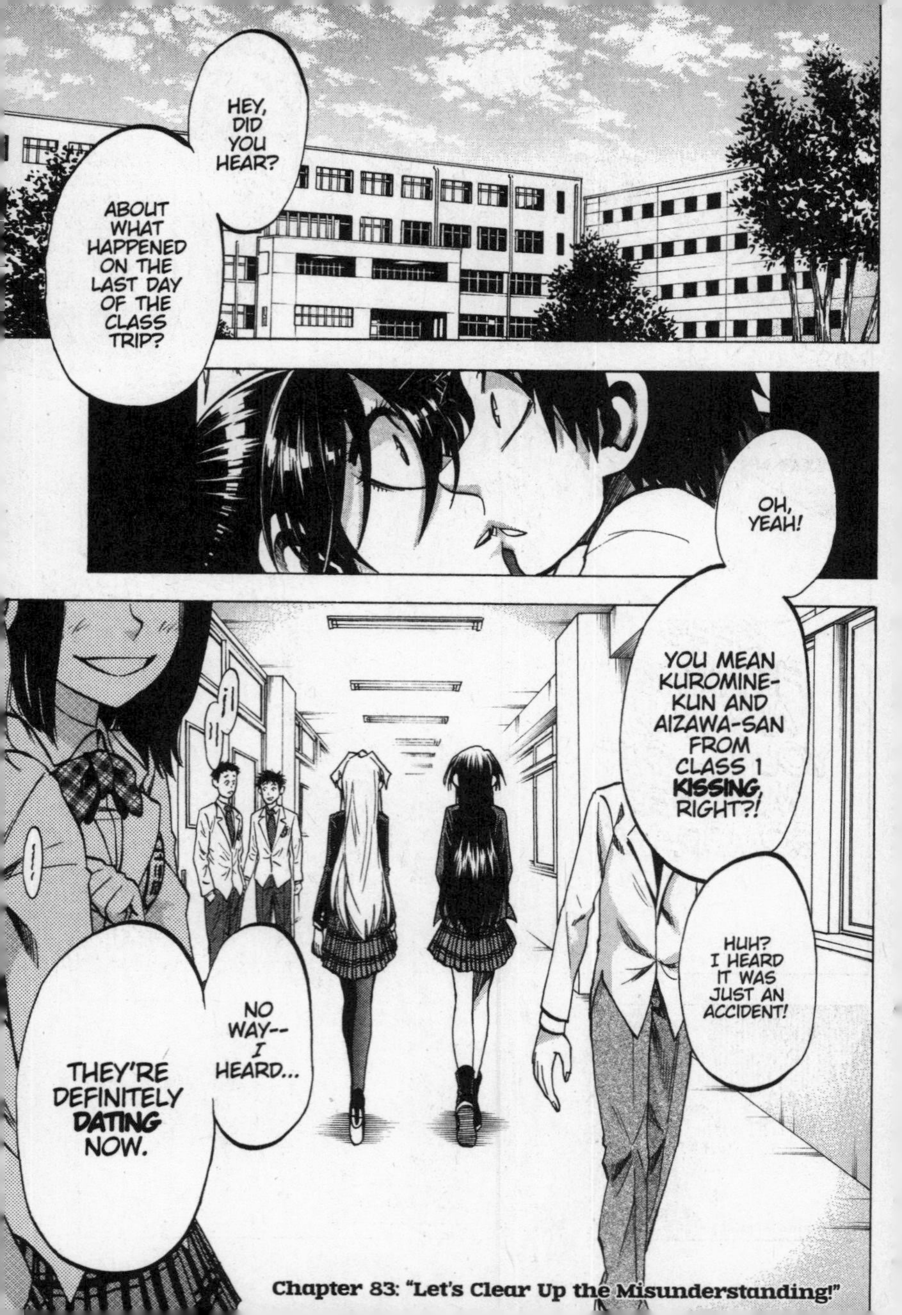
HEY, DID YOU HEAR?
ABOUT WHAT HAPPENED ON THE LAST DAY OF THE CLASS TRIP?
OH, YEAH!
YOU MEAN KUROMINE-KUN AND AIZAWA-SAN FROM CLASS 1 **KISSING**, RIGHT?!
HUH? I HEARD IT WAS JUST AN ACCIDENT!
NO WAY-- I HEARD...
THEY'RE DEFINITELY **DATING** NOW.

Chapter 83: "Let's Clear Up the Misunderstanding!"

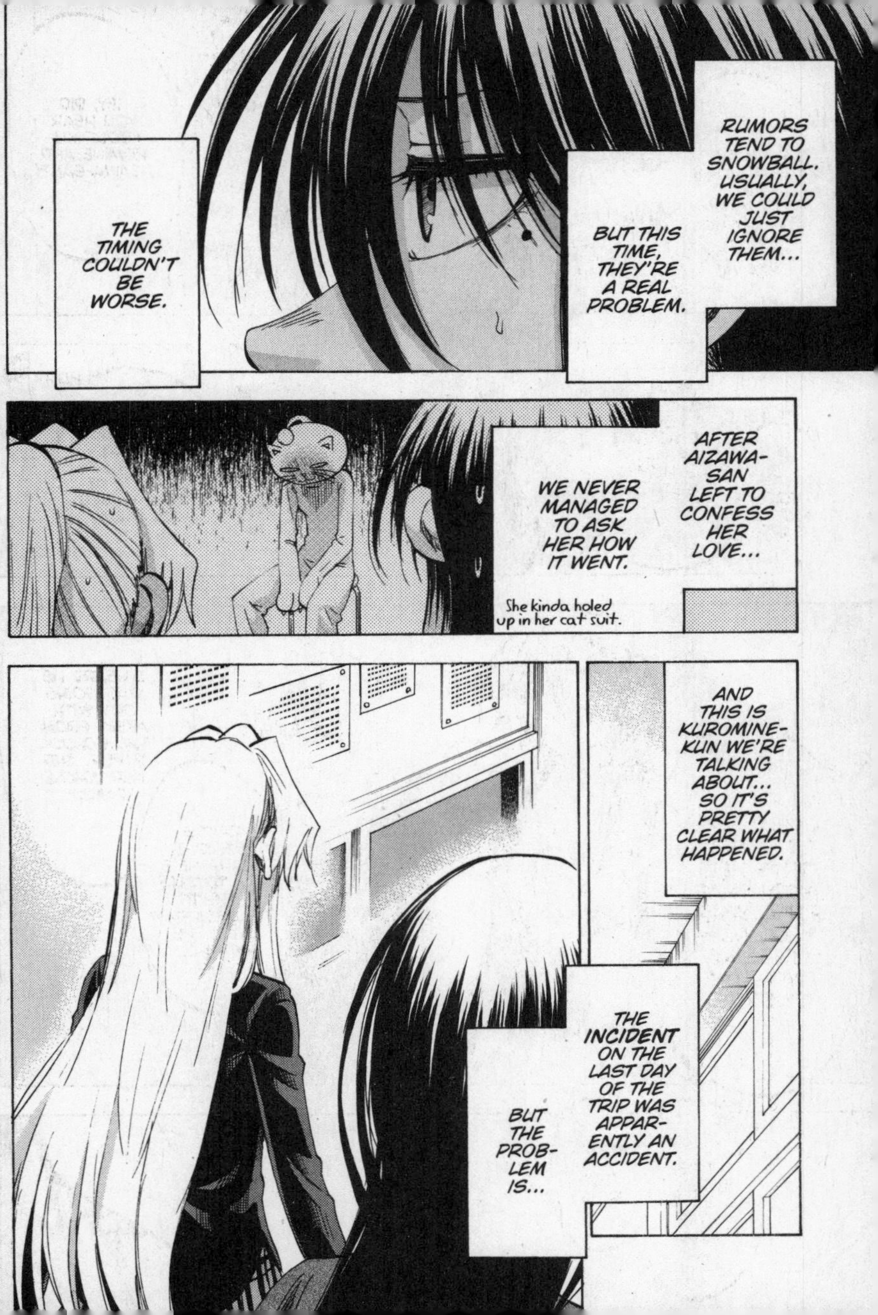
RUMORS TEND TO SNOWBALL. USUALLY, WE COULD JUST IGNORE THEM...
BUT THIS TIME, THEY'RE A REAL PROBLEM.
THE TIMING COULDN'T BE WORSE.
AFTER AIZAWA-SAN LEFT TO CONFESS HER LOVE...
WE NEVER MANAGED TO ASK HER HOW IT WENT.
She kinda holed up in her cat suit.
AND THIS IS KUROMINE-KUN WE'RE TALKING ABOUT... SO IT'S PRETTY CLEAR WHAT HAPPENED.
THE INCIDENT ON THE LAST DAY OF THE TRIP WAS APPARENTLY AN ACCIDENT.
BUT THE PROBLEM IS...

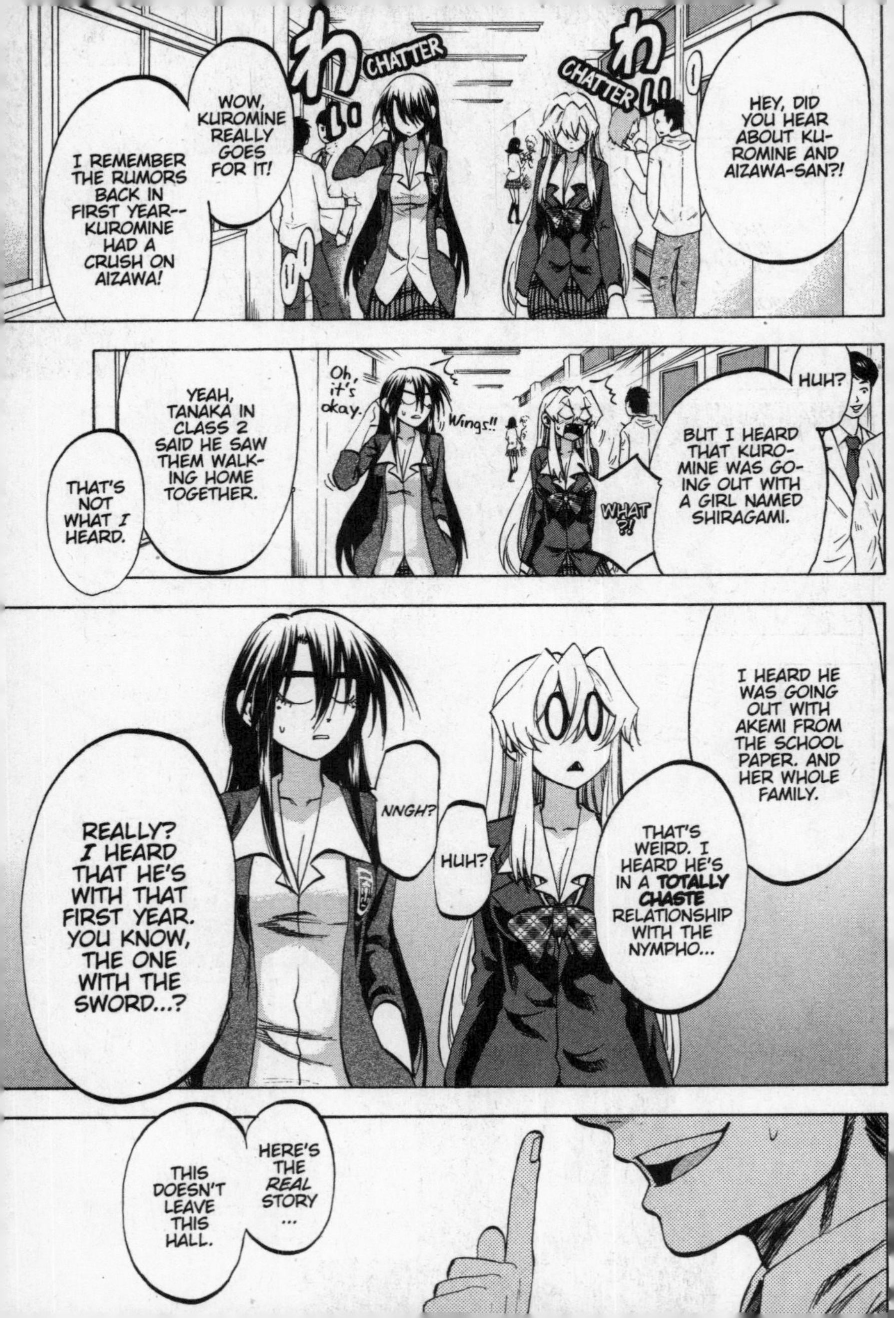
HEY, DID YOU HEAR ABOUT KU-ROMINE AND AIZAWA-SAN?!
わ CHATTER
わ CHATTER
WOW, KUROMINE REALLY GOES FOR IT!
I REMEMBER THE RUMORS BACK IN FIRST YEAR-- KUROMINE HAD A CRUSH ON AIZAWA!
HUH?
BUT I HEARD THAT KURO-MINE WAS GO-ING OUT WITH A GIRL NAMED SHIRAGAMI.
WHAT?!
Wings!!
Oh, it's okay.
YEAH, TANAKA IN CLASS 2 SAID HE SAW THEM WALK-ING HOME TOGETHER.
THAT'S NOT WHAT *I* HEARD.
I HEARD HE WAS GOING OUT WITH AKEMI FROM THE SCHOOL PAPER. AND HER WHOLE FAMILY.
THAT'S WEIRD. I HEARD HE'S IN A **TOTALLY CHASTE** RELATIONSHIP WITH THE NYMPHO...
HUH?
NNGH?
REALLY? *I* HEARD THAT HE'S WITH THAT FIRST YEAR. YOU KNOW, THE ONE WITH THE SWORD...?
HERE'S THE *REAL* STORY ...
THIS DOESN'T LEAVE THIS HALL.

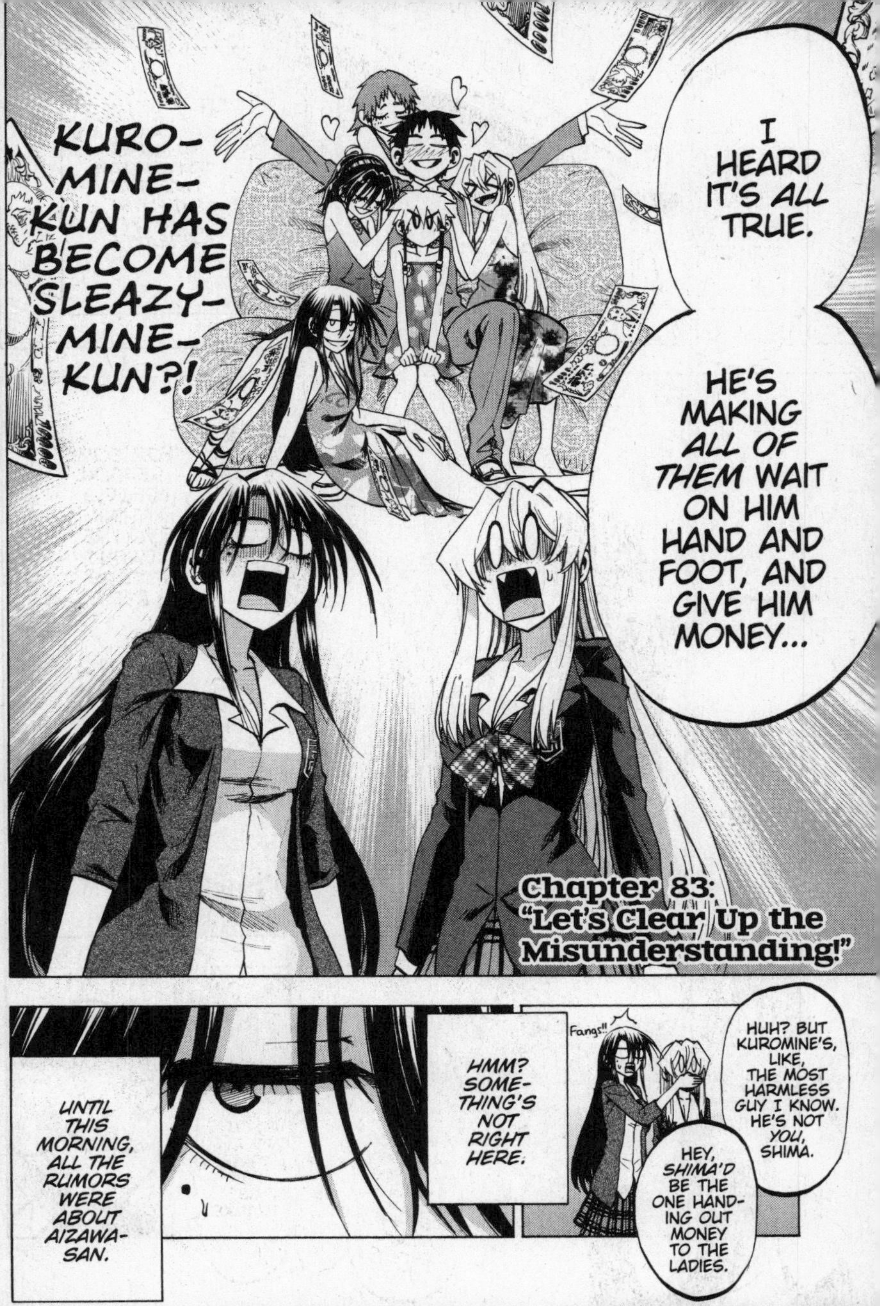
I HEARD IT'S ALL TRUE.
HE'S MAKING ALL OF THEM WAIT ON HIM HAND AND FOOT, AND GIVE HIM MONEY...
KURO-MINE-KUN HAS BECOME SLEAZY-MINE-KUN?!
Chapter 83: "Let's Clear Up the Misunderstanding!"
HUH? BUT KUROMINE'S, LIKE, THE MOST HARMLESS GUY I KNOW. HE'S NOT YOU, SHIMA.
Fangs!!
HEY, SHIMA'D BE THE ONE HANDING OUT MONEY TO THE LADIES.
HMM? SOMETHING'S NOT RIGHT HERE.
UNTIL THIS MORNING, ALL THE RUMORS WERE ABOUT AIZAWA-SAN.

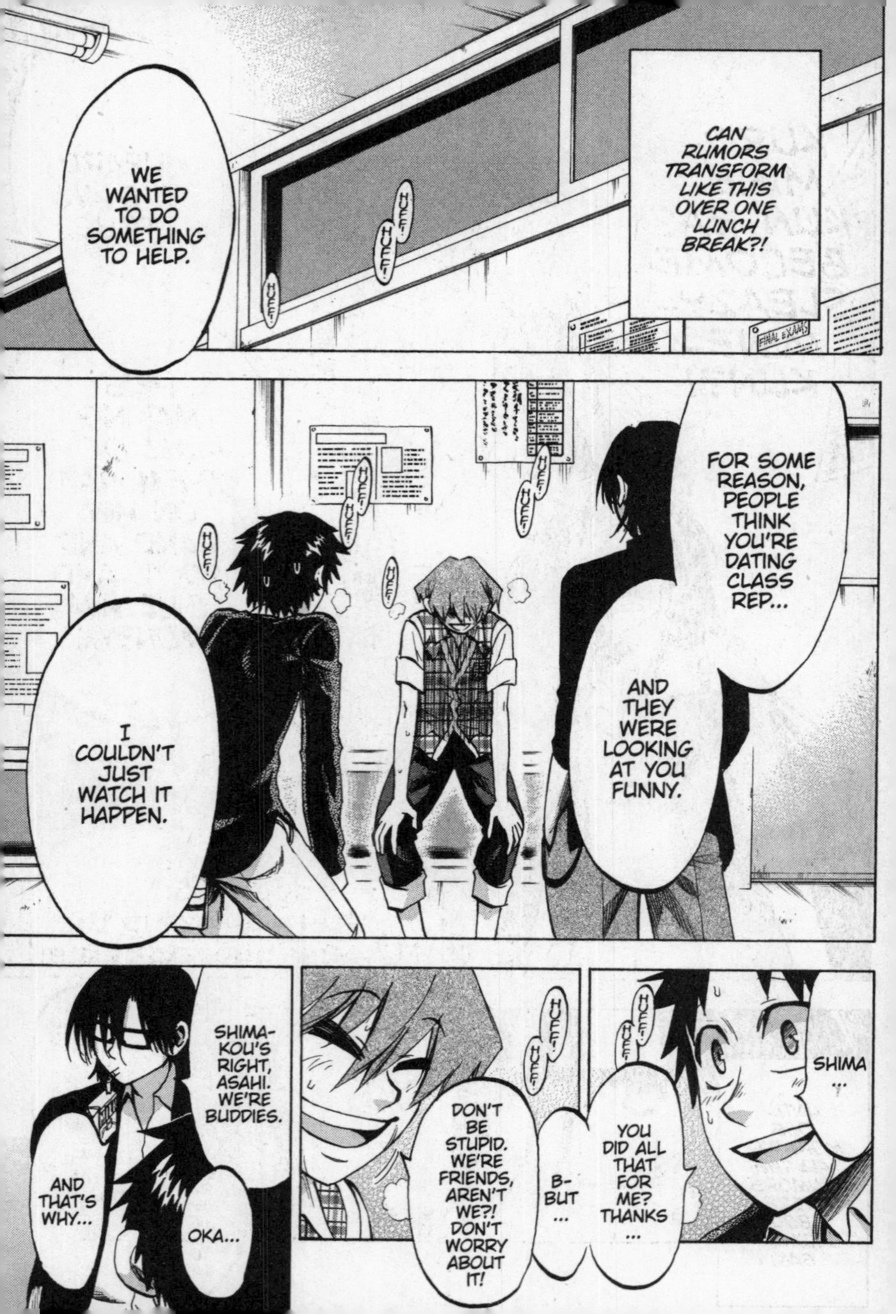
CAN RUMORS TRANSFORM LIKE THIS OVER ONE LUNCH BREAK?!
HUFF! HUFF!
HUFF!
WE WANTED TO DO SOMETHING TO HELP.
FOR SOME REASON, PEOPLE THINK YOU'RE DATING CLASS REP...
AND THEY WERE LOOKING AT YOU FUNNY.
HUFF! HUFF!
HUFF! HUFF!
HUFF!
HUFF!
I COULDN'T JUST WATCH IT HAPPEN.
HUFF! HUFF!
SHIMA...
YOU DID ALL THAT FOR ME? THANKS...
HUFF! HUFF!
B-BUT...
DON'T BE STUPID. WE'RE FRIENDS, AREN'T WE?! DON'T WORRY ABOUT IT!
SHIMAKOU'S RIGHT, ASAHI. WE'RE BUDDIES.
AND THAT'S WHY...
OKA...

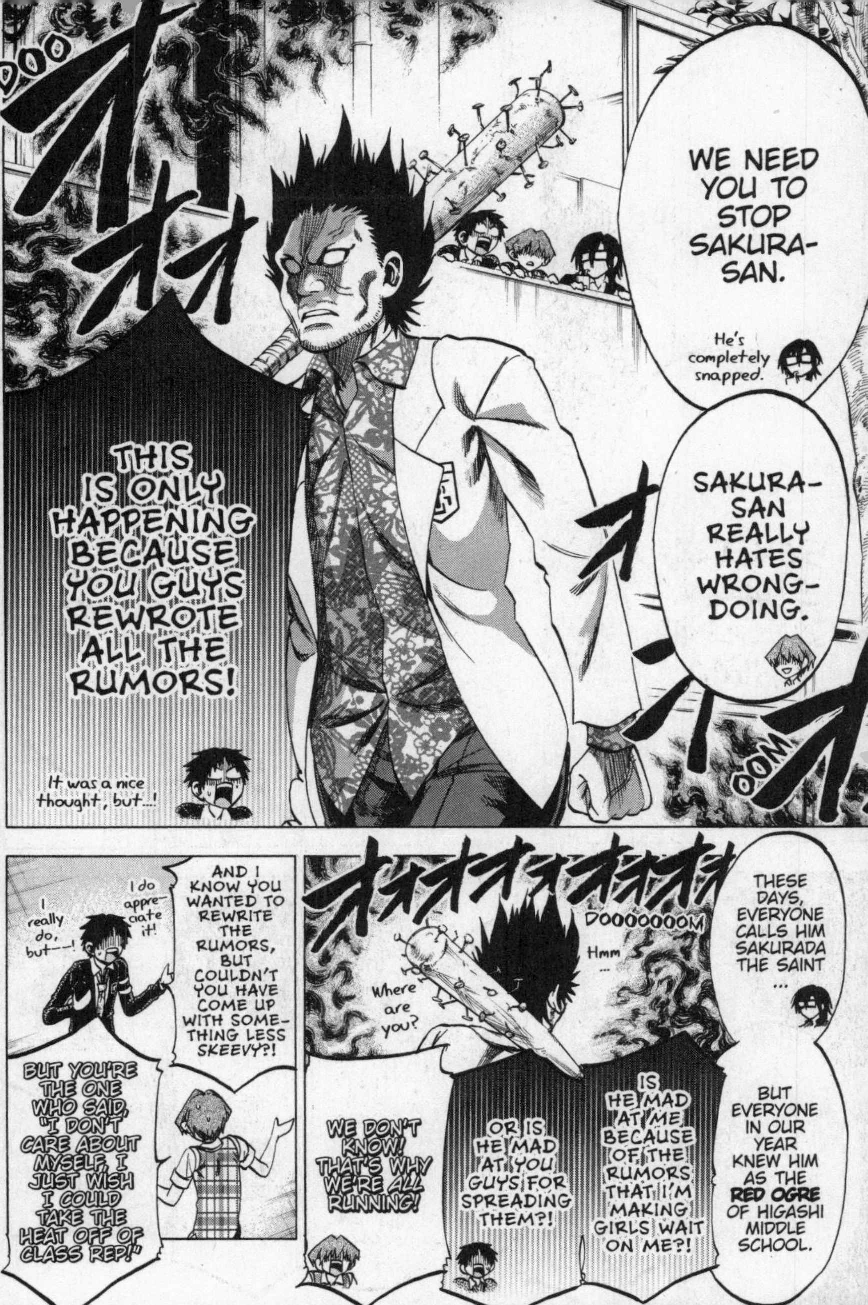
DOO
WE NEED YOU TO STOP SAKURA-SAN.
He's completely snapped.
SAKURA-SAN REALLY HATES WRONG-DOING.
OOM
THIS IS ONLY HAPPENING BECAUSE YOU GUYS REWROTE ALL THE RUMORS!
It was a nice thought, but...!
THESE DAYS, EVERYONE CALLS HIM SAKURADA THE SAINT...
DOOOOOOOM
Hmm...
Where are you?
BUT EVERYONE IN OUR YEAR KNEW HIM AS THE RED OGRE OF HIGASHI MIDDLE SCHOOL.
IS HE MAD AT ME BECAUSE OF THE RUMORS THAT I'M MAKING GIRLS WAIT ON ME?!
OR IS HE MAD AT YOU GUYS FOR SPREADING THEM?!
WE DON'T KNOW! THAT'S WHY WE'RE ALL RUNNING!
AND I KNOW YOU WANTED TO REWRITE THE RUMORS, BUT COULDN'T YOU HAVE COME UP WITH SOMETHING LESS SKEEVY?!
I do appreciate it!
I really do, but--!
BUT YOU'RE THE ONE WHO SAID, "I DON'T CARE ABOUT MYSELF, I JUST WISH I COULD TAKE THE HEAT OFF OF CLASS REP!"

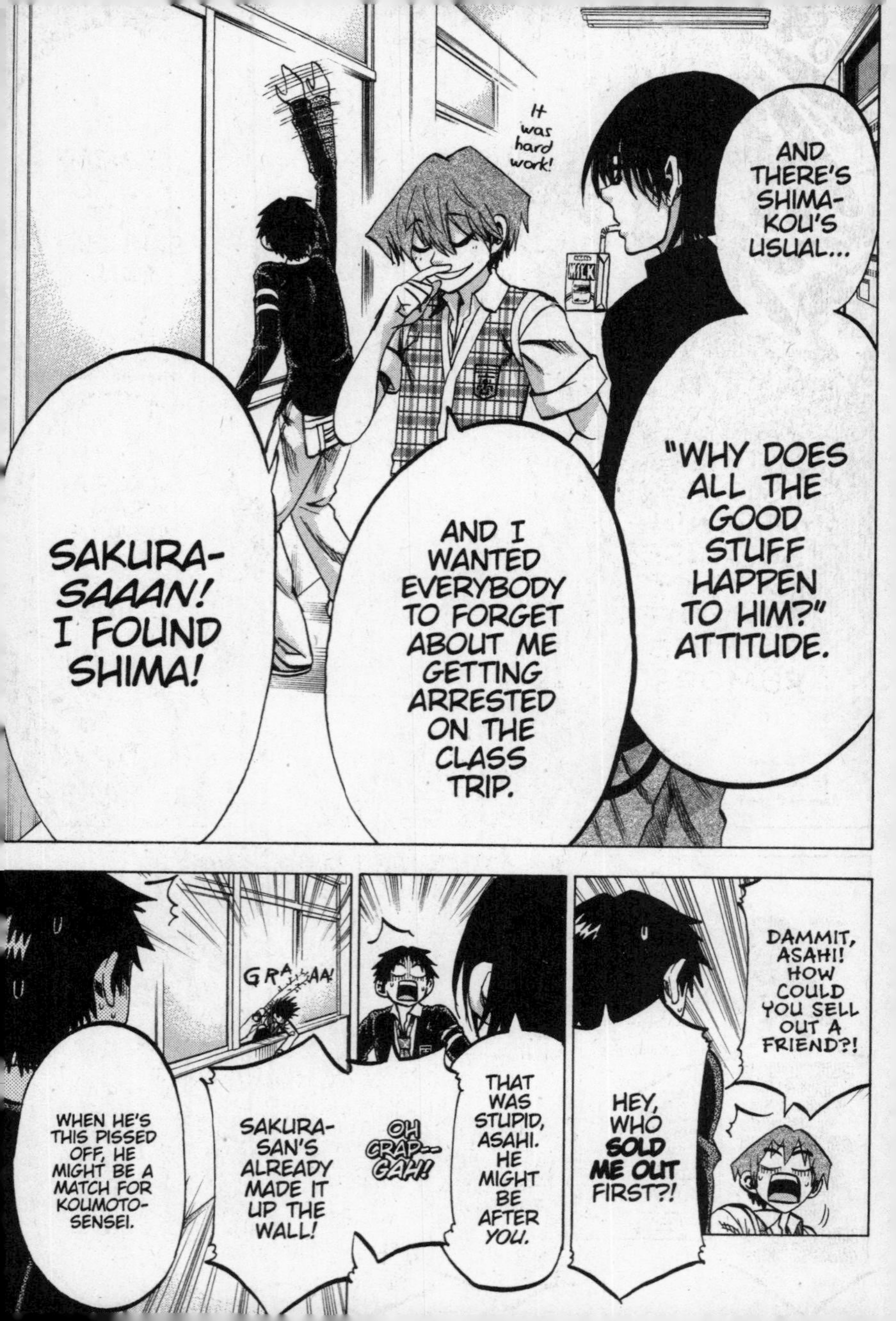
AND THERE'S SHIMA-KOU'S USUAL...
"WHY DOES ALL THE GOOD STUFF HAPPEN TO HIM?" ATTITUDE.
It was hard work!
AND I WANTED EVERYBODY TO FORGET ABOUT ME GETTING ARRESTED ON THE CLASS TRIP.
SAKURA-SAAAN! I FOUND SHIMA!
DAMMIT, ASAHI! HOW COULD YOU SELL OUT A FRIEND?!
HEY, WHO SOLD ME OUT FIRST?!
THAT WAS STUPID, ASAHI. HE MIGHT BE AFTER YOU.
OH CRAP-- GAH!
SAKURA-SAN'S ALREADY MADE IT UP THE WALL!
WHEN HE'S THIS PISSED OFF, HE MIGHT BE A MATCH FOR KOUMOTO-SENSEI.

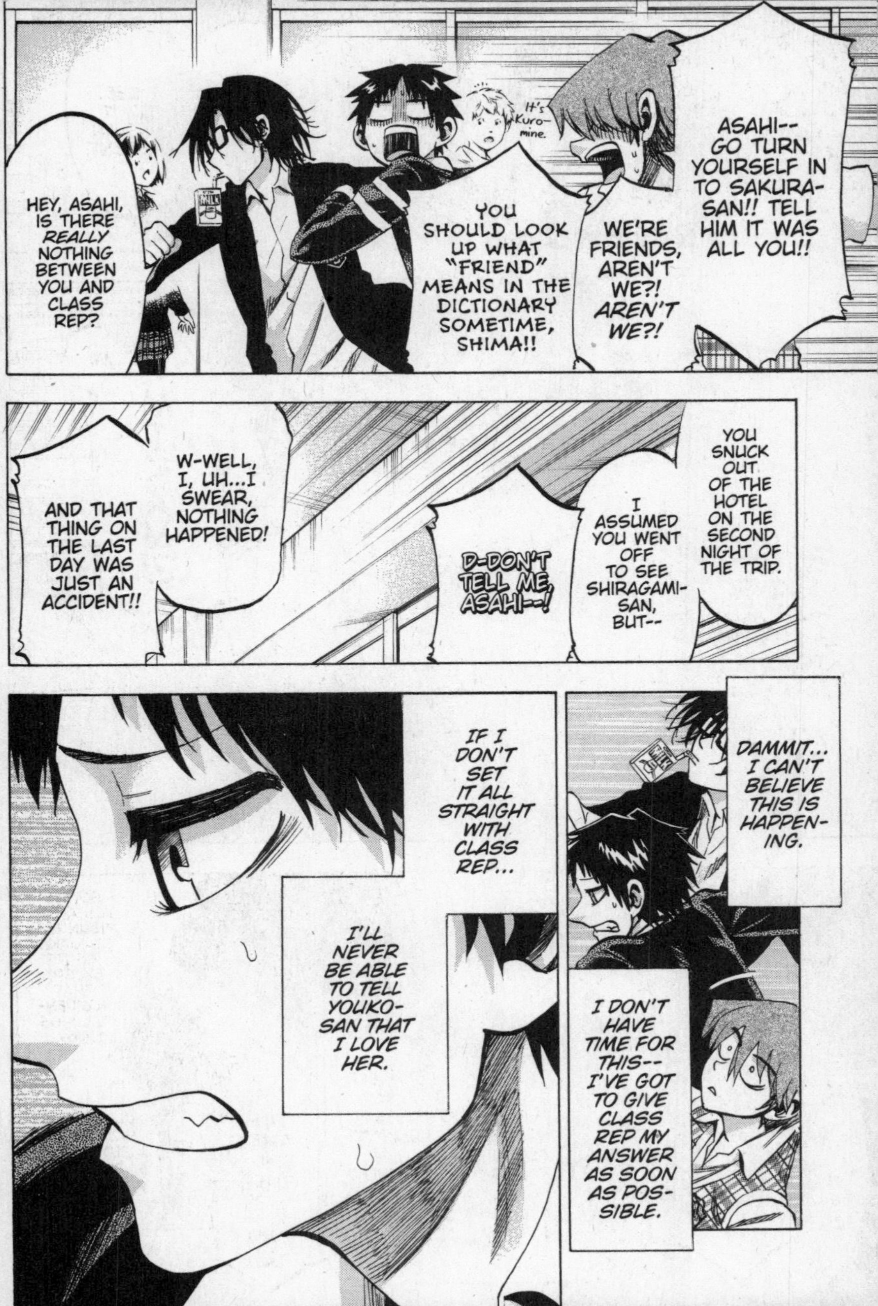
ASAHI-- GO TURN YOURSELF IN TO SAKURA-SAN!! TELL HIM IT WAS ALL YOU!!
It's Kuro-mine.
WE'RE FRIENDS, AREN'T WE?! AREN'T WE?!
YOU SHOULD LOOK UP WHAT "FRIEND" MEANS IN THE DICTIONARY SOMETIME, SHIMA!!
MILK
HEY, ASAHI, IS THERE REALLY NOTHING BETWEEN YOU AND CLASS REP?
YOU SNUCK OUT OF THE HOTEL ON THE SECOND NIGHT OF THE TRIP.
I ASSUMED YOU WENT OFF TO SEE SHIRAGAMI-SAN, BUT--
D-DON'T TELL ME, ASAHI--!
W-WELL, I, UH...I SWEAR, NOTHING HAPPENED!
AND THAT THING ON THE LAST DAY WAS JUST AN ACCIDENT!!
DAMMIT... I CAN'T BELIEVE THIS IS HAPPEN-ING.
I DON'T HAVE TIME FOR THIS-- I'VE GOT TO GIVE CLASS REP MY ANSWER AS SOON AS POS-SIBLE.
IF I DON'T SET IT ALL STRAIGHT WITH CLASS REP...
I'LL NEVER BE ABLE TO TELL YOUKO-SAN THAT I LOVE HER.

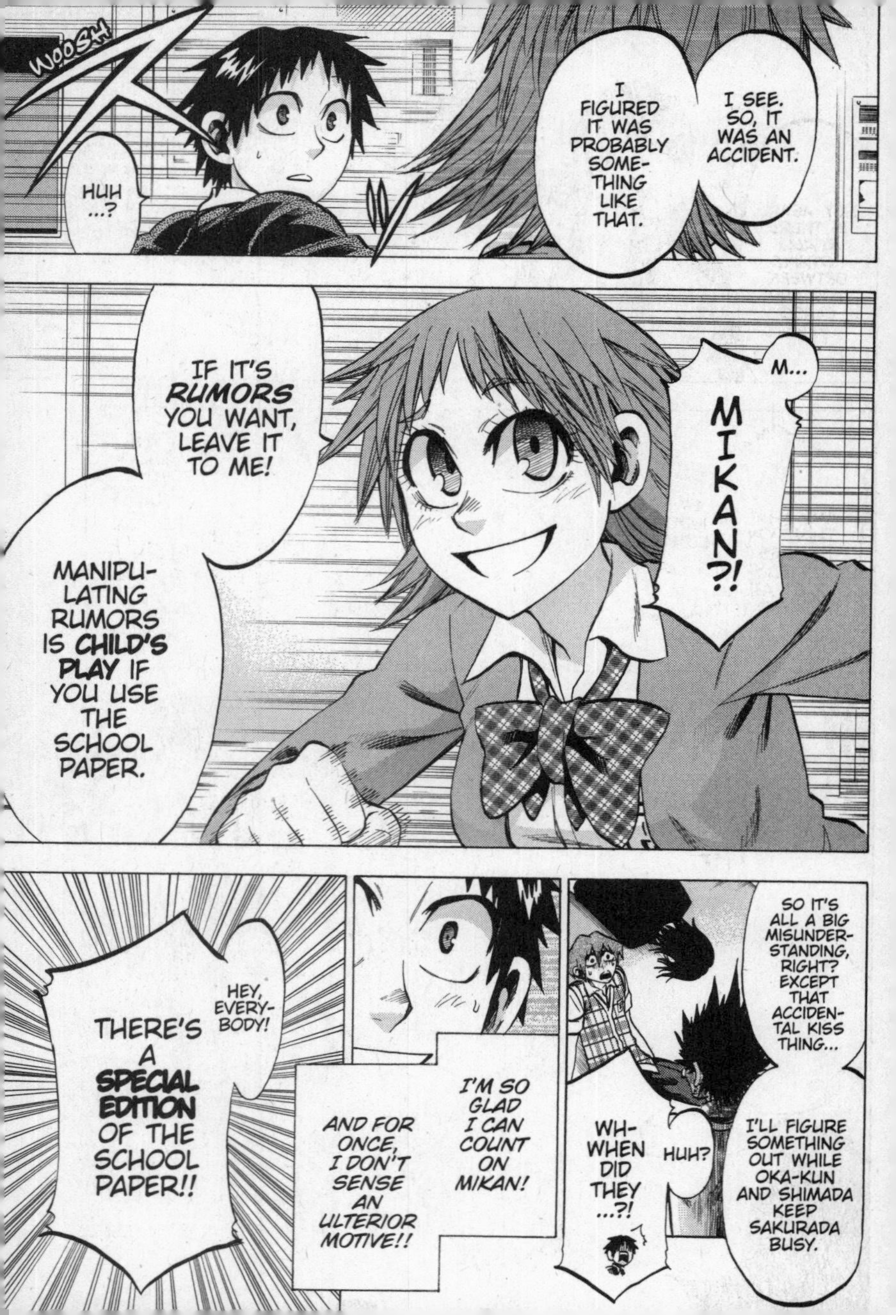
I SEE. SO, IT WAS AN ACCIDENT.
I FIGURED IT WAS PROBABLY SOMETHING LIKE THAT.
WOOSH
HUH ...?
M... MIKAN?!
IF IT'S RUMORS YOU WANT, LEAVE IT TO ME!
MANIPULATING RUMORS IS CHILD'S PLAY IF YOU USE THE SCHOOL PAPER.
SO IT'S ALL A BIG MISUNDERSTANDING, RIGHT? EXCEPT THAT ACCIDENTAL KISS THING...
I'LL FIGURE SOMETHING OUT WHILE OKA-KUN AND SHIMADA KEEP SAKURADA BUSY.
HUH?
WH- WHEN DID THEY ...?!
I'M SO GLAD I CAN COUNT ON MIKAN!
AND FOR ONCE, I DON'T SENSE AN ULTERIOR MOTIVE!!
HEY, EVERYBODY!
THERE'S A SPECIAL EDITION OF THE SCHOOL PAPER!!

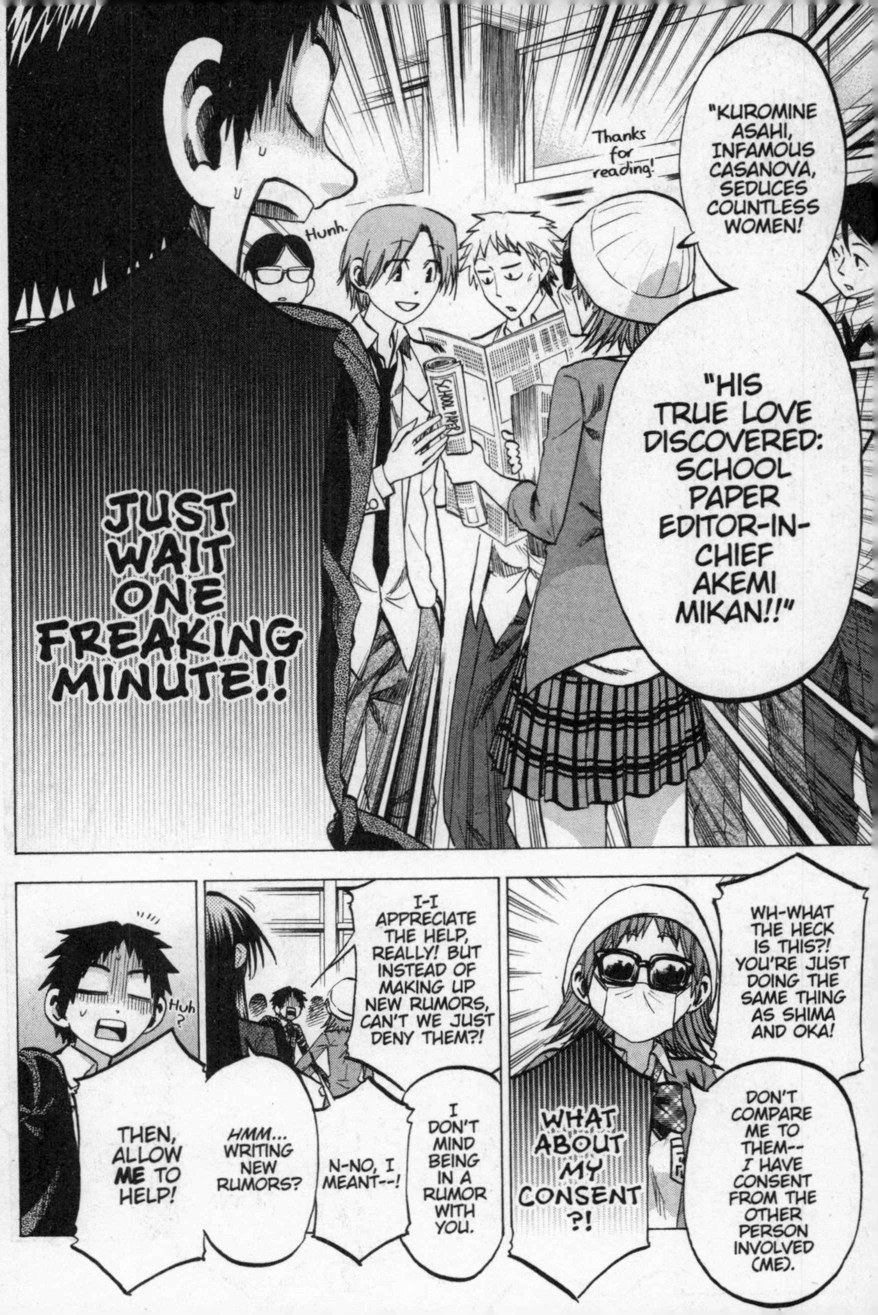
"KUROMINE ASAHI, INFAMOUS CASANOVA, SEDUCES COUNTLESS WOMEN!
"HIS TRUE LOVE DISCOVERED: SCHOOL PAPER EDITOR-IN-CHIEF AKEMI MIKAN!!"
Thanks for reading!
SCHOOL PAPER
Hunh.
JUST WAIT ONE FREAKING MINUTE!!
WH-WHAT THE HECK IS THIS?! YOU'RE JUST DOING THE SAME THING AS SHIMA AND OKA!
DON'T COMPARE ME TO THEM-- *I* HAVE CONSENT FROM THE OTHER PERSON INVOLVED (ME).
WHAT ABOUT MY CONSENT?!
I-I APPRECIATE THE HELP, REALLY! BUT INSTEAD OF MAKING UP NEW RUMORS, CAN'T WE JUST DENY THEM?!
I DON'T MIND BEING IN A RUMOR WITH YOU.
N-NO, I MEANT--!
Huh?
HMM... WRITING NEW RUMORS?
THEN, ALLOW **ME** TO HELP!

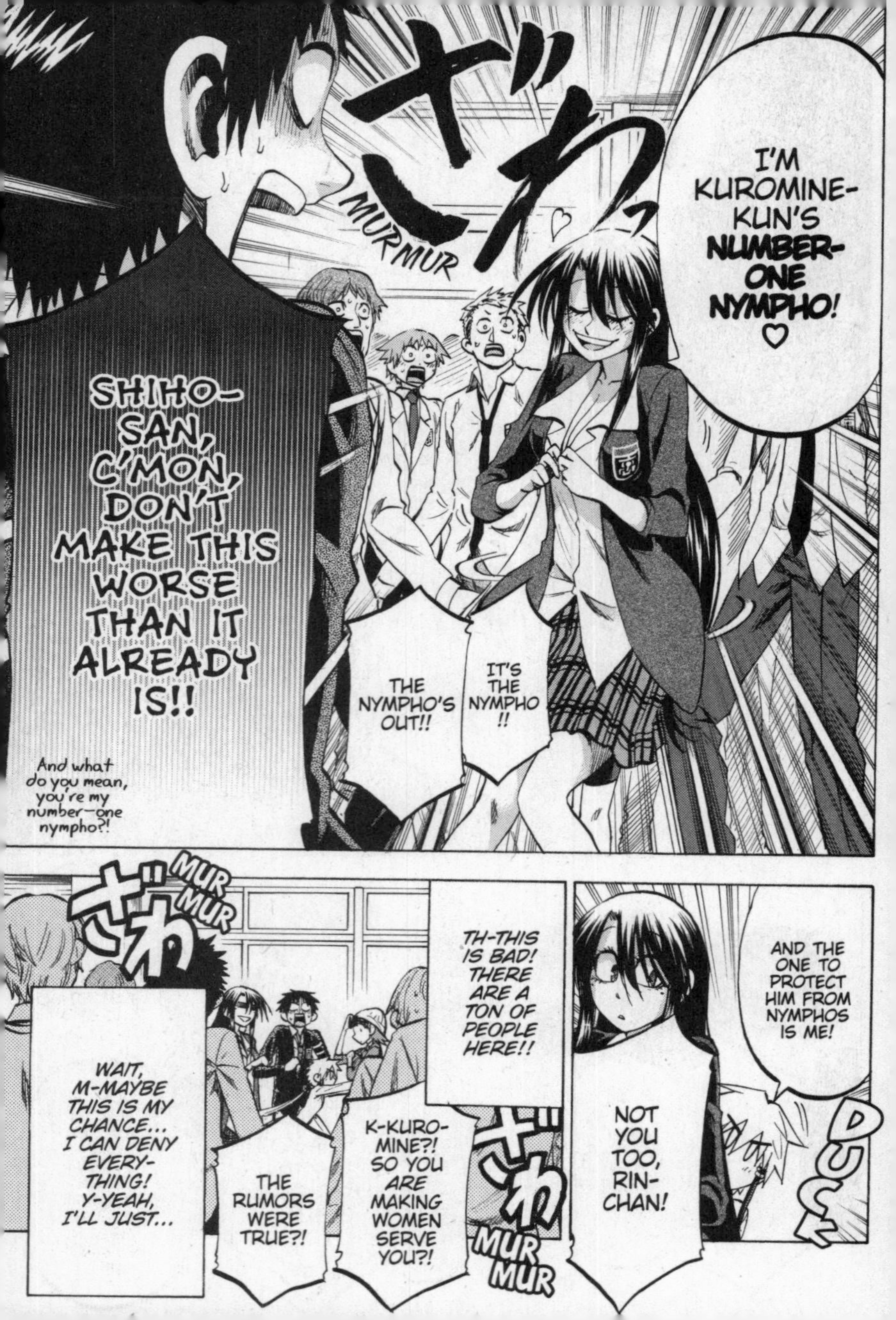
I'M KUROMINE-KUN'S NUMBER-ONE NYMPHO! ♡
MURMUR
IT'S THE NYMPHO!!
THE NYMPHO'S OUT!!
SHIHO-SAN, C'MON, DON'T MAKE THIS WORSE THAN IT ALREADY IS!!
And what do you mean, you're my number-one nympho?!
AND THE ONE TO PROTECT HIM FROM NYMPHOS IS ME!
DUCK
NOT YOU TOO, RIN-CHAN!
TH-THIS IS BAD! THERE ARE A TON OF PEOPLE HERE!!
MUR MUR
K-KURO-MINE?! SO YOU ARE MAKING WOMEN SERVE YOU?!
THE RUMORS WERE TRUE?!
WAIT, M-MAYBE THIS IS MY CHANCE... I CAN DENY EVERY-THING! Y-YEAH, I'LL JUST...
MUR MUR

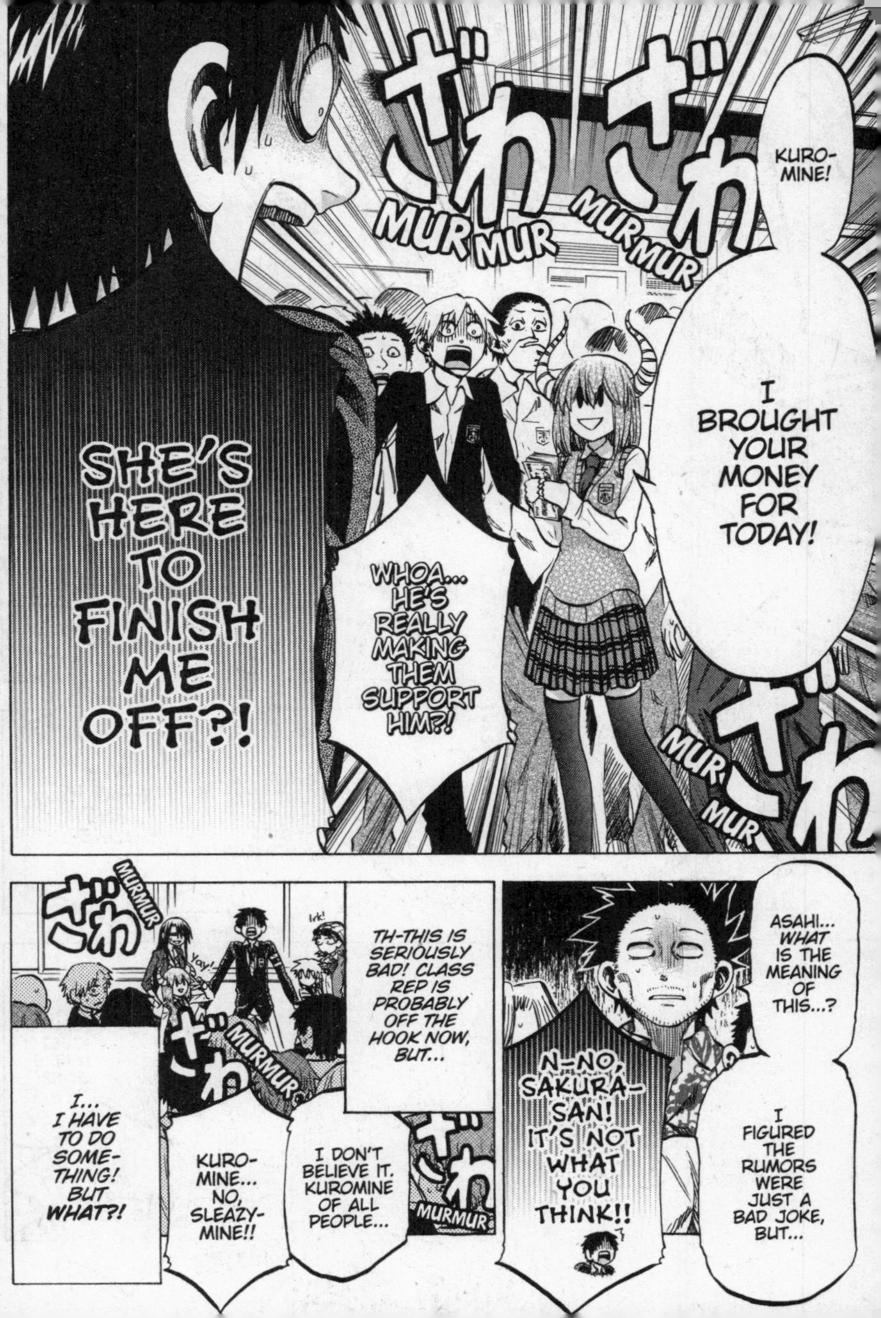
ざわざわ
MUR MUR MUR MUR
KURO-MINE!
I BROUGHT YOUR MONEY FOR TODAY!
ざわ
MUR MUR
WHOA... HE'S REALLY MAKING THEM SUPPORT HIM?!
SHE'S HERE TO FINISH ME OFF?!
ASAHI... WHAT IS THE MEANING OF THIS...?
I FIGURED THE RUMORS WERE JUST A BAD JOKE, BUT...
N-NO, SAKURA-SAN! IT'S NOT WHAT YOU THINK!!
TH-THIS IS SERIOUSLY BAD! CLASS REP IS PROBABLY OFF THE HOOK NOW, BUT...
ざわ
MURMUR
I DON'T BELIEVE IT. KUROMINE OF ALL PEOPLE...
KURO-MINE... NO, SLEAZY-MINE!!
ざわ
MURMUR
Irk!
Yay!
ざわ
MURMUR
I... I HAVE TO DO SOMETHING! BUT *WHAT*?!

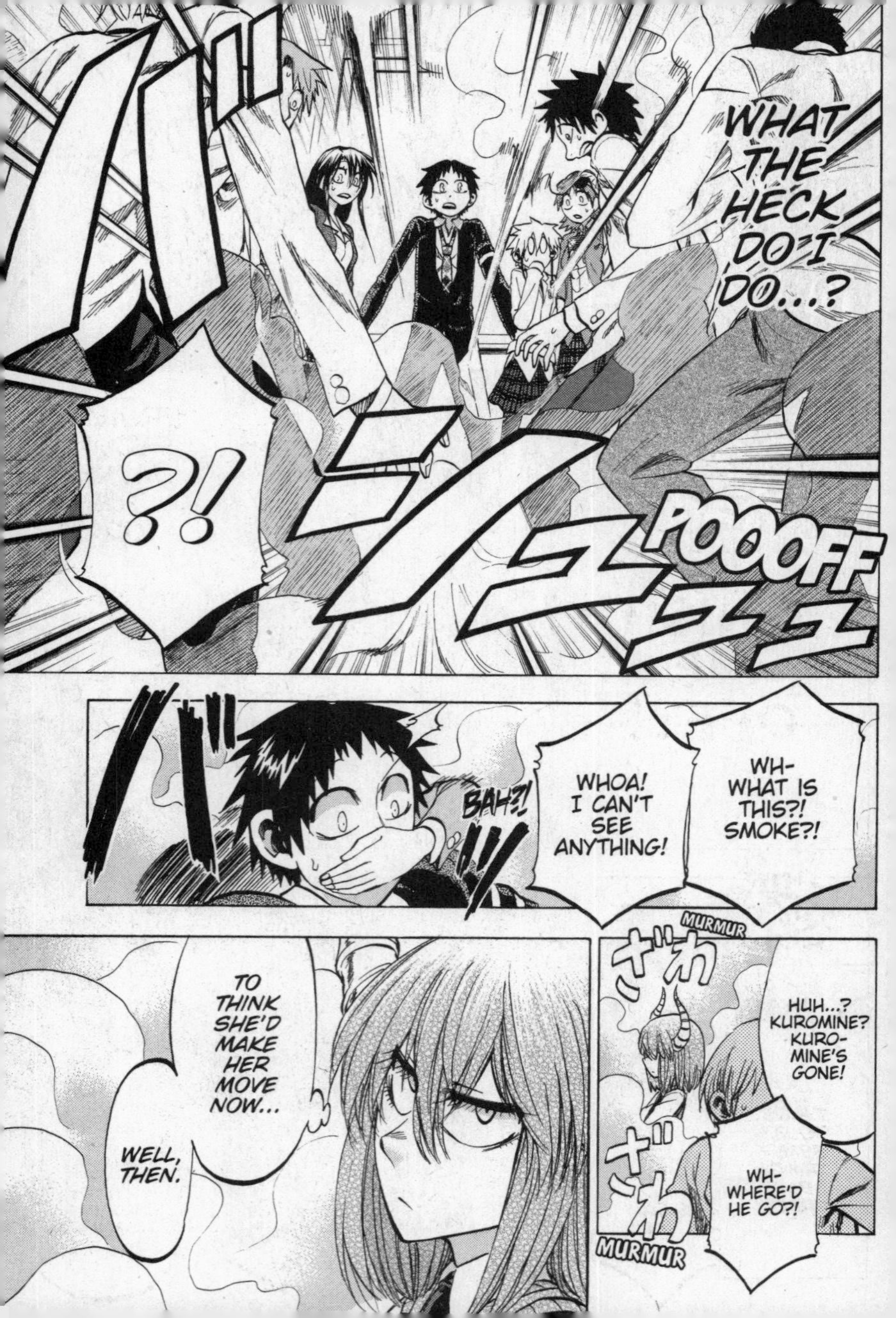
WHAT THE HECK DO I DO...?
?!
POOOFF
WH- WHAT IS THIS?! SMOKE?!
WHOA! I CAN'T SEE ANYTHING!
BAH?!
MURMUR
ざわ
HUH...? KUROMINE? KURO-MINE'S GONE!
ざわ
WH- WHERE'D HE GO?!
MURMUR
TO THINK SHE'D MAKE HER MOVE NOW...
WELL, THEN.

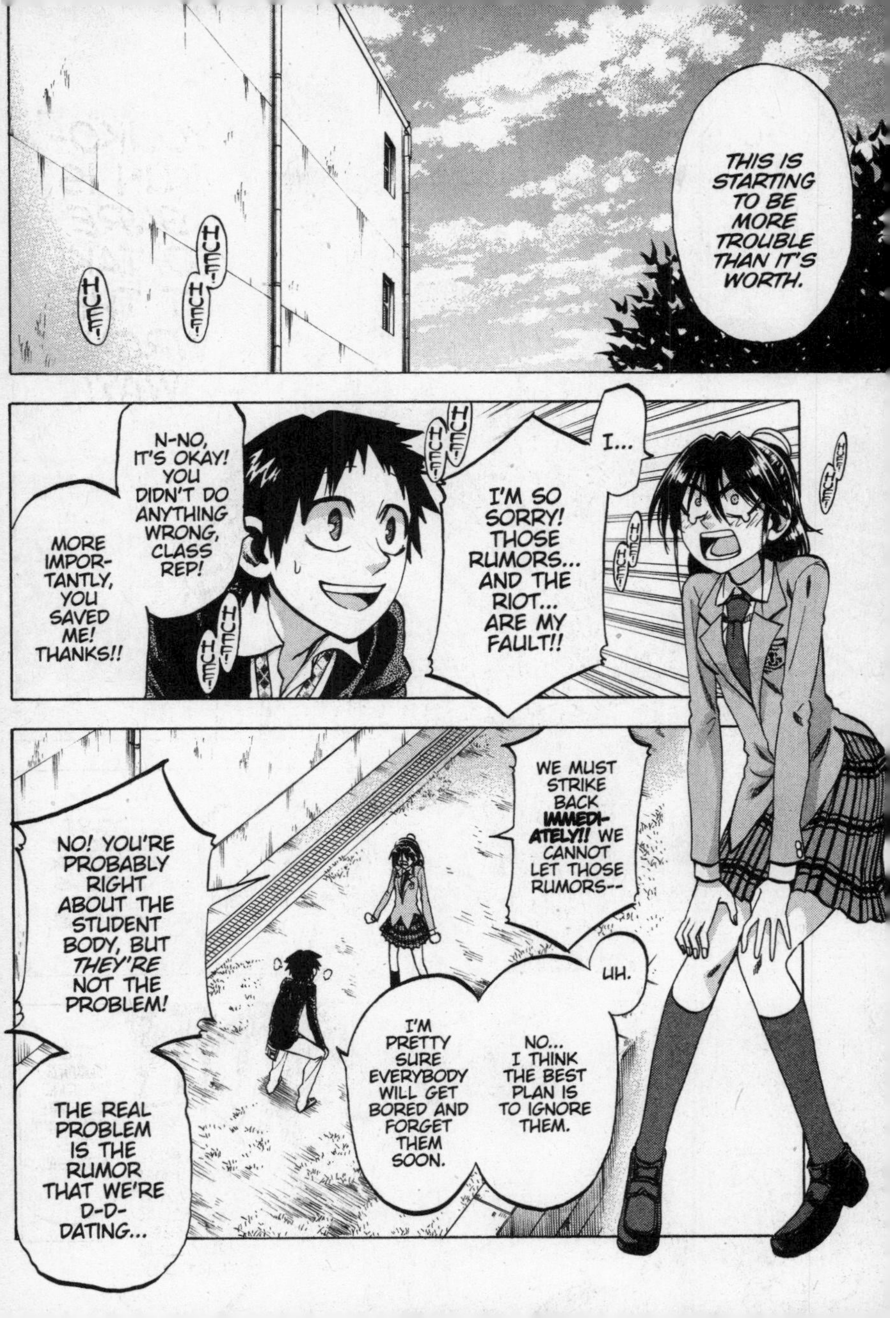
THIS IS STARTING TO BE MORE TROUBLE THAN IT'S WORTH.
HUFF! HUFF!
HUFF!
HUFF! HUFF!
I...
I'M SO SORRY! THOSE RUMORS... AND THE RIOT... ARE MY FAULT!!
HUFF! HUFF!
HUFF! HUFF!
HUFF! HUFF!
N-NO, IT'S OKAY! YOU DIDN'T DO ANYTHING WRONG, CLASS REP!
MORE IMPOR-TANTLY, YOU SAVED ME! THANKS!!
WE MUST STRIKE BACK **IMMEDI-ATELY!!** WE CANNOT LET THOSE RUMORS--
UH.
NO... I THINK THE BEST PLAN IS TO IGNORE THEM.
I'M PRETTY SURE EVERYBODY WILL GET BORED AND FORGET THEM SOON.
NO! YOU'RE PROBABLY RIGHT ABOUT THE STUDENT BODY, BUT *THEY'RE* NOT THE PROBLEM!
THE REAL PROBLEM IS THE RUMOR THAT WE'RE D-D-DATING...

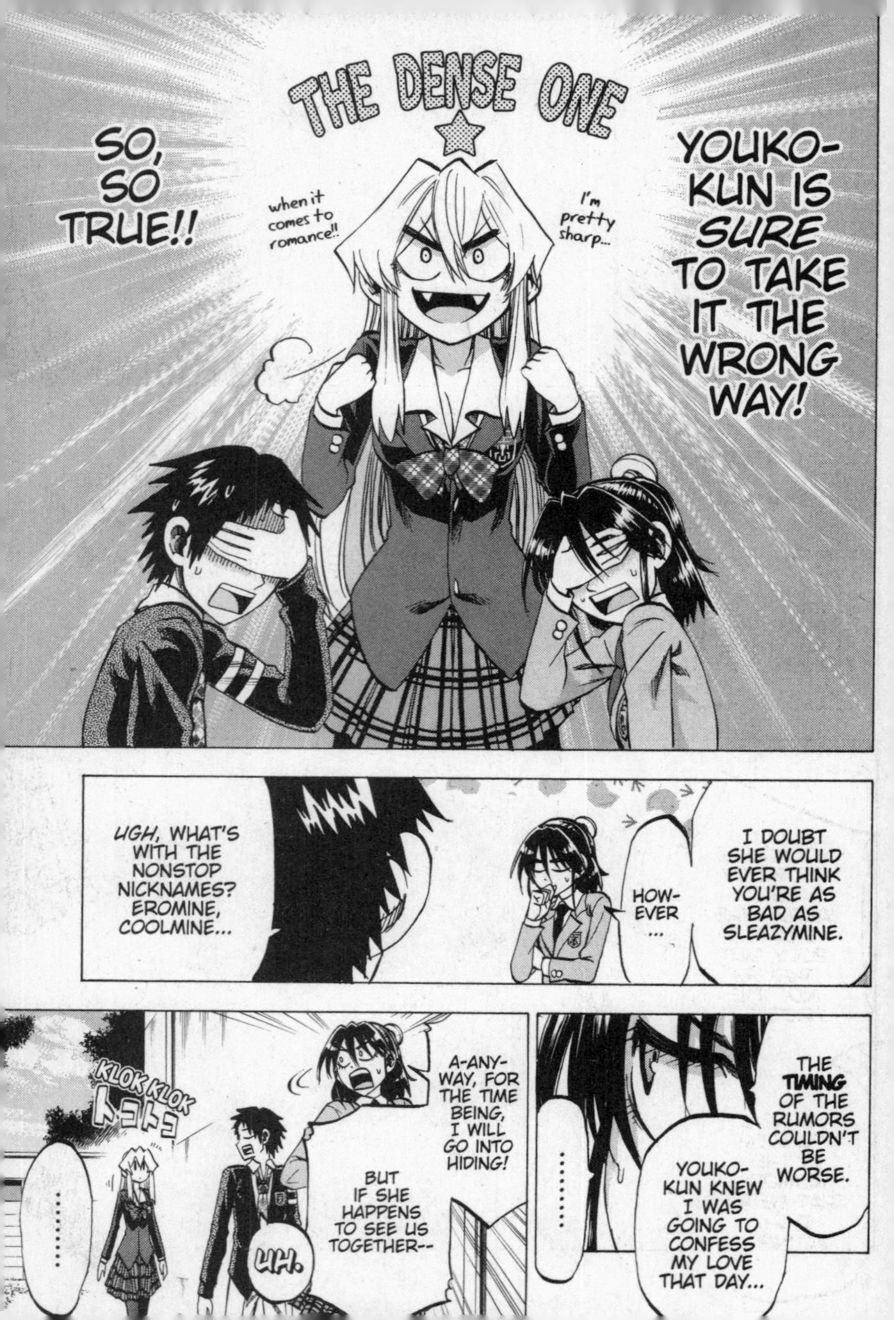
THE DENSE ONE
YOUKO-KUN IS SURE TO TAKE IT THE WRONG WAY!
I'm pretty sharp...
when it comes to romance!!
SO, SO TRUE!!
I DOUBT SHE WOULD EVER THINK YOU'RE AS BAD AS SLEAZYMINE.
HOW-EVER ...
UGH, WHAT'S WITH THE NONSTOP NICKNAMES? EROMINE, COOLMINE...
THE TIMING OF THE RUMORS COULDN'T BE WORSE.
YOUKO-KUN KNEW I WAS GOING TO CONFESS MY LOVE THAT DAY...
......
A-ANYWAY, FOR THE TIME BEING, I WILL GO INTO HIDING!
BUT IF SHE HAPPENS TO SEE US TOGETHER--
UH.
KLOK KLOK
......

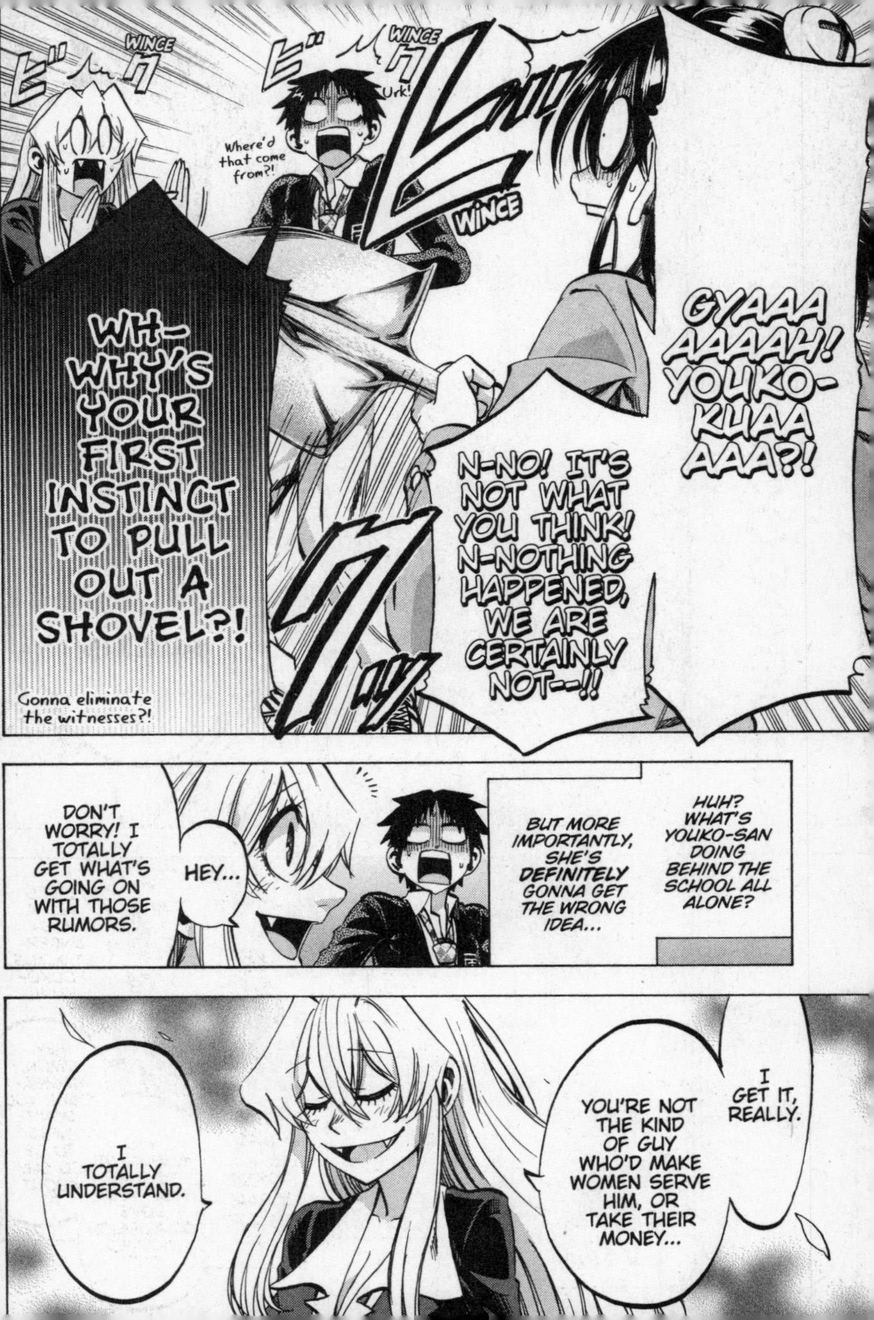
GYAAA AAAAH! YOUKO-KUAA AAA?!
N-NO! IT'S NOT WHAT YOU THINK! N-NOTHING HAPPENED, WE ARE CERTAINLY NOT--!!
WINCE
WINCE
Urk!
WINCE
Where'd that come from?!
WH-WHY'S YOUR FIRST INSTINCT TO PULL OUT A SHOVEL?!
Gonna eliminate the witnesses?!
HUH? WHAT'S YOUKO-SAN DOING BEHIND THE SCHOOL ALL ALONE?
BUT MORE IMPORTANTLY, SHE'S DEFINITELY GONNA GET THE WRONG IDEA...
HEY...
DON'T WORRY! I TOTALLY GET WHAT'S GOING ON WITH THOSE RUMORS.
I GET IT, REALLY.
YOU'RE NOT THE KIND OF GUY WHO'D MAKE WOMEN SERVE HIM, OR TAKE THEIR MONEY...
I TOTALLY UNDERSTAND.

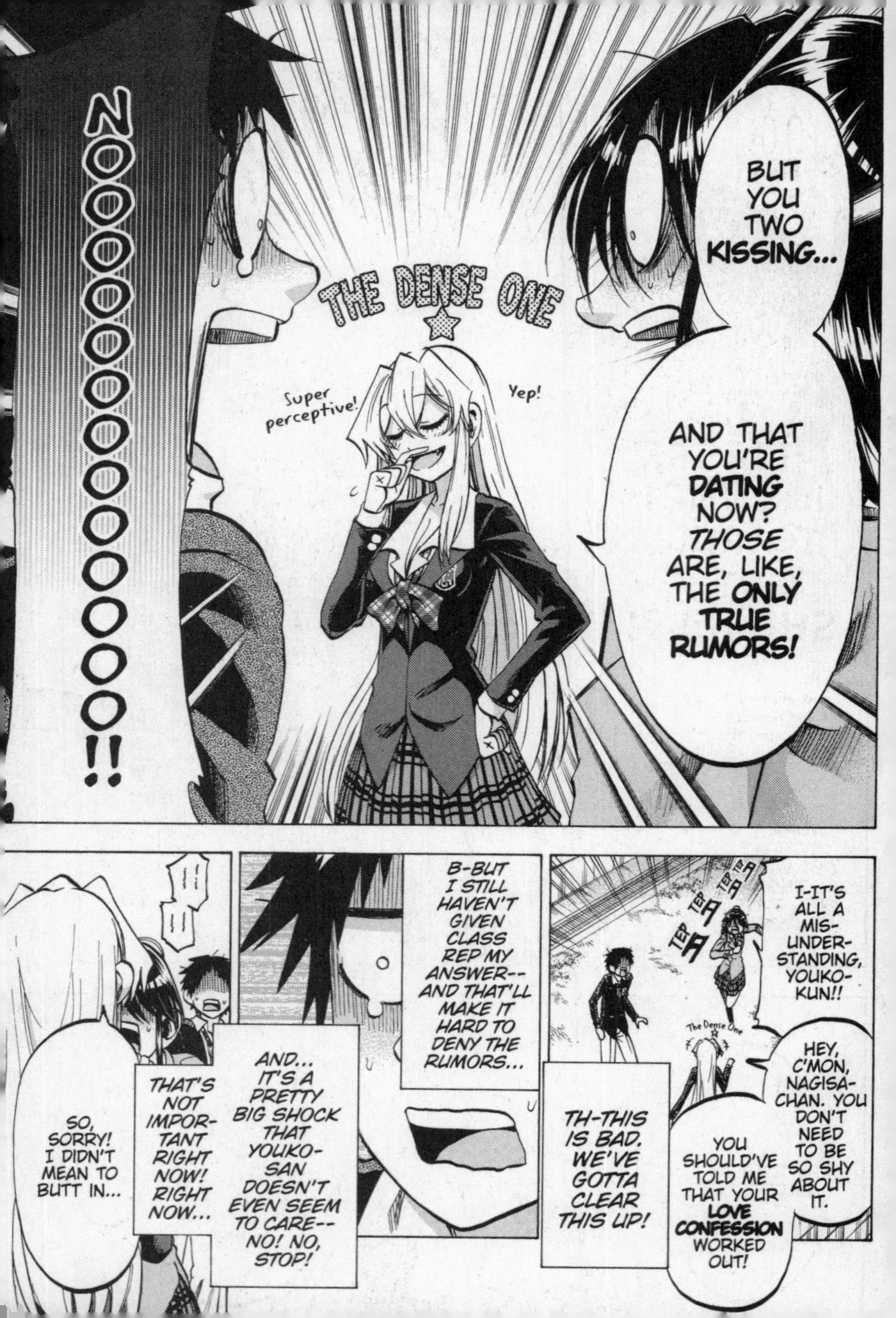
BUT YOU TWO KISSING...
AND THAT YOU'RE DATING NOW? THOSE ARE, LIKE, THE ONLY TRUE RUMORS!
THE DENSE ONE ☆
Yep!
Super perceptive!
NOOOOOOOOOOOOOOOOOO!!
TEP TEP TEP TEP
I-IT'S ALL A MIS-UNDERSTANDING, YOUKO-KUN!!
The Dense One
HEY, C'MON, NAGISA-CHAN. YOU DON'T NEED TO BE SO SHY ABOUT IT.
YOU SHOULD'VE TOLD ME THAT YOUR LOVE CONFESSION WORKED OUT!
TH-THIS IS BAD. WE'VE GOTTA CLEAR THIS UP!
B-BUT I STILL HAVEN'T GIVEN CLASS REP MY ANSWER--AND THAT'LL MAKE IT HARD TO DENY THE RUMORS...
AND... IT'S A PRETTY BIG SHOCK THAT YOUKO-SAN DOESN'T EVEN SEEM TO CARE--NO! NO, STOP!
THAT'S NOT IMPORTANT RIGHT NOW! RIGHT NOW...
!!
SO, SORRY! I DIDN'T MEAN TO BUTT IN...

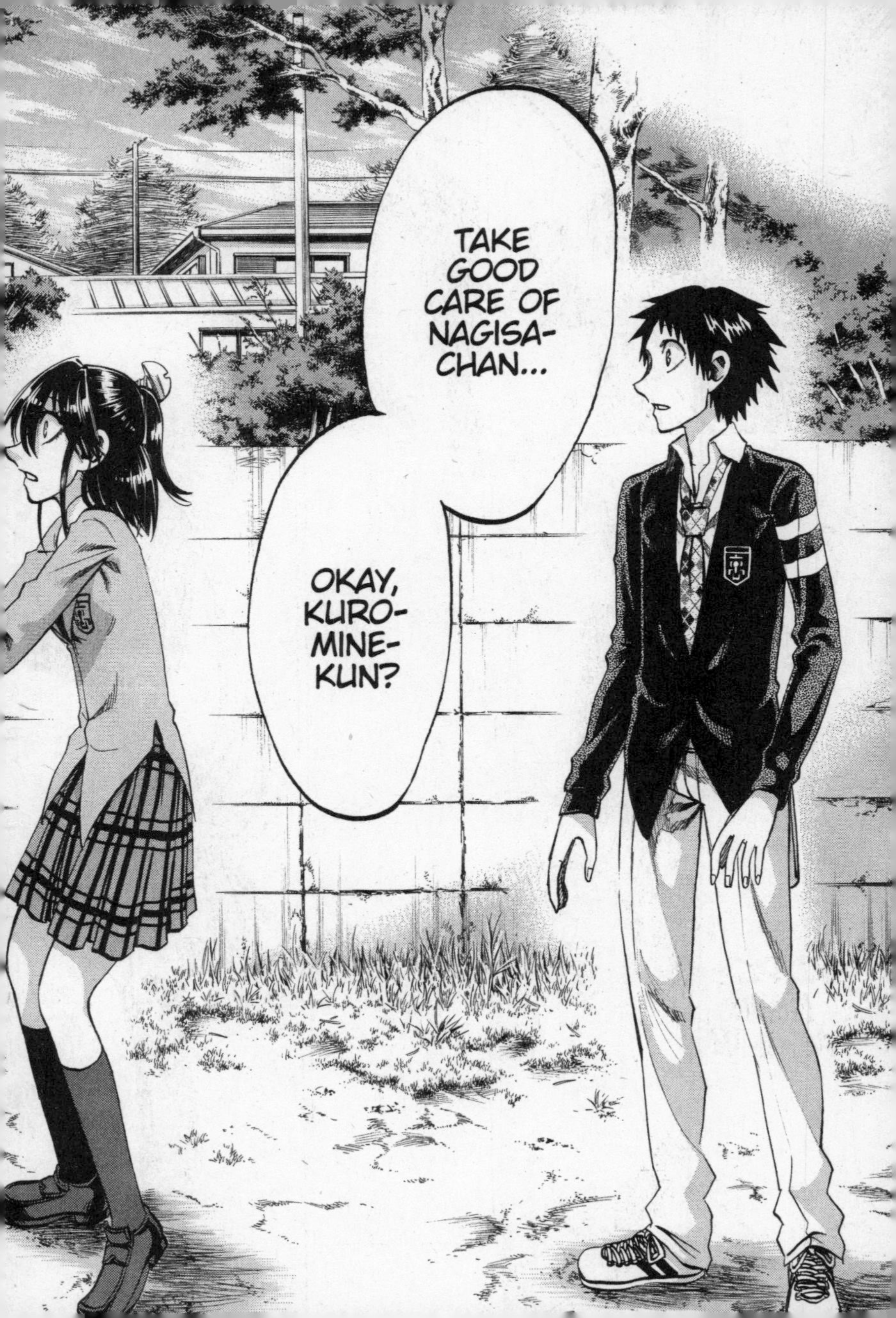
TAKE GOOD CARE OF NAGISA-CHAN...
OKAY, KURO-MINE-KUN?

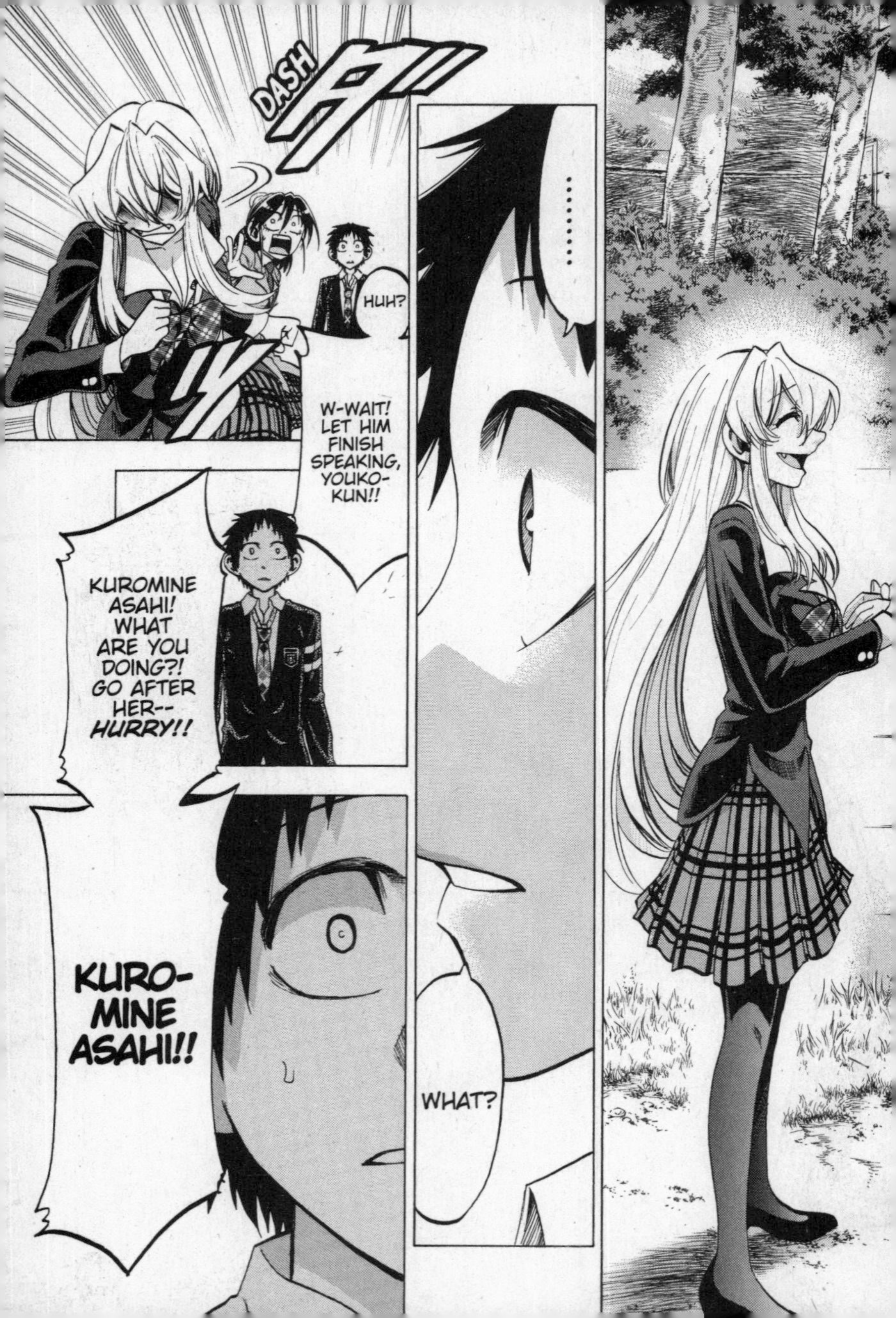
......
WHAT?
DASH
HUH?
W-WAIT! LET HIM FINISH SPEAKING, YOUKO-KUN!!
KUROMINE ASAHI! WHAT ARE YOU DOING?! GO AFTER HER-- HURRY!!
KURO-MINE ASAHI!!

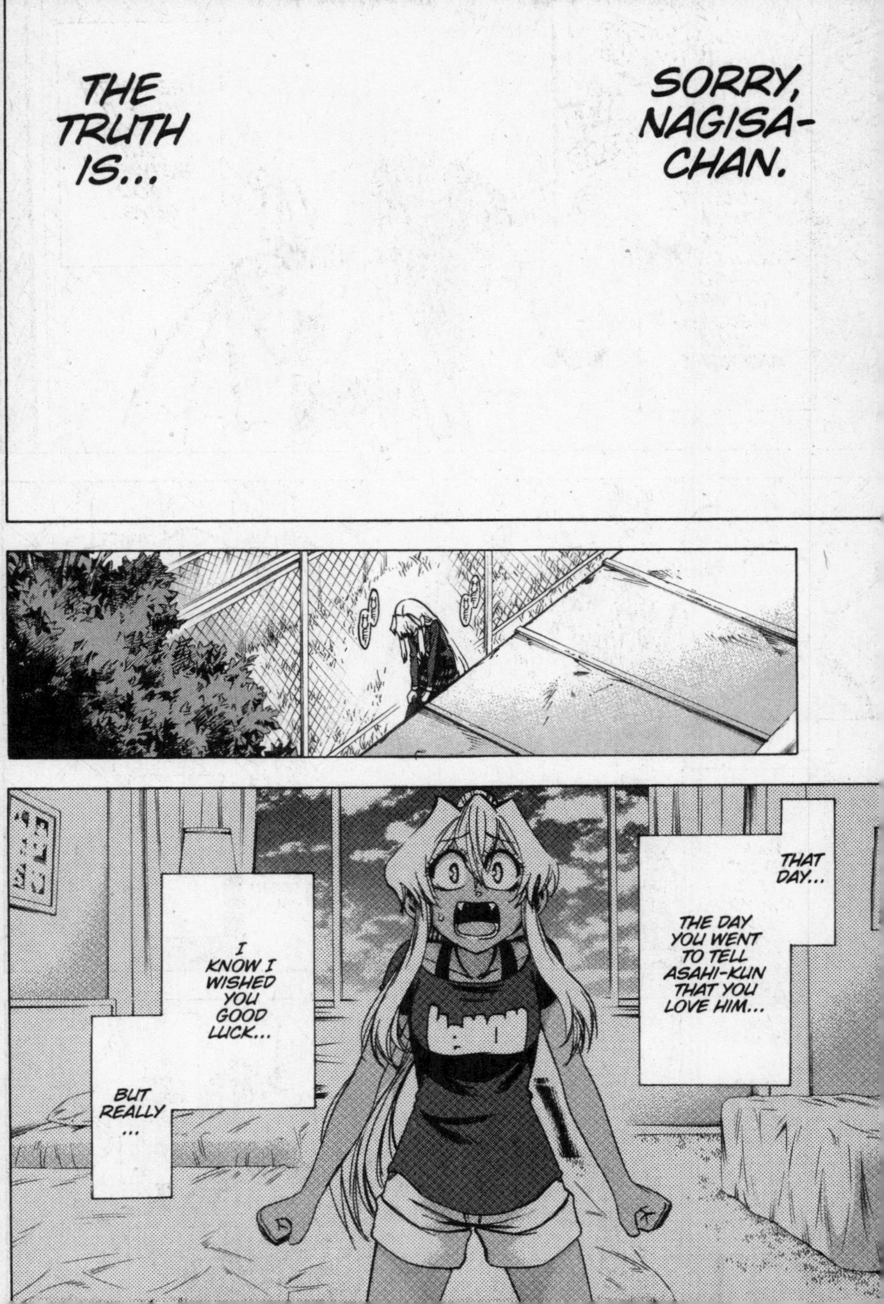
SORRY, NAGISA-CHAN.
THE TRUTH IS...
THAT DAY...
THE DAY YOU WENT TO TELL ASAHI-KUN THAT YOU LOVE HIM...
I KNOW I WISHED YOU GOOD LUCK...
BUT REALLY ...

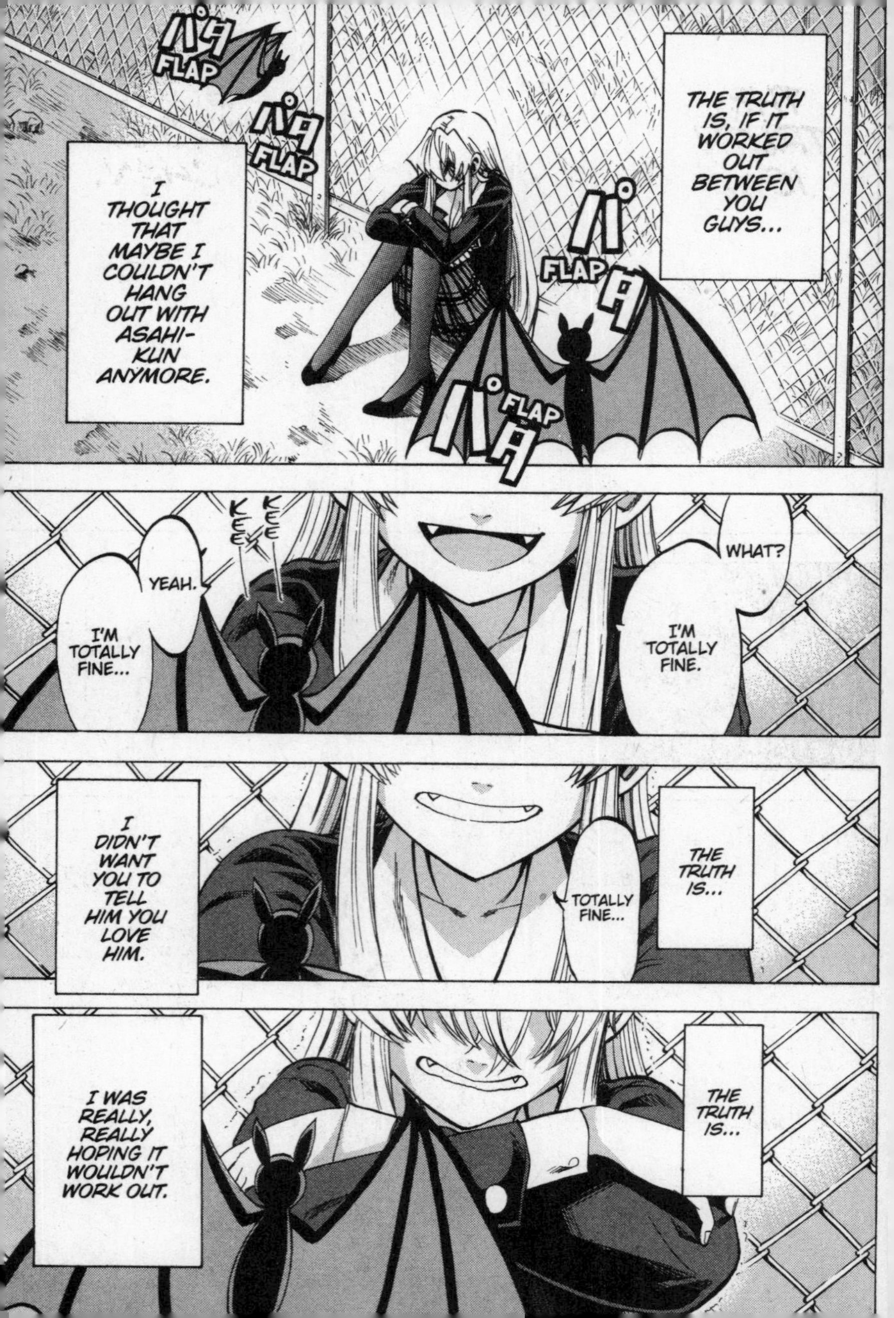
THE TRUTH IS, IF IT WORKED OUT BETWEEN YOU GUYS...
パ FLAP
パ
タ
FLAP
パ
タ
パタ
FLAP
パタ
FLAP
I THOUGHT THAT MAYBE I COULDN'T HANG OUT WITH ASAHI-KUN ANYMORE.
WHAT?
I'M TOTALLY FINE.
KEE
KEE
YEAH.
I'M TOTALLY FINE...
THE TRUTH IS...
TOTALLY FINE...
I DIDN'T WANT YOU TO TELL HIM YOU LOVE HIM.
THE TRUTH IS...
I WAS REALLY, REALLY HOPING IT WOULDN'T WORK OUT.

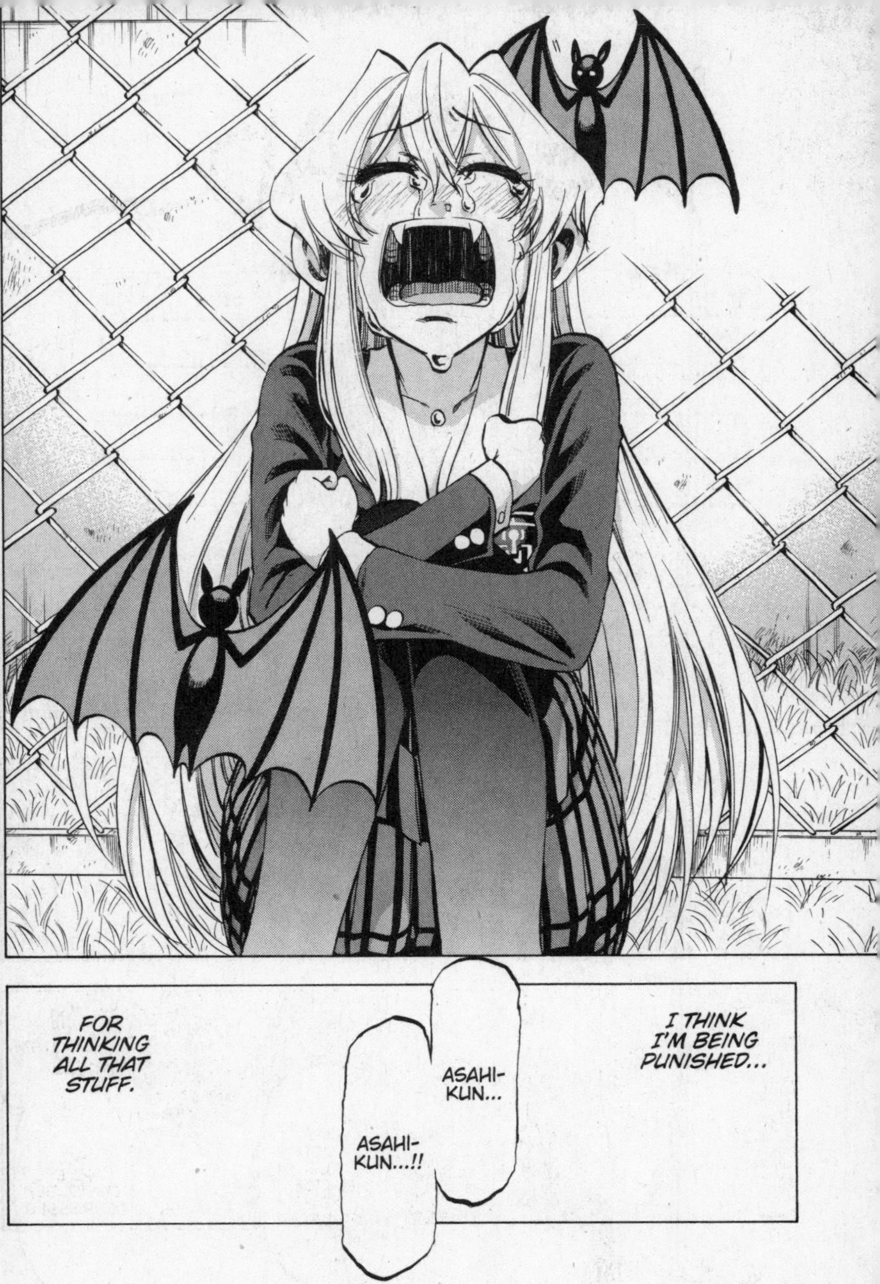
I THINK I'M BEING PUNISHED...
ASAHI-KUN...
ASAHI-KUN...!!
FOR THINKING ALL THAT STUFF.

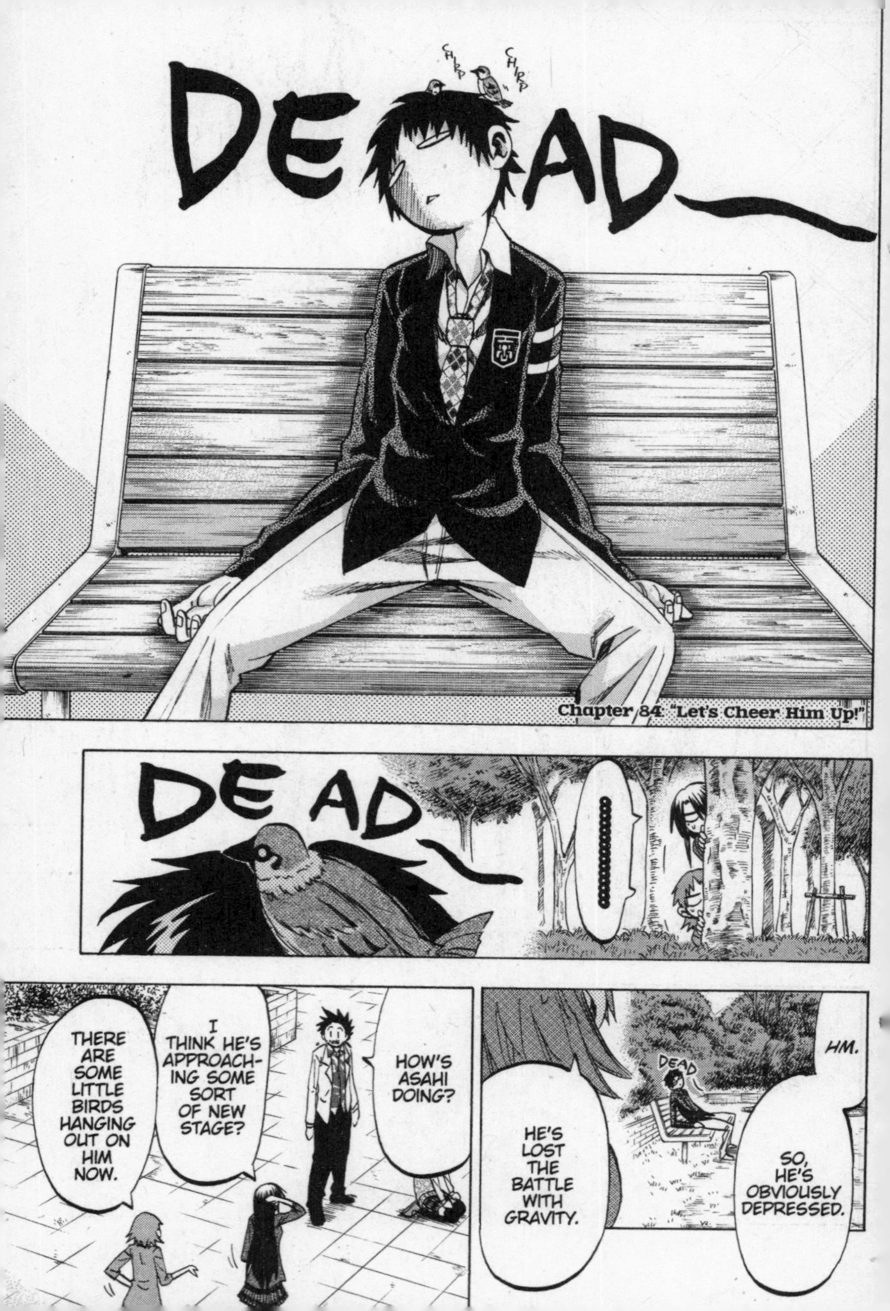
CHIRP
CHIRP
DEAD
Chapter 84: "Let's Cheer Him Up!"
DEAD
....
HM.
SO, HE'S OBVIOUSLY DEPRESSED.
DEAD
HE'S LOST THE BATTLE WITH GRAVITY.
HOW'S ASAHI DOING?
I THINK HE'S APPROACHING SOME SORT OF NEW STAGE?
THERE ARE SOME LITTLE BIRDS HANGING OUT ON HIM NOW.

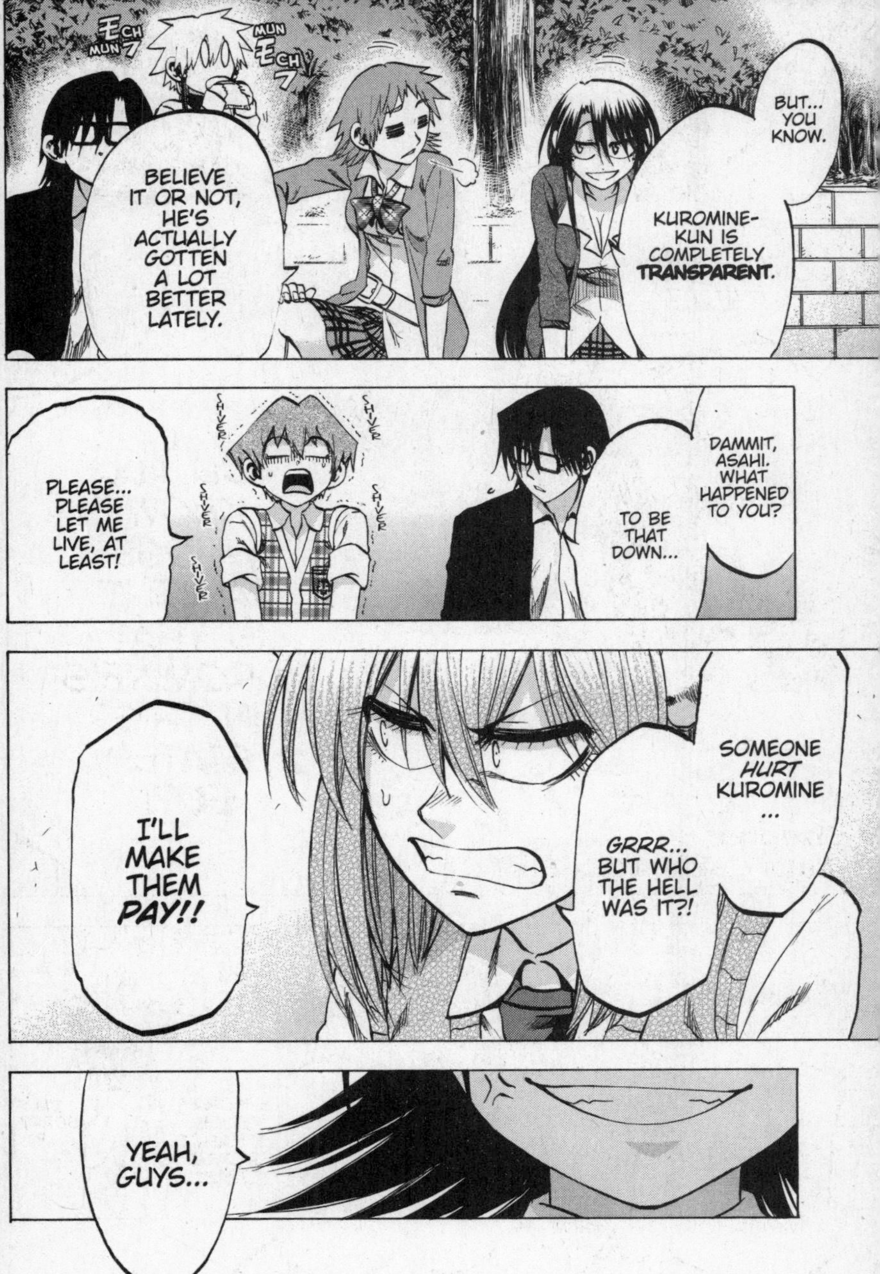
BUT... YOU KNOW.
KUROMINE-KUN IS COMPLETELY **TRANSPARENT.**
BELIEVE IT OR NOT, HE'S ACTUALLY GOTTEN A LOT BETTER LATELY.
DAMMIT, ASAHI. WHAT HAPPENED TO YOU?
TO BE THAT DOWN...
SHIVER SHIVER SHIVER SHIVER SHIVER
PLEASE... PLEASE LET ME LIVE, AT LEAST!
SOMEONE *HURT* KUROMINE...
GRRR... BUT WHO THE HELL WAS IT?!
I'LL MAKE THEM *PAY!!*
YEAH, GUYS...

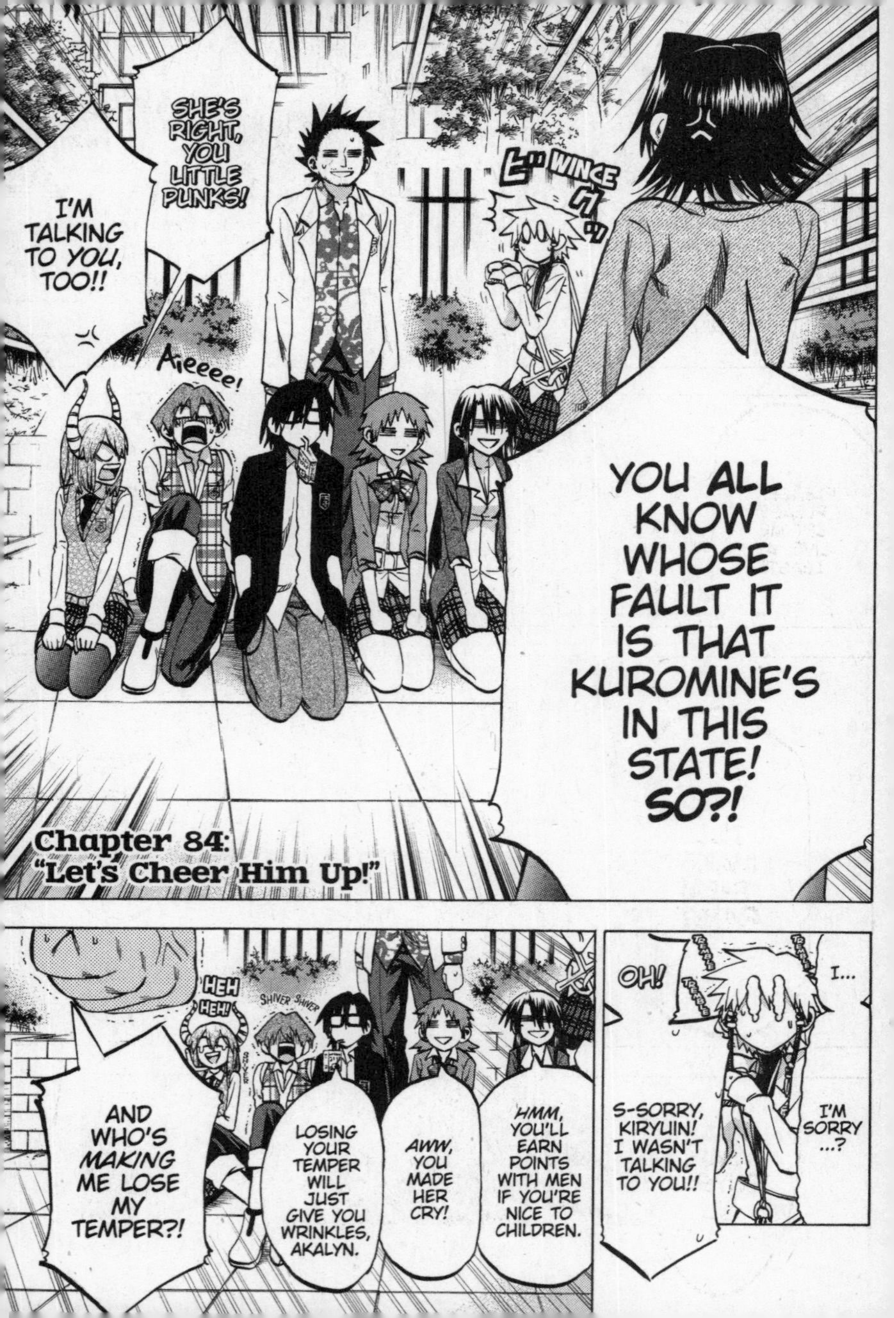
YOU ALL KNOW WHOSE FAULT IT IS THAT KUROMINE'S IN THIS STATE! SO?!
WINCE
SHE'S RIGHT, YOU LITTLE PUNKS!
I'M TALKING TO YOU, TOO!!
Aieeee!
Chapter 84: "Let's Cheer Him Up!"
TREMBLE
TREMBLE
TREMBLE
I...
I'M SORRY ...?
OH!
S-SORRY, KIRYUIN! I WASN'T TALKING TO YOU!!
HMM, YOU'LL EARN POINTS WITH MEN IF YOU'RE NICE TO CHILDREN.
AWW, YOU MADE HER CRY!
LOSING YOUR TEMPER WILL JUST GIVE YOU WRINKLES, AKALYN.
SHIVER SHIVER
SHIVER
HEH HEH!
AND WHO'S MAKING ME LOSE MY TEMPER?!

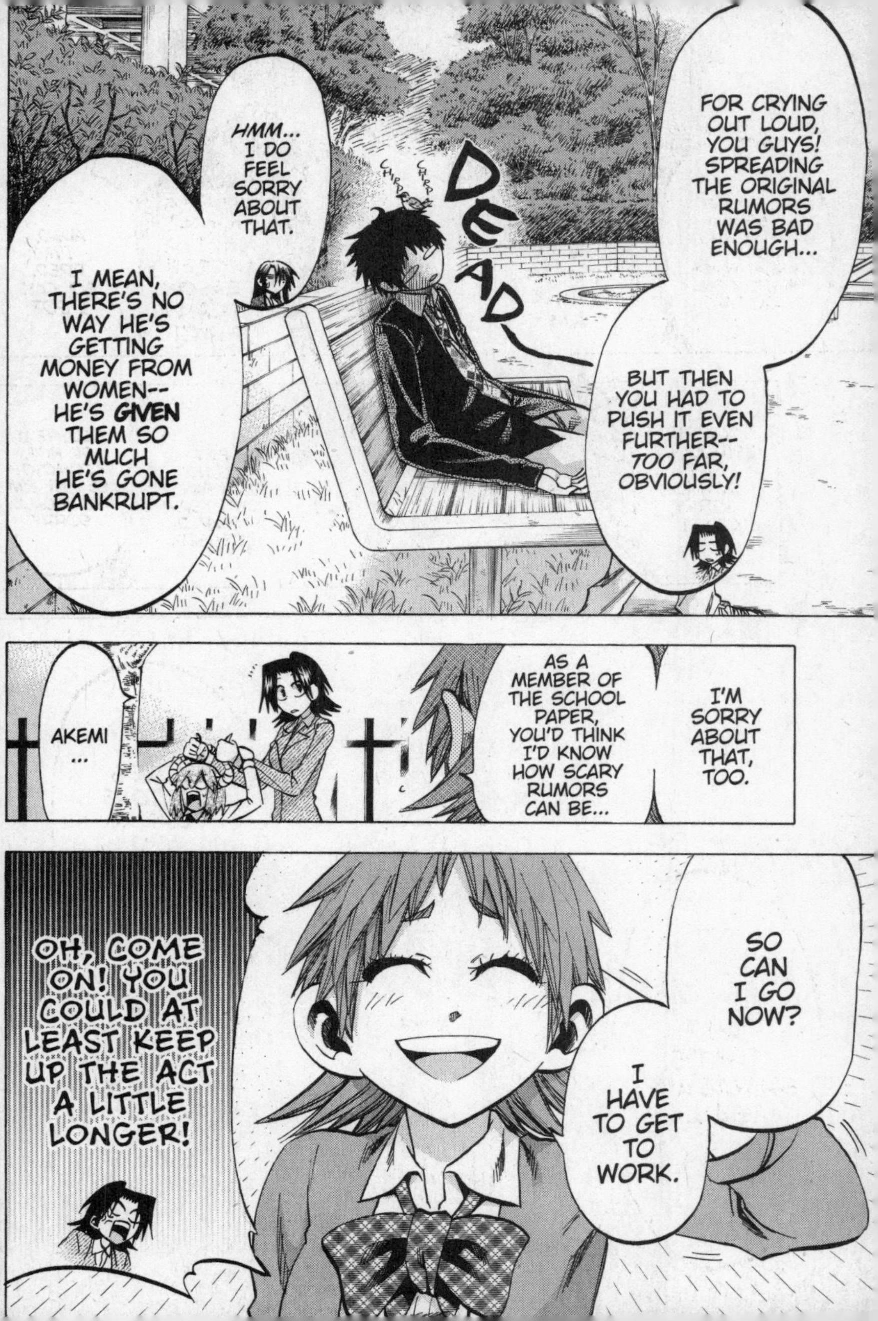
FOR CRYING OUT LOUD, YOU GUYS! SPREADING THE ORIGINAL RUMORS WAS BAD ENOUGH...
BUT THEN YOU HAD TO PUSH IT EVEN FURTHER-- *TOO* FAR, OBVIOUSLY!
DEAD
CHIRP
CHIRP
HMM... I DO FEEL SORRY ABOUT THAT.
I MEAN, THERE'S NO WAY HE'S GETTING MONEY FROM WOMEN-- HE'S **GIVEN** THEM SO MUCH HE'S GONE BANKRUPT.
I'M SORRY ABOUT THAT, TOO.
AS A MEMBER OF THE SCHOOL PAPER, YOU'D THINK I'D KNOW HOW SCARY RUMORS CAN BE...
AKEMI...
SO CAN I GO NOW?
I HAVE TO GET TO WORK.
OH, COME ON! YOU COULD AT LEAST KEEP UP THE ACT A LITTLE LONGER!

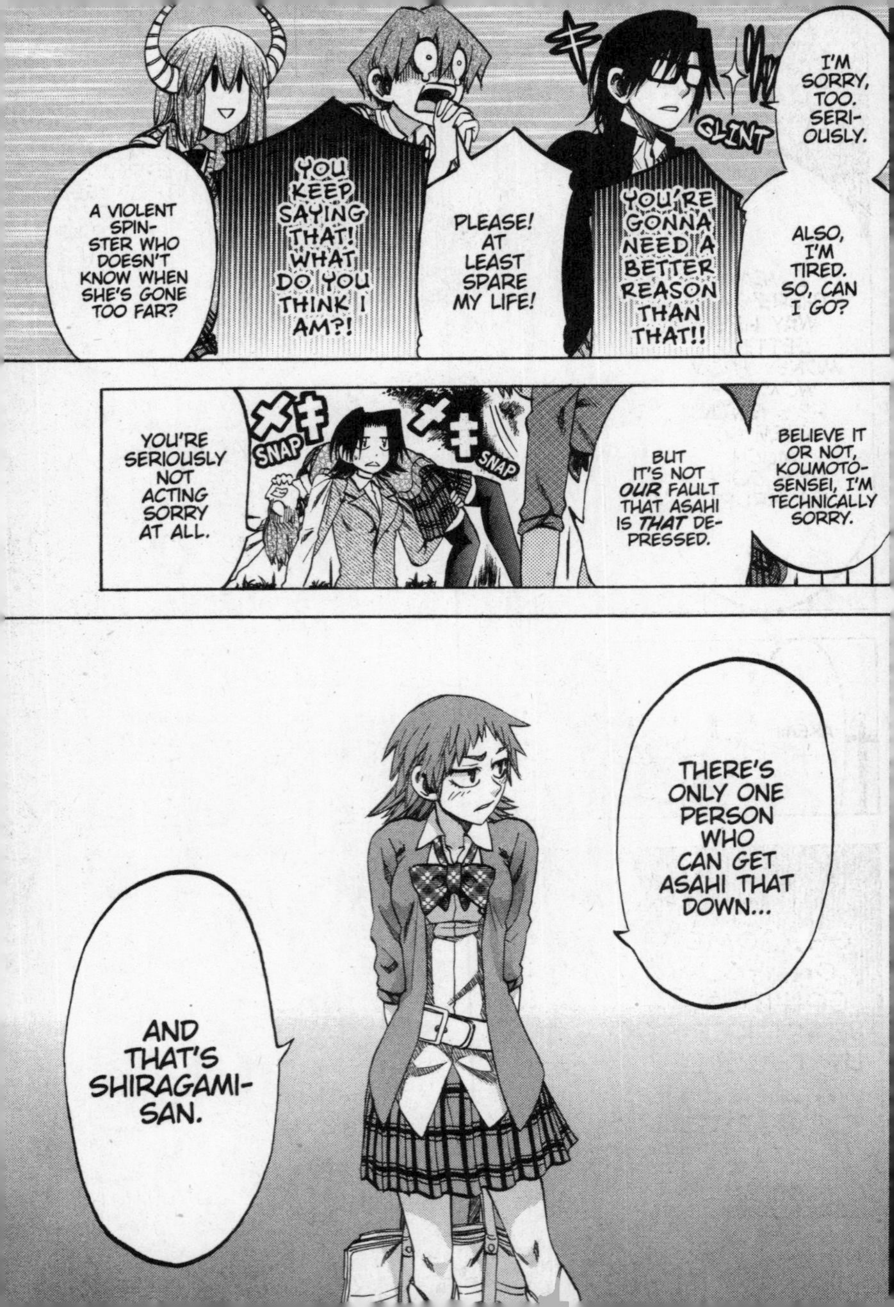
I'M SORRY, TOO. SERIOUSLY.
ALSO, I'M TIRED. SO, CAN I GO?
GLINT
YOU'RE GONNA NEED A BETTER REASON THAN THAT!!
PLEASE! AT LEAST SPARE MY LIFE!
YOU KEEP SAYING THAT! WHAT DO YOU THINK I AM?!
A VIOLENT SPINSTER WHO DOESN'T KNOW WHEN SHE'S GONE TOO FAR?
BELIEVE IT OR NOT, KOUMOTO-SENSEI, I'M TECHNICALLY SORRY.
BUT IT'S NOT OUR FAULT THAT ASAHI IS THAT DEPRESSED.
SNAP
SNAP
YOU'RE SERIOUSLY NOT ACTING SORRY AT ALL.
THERE'S ONLY ONE PERSON WHO CAN GET ASAHI THAT DOWN...
AND THAT'S SHIRAGAMI-SAN.

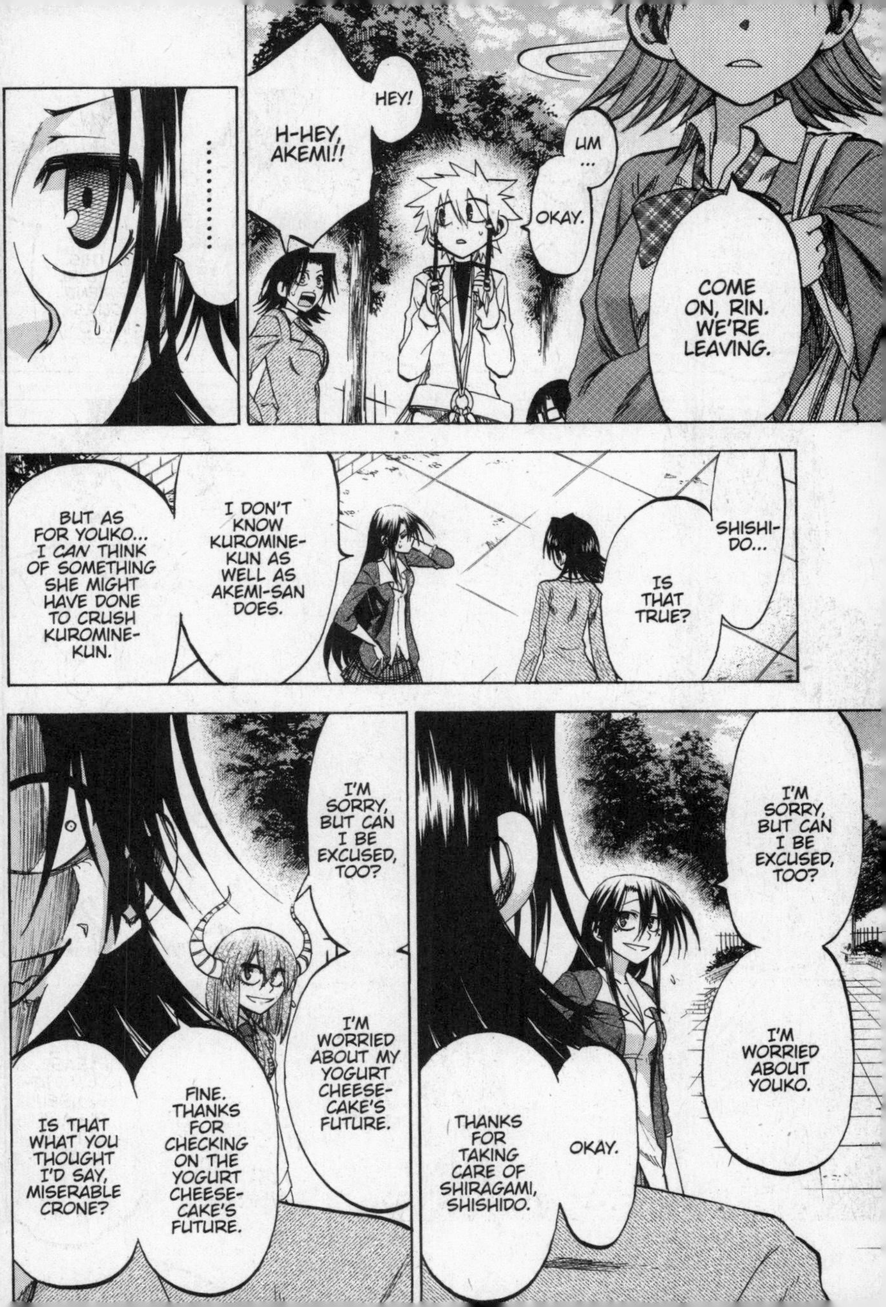
COME ON, RIN. WE'RE LEAVING.
UM ... OKAY.
HEY!
H-HEY, AKEMI!!
......
SHISHIDO... IS THAT TRUE?
I DON'T KNOW KUROMINE-KUN AS WELL AS AKEMI-SAN DOES.
BUT AS FOR YOUKO... I CAN THINK OF SOMETHING SHE MIGHT HAVE DONE TO CRUSH KUROMINE-KUN.
I'M SORRY, BUT CAN I BE EXCUSED, TOO?
I'M WORRIED ABOUT YOUKO.
OKAY.
THANKS FOR TAKING CARE OF SHIRAGAMI, SHISHIDO.
I'M SORRY, BUT CAN I BE EXCUSED, TOO?
I'M WORRIED ABOUT MY YOGURT CHEESE-CAKE'S FUTURE.
FINE. THANKS FOR CHECKING ON THE YOGURT CHEESE-CAKE'S FUTURE.
IS THAT WHAT YOU THOUGHT I'D SAY, MISERABLE CRONE?

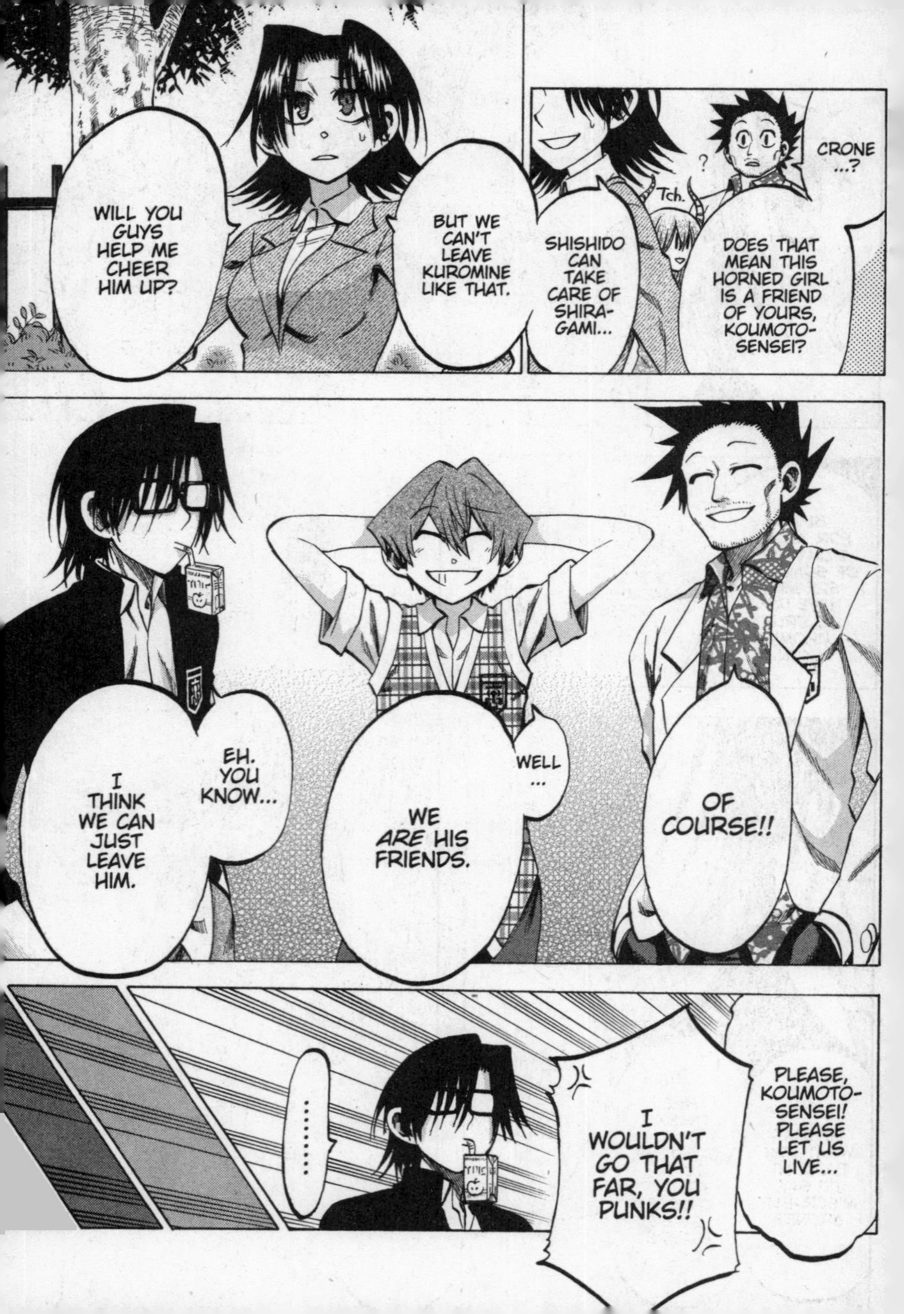
CRONE ...?
?
Tch.
DOES THAT MEAN THIS HORNED GIRL IS A FRIEND OF YOURS, KOUMOTO-SENSEI?
SHISHIDO CAN TAKE CARE OF SHIRA-GAMI...
BUT WE CAN'T LEAVE KUROMINE LIKE THAT.
WILL YOU GUYS HELP ME CHEER HIM UP?
OF COURSE!!
WELL ...
WE *ARE* HIS FRIENDS.
EH. YOU KNOW...
I THINK WE CAN JUST LEAVE HIM.
PLEASE, KOUMOTO-SENSEI! PLEASE LET US LIVE...
I WOULDN'T GO THAT FAR, YOU PUNKS!!
......

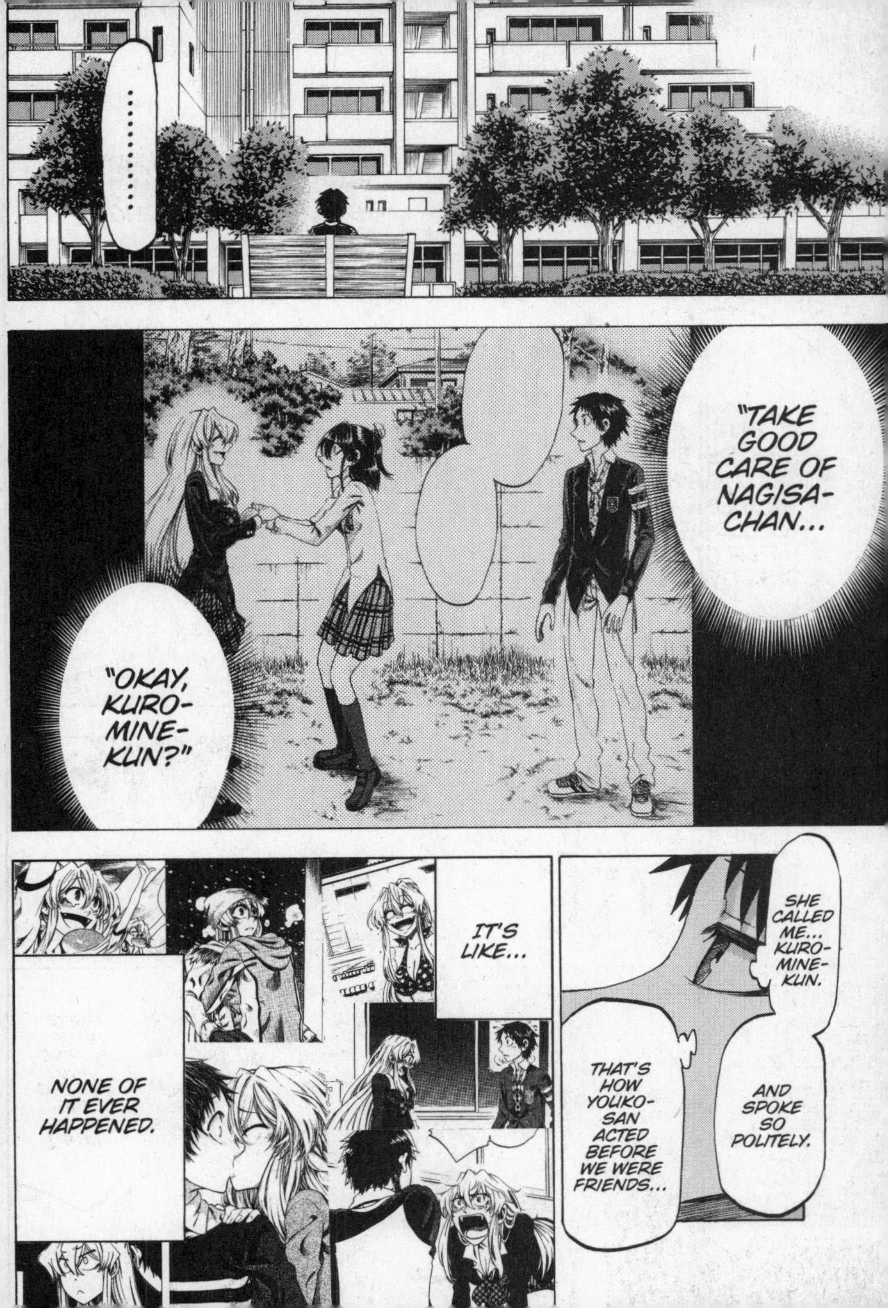
......
"TAKE GOOD CARE OF NAGISA-CHAN...
"OKAY, KUROMINE-KUN?"
SHE CALLED ME... KUROMINE-KUN.
AND SPOKE SO POLITELY.
THAT'S HOW YOUKO-SAN ACTED BEFORE WE WERE FRIENDS...
IT'S LIKE...
NONE OF IT EVER HAPPENED.

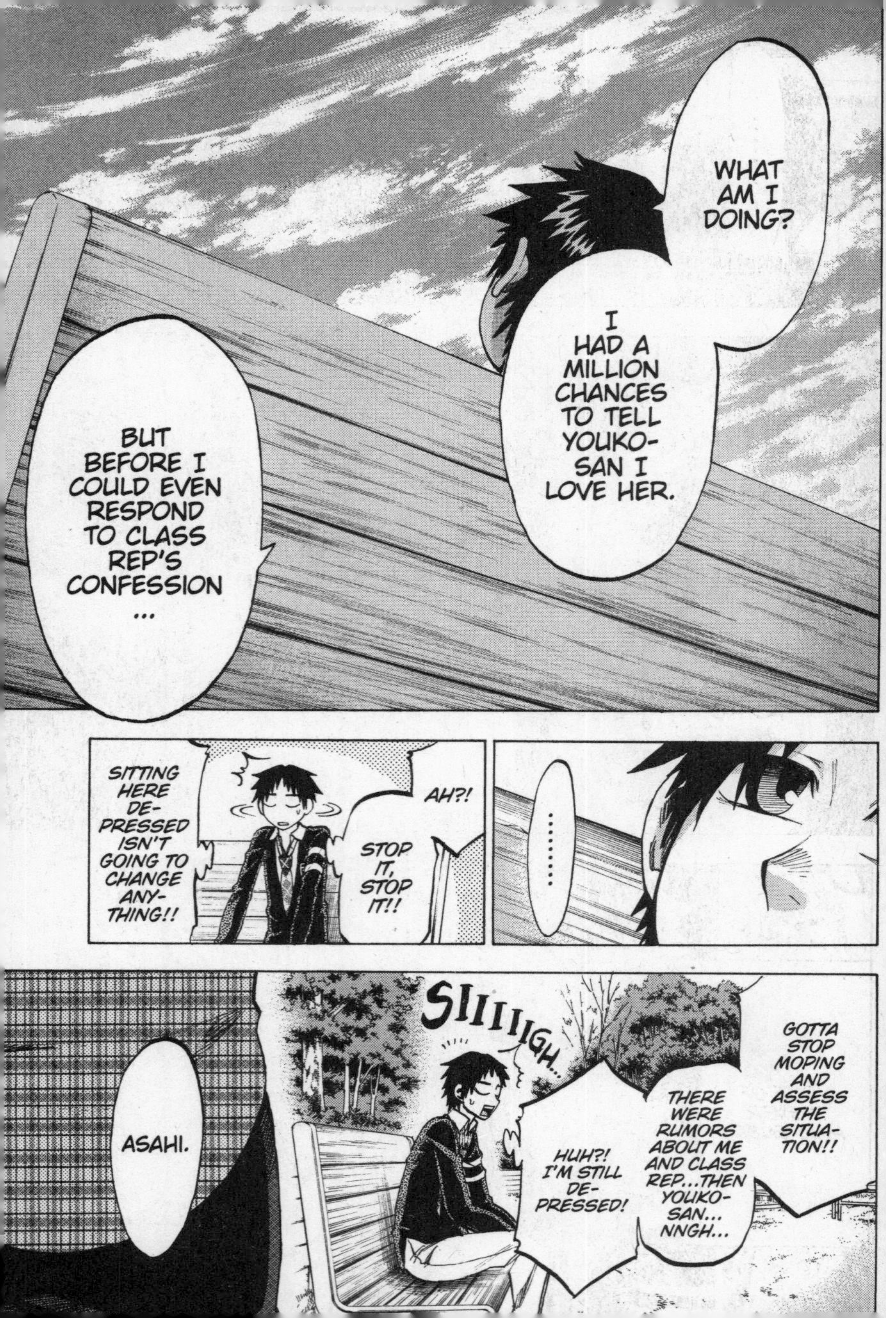
WHAT AM I DOING?
I HAD A MILLION CHANCES TO TELL YOUKO-SAN I LOVE HER.
BUT BEFORE I COULD EVEN RESPOND TO CLASS REP'S CONFESSION...
......
SITTING HERE DE-PRESSED ISN'T GOING TO CHANGE ANY-THING!!
AH?!
STOP IT, STOP IT!!
GOTTA STOP MOPING AND ASSESS THE SITUA-TION!!
THERE WERE RUMORS ABOUT ME AND CLASS REP...THEN YOUKO-SAN... NNGH...
SIIIIIGH...
HUH?! I'M STILL DE-PRESSED!
ASAHI.

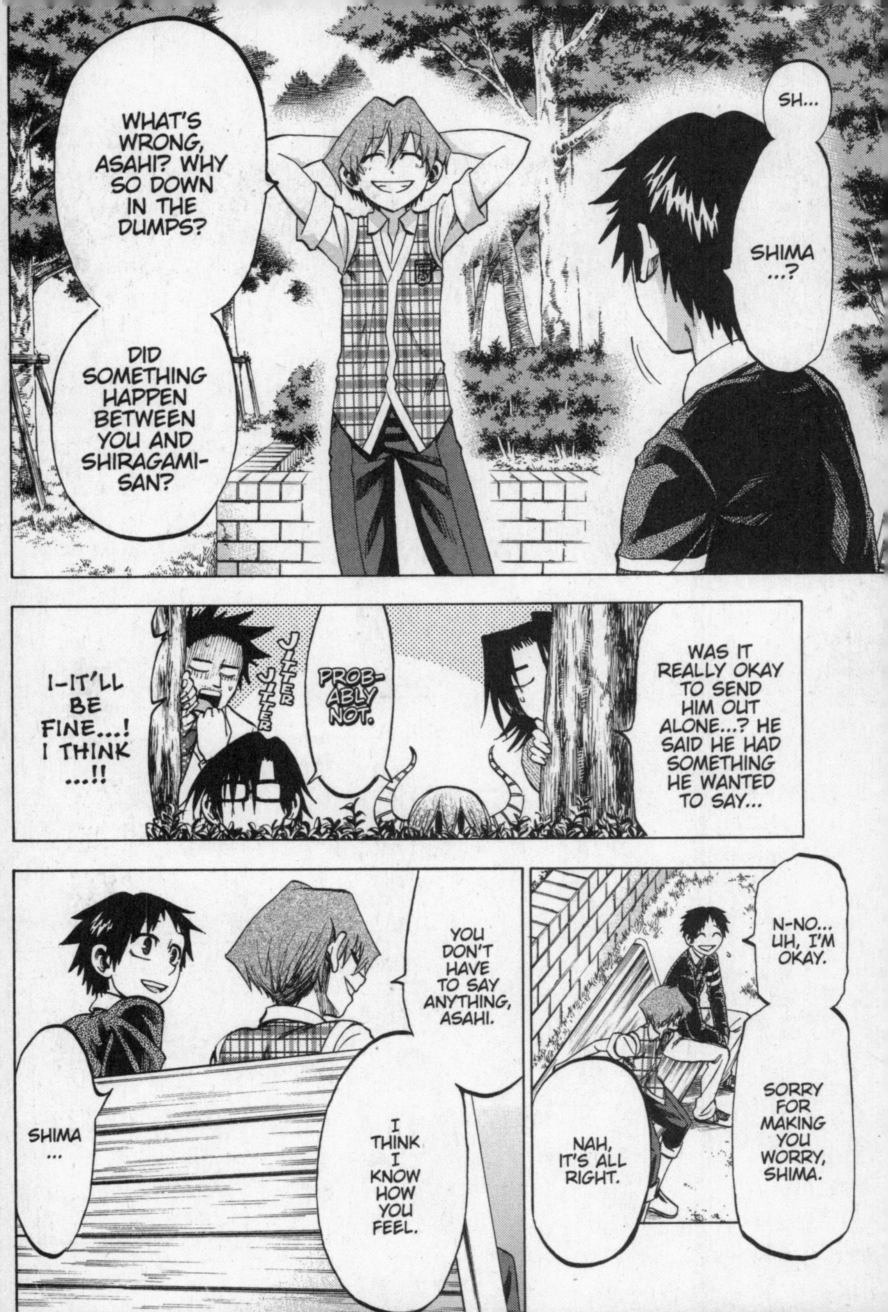
SH...
SHIMA ...?
WHAT'S WRONG, ASAHI? WHY SO DOWN IN THE DUMPS?
DID SOMETHING HAPPEN BETWEEN YOU AND SHIRAGAMI-SAN?
WAS IT REALLY OKAY TO SEND HIM OUT ALONE...? HE SAID HE HAD SOMETHING HE WANTED TO SAY...
PROBABLY NOT.
JITTER JITTER
I-IT'LL BE FINE...! I THINK ...!!
N-NO... UH, I'M OKAY.
SORRY FOR MAKING YOU WORRY, SHIMA.
NAH, IT'S ALL RIGHT.
YOU DON'T HAVE TO SAY ANYTHING, ASAHI.
I THINK I KNOW HOW YOU FEEL.
SHIMA ...

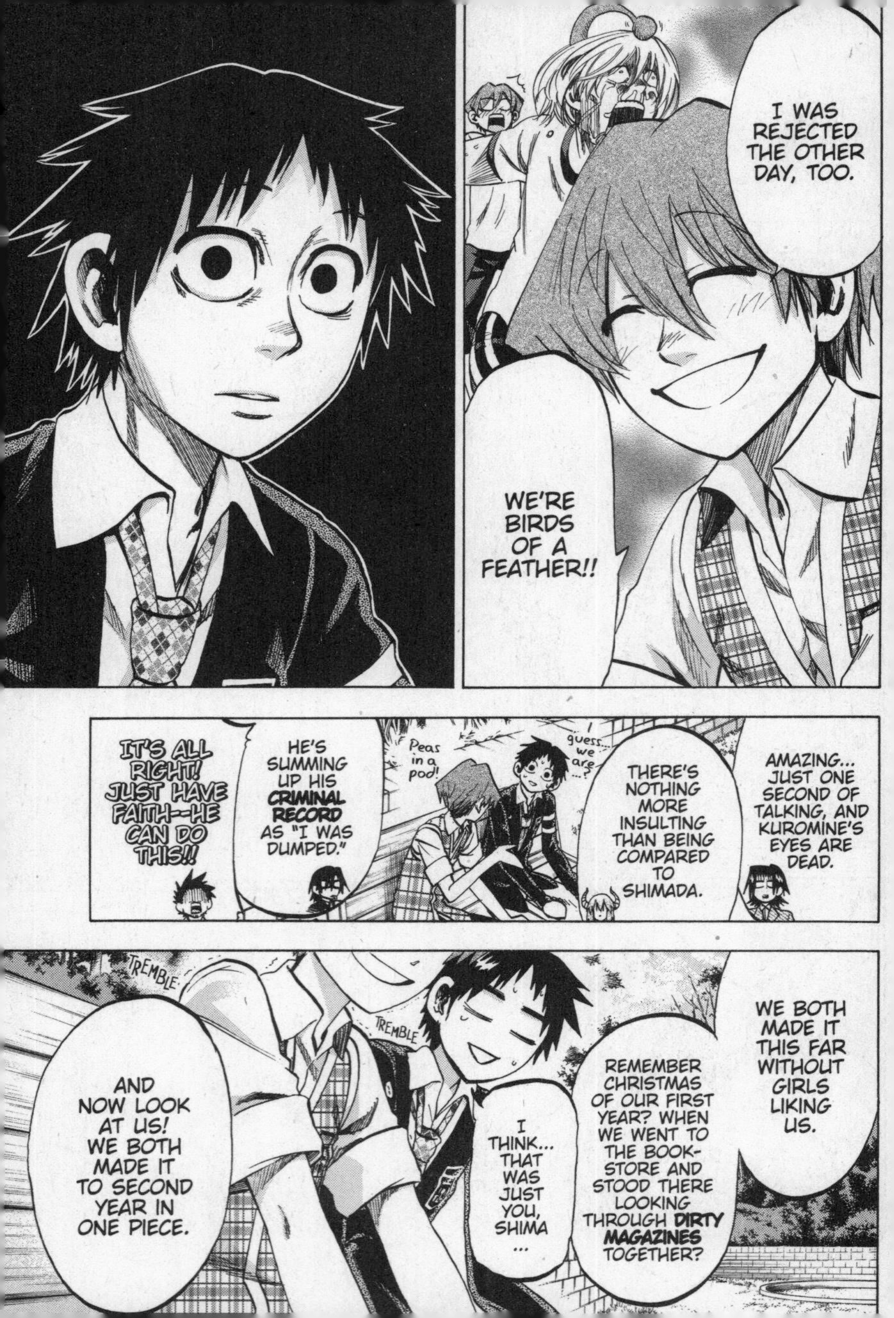
I WAS REJECTED THE OTHER DAY, TOO.
WE'RE BIRDS OF A FEATHER!!
AMAZING... JUST ONE SECOND OF TALKING, AND KUROMINE'S EYES ARE DEAD.
I guess... we are...?
THERE'S NOTHING MORE INSULTING THAN BEING COMPARED TO SHIMADA.
Peas in a pod!
HE'S SUMMING UP HIS **CRIMINAL RECORD** AS "I WAS DUMPED."
IT'S ALL RIGHT! JUST HAVE FAITH--HE CAN DO THIS!!
WE BOTH MADE IT THIS FAR WITHOUT GIRLS LIKING US.
REMEMBER CHRISTMAS OF OUR FIRST YEAR? WHEN WE WENT TO THE BOOK-STORE AND STOOD THERE LOOKING THROUGH **DIRTY MAGAZINES** TOGETHER?
I THINK... THAT WAS JUST YOU, SHIMA...
TREMBLE
TREMBLE
AND NOW LOOK AT US! WE BOTH MADE IT TO SECOND YEAR IN ONE PIECE.

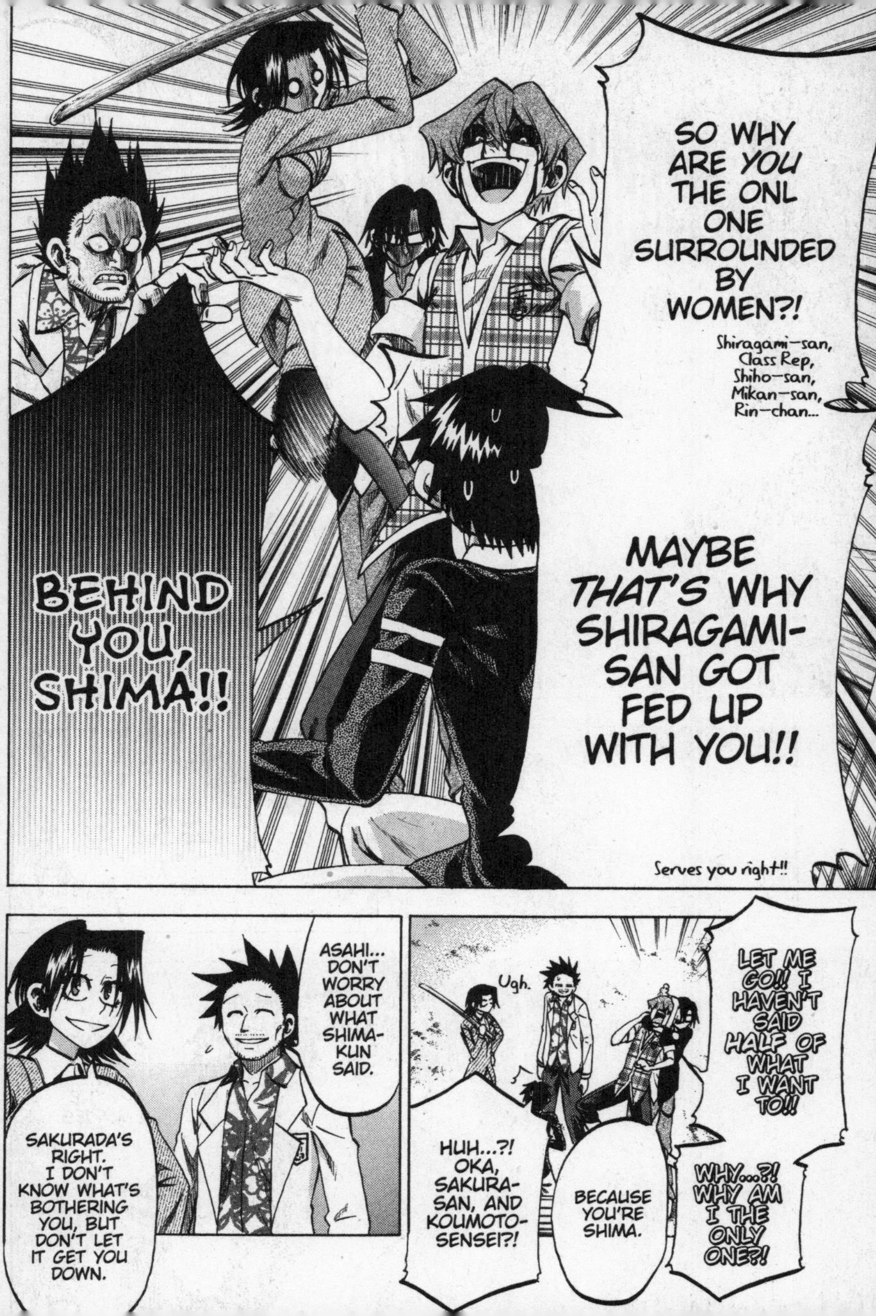
SO WHY ARE YOU THE ONL ONE SURROUNDED BY WOMEN?!
Shiragami-san, Class Rep, Shiho-san, Mikan-san, Rin-chan...
MAYBE THAT'S WHY SHIRAGAMI-SAN GOT FED UP WITH YOU!!
BEHIND YOU, SHIMA!!
Serves you right!!
LET ME GO!! I HAVEN'T SAID HALF OF WHAT I WANT TO!!
Ugh.
WHY...?! WHY AM I THE ONLY ONE?!
BECAUSE YOU'RE SHIMA.
HUH...?! OKA, SAKURA-SAN, AND KOUMOTO-SENSEI?!
ASAHI... DON'T WORRY ABOUT WHAT SHIMA-KUN SAID.
SAKURADA'S RIGHT. I DON'T KNOW WHAT'S BOTHERING YOU, BUT DON'T LET IT GET YOU DOWN.

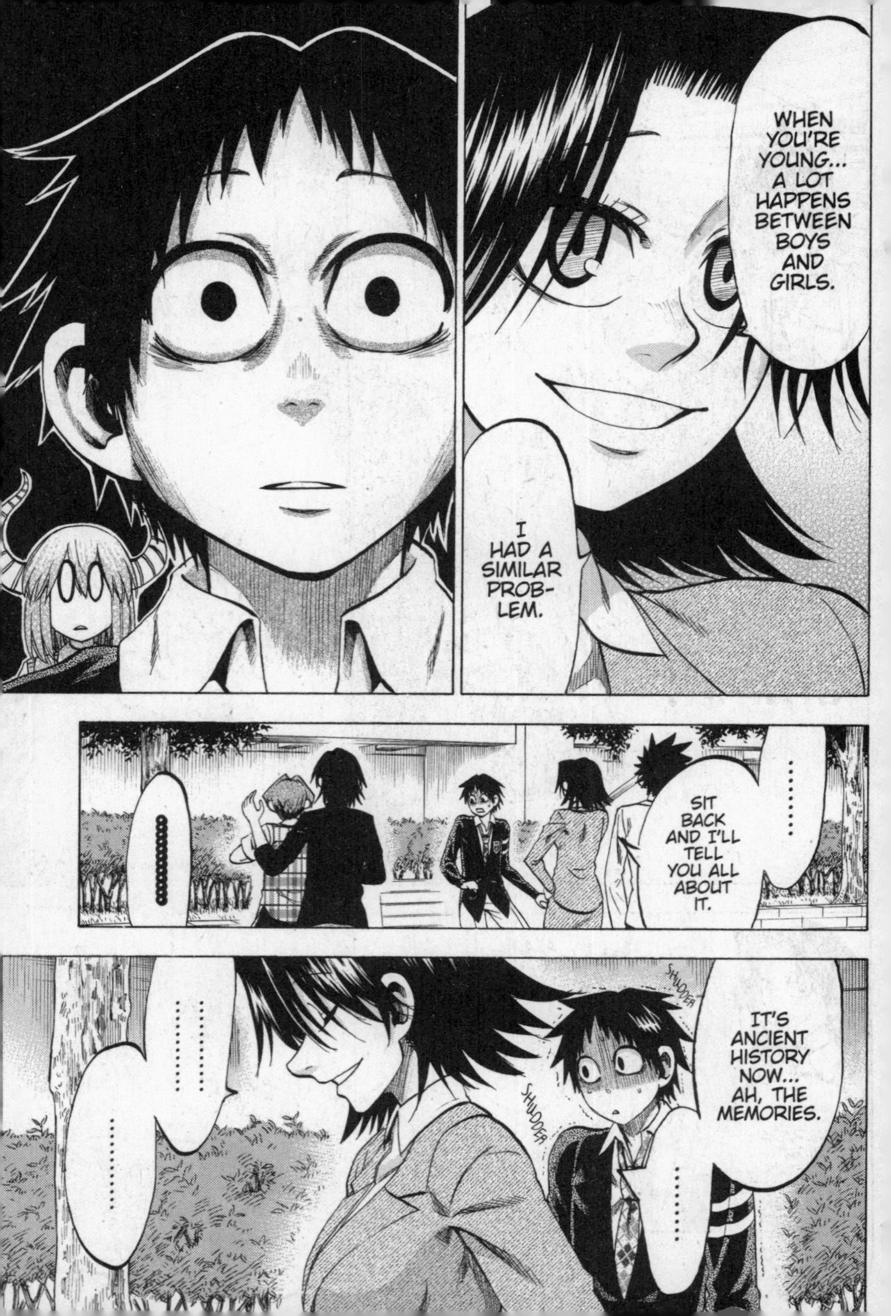
WHEN YOU'RE YOUNG... A LOT HAPPENS BETWEEN BOYS AND GIRLS.
I HAD A SIMILAR PROB-LEM.
......
SIT BACK AND I'LL TELL YOU ALL ABOUT IT.
....
IT'S ANCIENT HISTORY NOW... AH, THE MEMORIES.
SHUDDER
SHUDDER
......
......
......

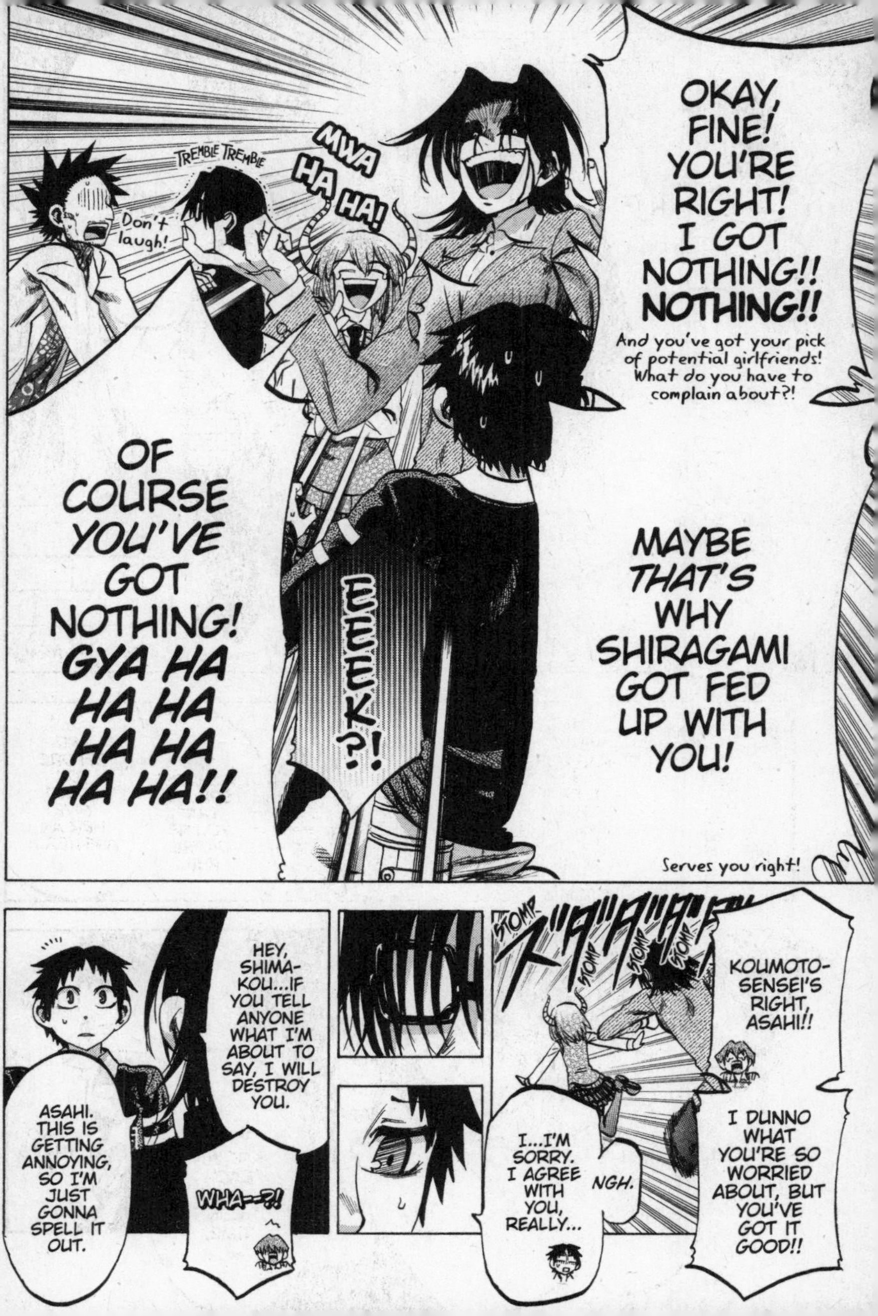
OKAY, FINE! YOU'RE RIGHT! I GOT NOTHING!! NOTHING!!
And you've got your pick of potential girlfriends! What do you have to complain about?!
MWA HA HA!
TREMBLE TREMBLE
Don't laugh!
MAYBE THAT'S WHY SHIRAGAMI GOT FED UP WITH YOU!
EEEEK?!
OF COURSE YOU'VE GOT NOTHING! GYA HA HA HA HA HA HA HA!!
Serves you right!
STOMP STOMP STOMP STOMP
KOUMOTO-SENSEI'S RIGHT, ASAHI!!
I DUNNO WHAT YOU'RE SO WORRIED ABOUT, BUT YOU'VE GOT IT GOOD!!
I...I'M SORRY. I AGREE WITH YOU, REALLY...
NGH.
HEY, SHIMA-KOU...IF YOU TELL ANYONE WHAT I'M ABOUT TO SAY, I WILL DESTROY YOU.
ASAHI. THIS IS GETTING ANNOYING, SO I'M JUST GONNA SPELL IT OUT.
WHA--?!

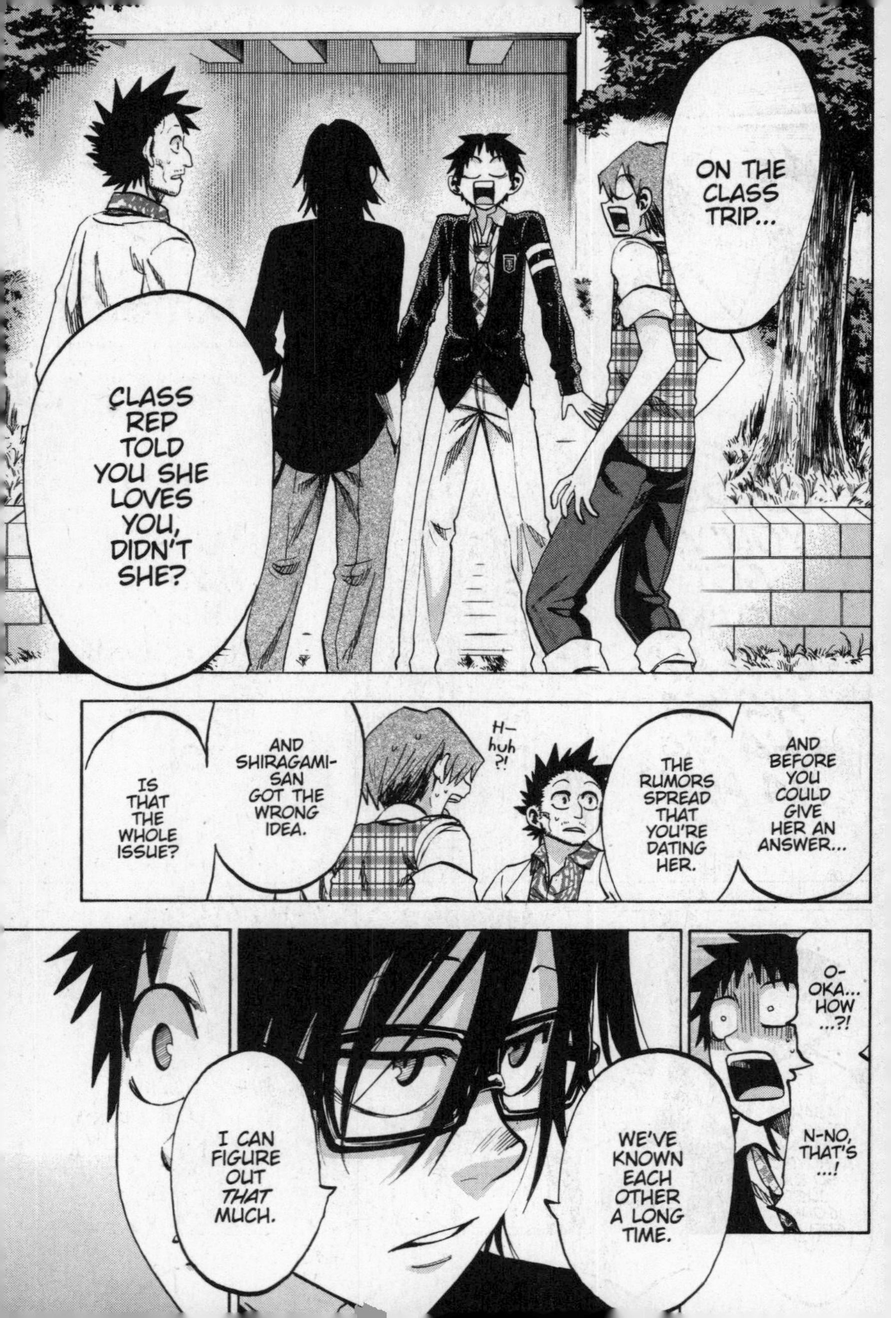
ON THE CLASS TRIP...
CLASS REP TOLD YOU SHE LOVES YOU, DIDN'T SHE?
AND BEFORE YOU COULD GIVE HER AN ANSWER...
THE RUMORS SPREAD THAT YOU'RE DATING HER.
H-huh ?!
AND SHIRAGAMI-SAN GOT THE WRONG IDEA.
IS THAT THE WHOLE ISSUE?
O-OKA... HOW ...?!
N-NO, THAT'S ...!
WE'VE KNOWN EACH OTHER A LONG TIME.
I CAN FIGURE OUT *THAT* MUCH.

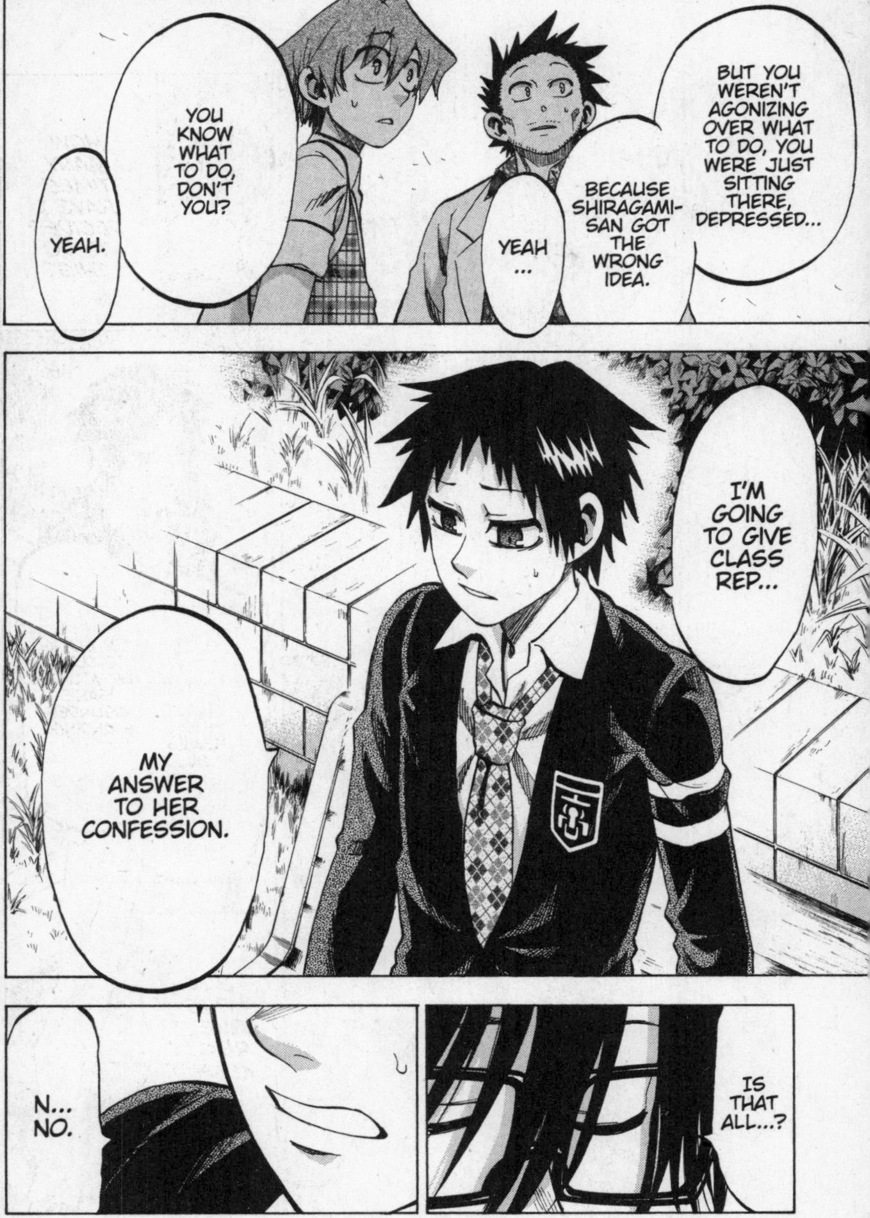
BUT YOU WEREN'T AGONIZING OVER WHAT TO DO, YOU WERE JUST SITTING THERE, DEPRESSED...
BECAUSE SHIRAGAMI-SAN GOT THE WRONG IDEA.
YEAH...
YOU KNOW WHAT TO DO, DON'T YOU?
YEAH.
I'M GOING TO GIVE CLASS REP...
MY ANSWER TO HER CONFESSION.
IS THAT ALL...?
N... NO.

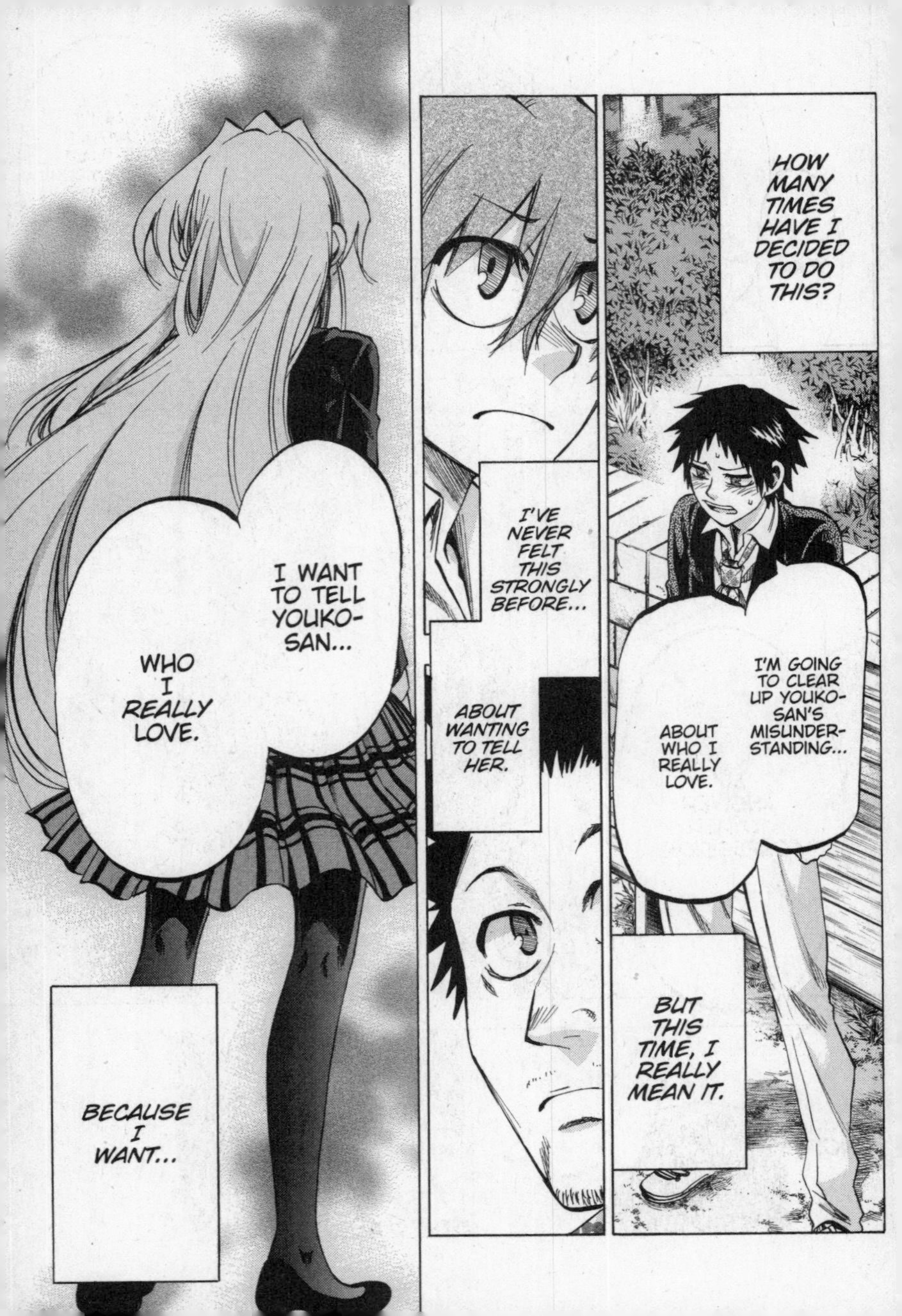
HOW MANY TIMES HAVE I DECIDED TO DO THIS?
I'M GOING TO CLEAR UP YOUKO-SAN'S MISUNDERSTANDING...
ABOUT WHO I REALLY LOVE.
BUT THIS TIME, I REALLY MEAN IT.
I'VE NEVER FELT THIS STRONGLY BEFORE...
ABOUT WANTING TO TELL HER.
I WANT TO TELL YOUKO-SAN...
WHO I REALLY LOVE.
BECAUSE I WANT...

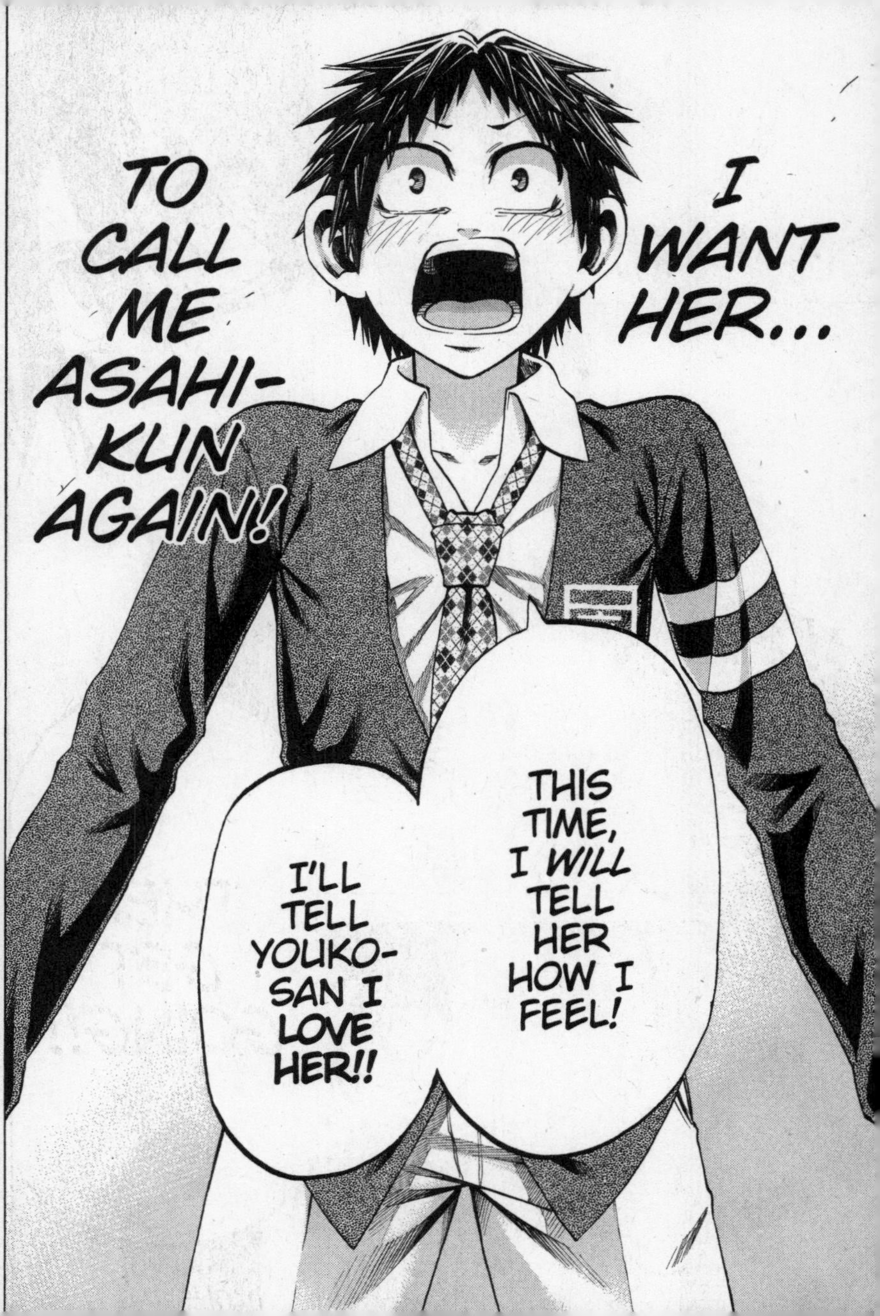
I WANT HER...
TO CALL ME ASAHI-KUN AGAIN!
THIS TIME, I *WILL* TELL HER HOW I FEEL!
I'LL TELL YOUKO-SAN I LOVE HER!!

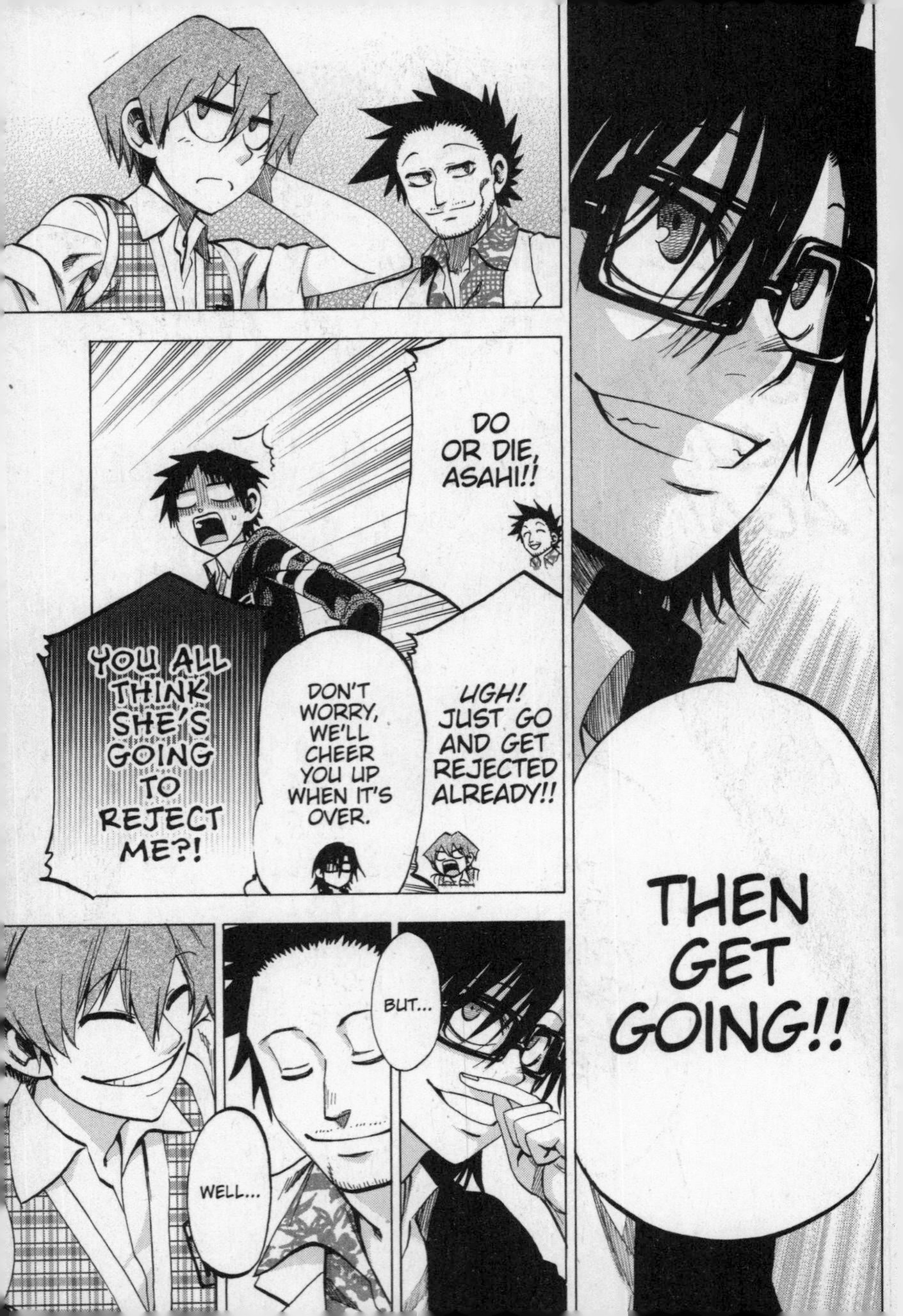
THEN GET GOING!!
DO OR DIE, ASAHI!!
UGH! JUST GO AND GET REJECTED ALREADY!!
DON'T WORRY, WE'LL CHEER YOU UP WHEN IT'S OVER.
YOU ALL THINK SHE'S GOING TO REJECT ME?!
BUT...
WELL...

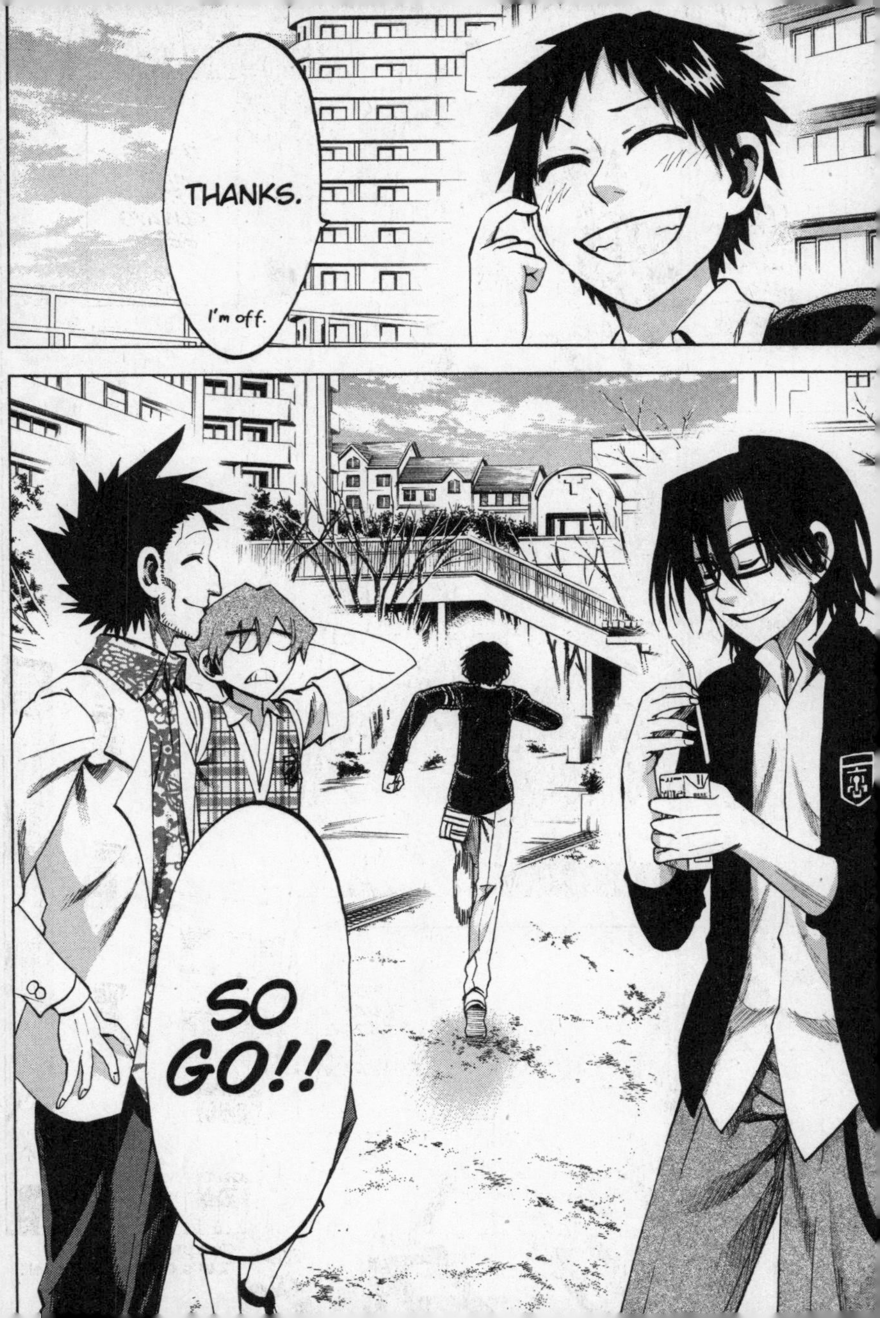
THANKS.
I'm off.
SO GO!!

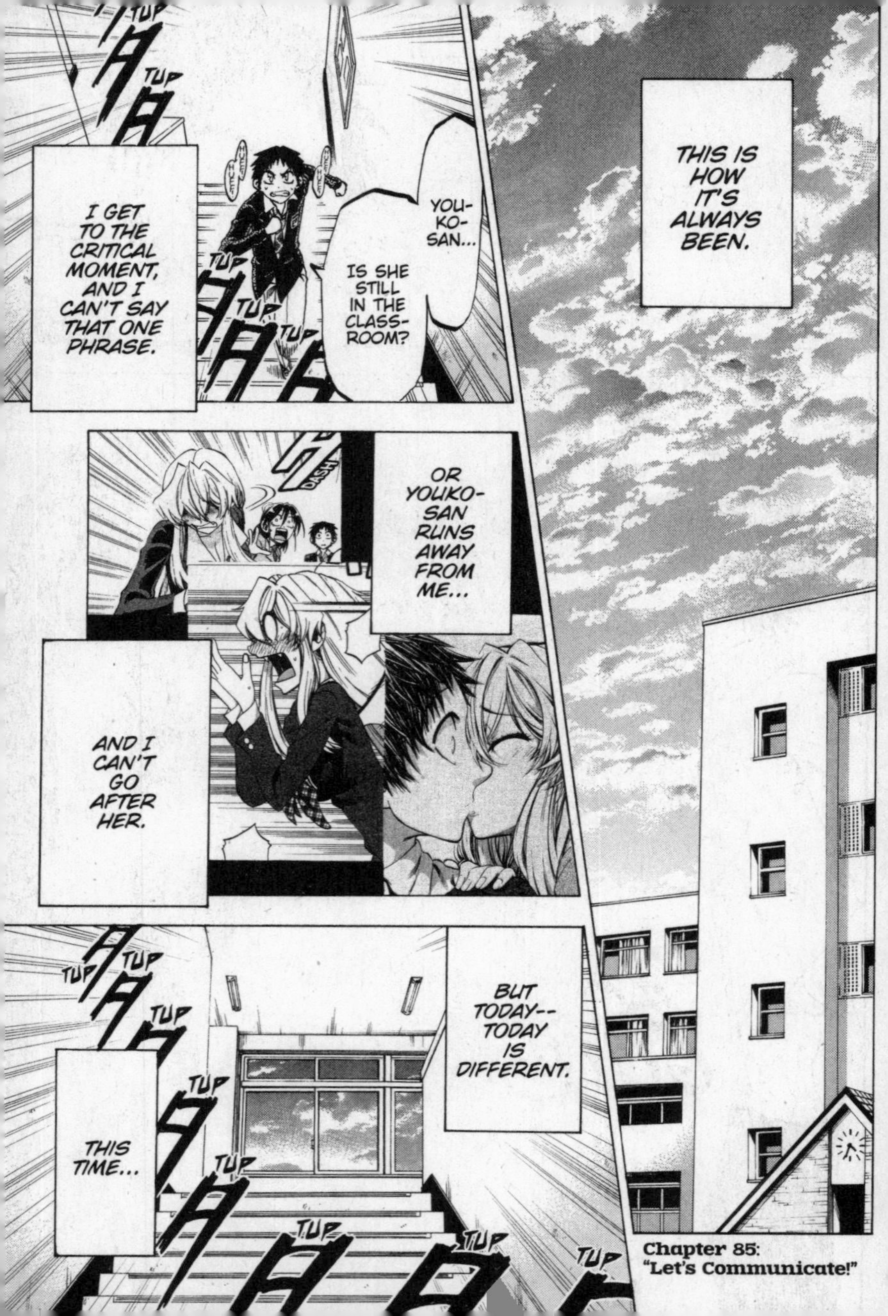
THIS IS HOW IT'S ALWAYS BEEN.
TUP TUP
YOUKO-SAN...
IS SHE STILL IN THE CLASSROOM?
HUFF HUFF
I GET TO THE CRITICAL MOMENT, AND I CAN'T SAY THAT ONE PHRASE.
TUP TUP TUP
OR YOUKO-SAN RUNS AWAY FROM ME...
DASH
AND I CAN'T GO AFTER HER.
BUT TODAY-- TODAY IS DIFFERENT.
TUP TUP TUP
THIS TIME...
TUP TUP TUP TUP TUP
Chapter 85: "Let's Communicate!"

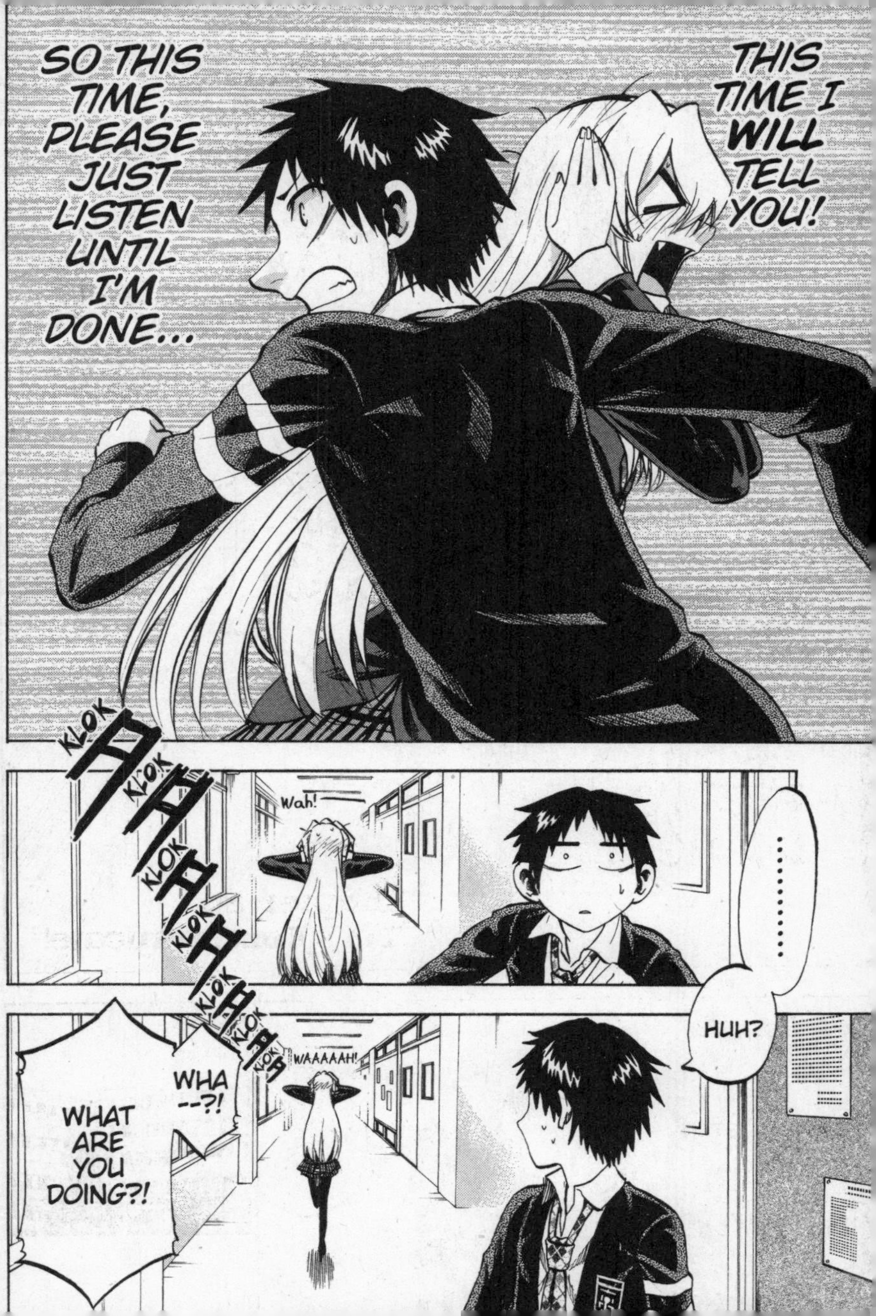
THIS TIME I **WILL** TELL YOU!
SO THIS TIME, PLEASE JUST LISTEN UNTIL I'M DONE...
......
Wah!
KLOK KLOK KLOK KLOK KLOK KLOK KLOK KLOK
HUH?
WAAAAAH!
WHA--?!
WHAT ARE YOU DOING?!

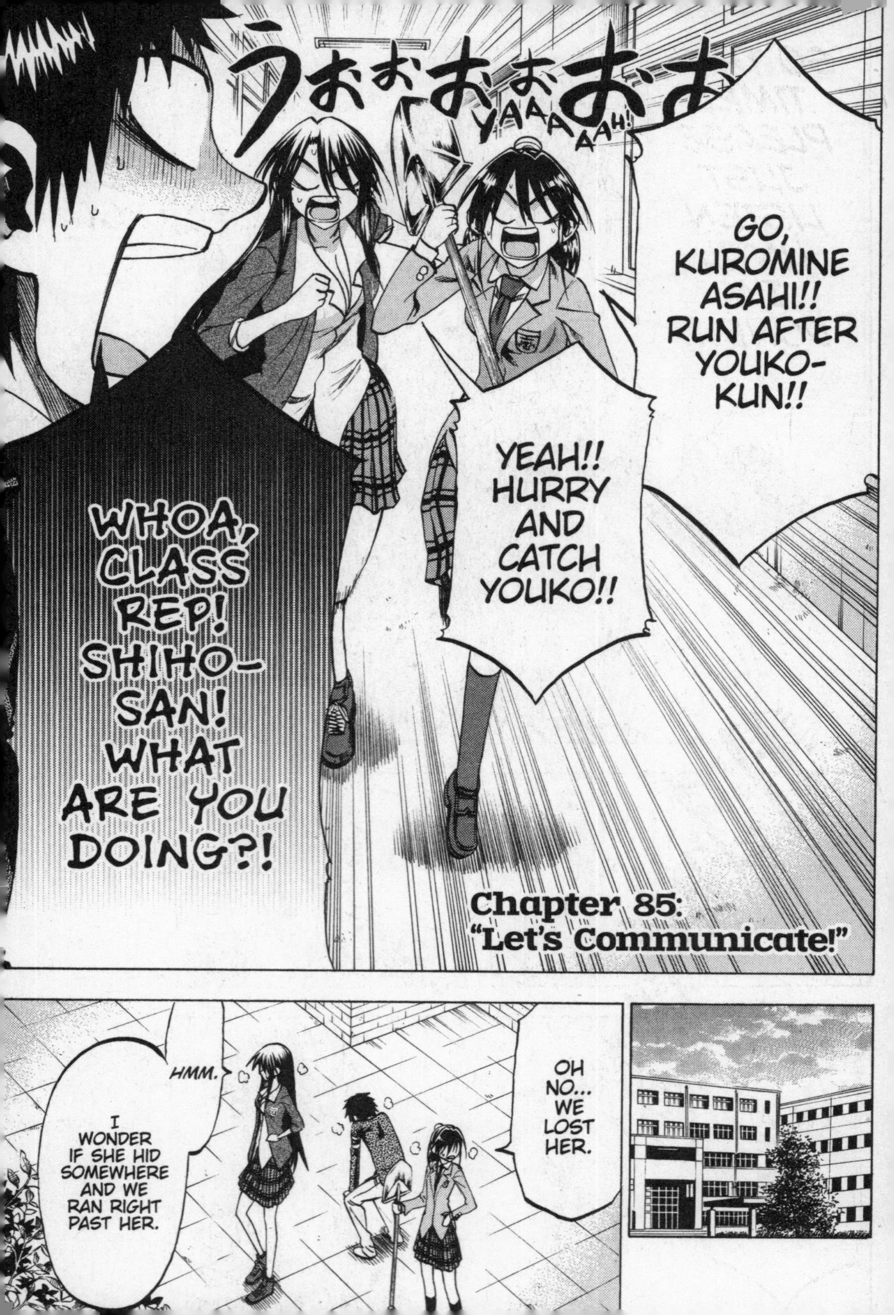
うおおおおお
YAAAAAH!
GO, KUROMINE ASAHI!! RUN AFTER YOUKO-KUN!!
YEAH!! HURRY AND CATCH YOUKO!!
WHOA, CLASS REP! SHIHO-SAN! WHAT ARE YOU DOING?!
Chapter 85: "Let's Communicate!"
OH NO... WE LOST HER.
HMM.
I WONDER IF SHE HID SOMEWHERE AND WE RAN RIGHT PAST HER.

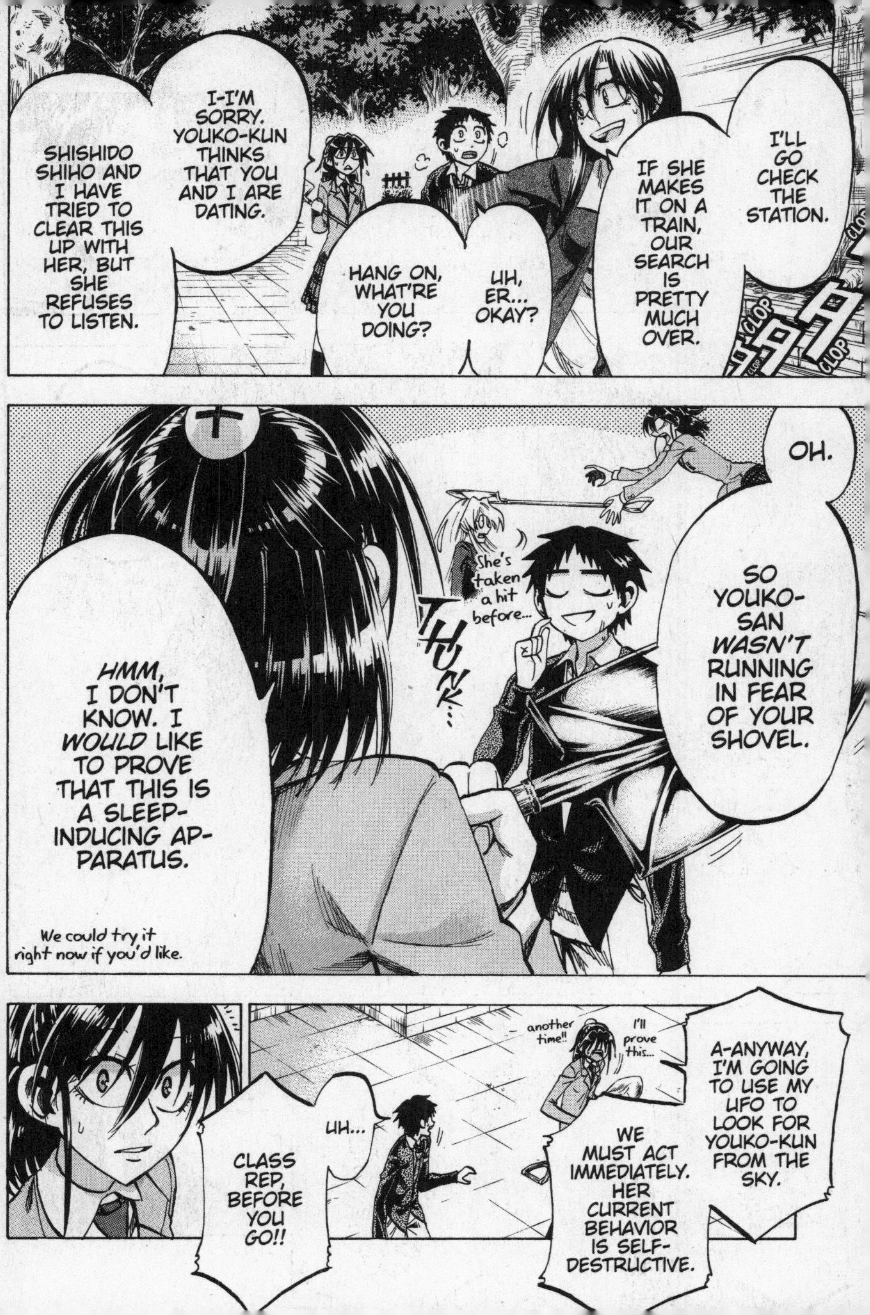
I'LL GO CHECK THE STATION.
IF SHE MAKES IT ON A TRAIN, OUR SEARCH IS PRETTY MUCH OVER.
CLOP CLOP CLOP CLOP
UH, ER... OKAY?
HANG ON, WHAT'RE YOU DOING?
I-I'M SORRY. YOUKO-KUN THINKS THAT YOU AND I ARE DATING.
SHISHIDO SHIHO AND I HAVE TRIED TO CLEAR THIS UP WITH HER, BUT SHE REFUSES TO LISTEN.
OH.
SO YOUKO-SAN *WASN'T* RUNNING IN FEAR OF YOUR SHOVEL.
She's taken a hit before...
THUNK...
HMM, I DON'T KNOW. I *WOULD* LIKE TO PROVE THAT THIS IS A SLEEP-INDUCING APPARATUS.
We could try it right now if you'd like.
A-ANYWAY, I'M GOING TO USE MY UFO TO LOOK FOR YOUKO-KUN FROM THE SKY.
I'll prove this...
another time!!
WE MUST ACT IMMEDIATELY. HER CURRENT BEHAVIOR IS SELF-DESTRUCTIVE.
UH...
CLASS REP, BEFORE YOU GO!!

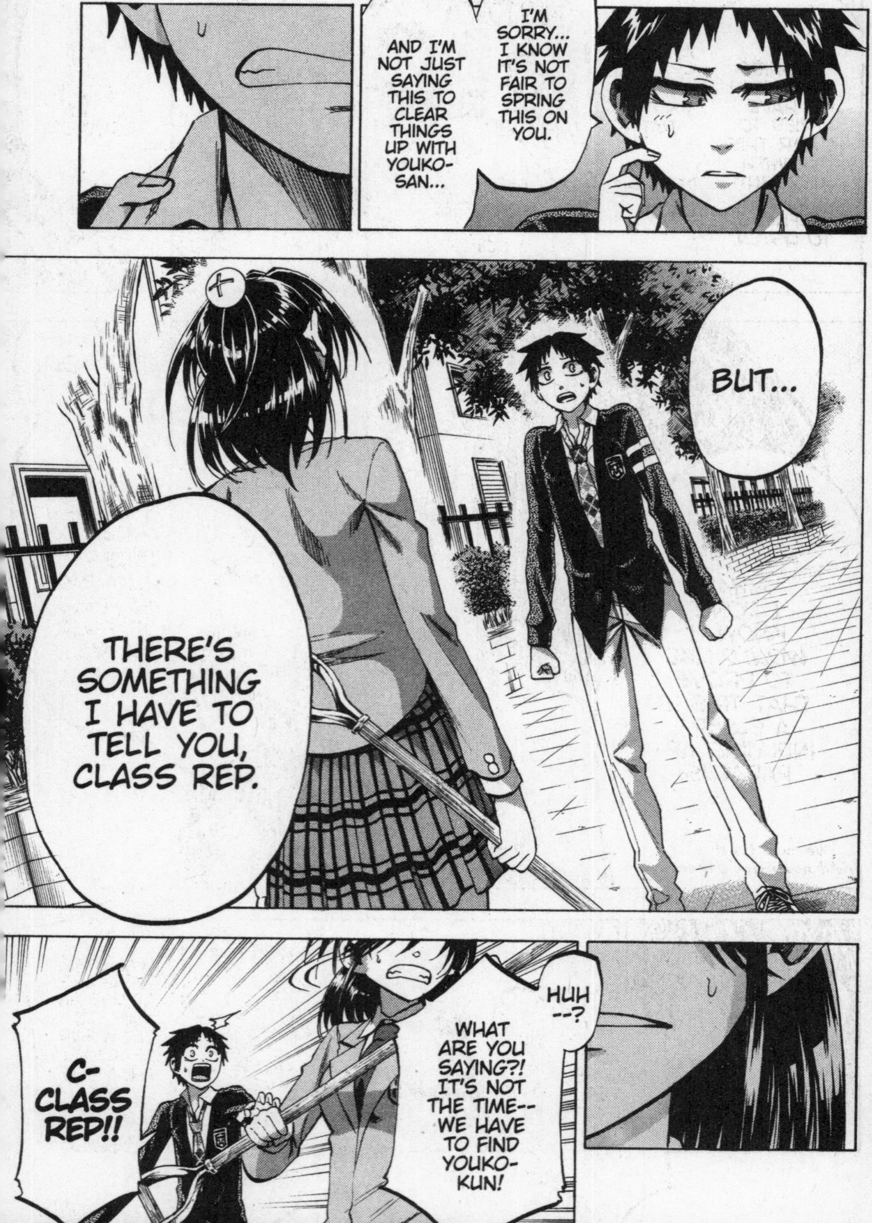
I'M SORRY... I KNOW IT'S NOT FAIR TO SPRING THIS ON YOU.
AND I'M NOT JUST SAYING THIS TO CLEAR THINGS UP WITH YOUKO-SAN...
BUT...
THERE'S SOMETHING I HAVE TO TELL YOU, CLASS REP.
HUH--?
WHAT ARE YOU SAYING?! IT'S NOT THE TIME--WE HAVE TO FIND YOUKO-KUN!
C-CLASS REP!!

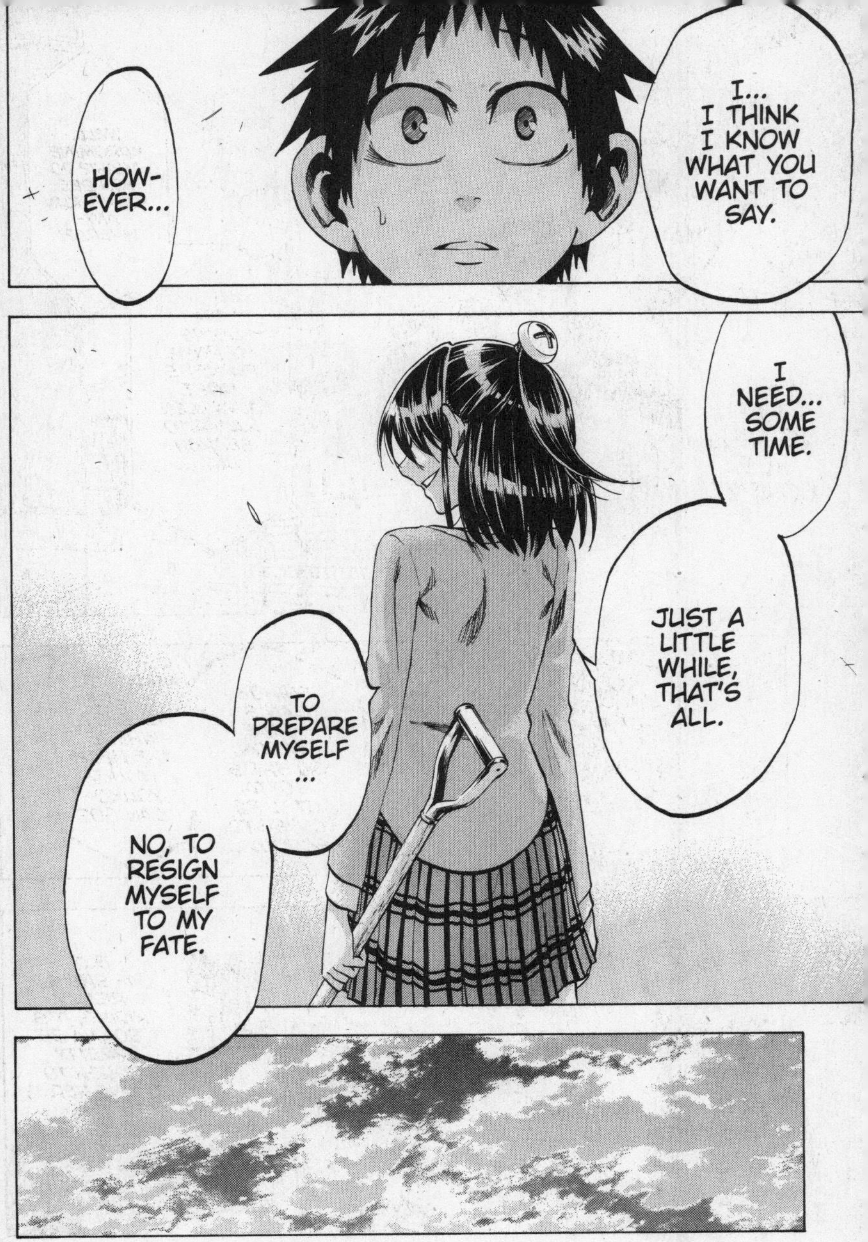
I... I THINK I KNOW WHAT YOU WANT TO SAY.
HOW-EVER...
I NEED... SOME TIME.
JUST A LITTLE WHILE, THAT'S ALL.
TO PREPARE MYSELF ...
NO, TO RESIGN MYSELF TO MY FATE.

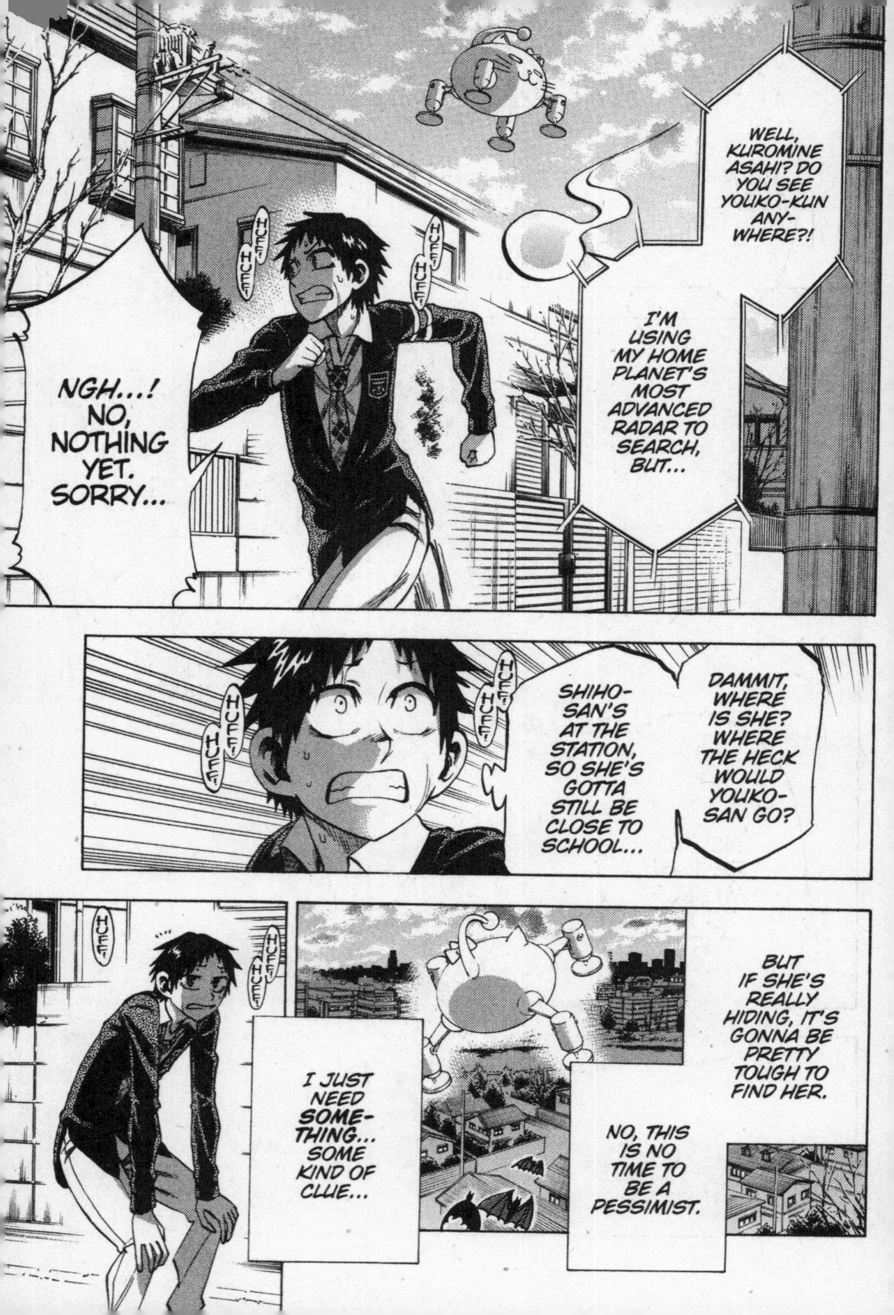
WELL, KUROMINE ASAHI? DO YOU SEE YOUKO-KUN ANY-WHERE?!
I'M USING MY HOME PLANET'S MOST ADVANCED RADAR TO SEARCH, BUT...
HUFF! HUFF!
HUFF! HUFF!
NGH...! NO, NOTHING YET. SORRY...
DAMMIT, WHERE IS SHE? WHERE THE HECK WOULD YOUKO-SAN GO?
SHIHO-SAN'S AT THE STATION, SO SHE'S GOTTA STILL BE CLOSE TO SCHOOL...
HUFF! HUFF!
HUFF! HUFF!
BUT IF SHE'S REALLY HIDING, IT'S GONNA BE PRETTY TOUGH TO FIND HER.
NO, THIS IS NO TIME TO BE A PESSIMIST.
I JUST NEED SOME-THING... SOME KIND OF CLUE...
HUFF! HUFF!
HUFF!

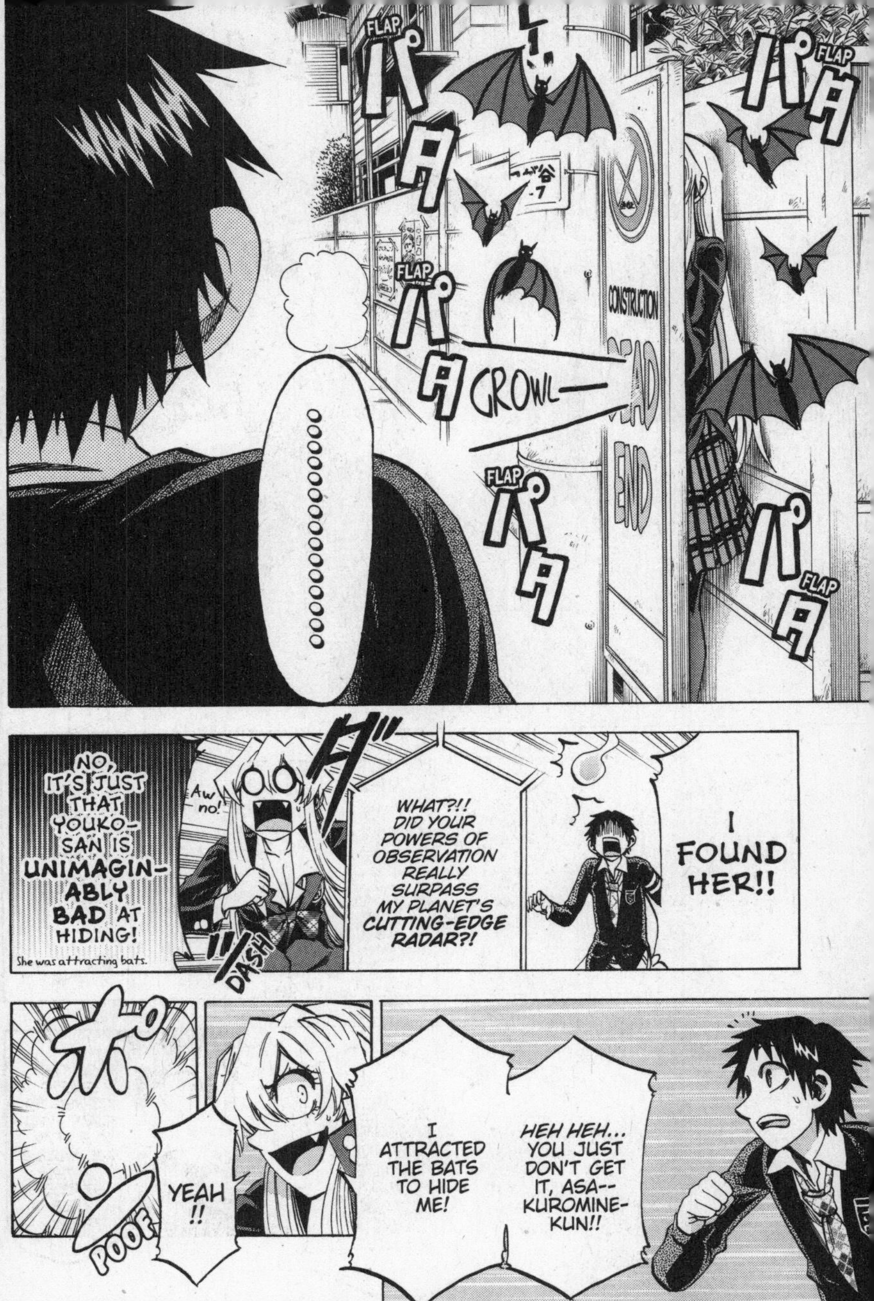
FLAP
パタ
FLAP
パタ
FLAP
パタ
CONSTRUCTION
DEAD END
GROWL—
FLAP
パタ
FLAP
パタ
....
I FOUND HER!!
WHAT?!! DID YOUR POWERS OF OBSERVATION REALLY SURPASS MY PLANET'S CUTTING-EDGE RADAR?!
Aw no!
DASH
NO, IT'S JUST THAT YOUKO-SAN IS UNIMAGIN-ABLY BAD AT HIDING!
She was attracting bats.
HEH HEH... YOU JUST DON'T GET IT, ASA-KUROMINE-KUN!!
I ATTRACTED THE BATS TO HIDE ME!
YEAH!!
POOF

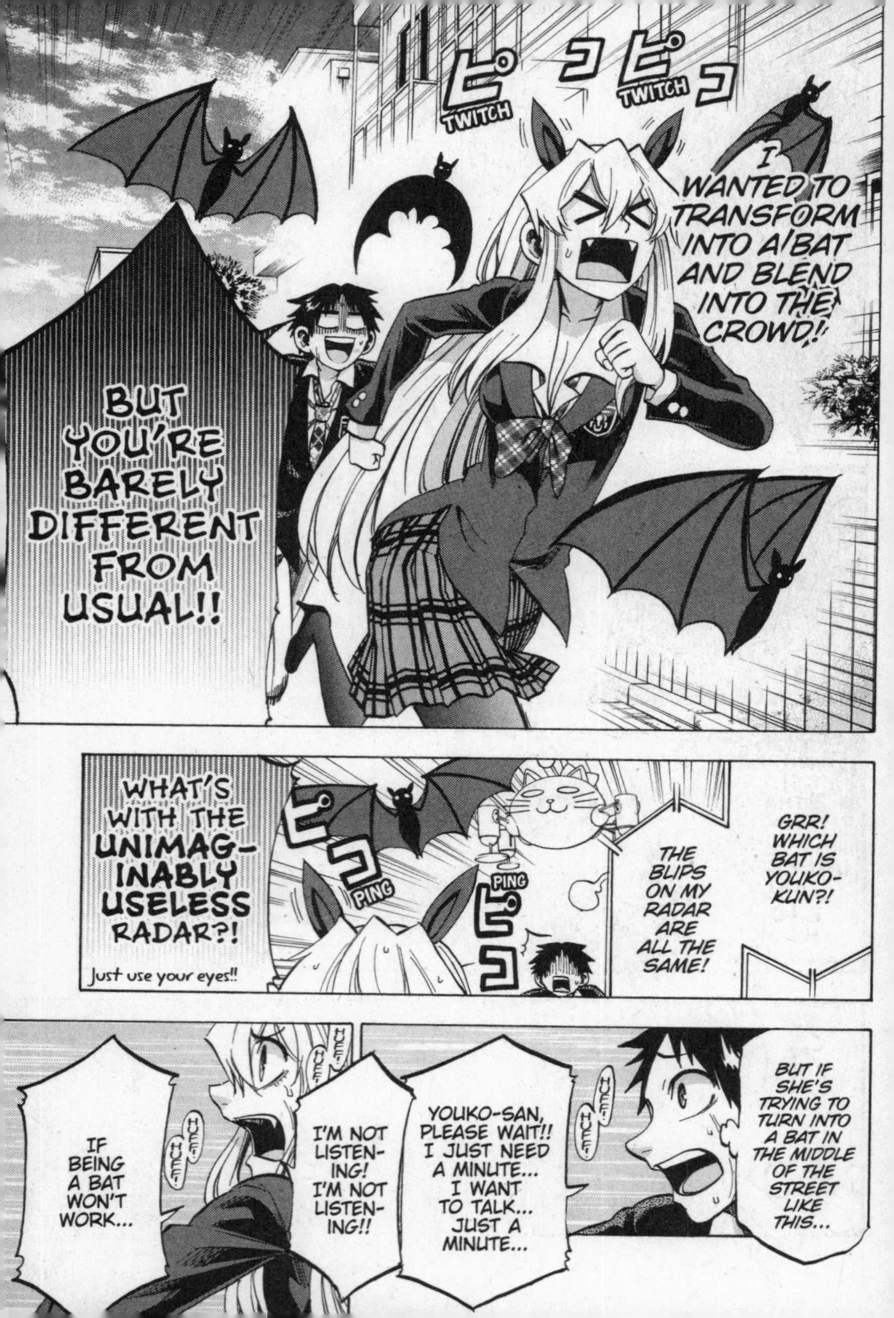
TWITCH
TWITCH
I WANTED TO TRANSFORM INTO A BAT AND BLEND INTO THE CROWD!
BUT YOU'RE BARELY DIFFERENT FROM USUAL!!
GRR! WHICH BAT IS YOUKO-KUN?!
THE BLIPS ON MY RADAR ARE ALL THE SAME!
PING
PING
WHAT'S WITH THE UNIMAGINABLY USELESS RADAR?!
Just use your eyes!!
BUT IF SHE'S TRYING TO TURN INTO A BAT IN THE MIDDLE OF THE STREET LIKE THIS...
HUFF! HUFF!
YOUKO-SAN, PLEASE WAIT!! I JUST NEED A MINUTE... I WANT TO TALK... JUST A MINUTE...
HUFF! HUFF!
I'M NOT LISTENING! I'M NOT LISTENING!!
IF BEING A BAT WON'T WORK...

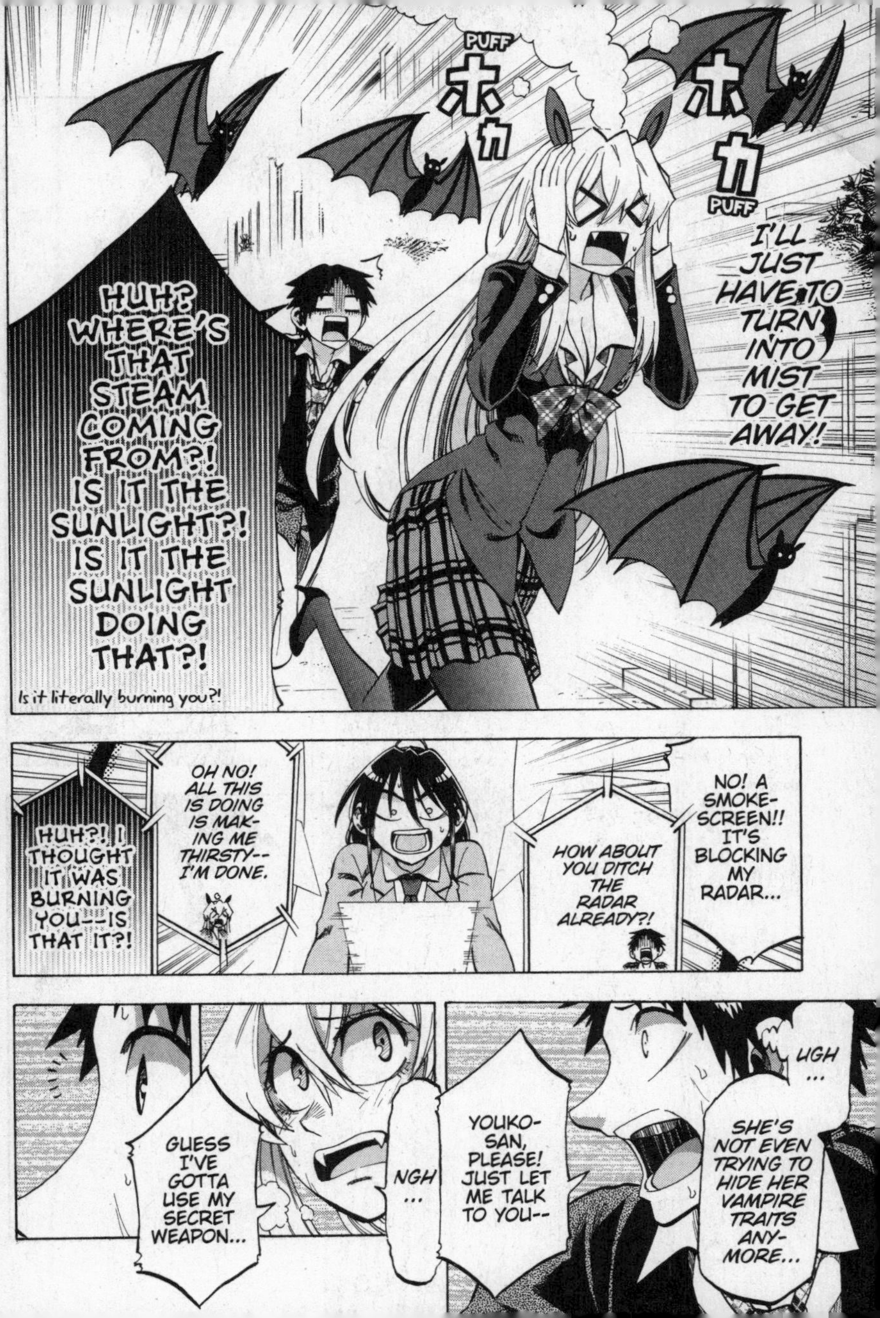
PUFF
ホカ
ホカ
PUFF
I'LL JUST HAVE TO TURN INTO MIST TO GET AWAY!
HUH? WHERE'S THAT STEAM COMING FROM?! IS IT THE SUNLIGHT?! IS IT THE SUNLIGHT DOING THAT?!
Is it literally burning you?!
NO! A SMOKE-SCREEN!! IT'S BLOCKING MY RADAR...
HOW ABOUT YOU DITCH THE RADAR ALREADY?!
OH NO! ALL THIS IS DOING IS MAKING ME THIRSTY--I'M DONE.
HUH?! I THOUGHT IT WAS BURNING YOU--IS THAT IT?!
UGH ...
SHE'S NOT EVEN TRYING TO HIDE HER VAMPIRE TRAITS ANYMORE...
YOUKO-SAN, PLEASE! JUST LET ME TALK TO YOU--
NGH ...
GUESS I'VE GOTTA USE MY SECRET WEAPON...

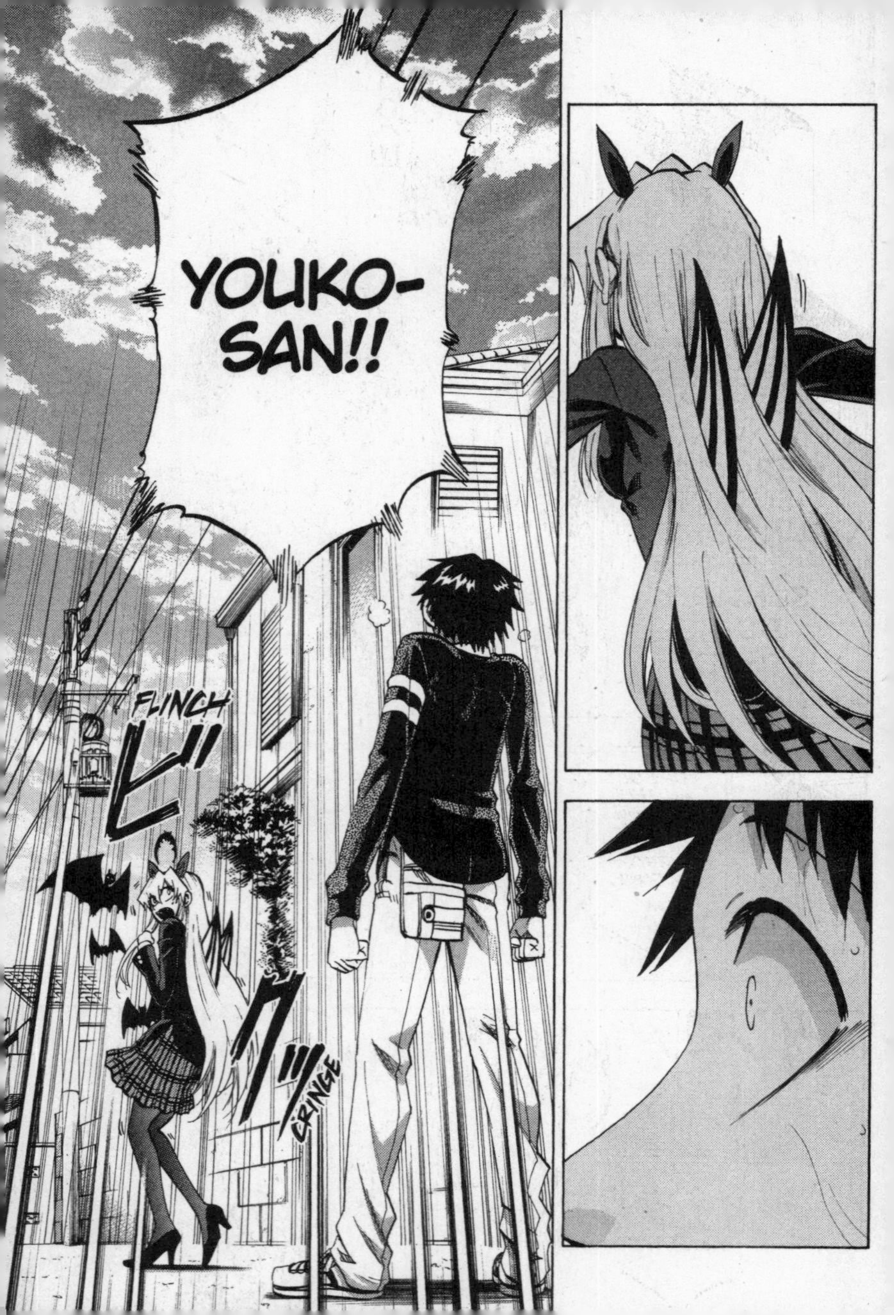
YOUKO-SAN!!
FLINCH
CRINGE

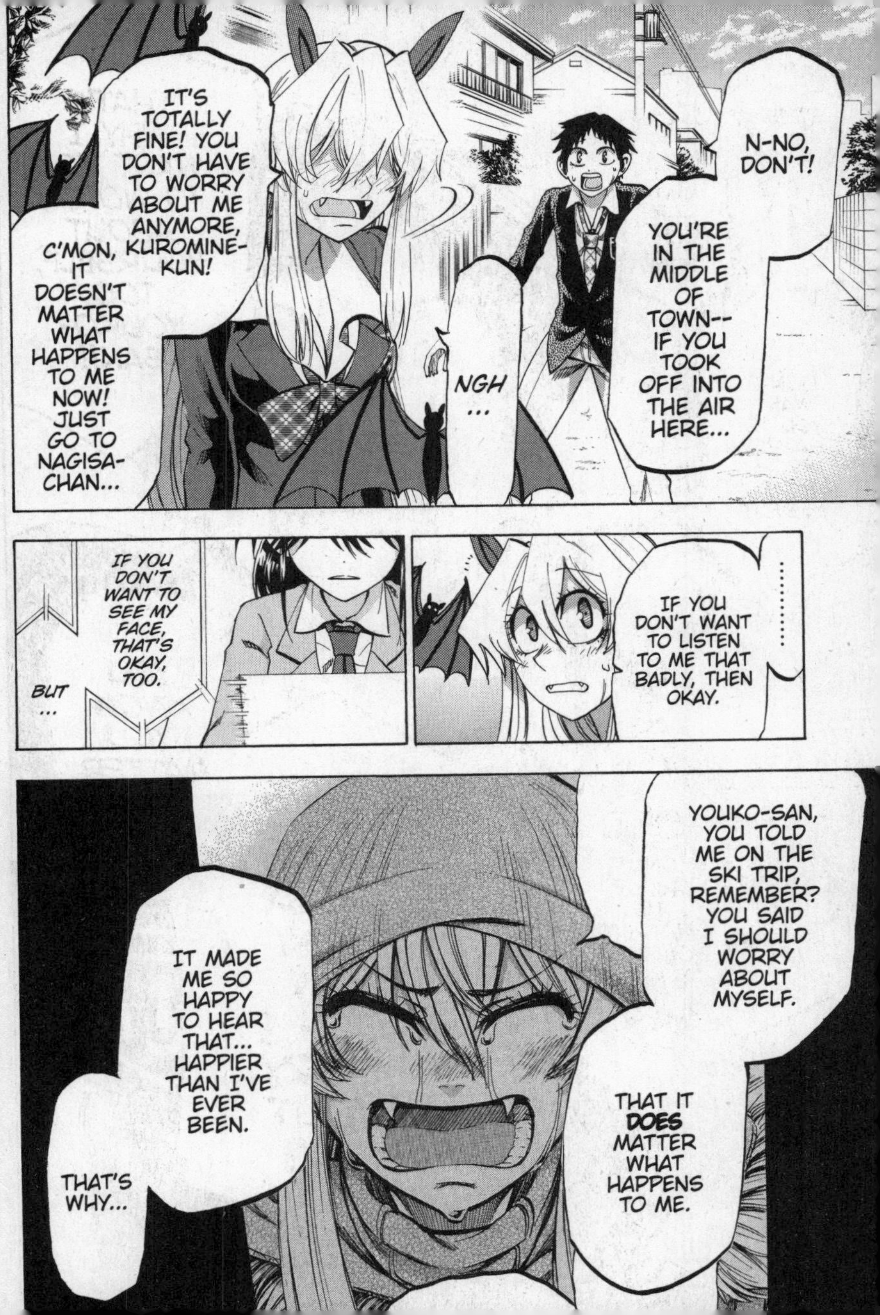
N-NO, DON'T!
YOU'RE IN THE MIDDLE OF TOWN-- IF YOU TOOK OFF INTO THE AIR HERE...
NGH...
IT'S TOTALLY FINE! YOU DON'T HAVE TO WORRY ABOUT ME ANYMORE, KUROMINE-KUN!
C'MON, IT DOESN'T MATTER WHAT HAPPENS TO ME NOW! JUST GO TO NAGISA-CHAN...
......
IF YOU DON'T WANT TO LISTEN TO ME THAT BADLY, THEN OKAY.
IF YOU DON'T WANT TO SEE MY FACE, THAT'S OKAY, TOO.
BUT...
YOUKO-SAN, YOU TOLD ME ON THE SKI TRIP, REMEMBER? YOU SAID I SHOULD WORRY ABOUT MYSELF.
THAT IT **DOES** MATTER WHAT HAPPENS TO ME.
IT MADE ME SO HAPPY TO HEAR THAT... HAPPIER THAN I'VE EVER BEEN.
THAT'S WHY...

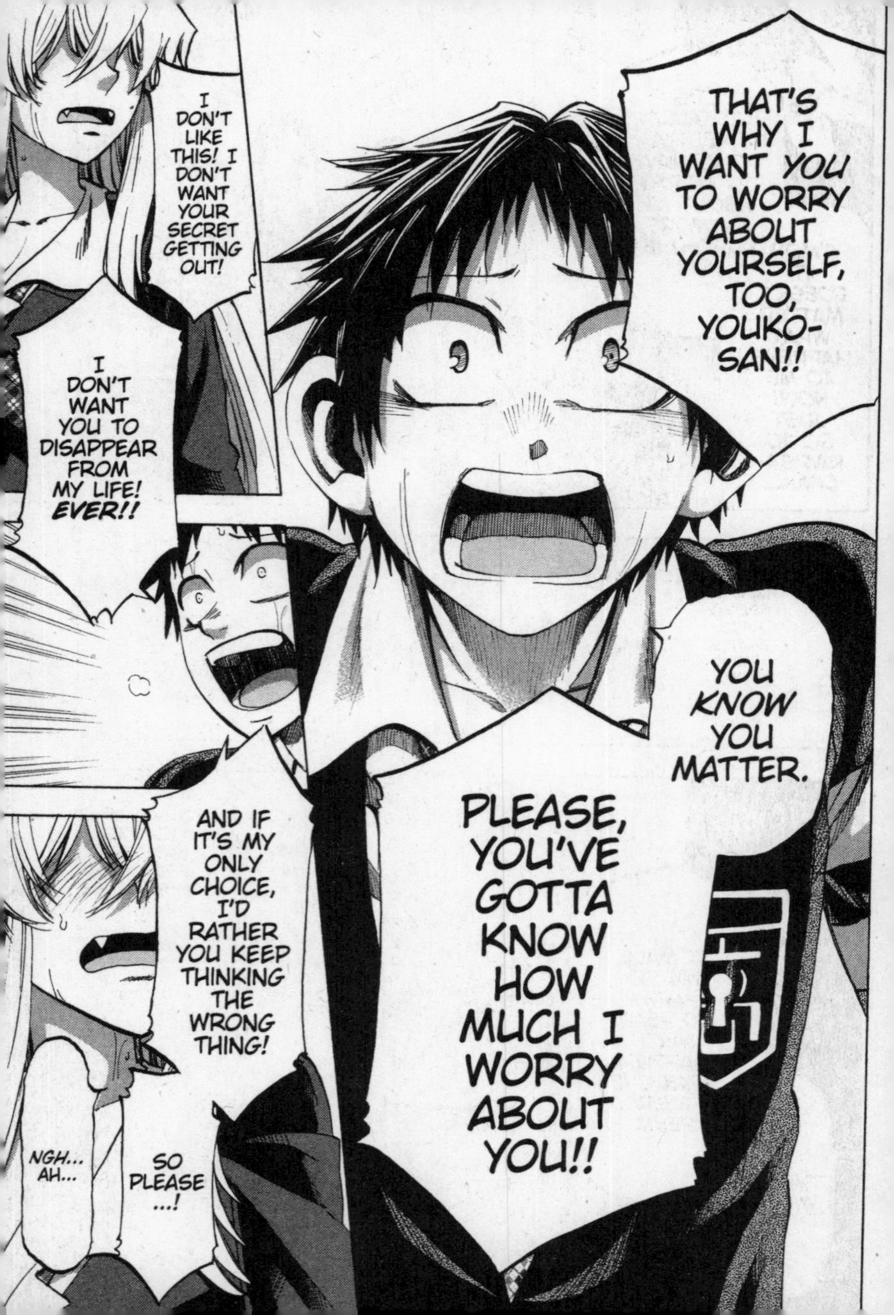
THAT'S WHY I WANT *YOU* TO WORRY ABOUT YOURSELF, TOO, YOUKO-SAN!!
YOU *KNOW* YOU MATTER.
PLEASE, YOU'VE GOTTA KNOW HOW MUCH I WORRY ABOUT YOU!!
I DON'T LIKE THIS! I DON'T WANT YOUR SECRET GETTING OUT!
I DON'T WANT YOU TO DISAPPEAR FROM MY LIFE! ***EVER!!***
AND IF IT'S MY ONLY CHOICE, I'D RATHER YOU KEEP THINKING THE WRONG THING!
SO PLEASE ...!
NGH... AH...

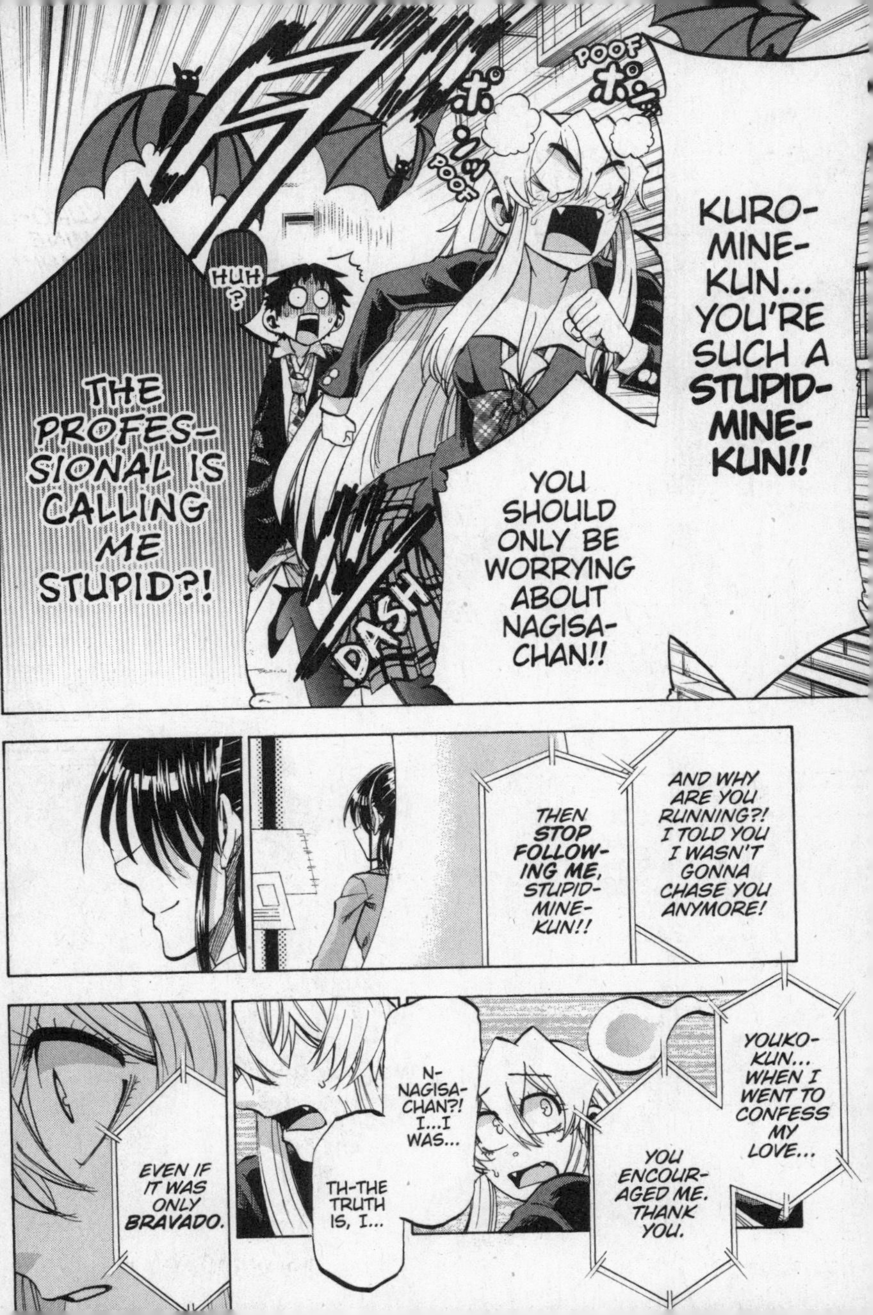
POOF
POOF
KURO-MINE-KUN... YOU'RE SUCH A STUPID-MINE-KUN!!
YOU SHOULD ONLY BE WORRYING ABOUT NAGISA-CHAN!!
DASH
HUH?
THE PROFES-SIONAL IS CALLING ME STUPID?!
AND WHY ARE YOU RUNNING?! I TOLD YOU I WASN'T GONNA CHASE YOU ANYMORE!
THEN STOP FOLLOW-ING ME, STUPID-MINE-KUN!!
YOUKO-KUN... WHEN I WENT TO CONFESS MY LOVE...
YOU ENCOUR-AGED ME. THANK YOU.
N-NAGISA-CHAN?! I...I WAS...
TH-THE TRUTH IS, I...
EVEN IF IT WAS ONLY BRAVADO.

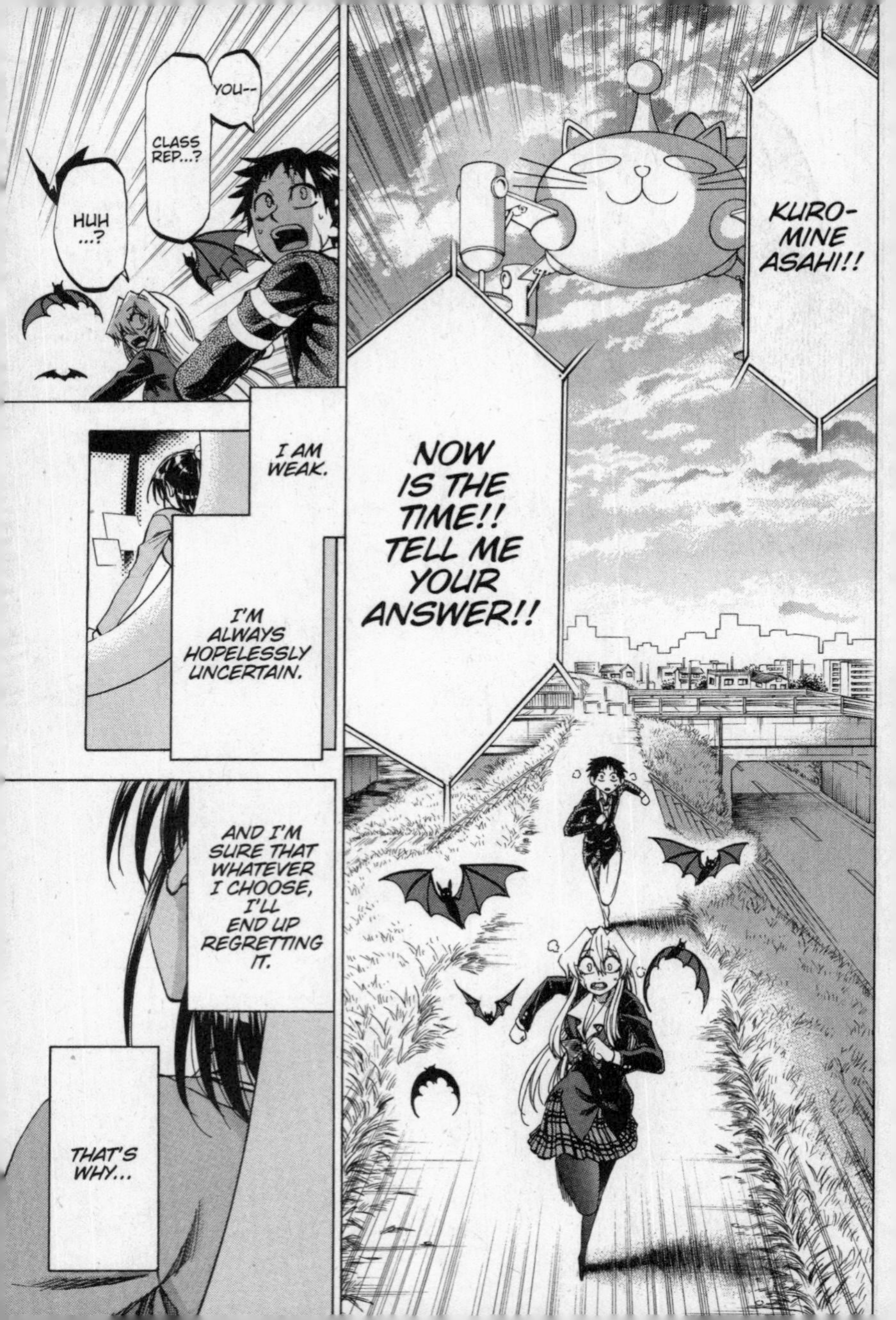
KURO-MINE ASAHI!!
NOW IS THE TIME!! TELL ME YOUR ANSWER!!
YOU--
CLASS REP...?
HUH ...?
I AM WEAK.
I'M ALWAYS HOPELESSLY UNCERTAIN.
AND I'M SURE THAT WHATEVER I CHOOSE, I'LL END UP REGRETTING IT.
THAT'S WHY...

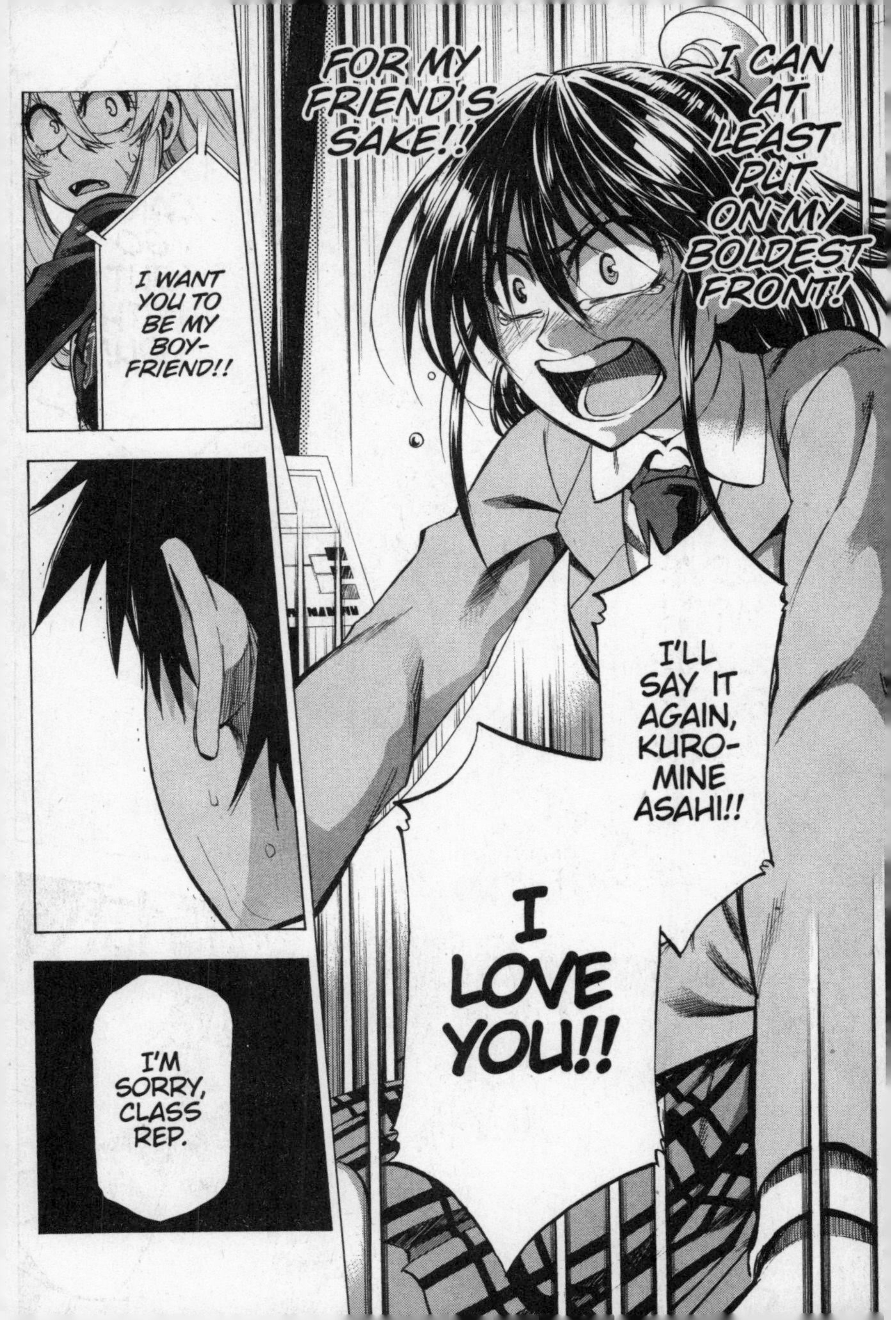
I CAN AT LEAST PUT ON MY BOLDEST FRONT!
FOR MY FRIEND'S SAKE!!
I'LL SAY IT AGAIN, KURO-MINE ASAHI!!
I LOVE YOU!!
I WANT YOU TO BE MY BOY-FRIEND!!
I'M SORRY, CLASS REP.

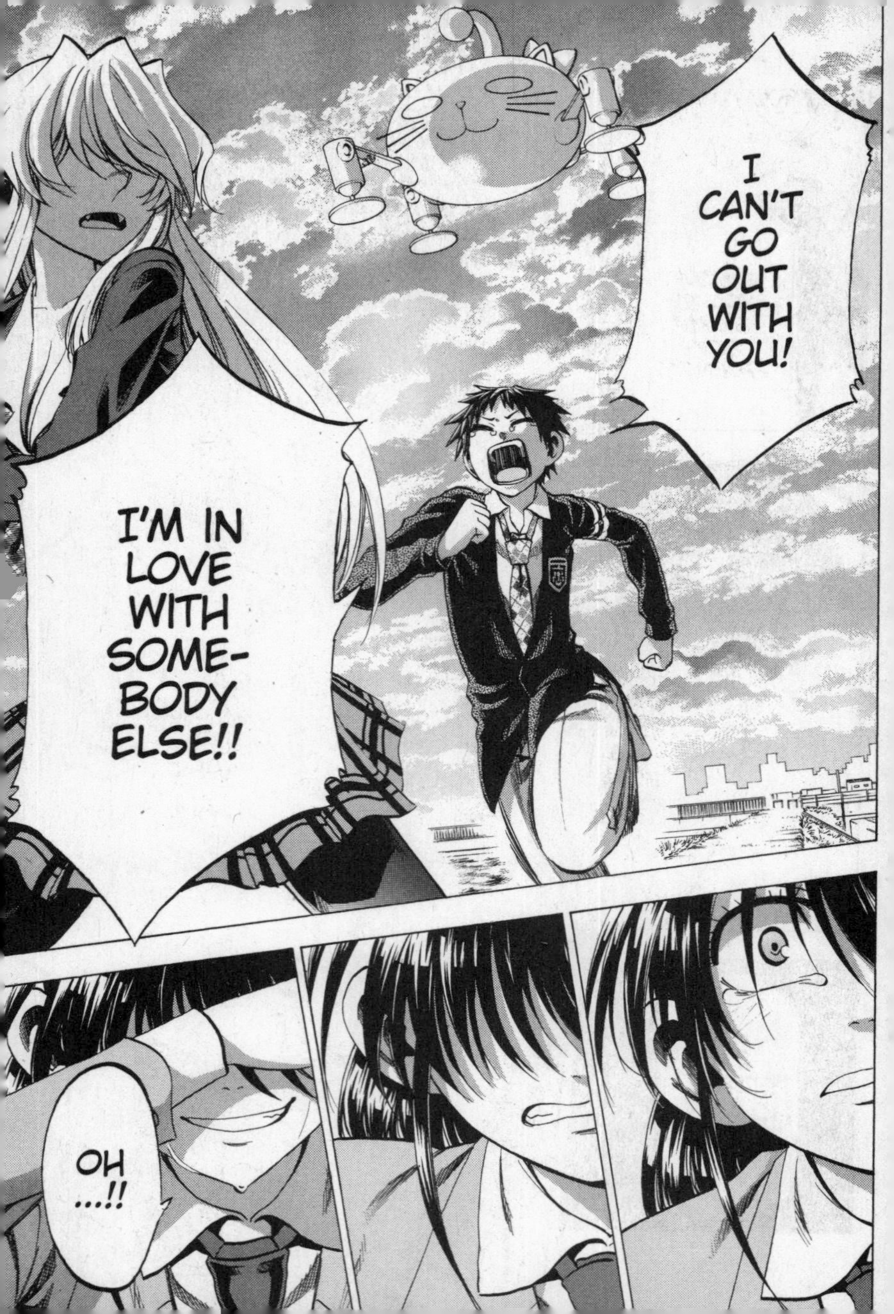
I CAN'T GO OUT WITH YOU!
I'M IN LOVE WITH SOMEBODY ELSE!!
OH ...!!

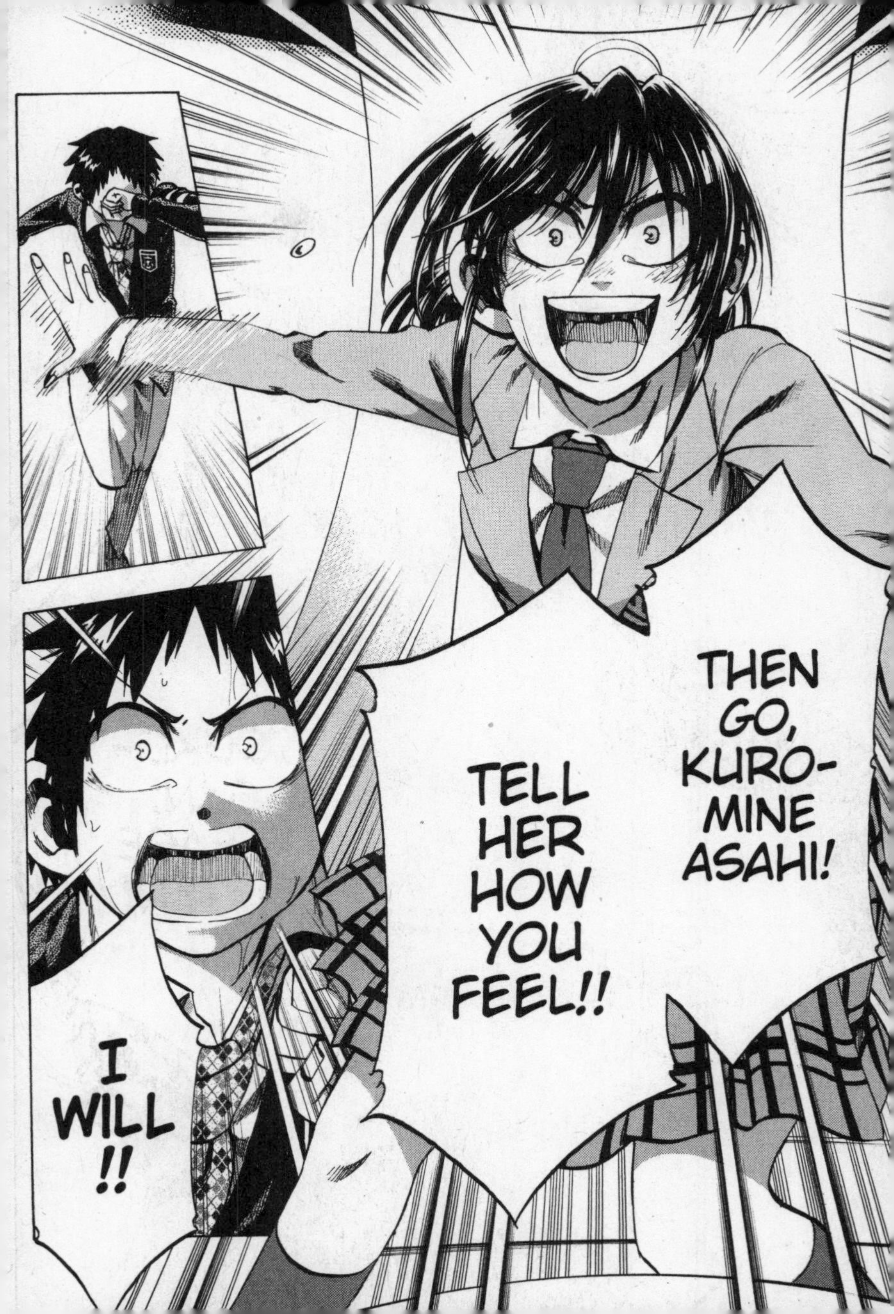
THEN GO, KURO-MINE ASAHI! TELL HER HOW YOU FEEL!!
I WILL!!

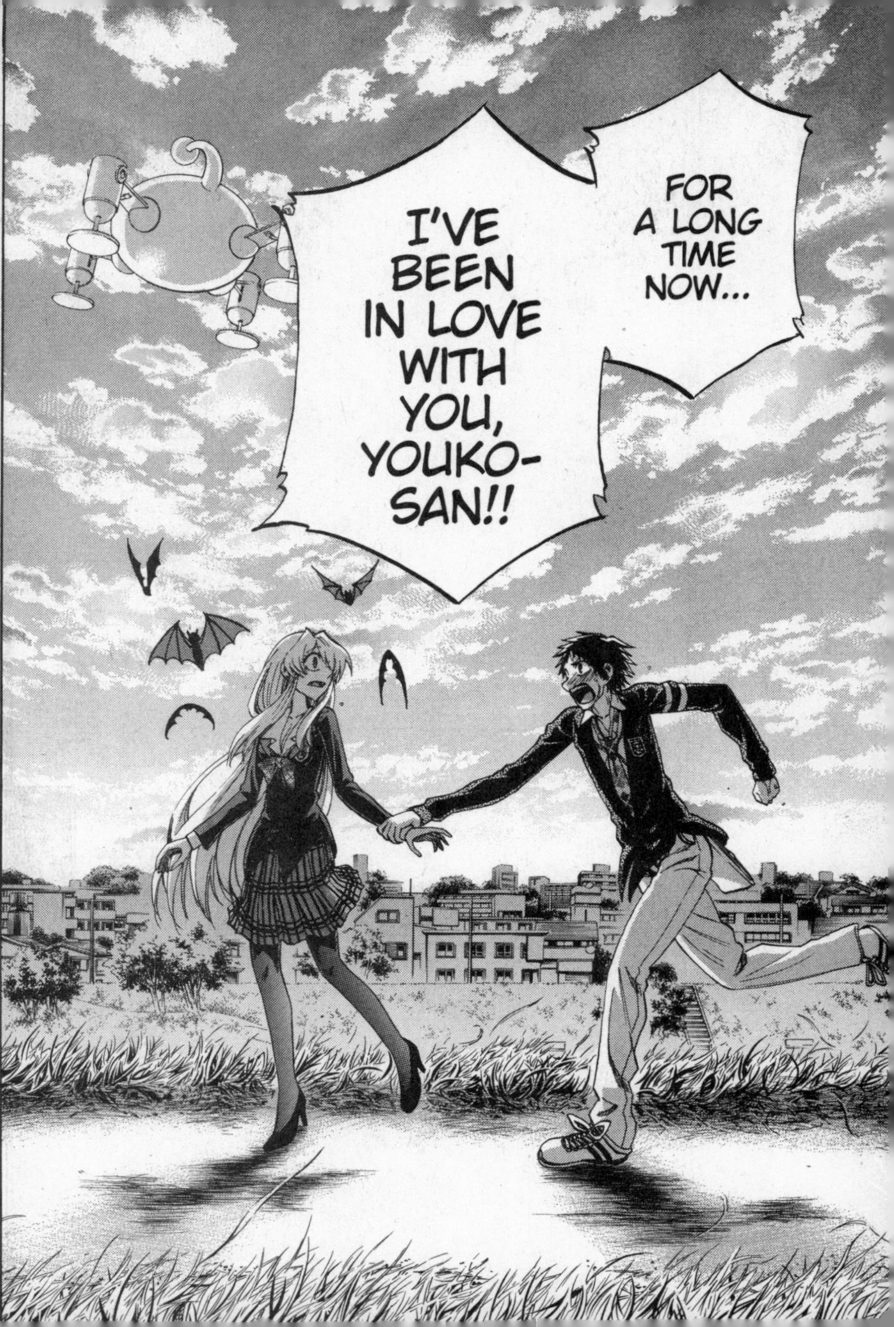
FOR A LONG TIME NOW...
I'VE BEEN IN LOVE WITH YOU, YOUKO-SAN!!

Chapter 86: "Let's Confess Our Love!!"

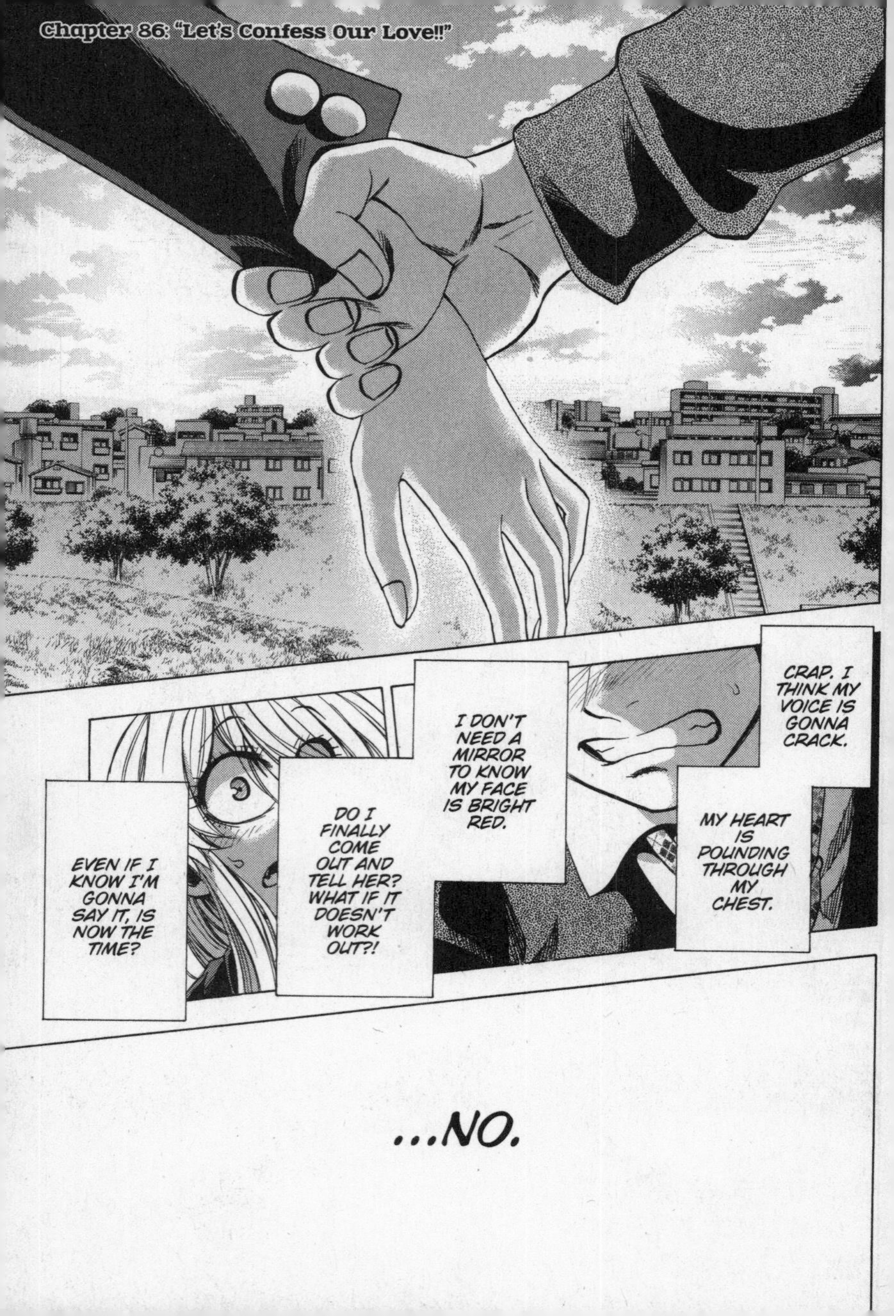
CRAP. I THINK MY VOICE IS GONNA CRACK.
MY HEART IS POUNDING THROUGH MY CHEST.
I DON'T NEED A MIRROR TO KNOW MY FACE IS BRIGHT RED.
DO I FINALLY COME OUT AND TELL HER? WHAT IF IT DOESN'T WORK OUT?!
EVEN IF I KNOW I'M GONNA SAY IT, IS NOW THE TIME?
...NO.

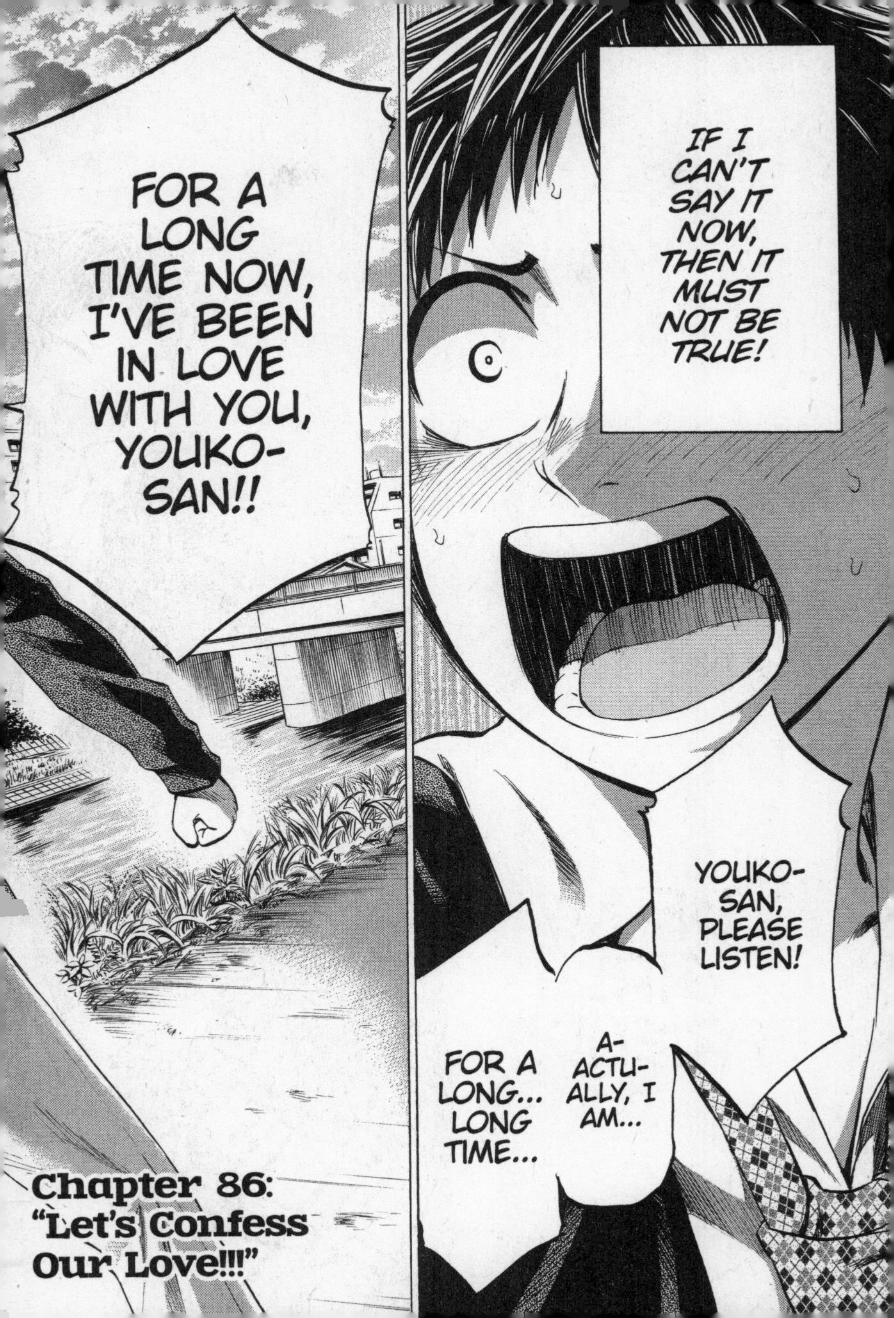
IF I CAN'T SAY IT NOW, THEN IT MUST NOT BE TRUE!
YOUKO-SAN, PLEASE LISTEN!
A-ACTU-ALLY, I AM...
FOR A LONG... LONG TIME...
FOR A LONG TIME NOW, I'VE BEEN IN LOVE WITH YOU, YOUKO-SAN!!
Chapter 86: "Let's Confess Our Love!!!"

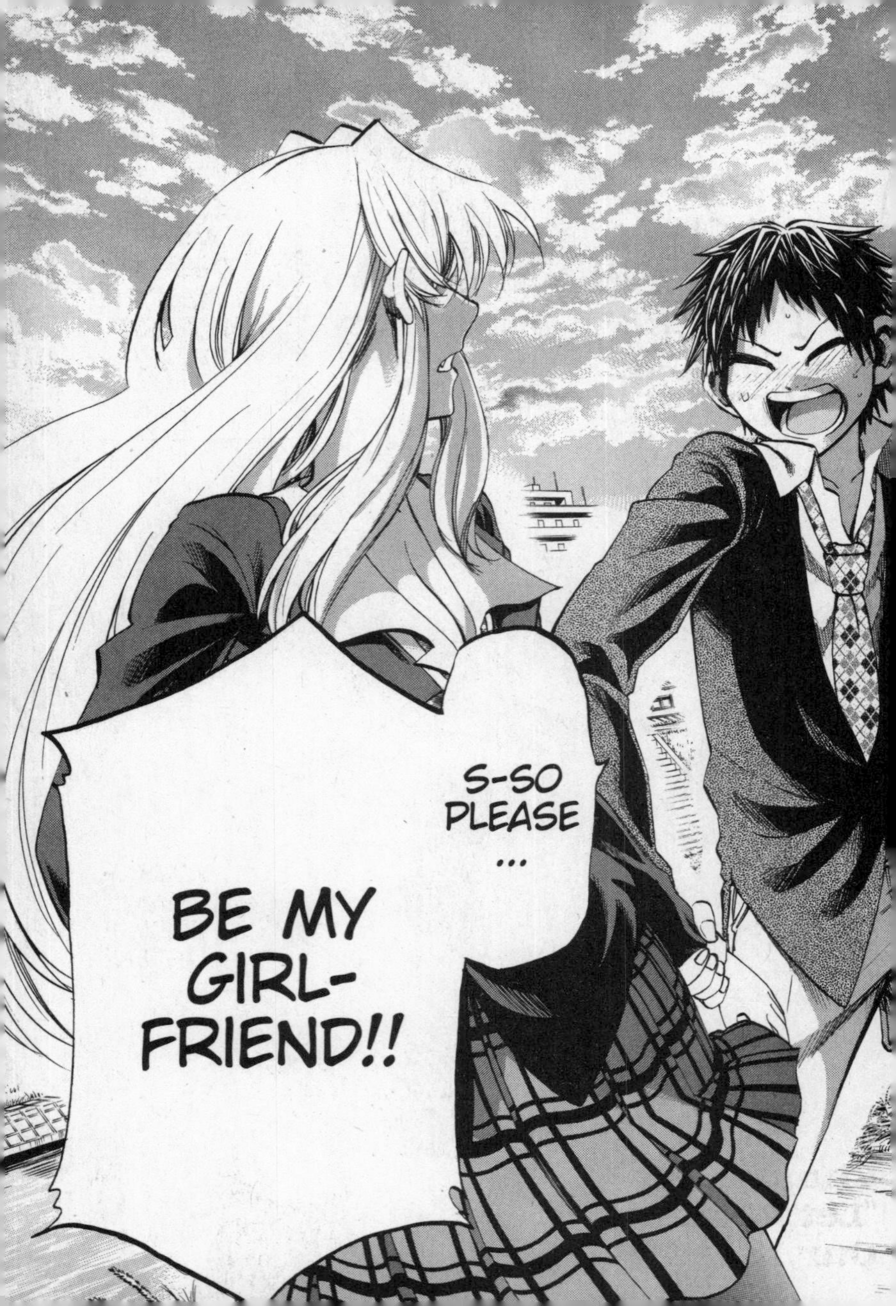
S-SO PLEASE ...
BE MY GIRL-FRIEND!!

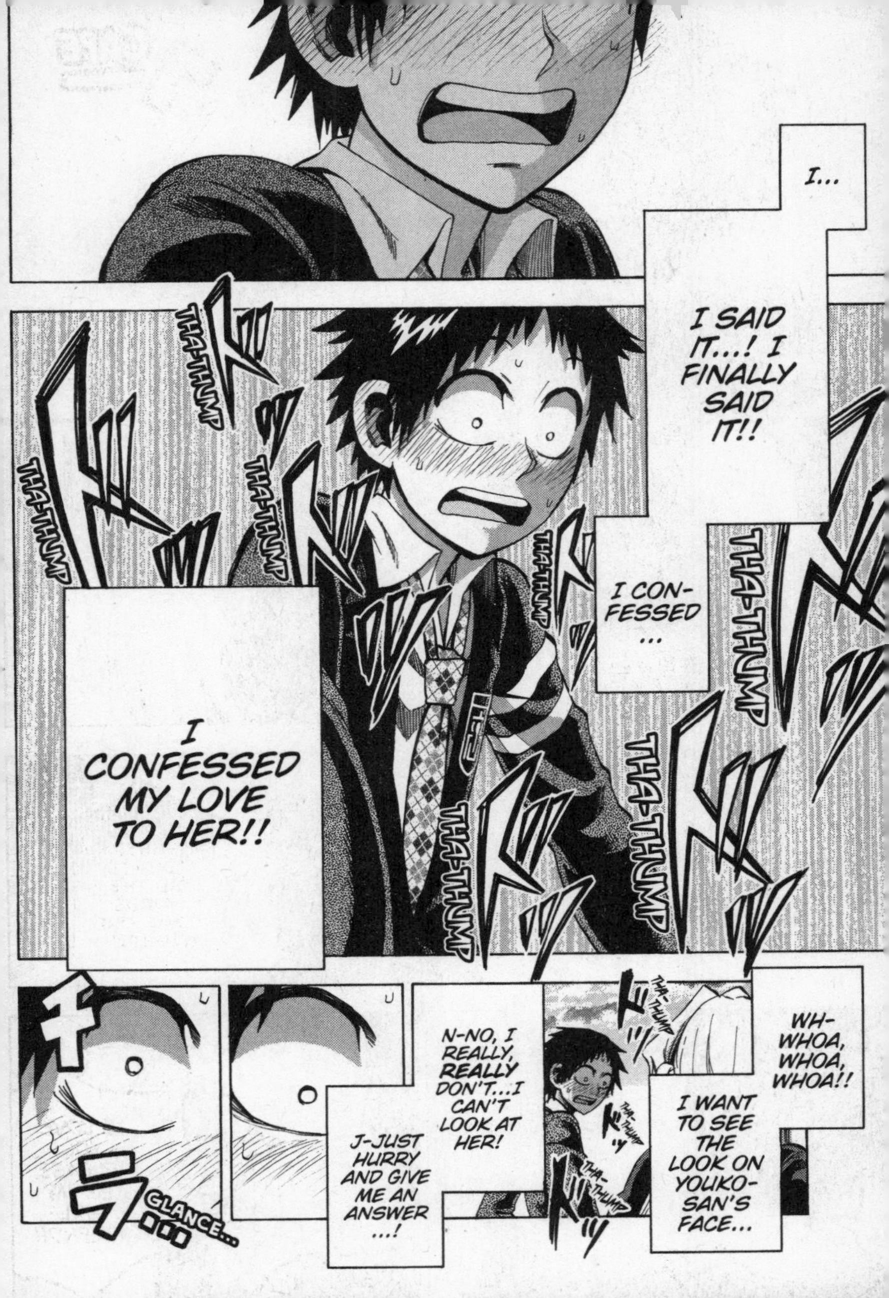
I...
I SAID IT...! I FINALLY SAID IT!!
THA-THUMP
THA-THUMP
THA-THUMP
THA-THUMP
I CON-FESSED ...
THA-THUMP
THA-THUMP
THA-THUMP
I CONFESSED MY LOVE TO HER!!
WH-WHOA, WHOA, WHOA!!
I WANT TO SEE THE LOOK ON YOUKO-SAN'S FACE...
THA-THUMP
THA-THUMP
THA-THUMP
N-NO, I REALLY, REALLY DON'T...I CAN'T LOOK AT HER!
J-JUST HURRY AND GIVE ME AN ANSWER ...!
GLANCE...

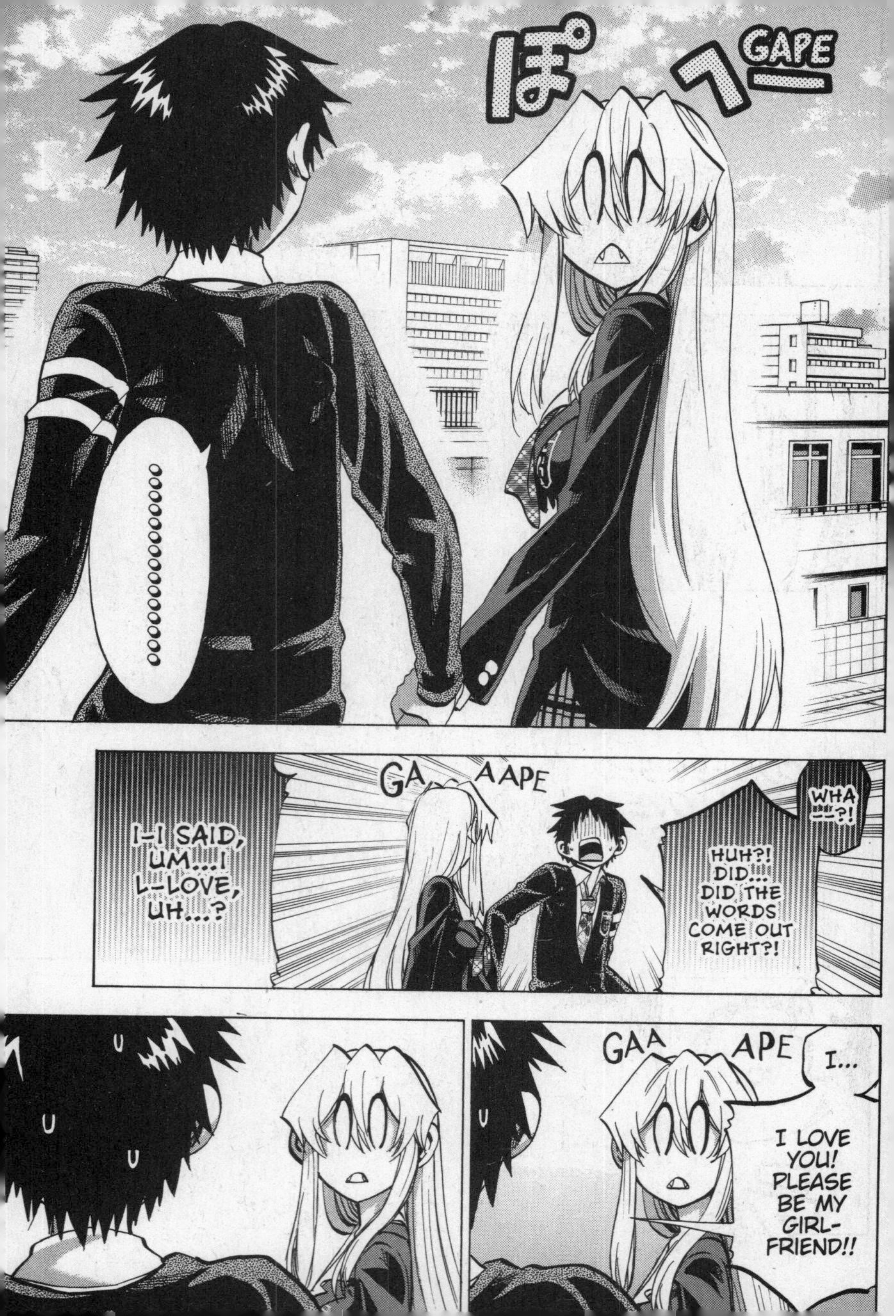
ぽへー
GAPE
WHA—?!
HUH?! DID... DID THE WORDS COME OUT RIGHT?!
GA AAPE
I-I SAID, UM...I L-LOVE, UH...?
GAA APE
I...
I LOVE YOU! PLEASE BE MY GIRL-FRIEND!!

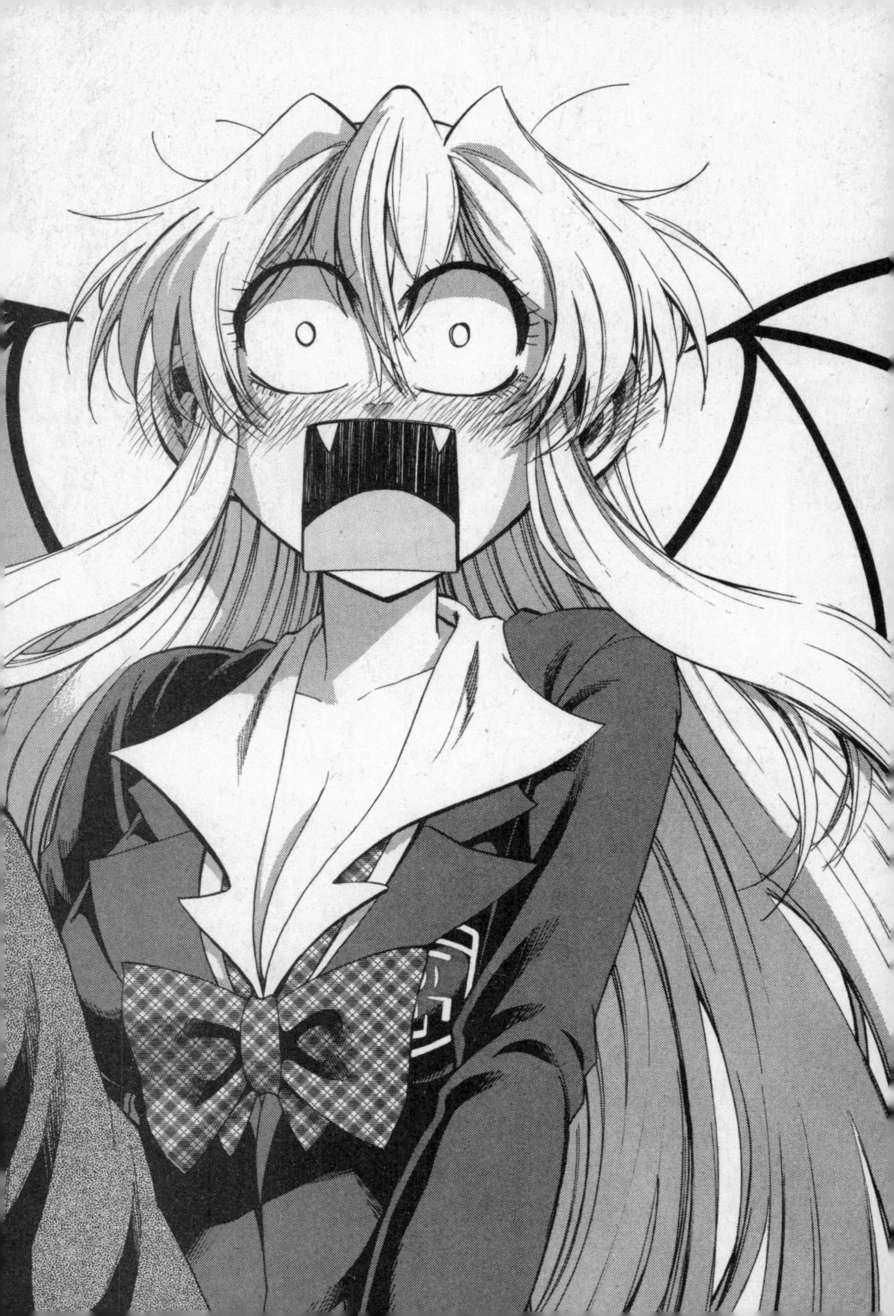

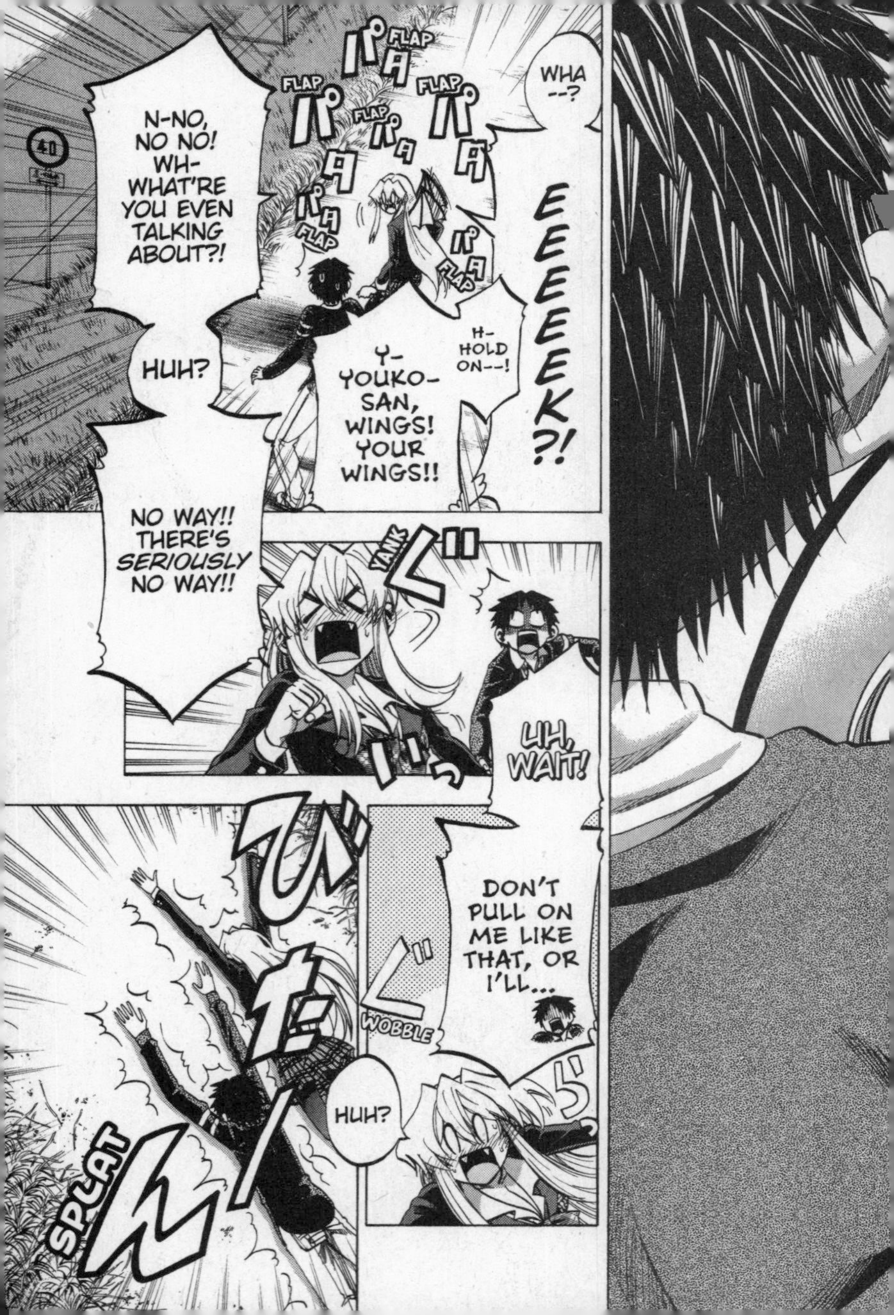
WHA --?
FLAP
FLAP
FLAP
FLAP
FLAP
FLAP
N-NO, NO NO! WH- WHAT'RE YOU EVEN TALKING ABOUT?!
EEEEEEEK?!
H-HOLD ON--!
Y-YOUKO-SAN, WINGS! YOUR WINGS!!
HUH?
NO WAY!! THERE'S *SERIOUSLY* NO WAY!!
YANK
UH, WAIT!
DON'T PULL ON ME LIKE THAT, OR I'LL...
WOBBLE
HUH?
SPLAT

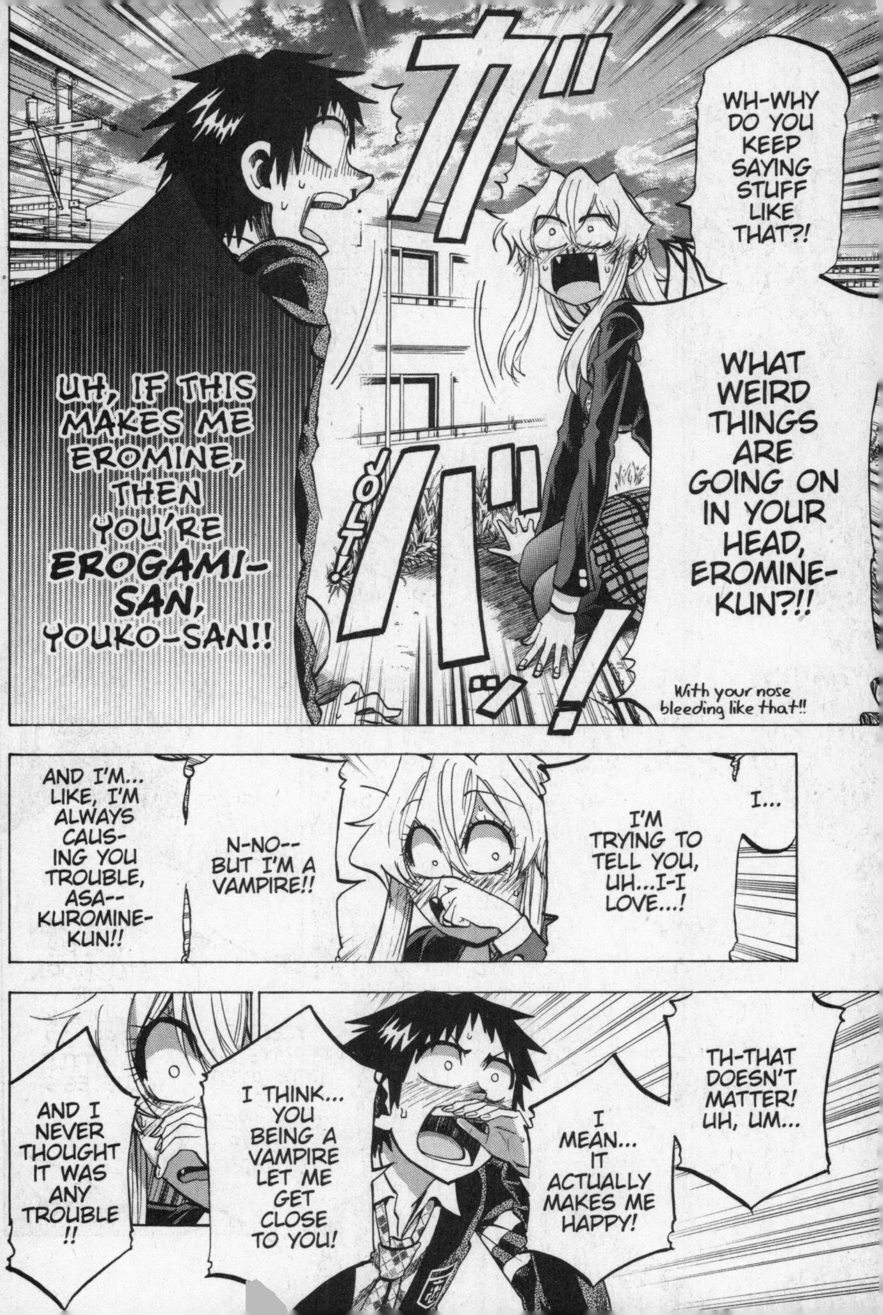
WH-WHY DO YOU KEEP SAYING STUFF LIKE THAT?!
WHAT WEIRD THINGS ARE GOING ON IN YOUR HEAD, EROMINE-KUN?!!
With your nose bleeding like that!!
JOLT!
UH, IF THIS MAKES ME EROMINE, THEN YOU'RE **EROGAMI-SAN**, YOUKO-SAN!!
I...
I'M TRYING TO TELL YOU, UH...I-I LOVE...!
N-NO-- BUT I'M A VAMPIRE!!
AND I'M... LIKE, I'M ALWAYS CAUSING YOU TROUBLE, ASA--KUROMINE-KUN!!
TH-THAT DOESN'T MATTER! UH, UM...
I MEAN... IT ACTUALLY MAKES ME HAPPY!
I THINK... YOU BEING A VAMPIRE LET ME GET CLOSE TO YOU!
AND I NEVER THOUGHT IT WAS ANY TROUBLE!!

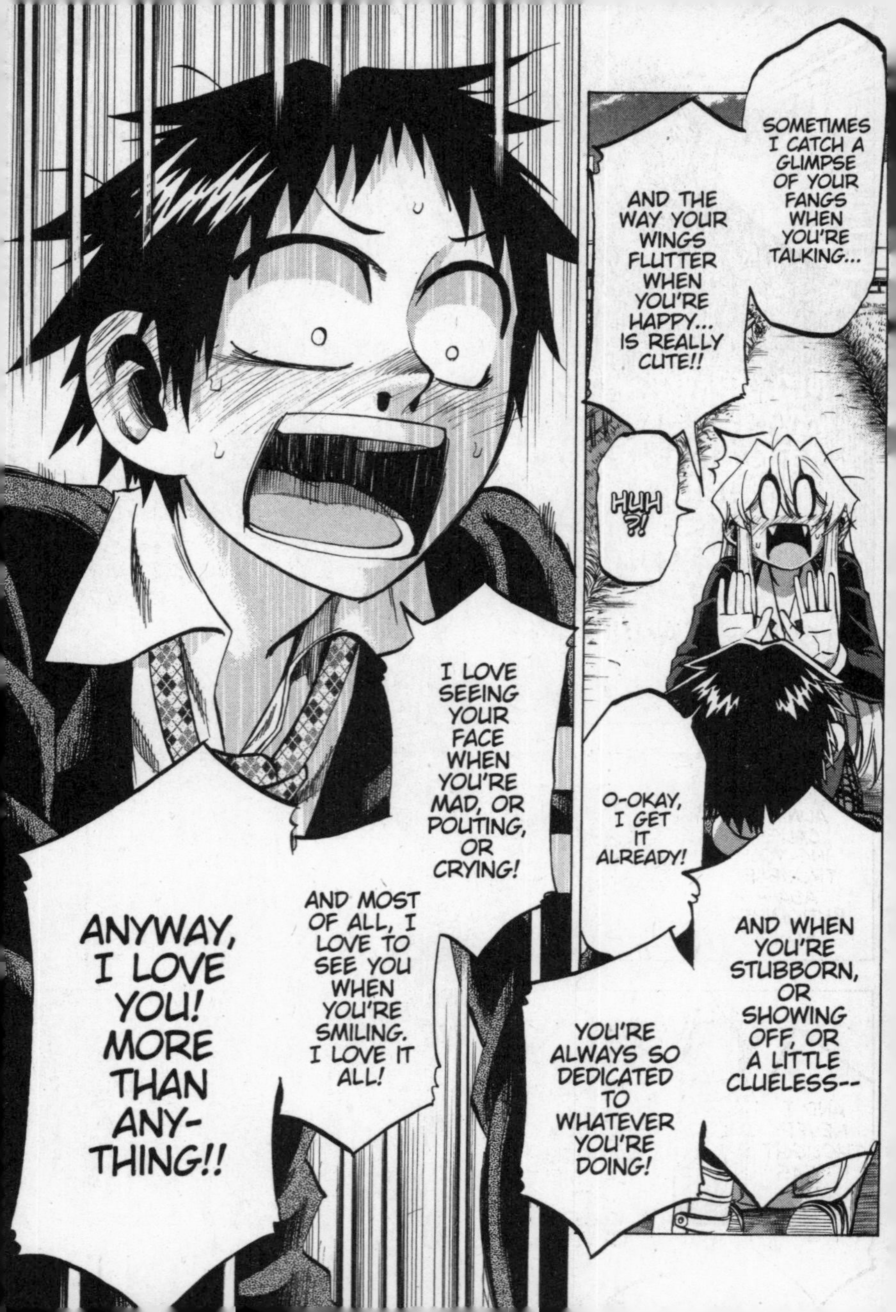
SOMETIMES I CATCH A GLIMPSE OF YOUR FANGS WHEN YOU'RE TALKING...
AND THE WAY YOUR WINGS FLUTTER WHEN YOU'RE HAPPY... IS REALLY CUTE!!
HUH ?!
I LOVE SEEING YOUR FACE WHEN YOU'RE MAD, OR POUTING, OR CRYING!
O-OKAY, I GET IT ALREADY!
AND WHEN YOU'RE STUBBORN, OR SHOWING OFF, OR A LITTLE CLUELESS--
YOU'RE ALWAYS SO DEDICATED TO WHATEVER YOU'RE DOING!
AND MOST OF ALL, I LOVE TO SEE YOU WHEN YOU'RE SMILING. I LOVE IT ALL!
ANYWAY, I LOVE YOU! MORE THAN ANY-THING!!

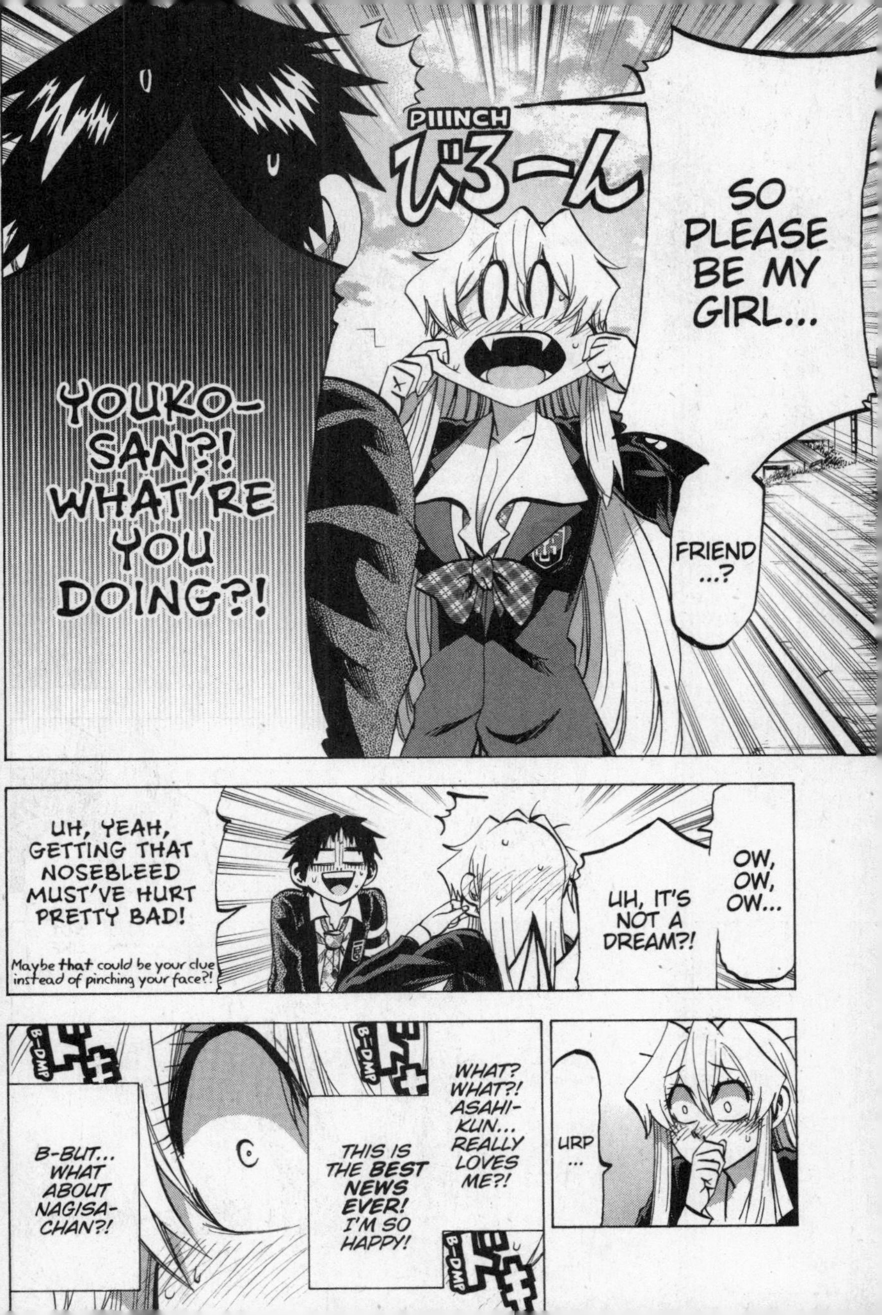
SO PLEASE BE MY GIRL...
FRIEND ...?
PIIINCH
びろーん
YOUKO-SAN?! WHAT'RE YOU DOING?!
OW, OW, OW...
UH, IT'S NOT A DREAM?!
UH, YEAH, GETTING THAT NOSEBLEED MUST'VE HURT PRETTY BAD!
Maybe that could be your clue instead of pinching your face?!
URP ...
WHAT? WHAT?! ASAHI-KUN... REALLY LOVES ME?!
B-DMP
THIS IS THE BEST NEWS EVER! I'M SO HAPPY!
B-DMP
B-BUT... WHAT ABOUT NAGISA-CHAN?!

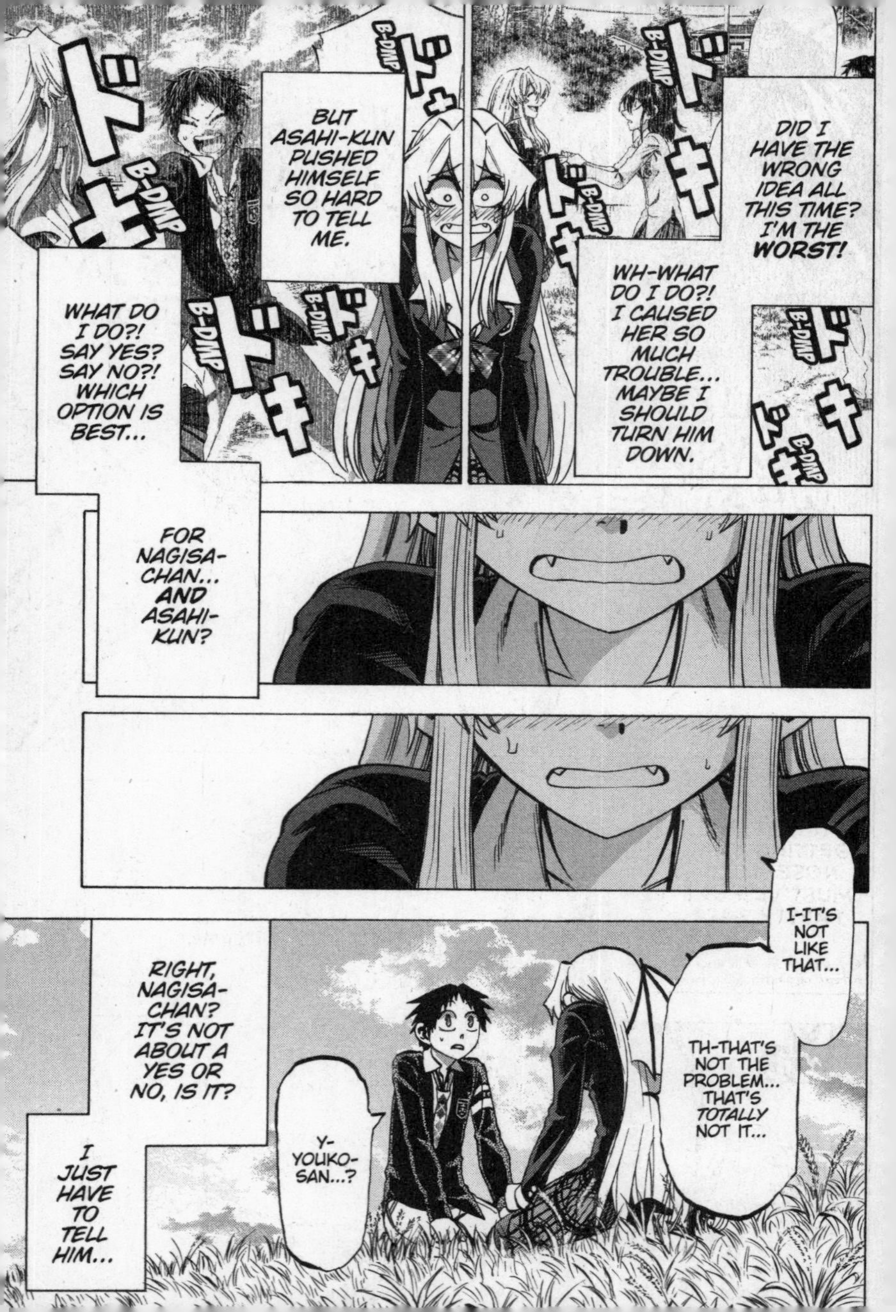
B-DMP
DID I HAVE THE WRONG IDEA ALL THIS TIME? I'M THE WORST!
B-DMP
WH-WHAT DO I DO?! I CAUSED HER SO MUCH TROUBLE... MAYBE I SHOULD TURN HIM DOWN.
B-DMP
B-DMP
B-DMP
BUT ASAHI-KUN PUSHED HIMSELF SO HARD TO TELL ME.
B-DMP
B-DMP
B-DMP
WHAT DO I DO?! SAY YES? SAY NO?! WHICH OPTION IS BEST...
FOR NAGISA-CHAN... AND ASAHI-KUN?
I-IT'S NOT LIKE THAT...
TH-THAT'S NOT THE PROBLEM... THAT'S TOTALLY NOT IT...
RIGHT, NAGISA-CHAN? IT'S NOT ABOUT A YES OR NO, IS IT?
Y-YOUKO-SAN...?
I JUST HAVE TO TELL HIM...

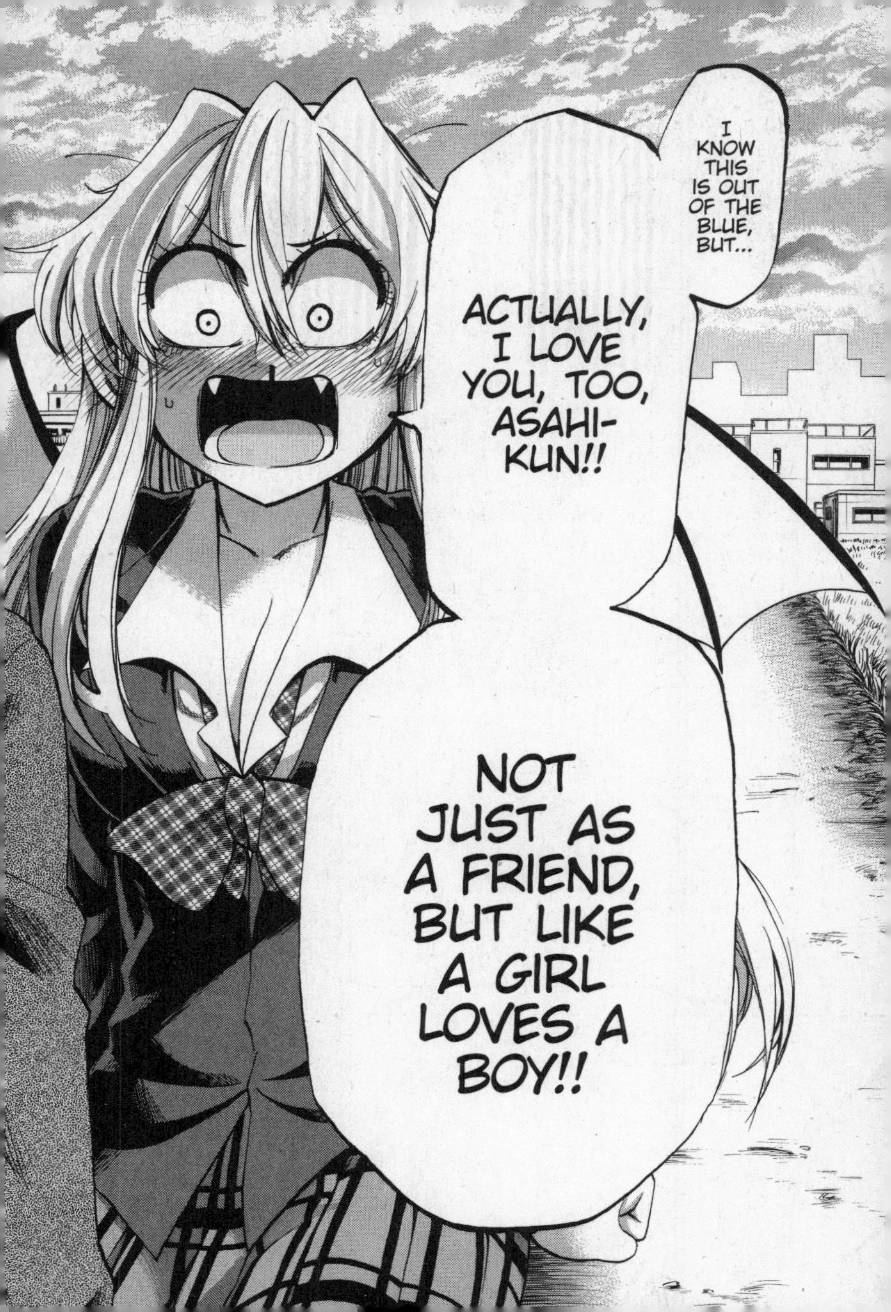
I KNOW THIS IS OUT OF THE BLUE, BUT...
ACTUALLY, I LOVE YOU, TOO, ASAHI-KUN!!
NOT JUST AS A FRIEND, BUT LIKE A GIRL LOVES A BOY!!

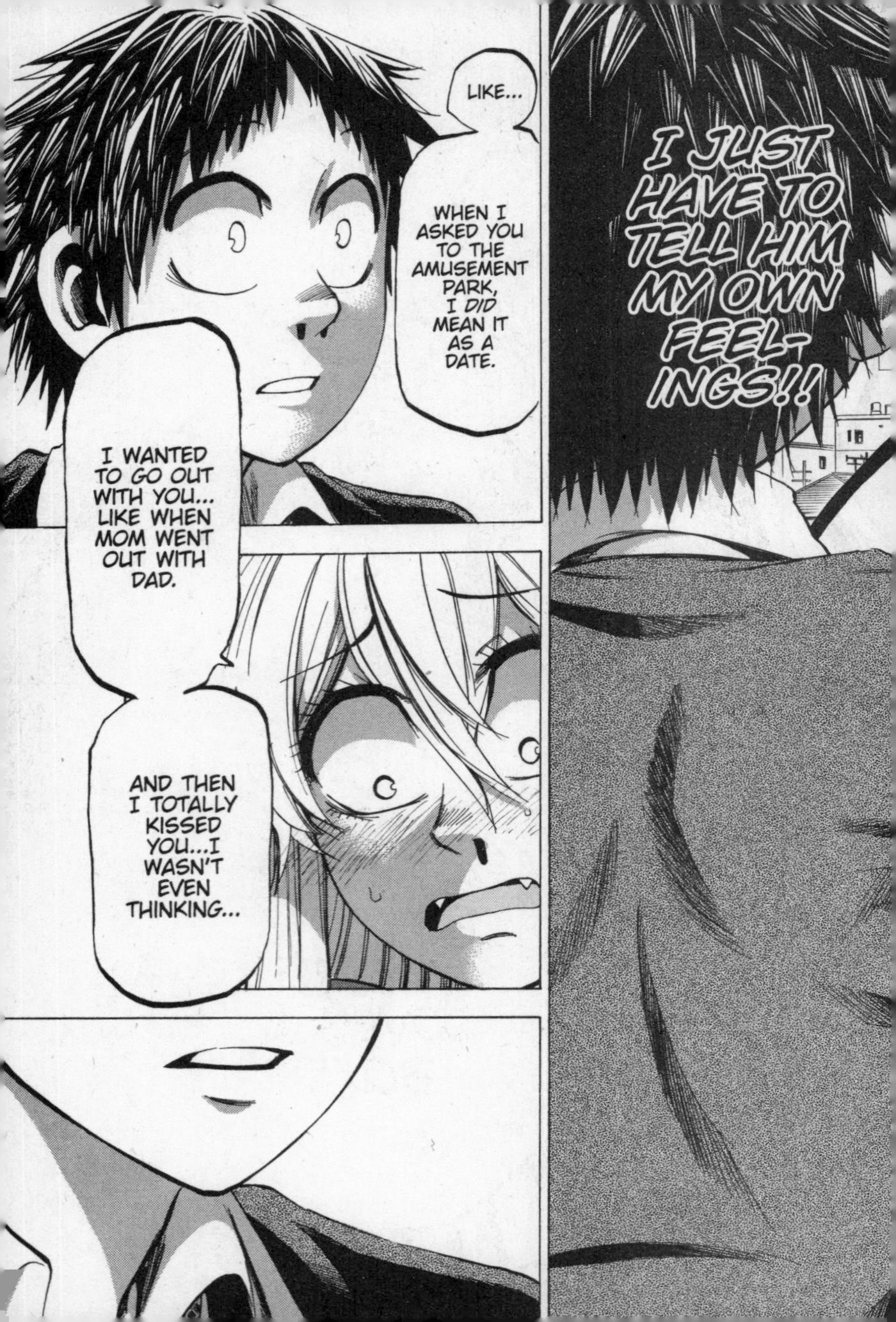
I JUST HAVE TO TELL HIM MY OWN FEEL-INGS!!
LIKE...
WHEN I ASKED YOU TO THE AMUSEMENT PARK, I *DID* MEAN IT AS A DATE.
I WANTED TO GO OUT WITH YOU... LIKE WHEN MOM WENT OUT WITH DAD.
AND THEN I TOTALLY KISSED YOU...I WASN'T EVEN THINKING...

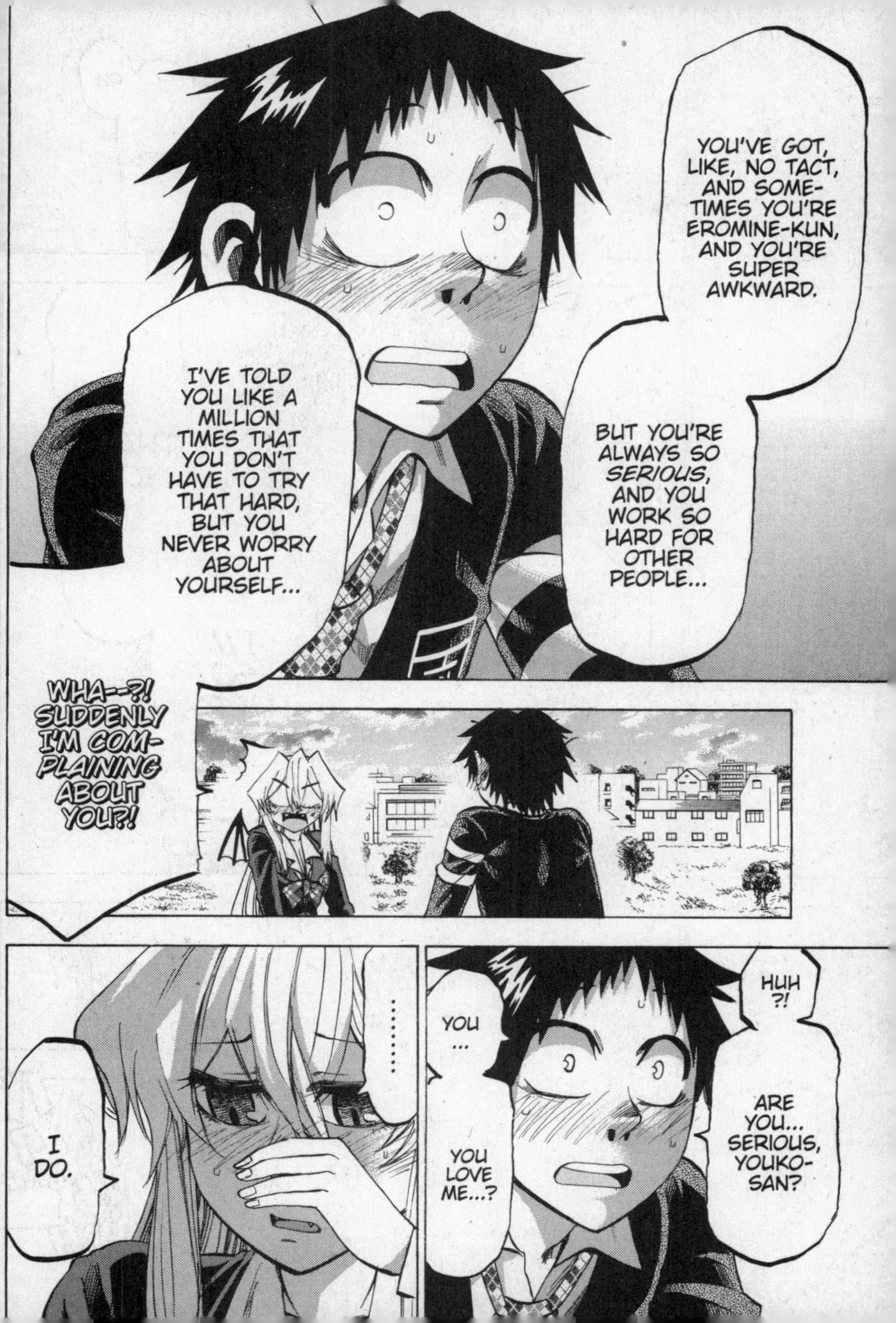
YOU'VE GOT, LIKE, NO TACT, AND SOME-TIMES YOU'RE EROMINE-KUN, AND YOU'RE SUPER AWKWARD.
BUT YOU'RE ALWAYS SO *SERIOUS*, AND YOU WORK SO HARD FOR OTHER PEOPLE...
I'VE TOLD YOU LIKE A MILLION TIMES THAT YOU DON'T HAVE TO TRY THAT HARD, BUT YOU NEVER WORRY ABOUT YOURSELF...
WHA--?! SUDDENLY I'M COM-PLAINING ABOUT YOU?!
HUH ?!
YOU ...
ARE YOU... SERIOUS, YOUKO-SAN?
YOU LOVE ME...?
......
I DO.

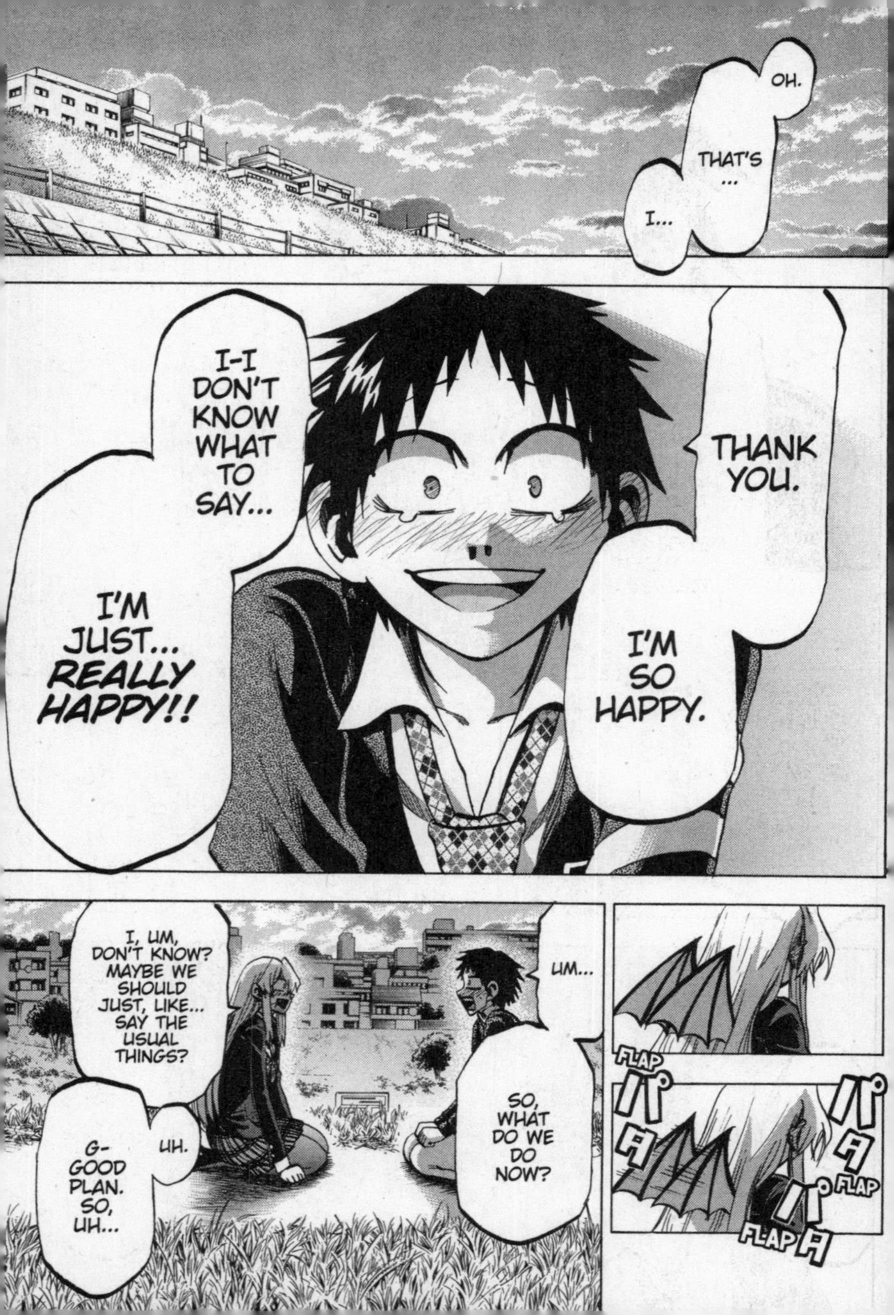

OH.
THAT'S...
I...
THANK YOU.
I'M SO HAPPY.
I-I DON'T KNOW WHAT TO SAY...
I'M JUST... REALLY HAPPY!!
パタ FLAP
パタ FLAP
パタ FLAP
UM...
SO, WHAT DO WE DO NOW?
I, UM, DON'T KNOW? MAYBE WE SHOULD JUST, LIKE... SAY THE USUAL THINGS?
UH.
G-GOOD PLAN. SO, UH...

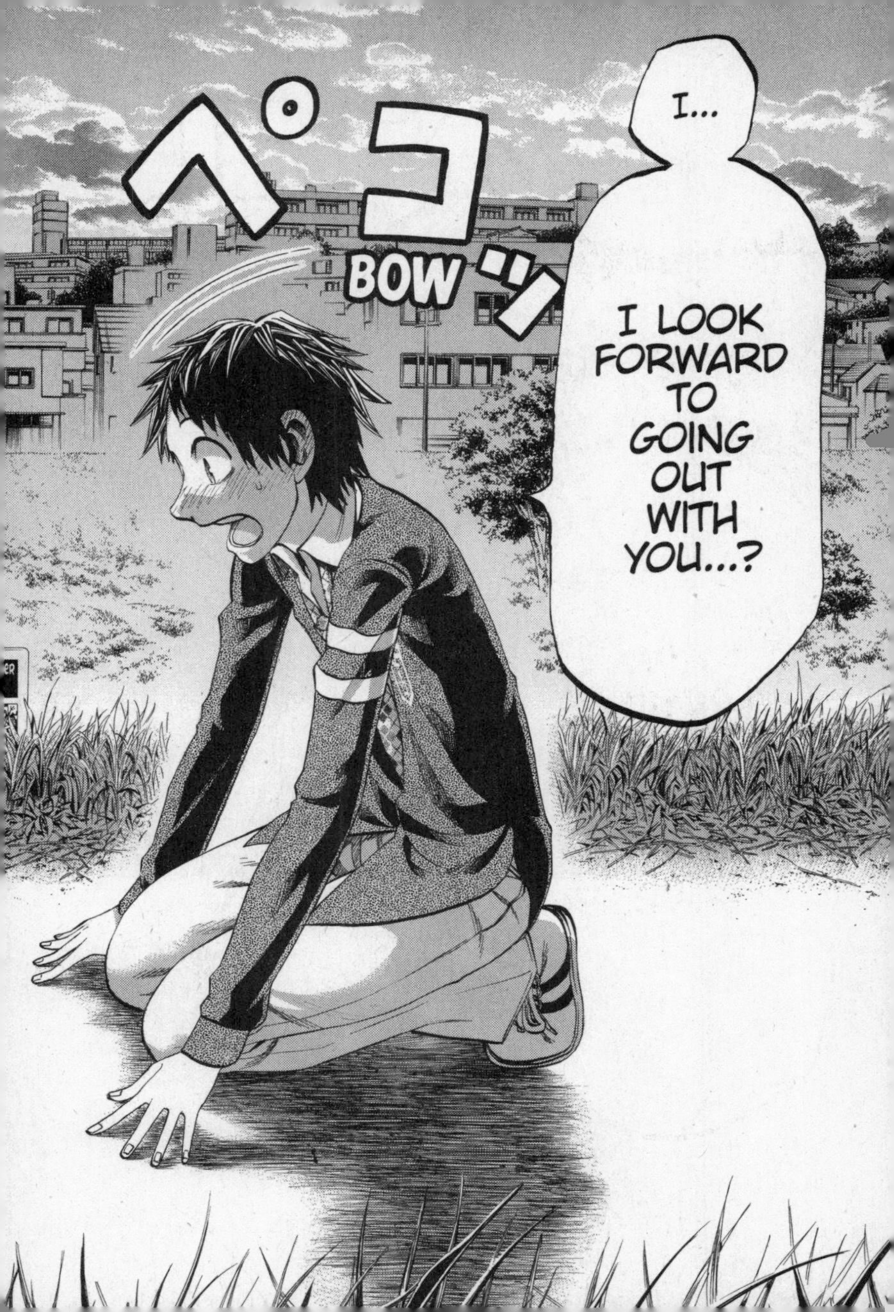
I...
I LOOK FORWARD TO GOING OUT WITH YOU...?
ペコッ
BOW

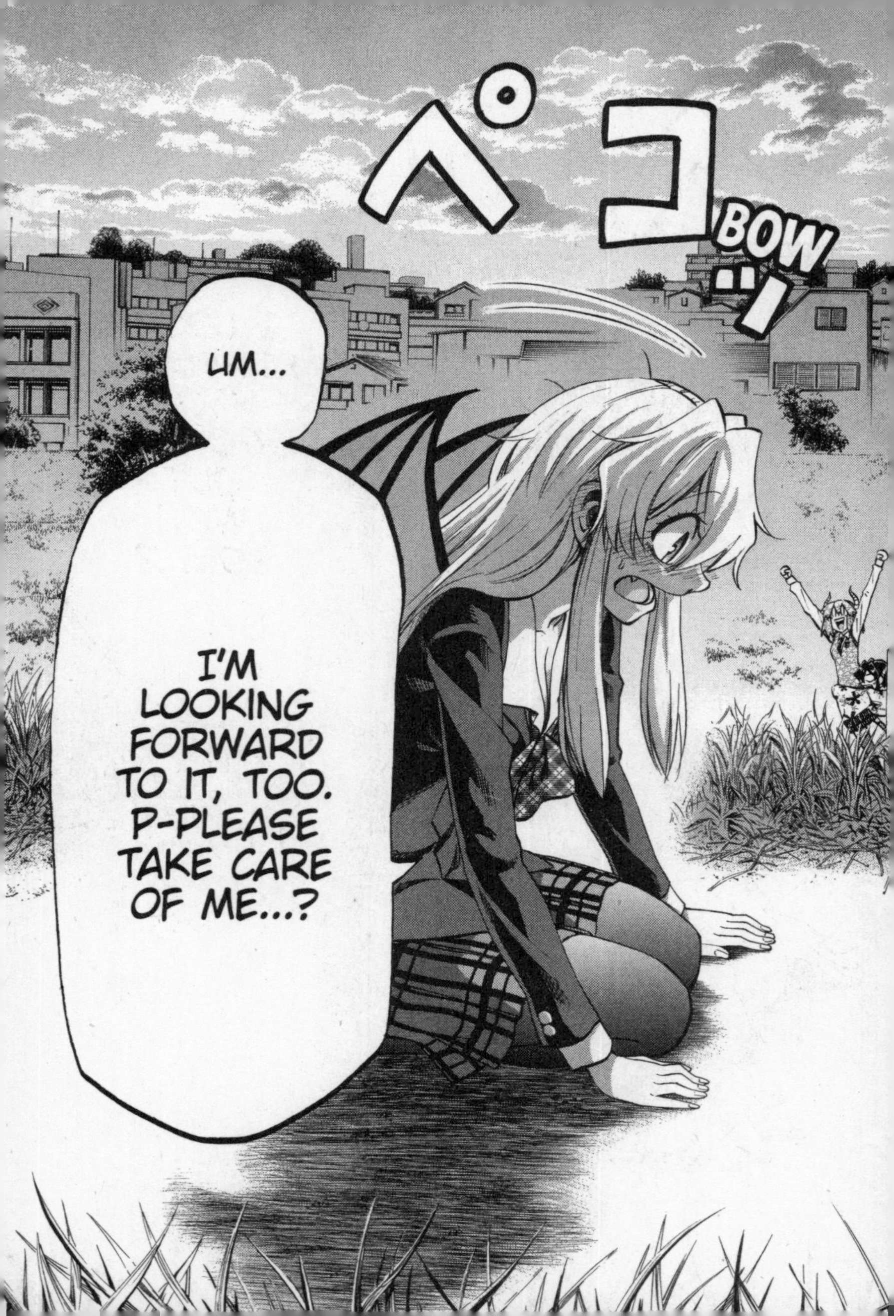
ペコ
BOW
UM...
I'M LOOKING FORWARD TO IT, TOO. P-PLEASE TAKE CARE OF ME...?

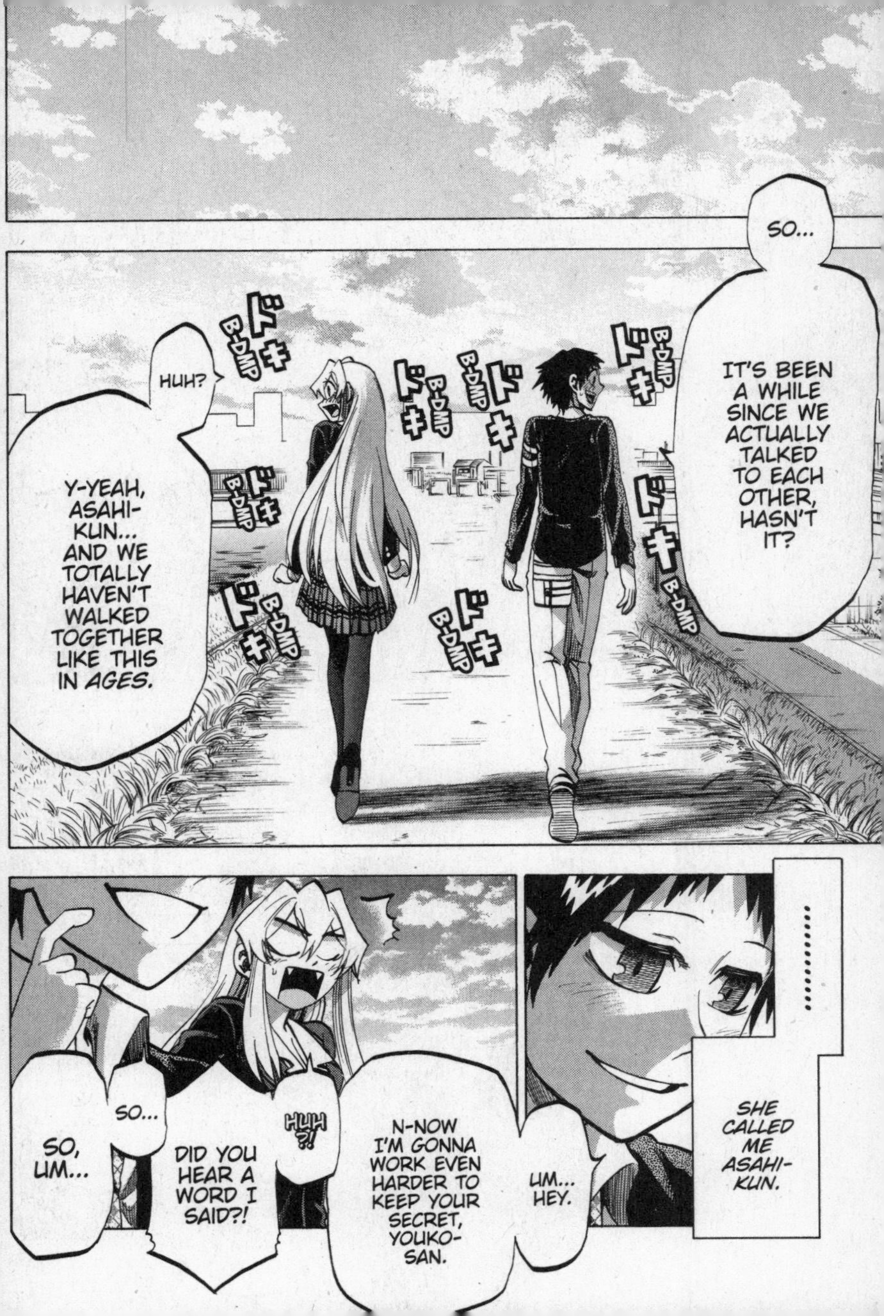
SO...
IT'S BEEN A WHILE SINCE WE ACTUALLY TALKED TO EACH OTHER, HASN'T IT?
ドキ B-DMP
ドキ B-DMP
ドキ B-DMP
ドキ B-DMP
ドキ B-DMP
ドキ B-DMP
ドキ B-DMP
ドキ B-DMP
HUH?
Y-YEAH, ASAHI-KUN... AND WE TOTALLY HAVEN'T WALKED TOGETHER LIKE THIS IN *AGES*.
......
SHE CALLED ME ASAHI-KUN.
UM... HEY.
N-NOW I'M GONNA WORK EVEN HARDER TO KEEP YOUR SECRET, YOUKO-SAN.
HUH ?!
DID YOU HEAR A WORD I SAID?!
SO...
SO, UM...

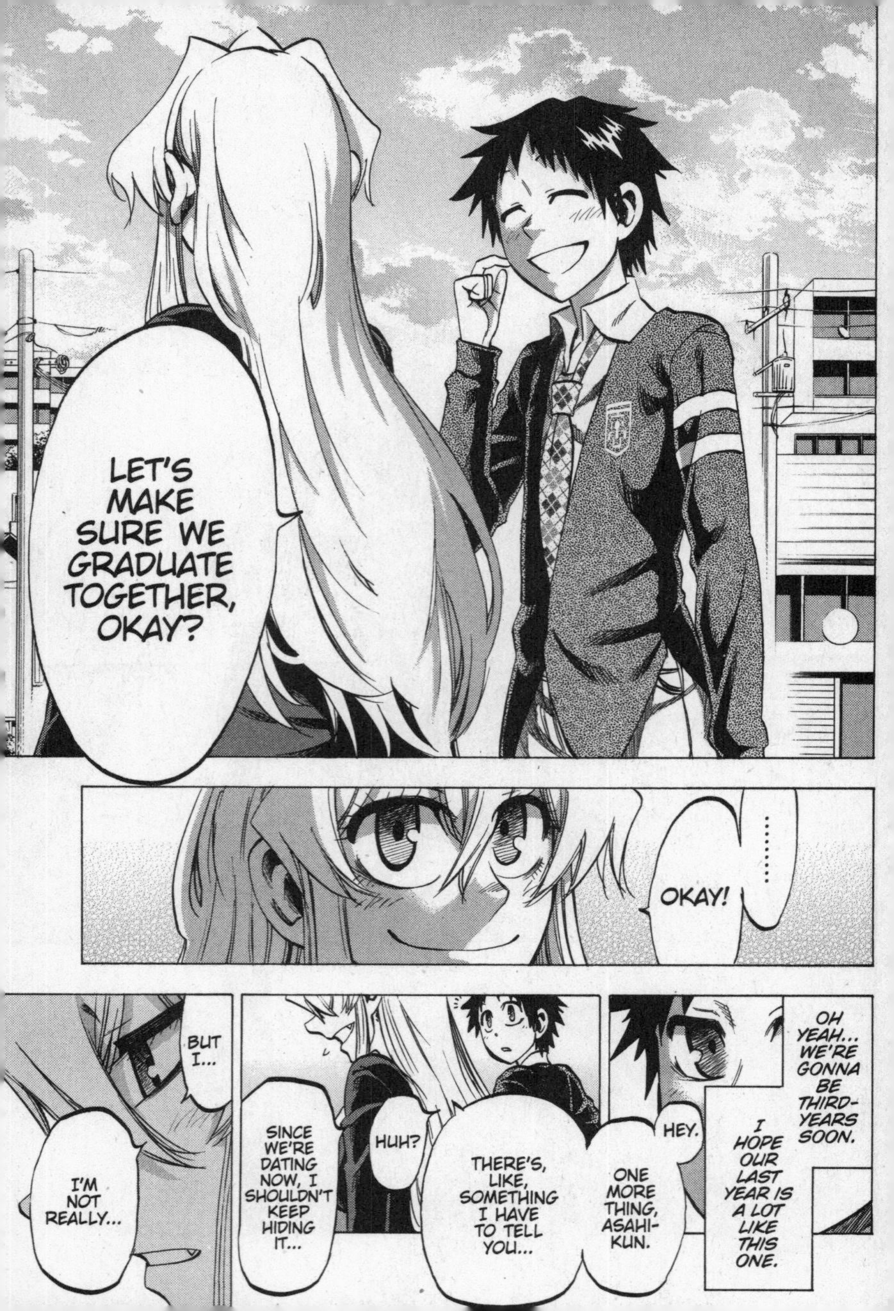
LET'S MAKE SURE WE GRADUATE TOGETHER, OKAY?
......
OKAY!
OH YEAH... WE'RE GONNA BE THIRD-YEARS SOON.
I HOPE OUR LAST YEAR IS A LOT LIKE THIS ONE.
HEY.
ONE MORE THING, ASAHI-KUN.
THERE'S, LIKE, SOMETHING I HAVE TO TELL YOU...
HUH?
SINCE WE'RE DATING NOW, I SHOULDN'T KEEP HIDING IT...
BUT I...
I'M NOT REALLY...

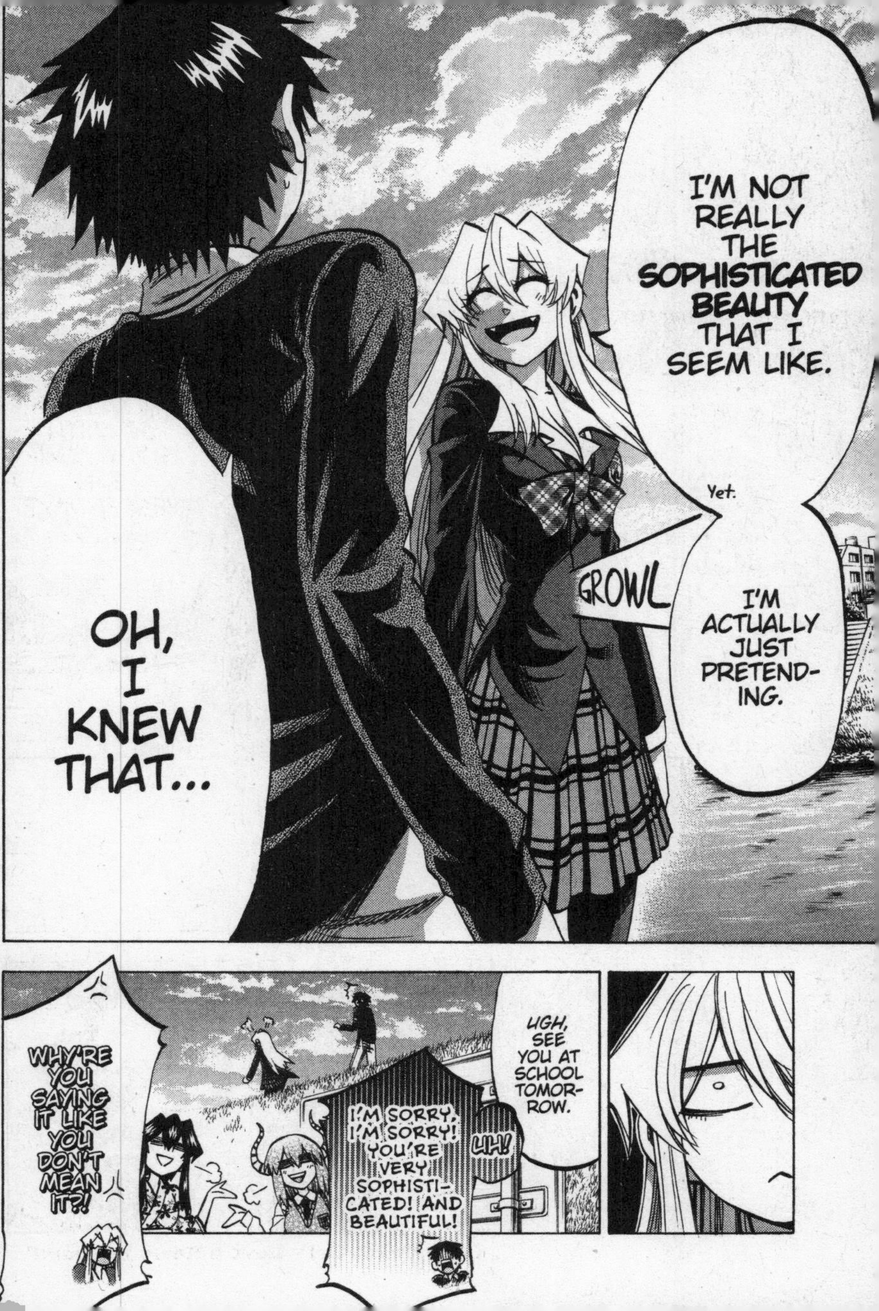
I'M NOT REALLY THE SOPHISTICATED BEAUTY THAT I SEEM LIKE.
Yet.
GROWL
I'M ACTUALLY JUST PRETEND-ING.
OH, I KNEW THAT...
UGH, SEE YOU AT SCHOOL TOMOR-ROW.
UH!
I'M SORRY, I'M SORRY! YOU'RE VERY SOPHISTI-CATED! AND BEAUTIFUL!
WHY'RE YOU SAYING IT LIKE YOU DON'T MEAN IT?!

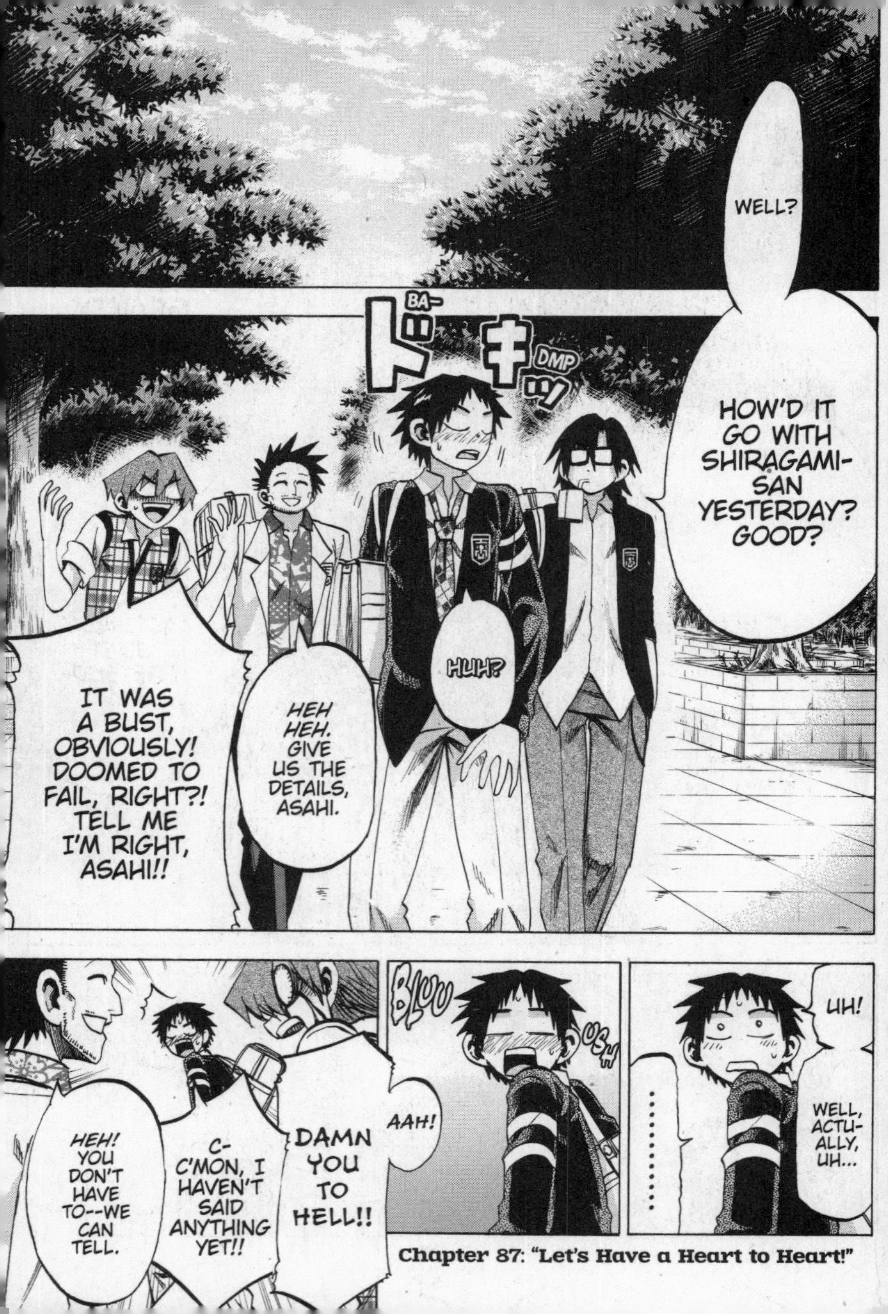
WELL?
HOW'D IT GO WITH SHIRAGAMI-SAN YESTERDAY? GOOD?
BA-
DMP
HUH?
HEH HEH. GIVE US THE DETAILS, ASAHI.
IT WAS A BUST, OBVIOUSLY! DOOMED TO FAIL, RIGHT?! TELL ME I'M RIGHT, ASAHI!!
UH!
WELL, ACTU-ALLY, UH...
......
BLUU
USH
AAH!
DAMN YOU TO HELL!!
C-C'MON, I HAVEN'T SAID ANYTHING YET!!
HEH! YOU DON'T HAVE TO--WE CAN TELL.

Chapter 87: "Let's Have a Heart to Heart!"

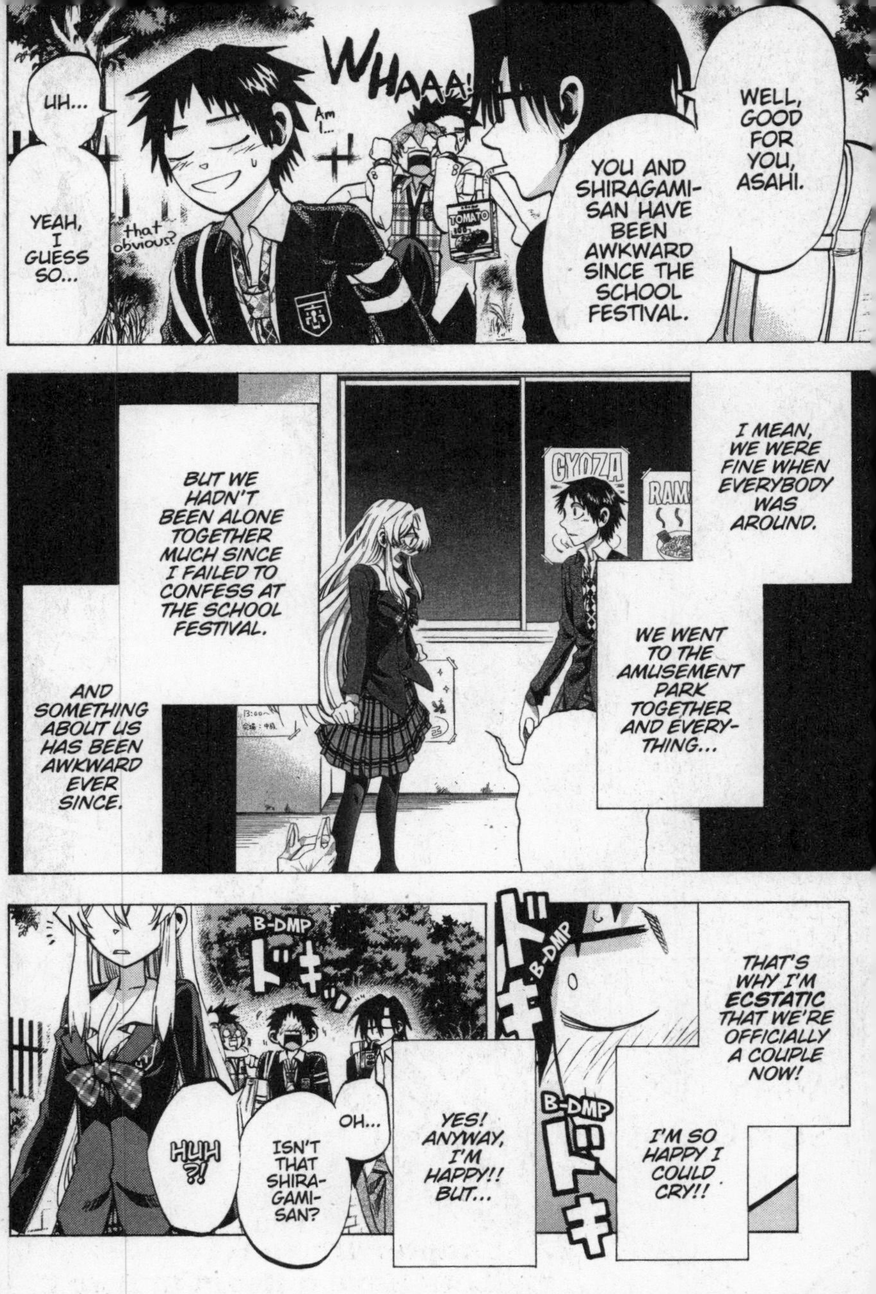
WELL, GOOD FOR YOU, ASAHI.
YOU AND SHIRAGAMI-SAN HAVE BEEN AWKWARD SINCE THE SCHOOL FESTIVAL.
WHAAAA!
Am I... that obvious?
UH...
YEAH, I GUESS SO...
I MEAN, WE WERE FINE WHEN EVERYBODY WAS AROUND.
WE WENT TO THE AMUSEMENT PARK TOGETHER AND EVERY-THING...
GYOZA
RAM
BUT WE HADN'T BEEN ALONE TOGETHER MUCH SINCE I FAILED TO CONFESS AT THE SCHOOL FESTIVAL.
AND SOMETHING ABOUT US HAS BEEN AWKWARD EVER SINCE.
THAT'S WHY I'M ECSTATIC THAT WE'RE OFFICIALLY A COUPLE NOW!
B-DMP
I'M SO HAPPY I COULD CRY!!
B-DMP
YES! ANYWAY, I'M HAPPY!! BUT...
B-DMP
OH...
ISN'T THAT SHIRA-GAMI-SAN?
HUH?!

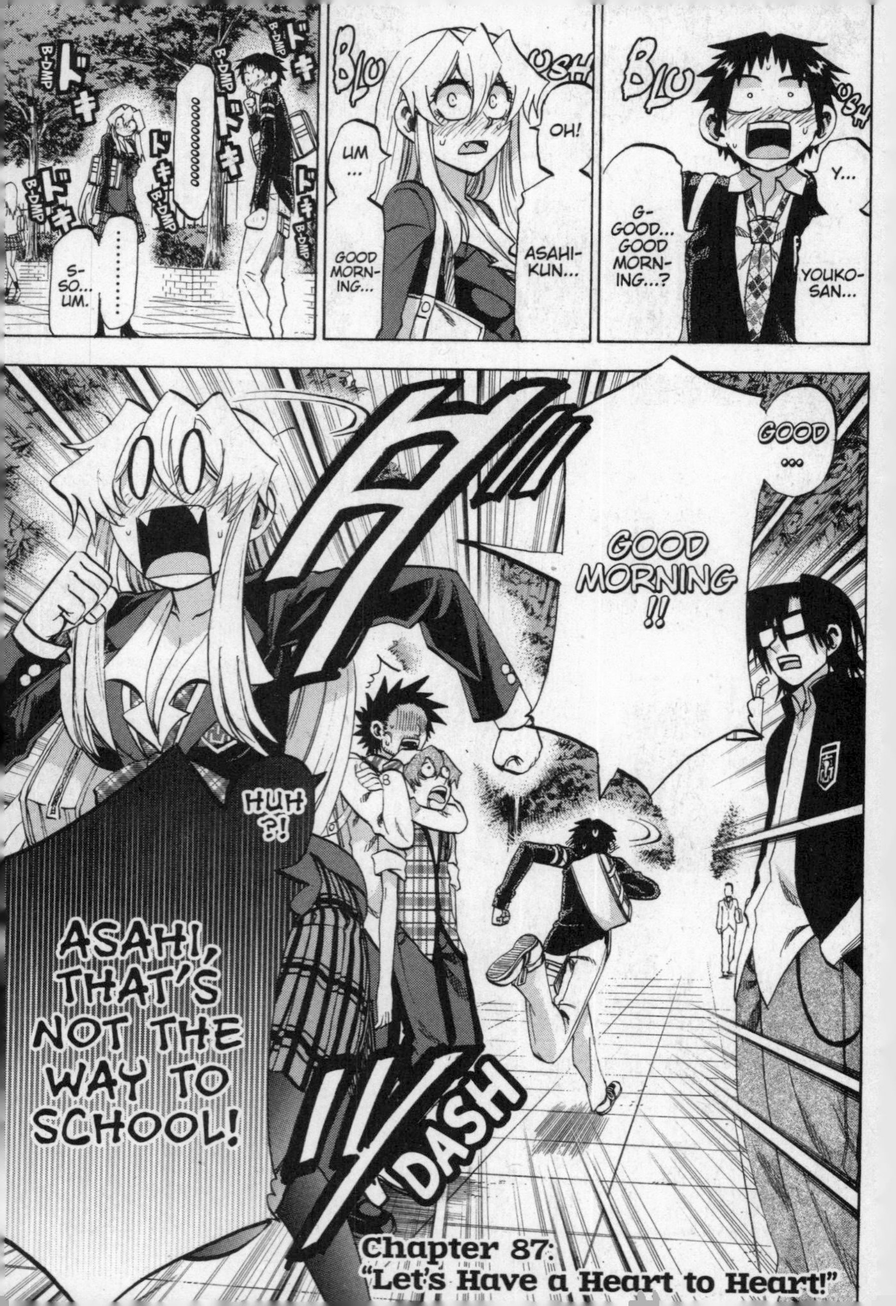
BLU
USH
Y... YOUKO-SAN...
G-GOOD... GOOD MORNING...?
BLU
USH
OH! ASAHI-KUN...
UM ... GOOD MORNING...
ドキ
B-DMP
ドキ
B-DMP
ドキ
B-DMP
ドキ
B-DMP
ドキ
B-DMP
oooooooooo
S-SO... UM.
....
GOOD ...
GOOD MORNING !!
HUH ?!
DASH
ASAHI, THAT'S NOT THE WAY TO SCHOOL!

Chapter 87: "Let's Have a Heart to Heart!"

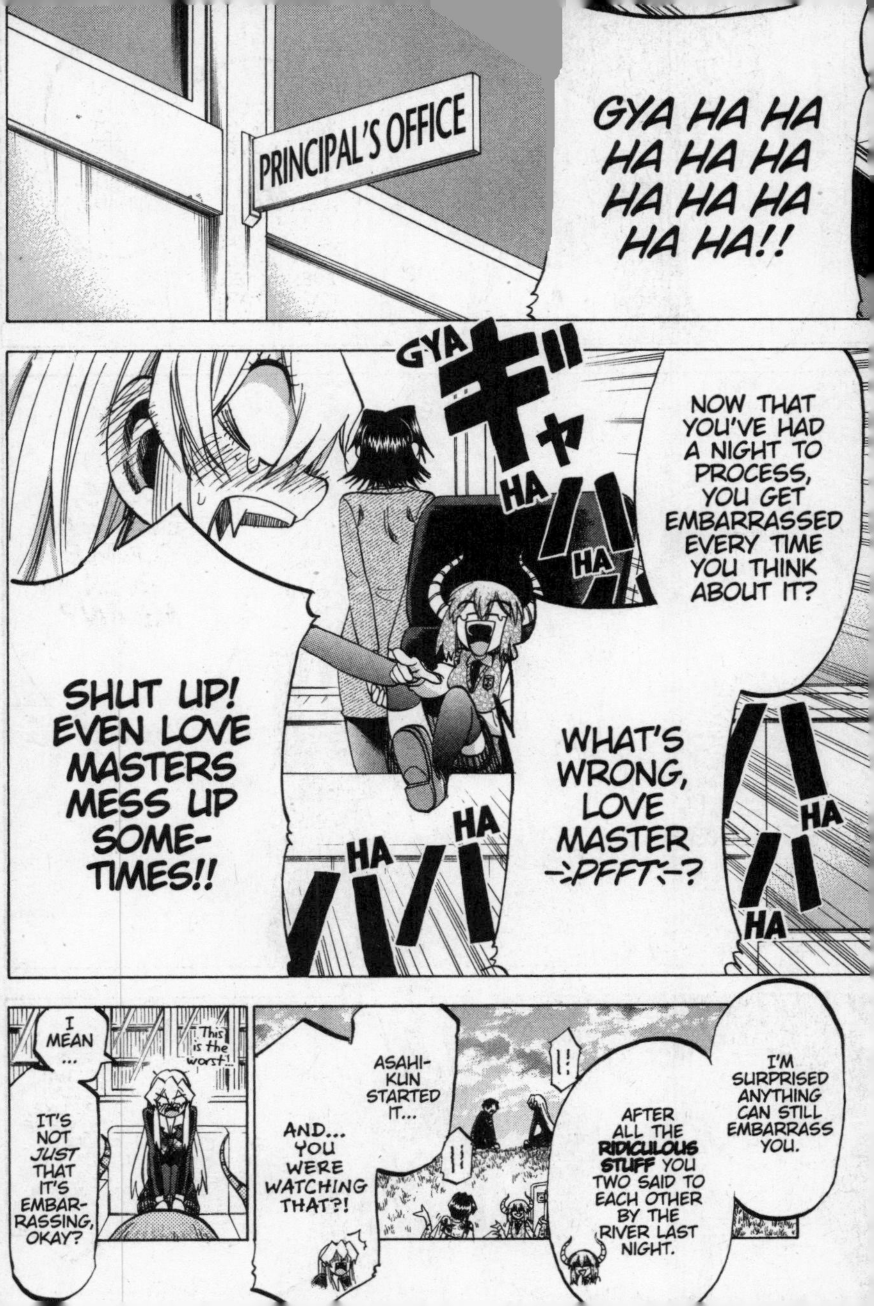

GYA HA HA HA HA HA HA HA HA HA HA!!
PRINCIPAL'S OFFICE
GYA
ギャ
NOW THAT YOU'VE HAD A NIGHT TO PROCESS, YOU GET EMBARRASSED EVERY TIME YOU THINK ABOUT IT?
HA HA
WHAT'S WRONG, LOVE MASTER -PFFT-?
HA HA
SHUT UP! EVEN LOVE MASTERS MESS UP SOME-TIMES!!
HA HA
I'M SURPRISED ANYTHING CAN STILL EMBARRASS YOU.
AFTER ALL THE RIDICULOUS STUFF YOU TWO SAID TO EACH OTHER BY THE RIVER LAST NIGHT.
!!
ASAHI-KUN STARTED IT...
AND... YOU WERE WATCHING THAT?!
!!
This is the worst...
I MEAN ...
IT'S NOT JUST THAT IT'S EMBAR-RASSING, OKAY?

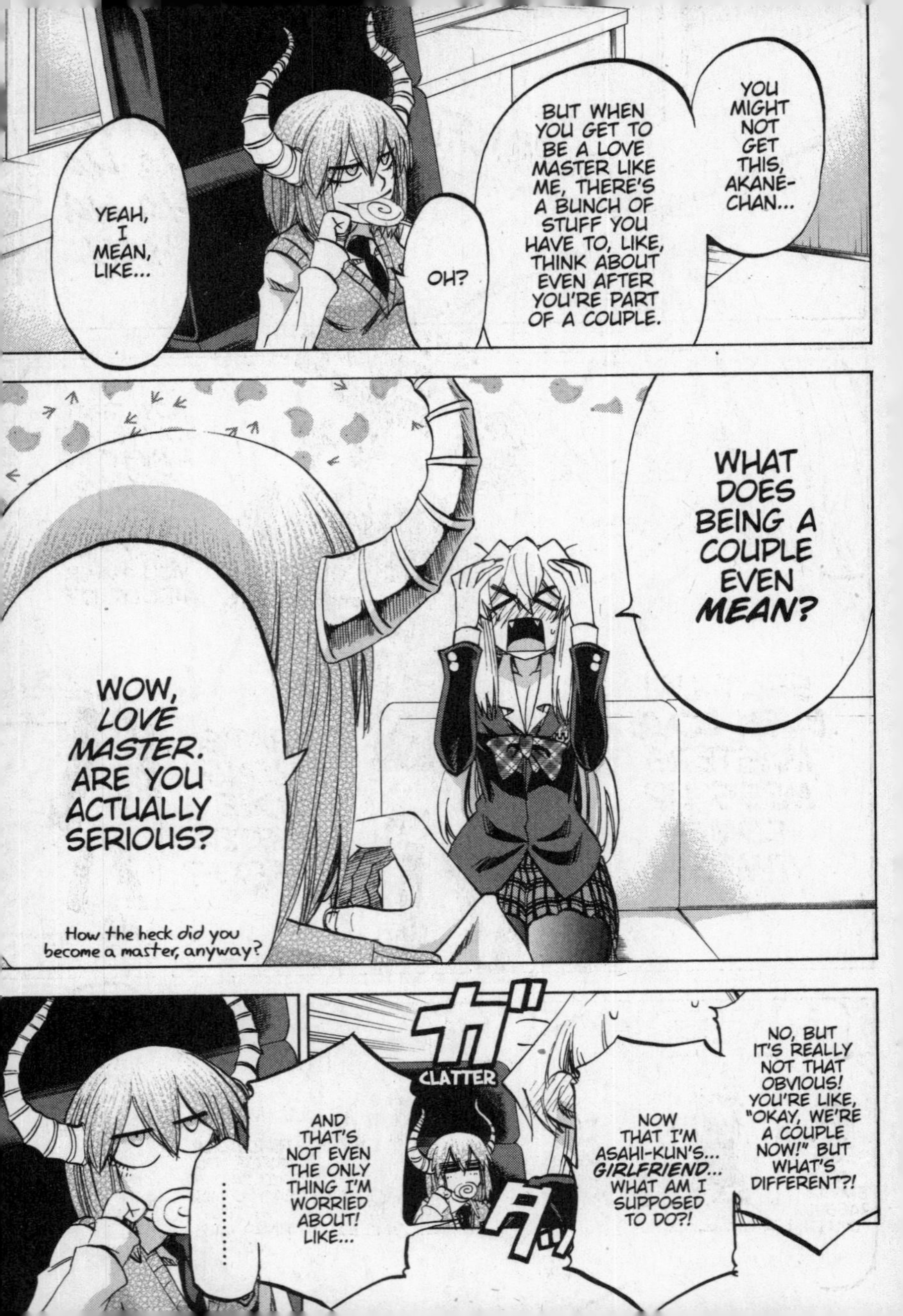
YOU MIGHT NOT GET THIS, AKANE-CHAN...
BUT WHEN YOU GET TO BE A LOVE MASTER LIKE ME, THERE'S A BUNCH OF STUFF YOU HAVE TO, LIKE, THINK ABOUT EVEN AFTER YOU'RE PART OF A COUPLE.
OH?
YEAH, I MEAN, LIKE...
WHAT DOES BEING A COUPLE EVEN MEAN?
WOW, LOVE MASTER. ARE YOU ACTUALLY SERIOUS?
How the heck did you become a master, anyway?
NO, BUT IT'S REALLY NOT THAT OBVIOUS! YOU'RE LIKE, "OKAY, WE'RE A COUPLE NOW!" BUT WHAT'S DIFFERENT?!
NOW THAT I'M ASAHI-KUN'S... GIRLFRIEND... WHAT AM I SUPPOSED TO DO?!
CLATTER
AND THAT'S NOT EVEN THE ONLY THING I'M WORRIED ABOUT! LIKE...
......

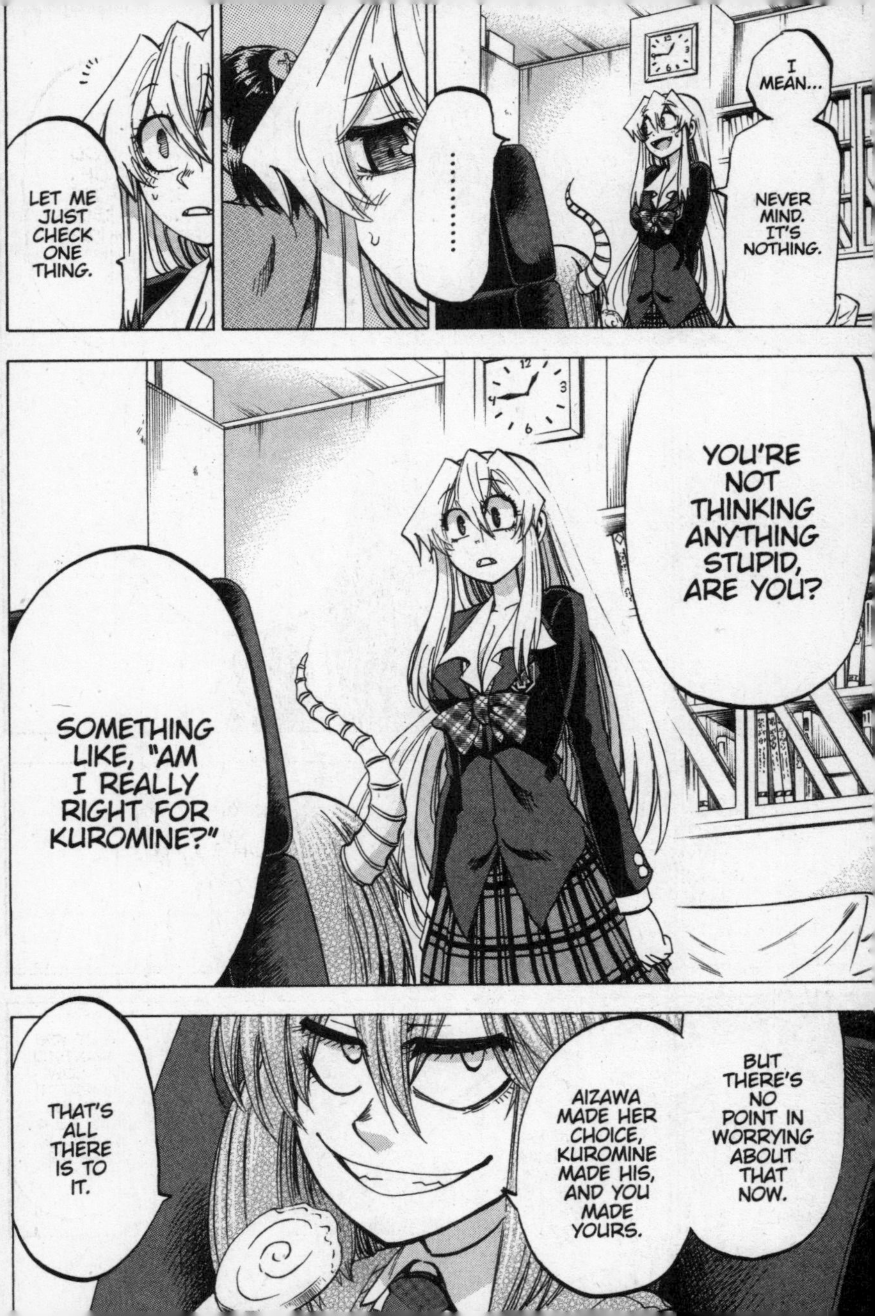
I MEAN...
NEVER MIND. IT'S NOTHING.
......
LET ME JUST CHECK ONE THING.
YOU'RE NOT THINKING ANYTHING STUPID, ARE YOU?
SOMETHING LIKE, "AM I REALLY RIGHT FOR KUROMINE?"
BUT THERE'S NO POINT IN WORRYING ABOUT THAT NOW.
AIZAWA MADE HER CHOICE, KUROMINE MADE HIS, AND YOU MADE YOURS.
THAT'S ALL THERE IS TO IT.

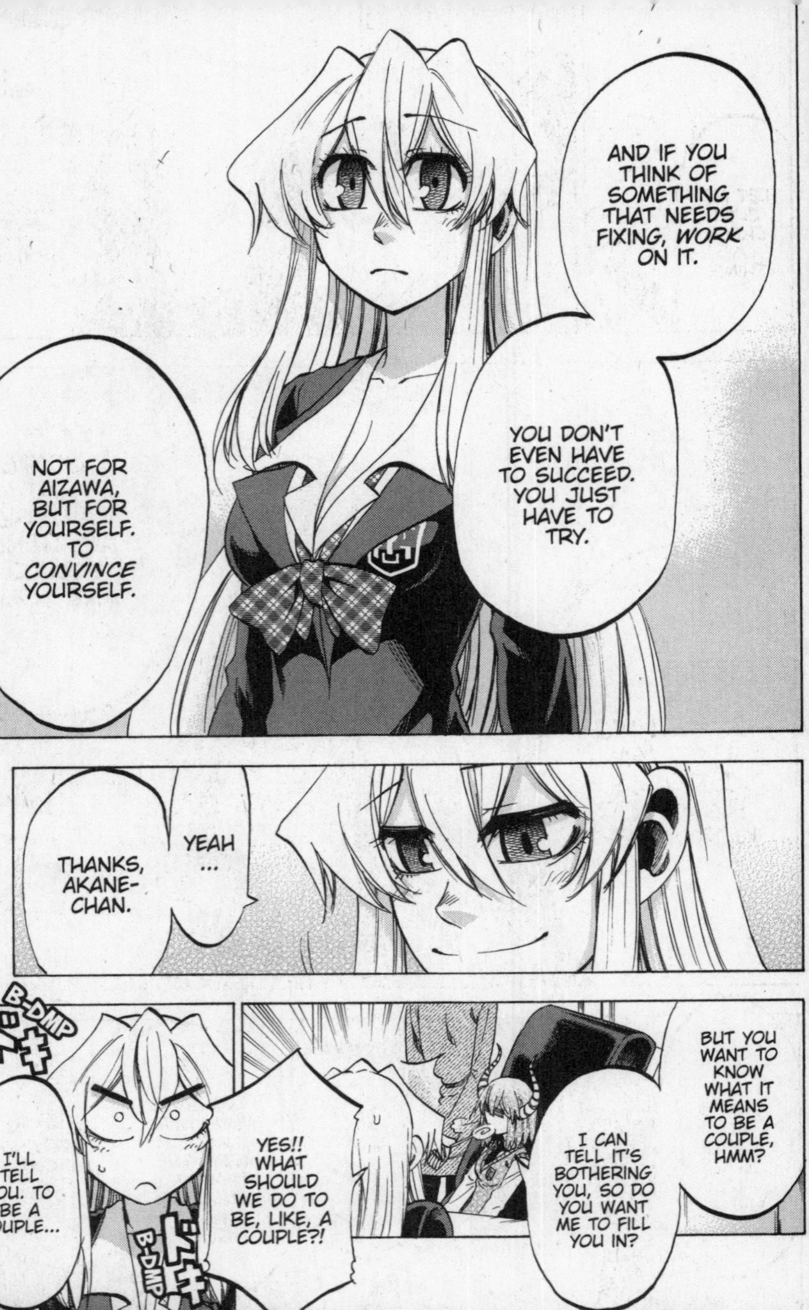
AND IF YOU THINK OF SOMETHING THAT NEEDS FIXING, *WORK* ON IT.
YOU DON'T EVEN HAVE TO SUCCEED. YOU JUST HAVE TO TRY.
NOT FOR AIZAWA, BUT FOR YOURSELF. TO *CONVINCE* YOURSELF.
YEAH ...
THANKS, AKANE-CHAN.
BUT YOU WANT TO KNOW WHAT IT MEANS TO BE A COUPLE, HMM?
I CAN TELL IT'S BOTHERING YOU, SO DO YOU WANT ME TO FILL YOU IN?
B-DMP
YES!! WHAT SHOULD WE DO TO BE, LIKE, A COUPLE?!
I'LL TELL YOU. TO BE A COUPLE...
B-DMP

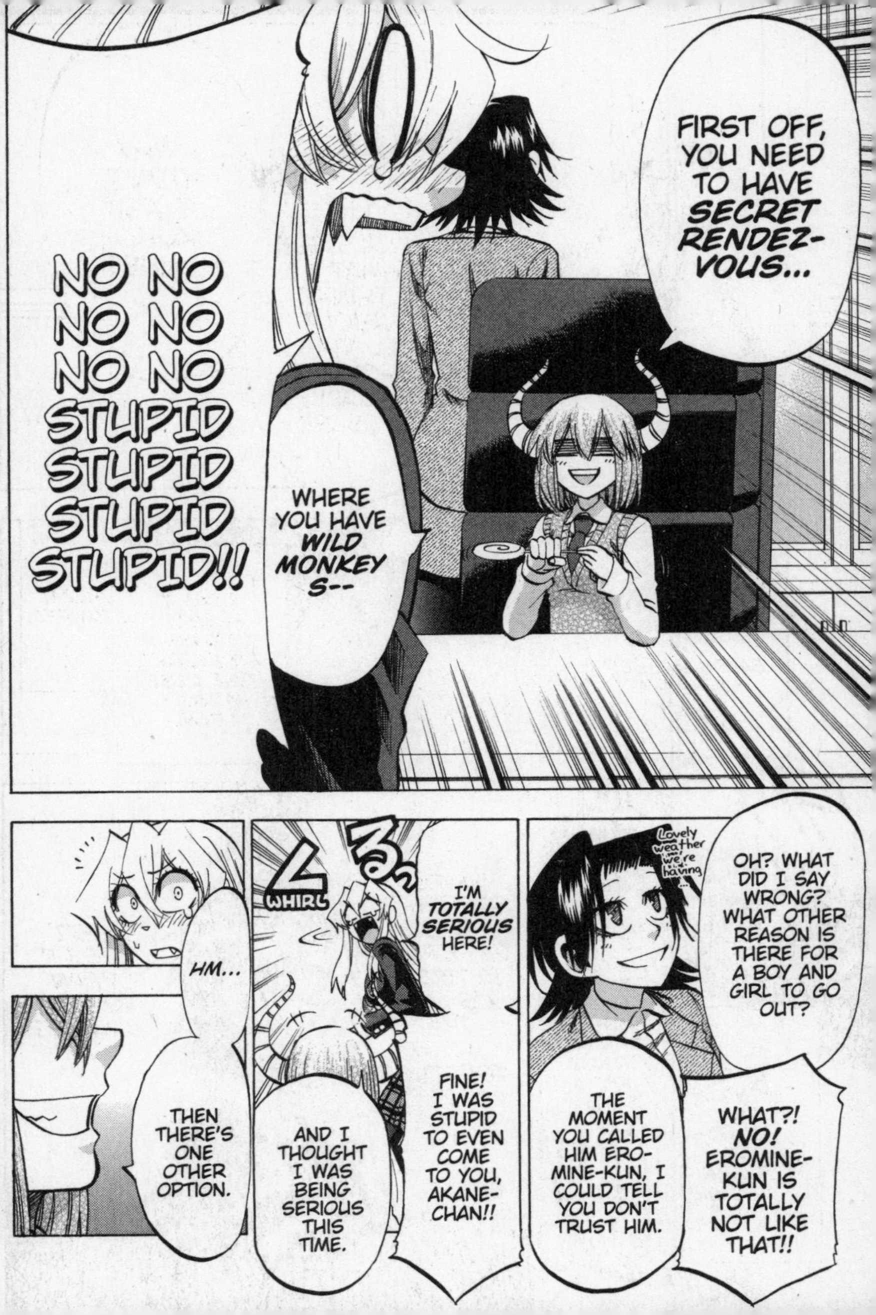
FIRST OFF, YOU NEED TO HAVE SECRET RENDEZ-VOUS...
WHERE YOU HAVE WILD MONKEY S--
NO NO NO NO NO NO STUPID STUPID STUPID STUPID!!
OH? WHAT DID I SAY WRONG? WHAT OTHER REASON IS THERE FOR A BOY AND GIRL TO GO OUT?
Lovely weather we're having...
WHAT?! NO! EROMINE-KUN IS TOTALLY NOT LIKE THAT!!
THE MOMENT YOU CALLED HIM ERO-MINE-KUN, I COULD TELL YOU DON'T TRUST HIM.
WHIRL
I'M TOTALLY SERIOUS HERE!
FINE! I WAS STUPID TO EVEN COME TO YOU, AKANE-CHAN!!
AND I THOUGHT I WAS BEING SERIOUS THIS TIME.
HM...
THEN THERE'S ONE OTHER OPTION.

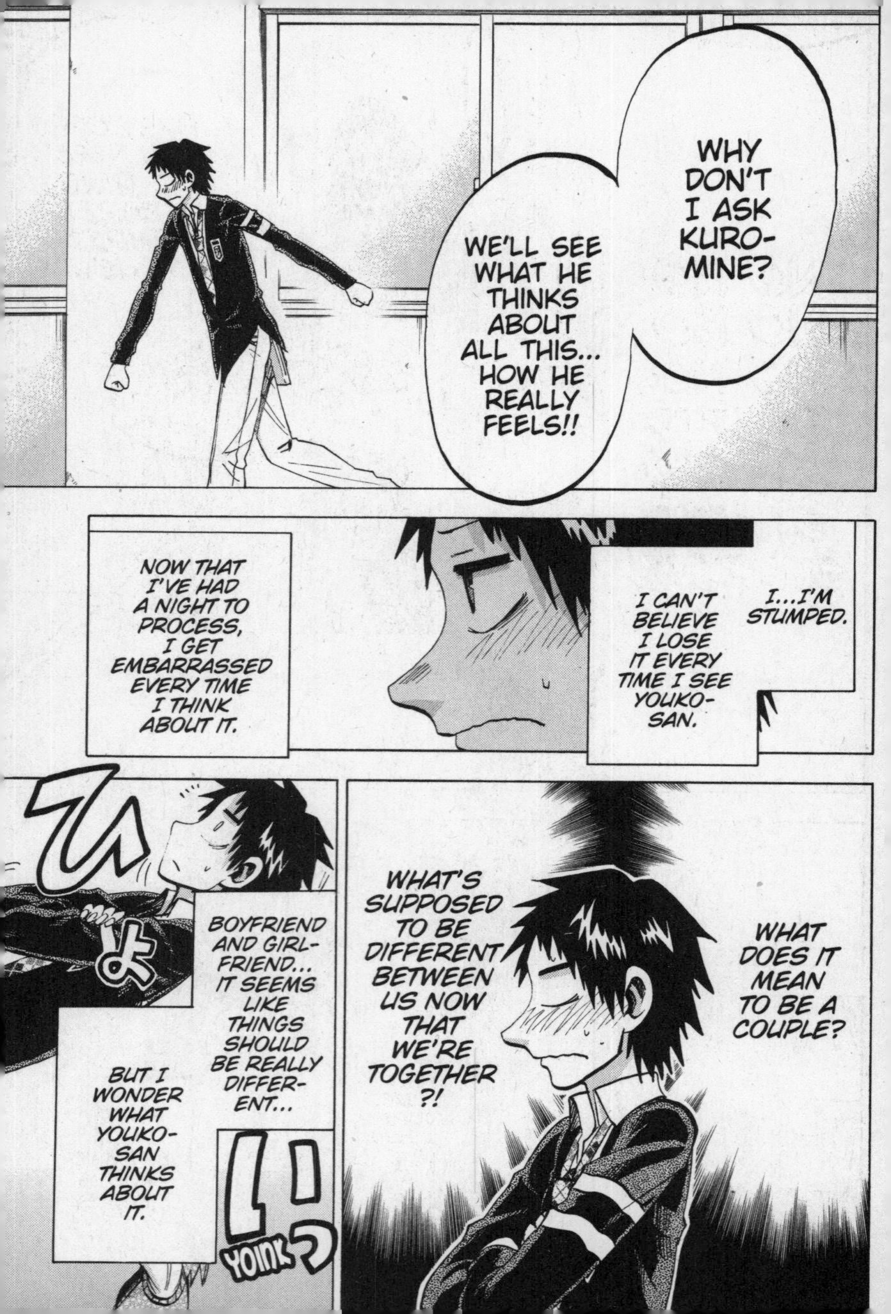
WHY DON'T I ASK KURO-MINE?
WE'LL SEE WHAT HE THINKS ABOUT ALL THIS... HOW HE REALLY FEELS!!
I...I'M STUMPED.
I CAN'T BELIEVE I LOSE IT EVERY TIME I SEE YOUKO-SAN.
NOW THAT I'VE HAD A NIGHT TO PROCESS, I GET EMBARRASSED EVERY TIME I THINK ABOUT IT.
WHAT DOES IT MEAN TO BE A COUPLE?
WHAT'S SUPPOSED TO BE DIFFERENT BETWEEN US NOW THAT WE'RE TOGETHER?!
ひょいっ
YOINK
BOYFRIEND AND GIRL-FRIEND... IT SEEMS LIKE THINGS SHOULD BE REALLY DIFFER-ENT...
BUT I WONDER WHAT YOUKO-SAN THINKS ABOUT IT.

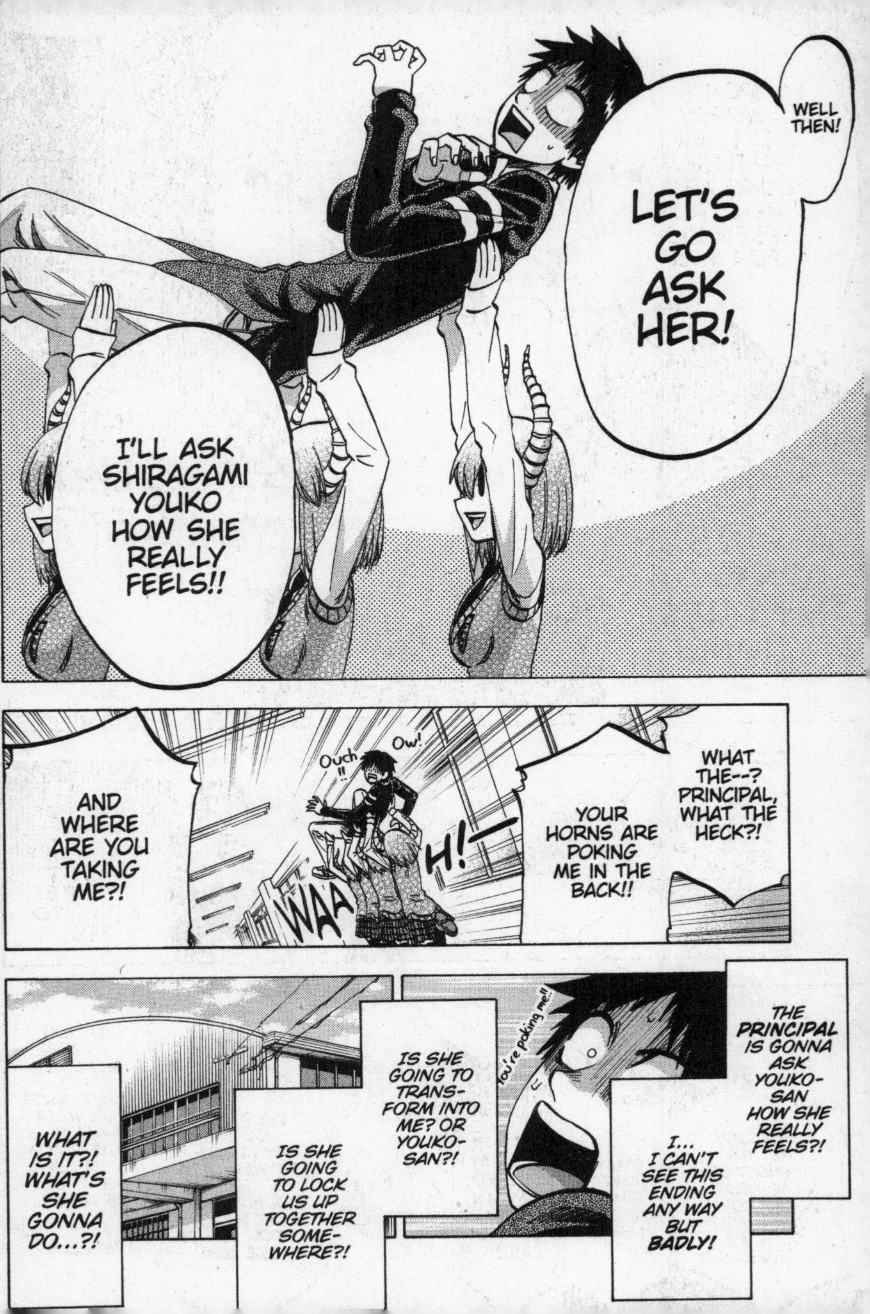
WELL THEN!
LET'S GO ASK HER!
I'LL ASK SHIRAGAMI YOUKO HOW SHE REALLY FEELS!!
WHAT THE--? PRINCIPAL, WHAT THE HECK?!
YOUR HORNS ARE POKING ME IN THE BACK!!
Ow!
Ouch!!
WAAH!—
AND WHERE ARE YOU TAKING ME?!
THE PRINCIPAL IS GONNA ASK YOUKO-SAN HOW SHE REALLY FEELS?!
I... I CAN'T SEE THIS ENDING ANY WAY BUT BADLY!
You're poking me!!
IS SHE GOING TO TRANSFORM INTO ME? OR YOUKO-SAN?!
IS SHE GOING TO LOCK US UP TOGETHER SOMEWHERE?!
WHAT IS IT?! WHAT'S SHE GONNA DO...?!

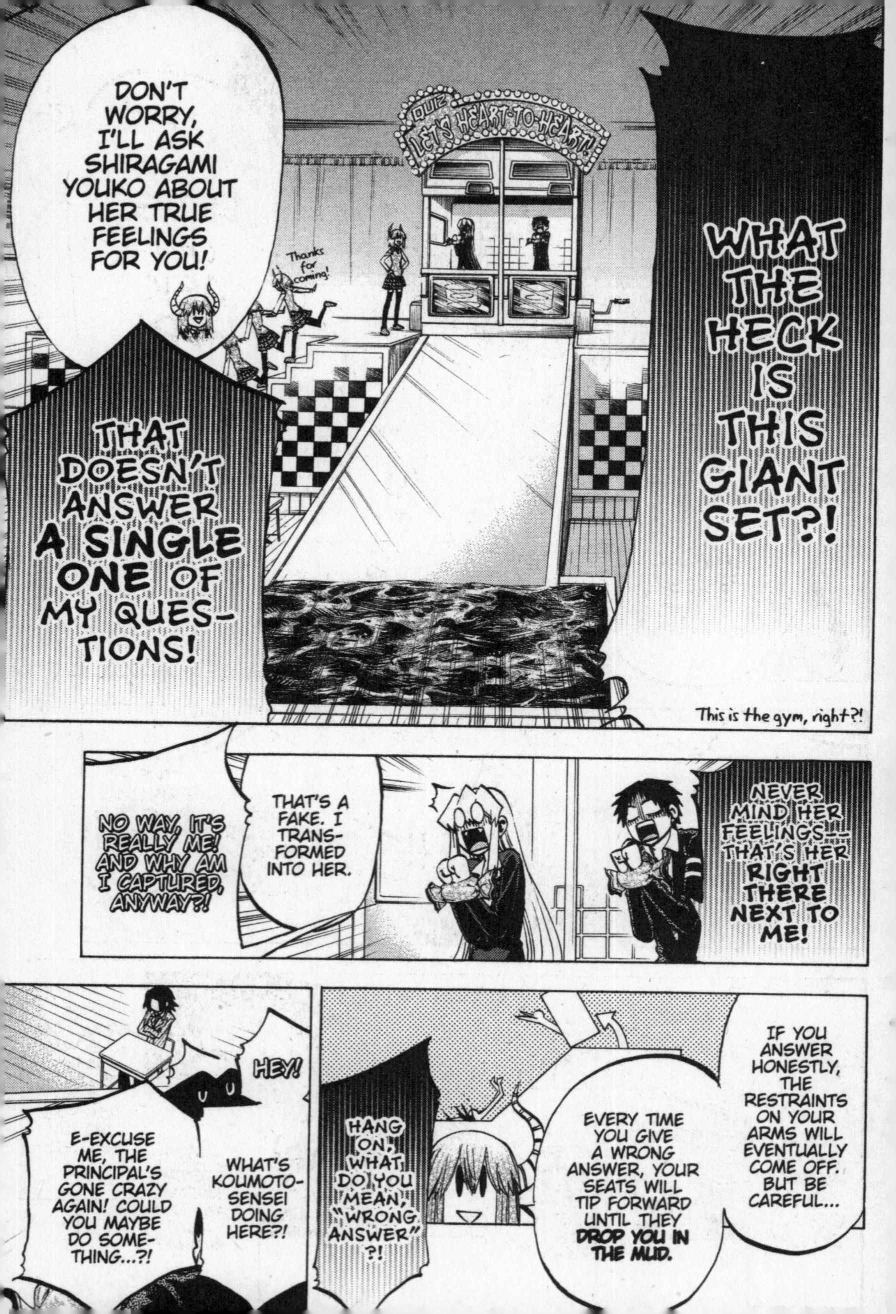
WHAT THE HECK IS THIS GIANT SET?!
QUIZ LET'S HEART-TO-HEART!
DON'T WORRY, I'LL ASK SHIRAGAMI YOUKO ABOUT HER TRUE FEELINGS FOR YOU!
Thanks for coming!
THAT DOESN'T ANSWER A SINGLE ONE OF MY QUES-TIONS!
This is the gym, right?!
NEVER MIND HER FEELINGS-- THAT'S HER RIGHT THERE NEXT TO ME!
THAT'S A FAKE. I TRANS-FORMED INTO HER.
NO WAY, IT'S REALLY ME! AND WHY AM I CAPTURED, ANYWAY?!
IF YOU ANSWER HONESTLY, THE RESTRAINTS ON YOUR ARMS WILL EVENTUALLY COME OFF. BUT BE CAREFUL...
EVERY TIME YOU GIVE A WRONG ANSWER, YOUR SEATS WILL TIP FORWARD UNTIL THEY DROP YOU IN THE MUD.
HANG ON, WHAT DO YOU MEAN, "WRONG ANSWER"?!
HEY!
WHAT'S KOUMOTO-SENSEI DOING HERE?!
E-EXCUSE ME, THE PRINCIPAL'S GONE CRAZY AGAIN! COULD YOU MAYBE DO SOME-THING...?!

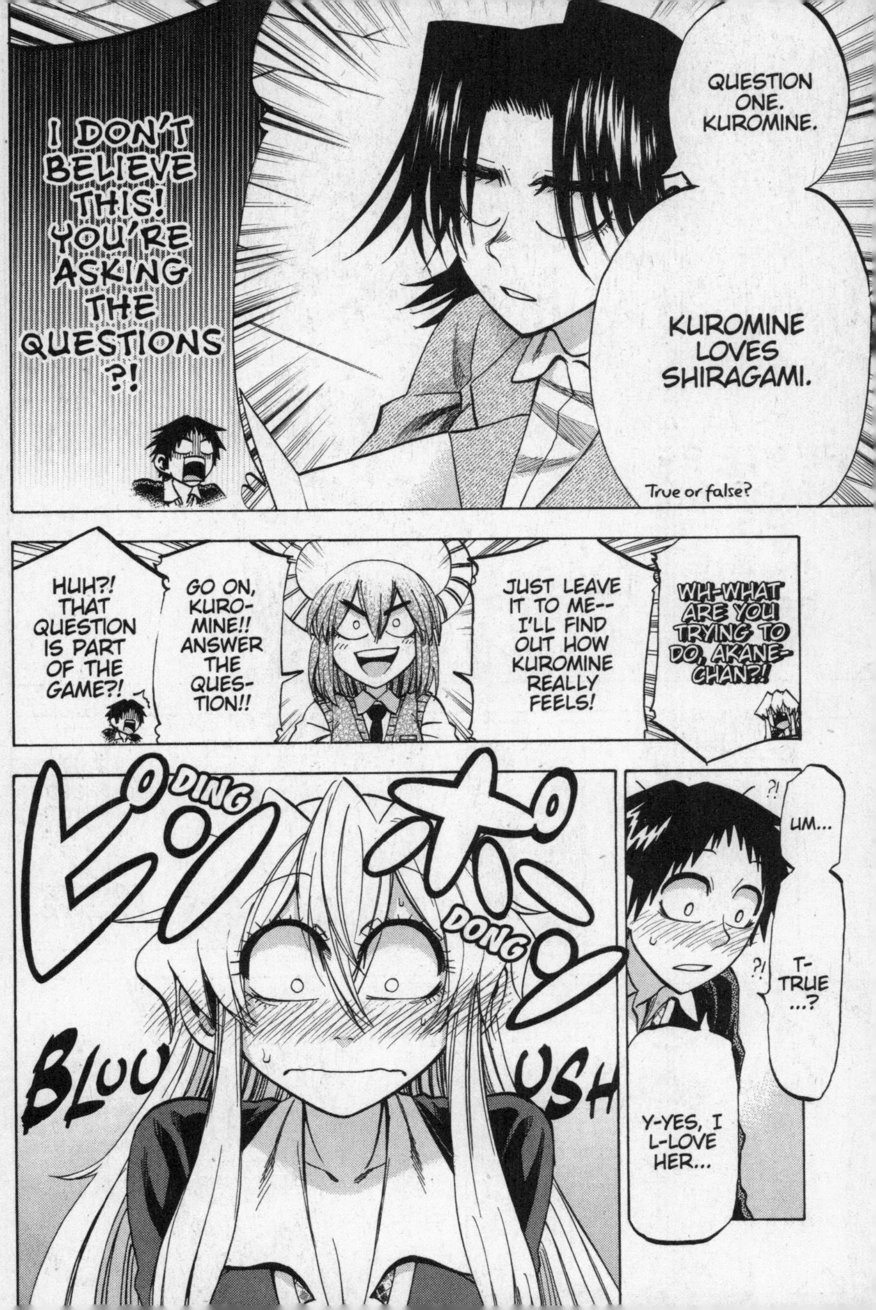
QUESTION ONE. KUROMINE.
KUROMINE LOVES SHIRAGAMI.
True or false?
I DON'T BELIEVE THIS! YOU'RE ASKING THE QUESTIONS?!
WH-WHAT ARE YOU TRYING TO DO, AKANE-CHAN?!
JUST LEAVE IT TO ME-- I'LL FIND OUT HOW KUROMINE REALLY FEELS!
GO ON, KURO-MINE!! ANSWER THE QUES-TION!!
HUH?! THAT QUESTION IS PART OF THE GAME?!
?!
UM...
?!
T-TRUE ...?
Y-YES, I L-LOVE HER...
DING
DONG
BLUU USH

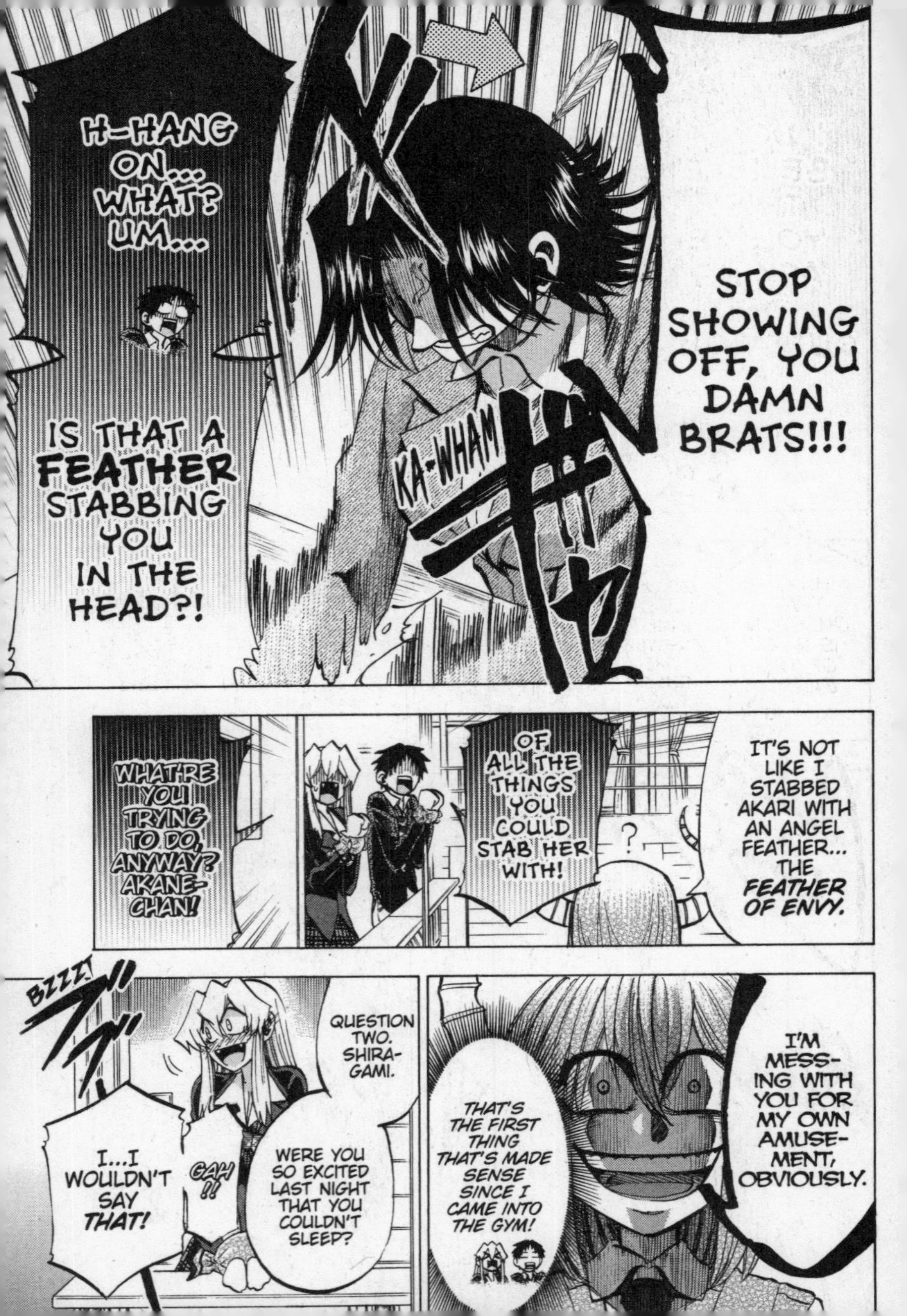
STOP SHOWING OFF, YOU DAMN BRATS!!!
KA-WHAM
H-HANG ON... WHAT? UM...
IS THAT A **FEATHER** STABBING YOU IN THE HEAD?!
IT'S NOT LIKE I STABBED AKARI WITH AN ANGEL FEATHER... THE *FEATHER OF ENVY.*
?
OF ALL THE THINGS YOU COULD STAB HER WITH!
WHAT'RE YOU TRYING TO DO, ANYWAY? AKANE-CHAN!
I'M MESSING WITH YOU FOR MY OWN AMUSEMENT, OBVIOUSLY.
THAT'S THE FIRST THING THAT'S MADE SENSE SINCE I CAME INTO THE GYM!
QUESTION TWO. SHIRAGAMI.
WERE YOU SO EXCITED LAST NIGHT THAT YOU COULDN'T SLEEP?
BZZZT
GAH!!
I...I WOULDN'T SAY *THAT*!

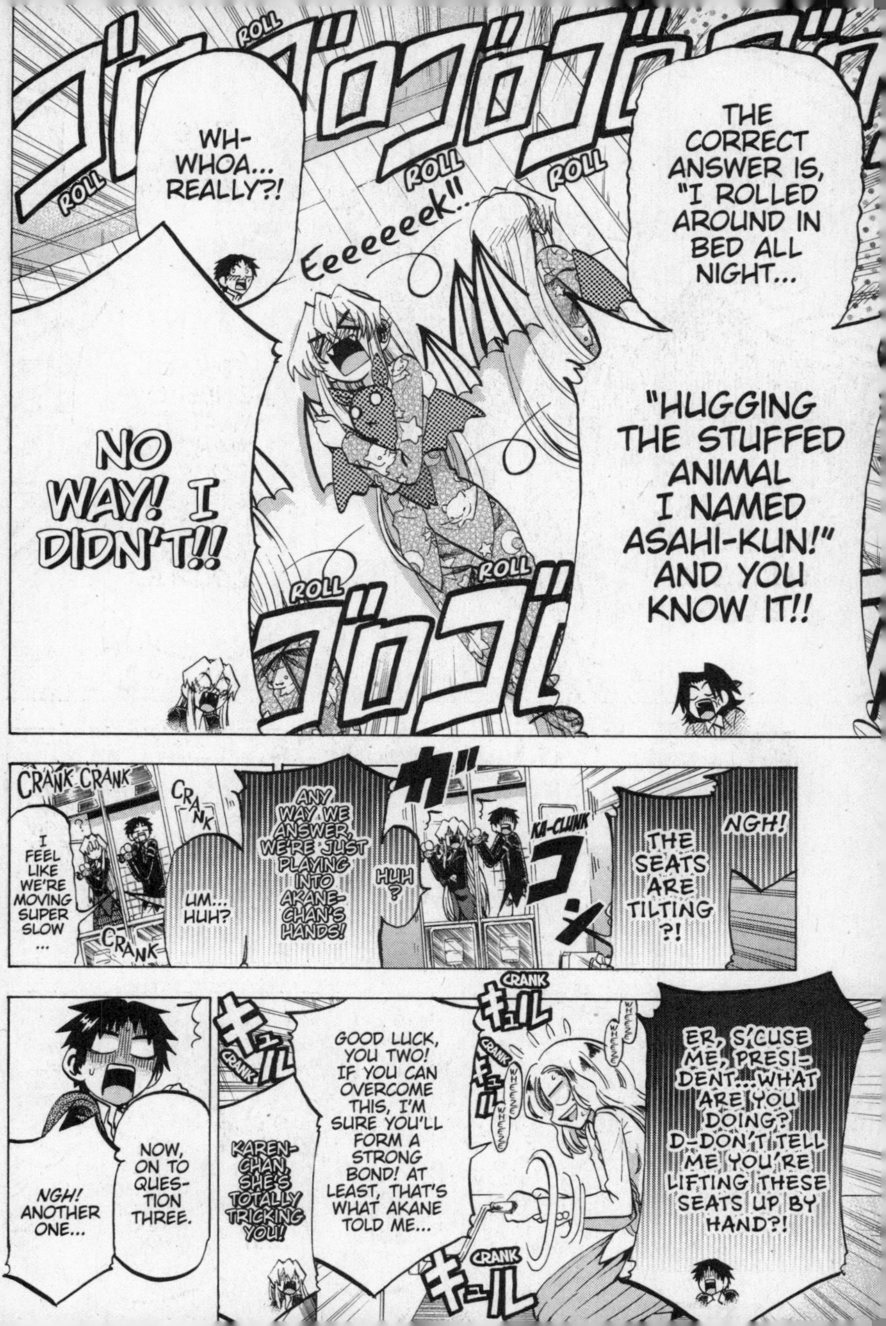
ROLL
ROLL
ROLL
ROLL
THE CORRECT ANSWER IS, "I ROLLED AROUND IN BED ALL NIGHT...
"HUGGING THE STUFFED ANIMAL I NAMED ASAHI-KUN!" AND YOU KNOW IT!!
Eeeeeeek!!...
WH-WHOA... REALLY?!
ROLL
ROLL
NO WAY! I DIDN'T!!
NGH!
THE SEATS ARE TILTING?!
KA-CLUNK
ANY WAY WE ANSWER, WE'RE JUST PLAYING INTO AKANE-CHAN'S HANDS!
HUH?
CRANK CRANK
CRANK
I FEEL LIKE WE'RE MOVING SUPER SLOW...
UM... HUH?
CRANK
ER, S'CUSE ME, PRESI-DENT... WHAT ARE YOU DOING? D-DON'T TELL ME YOU'RE LIFTING THESE SEATS UP BY HAND?!
WHEEZE
WHEEZE
WHEEZE
WHEEZE
CRANK
CRANK
GOOD LUCK, YOU TWO! IF YOU CAN OVERCOME THIS, I'M SURE YOU'LL FORM A STRONG BOND! AT LEAST, THAT'S WHAT AKANE TOLD ME...
CRANK
KAREN-CHAN, SHE'S TOTALLY TRICKING YOU!
CRANK
NOW, ON TO QUES-TION THREE.
NGH! ANOTHER ONE...

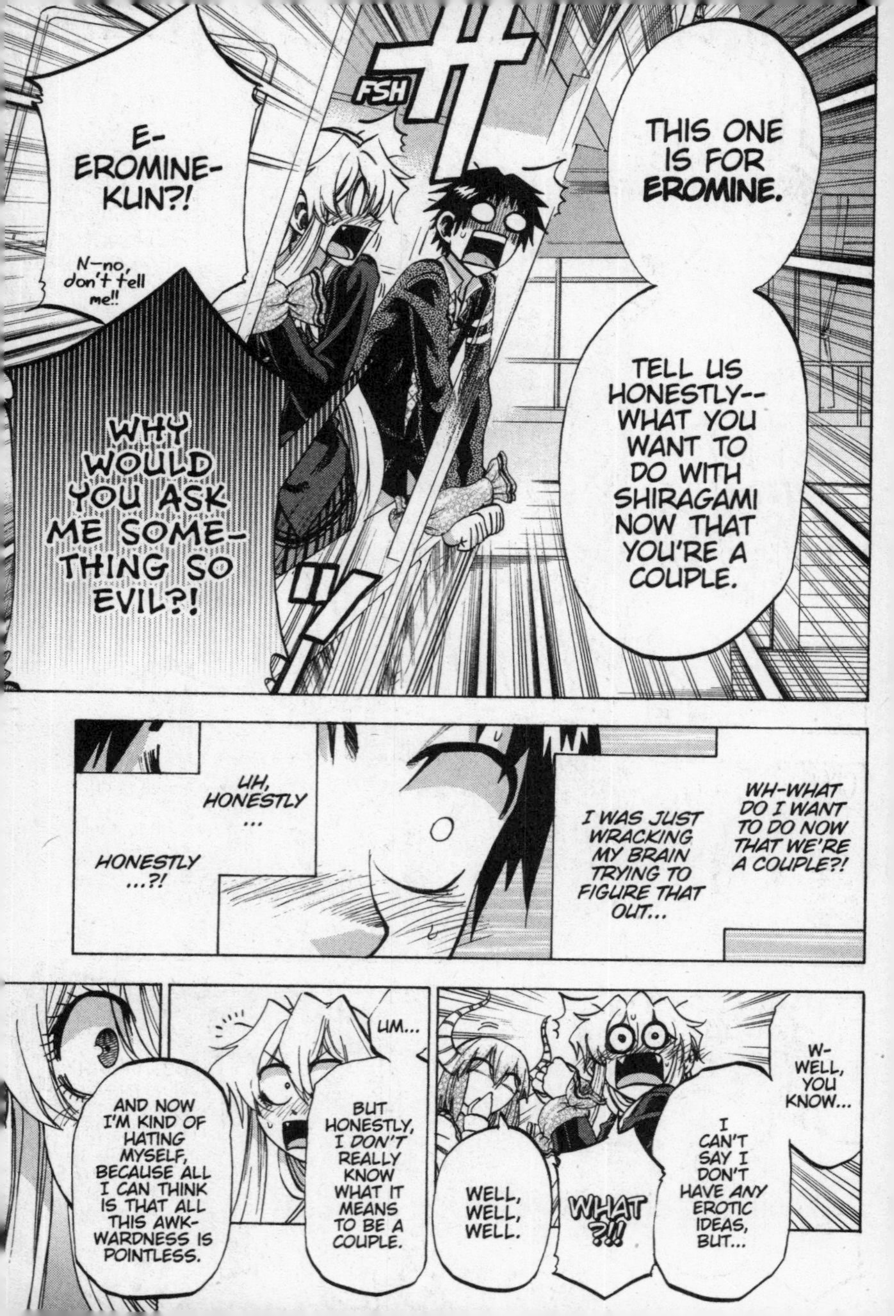
FSH
THIS ONE IS FOR EROMINE.
TELL US HONESTLY-- WHAT YOU WANT TO DO WITH SHIRAGAMI NOW THAT YOU'RE A COUPLE.
E-EROMINE-KUN?!
N-no, don't tell me!!
WHY WOULD YOU ASK ME SOME-THING SO EVIL?!
WH-WHAT DO I WANT TO DO NOW THAT WE'RE A COUPLE?!
I WAS JUST WRACKING MY BRAIN TRYING TO FIGURE THAT OUT...
UH, HONESTLY ...
HONESTLY ...?!
W-WELL, YOU KNOW...
I CAN'T SAY I DON'T HAVE ANY EROTIC IDEAS, BUT...
WHAT ?!!
WELL, WELL, WELL.
UM...
BUT HONESTLY, I DON'T REALLY KNOW WHAT IT MEANS TO BE A COUPLE.
AND NOW I'M KIND OF HATING MYSELF, BECAUSE ALL I CAN THINK IS THAT ALL THIS AWK-WARDNESS IS POINTLESS.

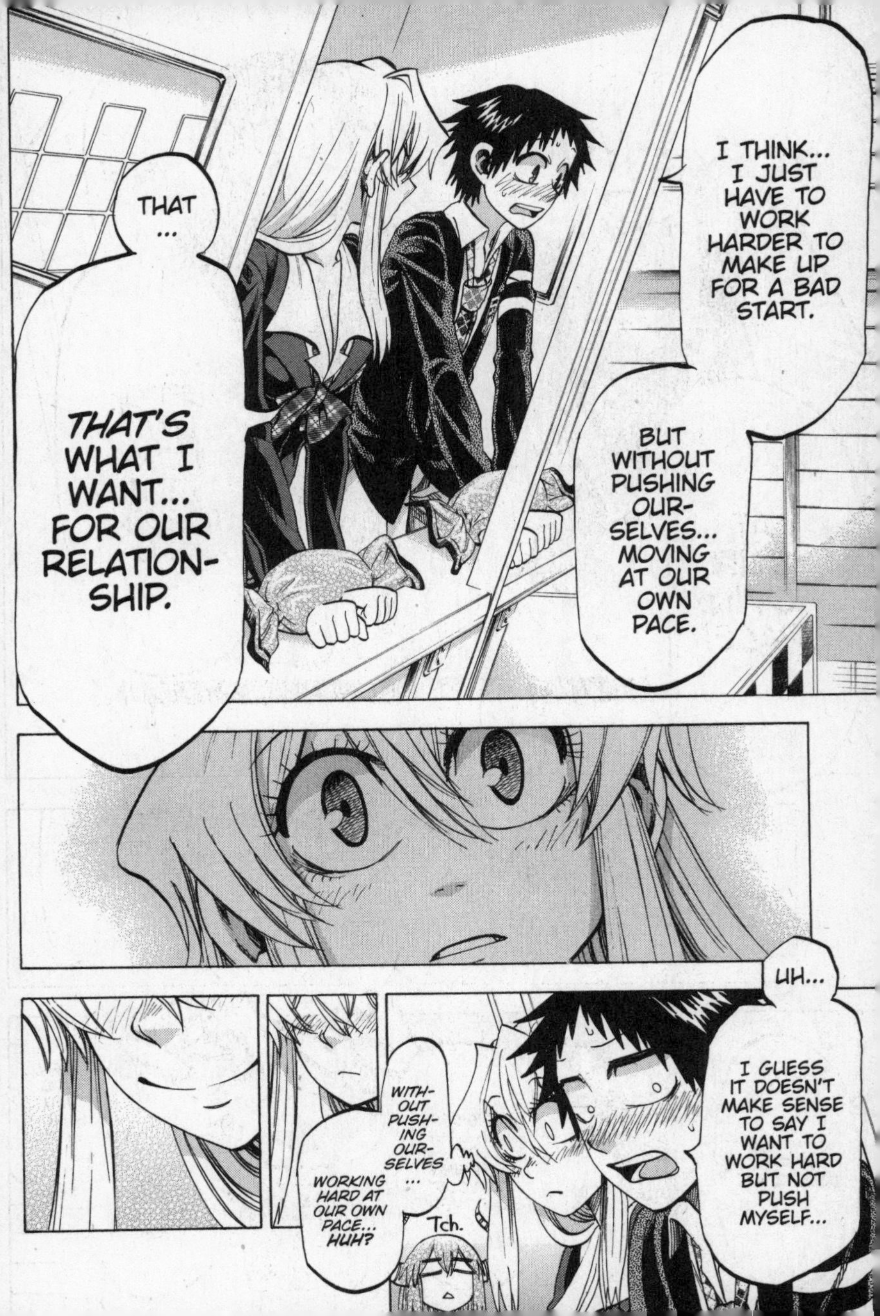
I THINK... I JUST HAVE TO WORK HARDER TO MAKE UP FOR A BAD START.
BUT WITHOUT PUSHING OURSELVES... MOVING AT OUR OWN PACE.
THAT ...
THAT'S WHAT I WANT... FOR OUR RELATIONSHIP.
UH...
I GUESS IT DOESN'T MAKE SENSE TO SAY I WANT TO WORK HARD BUT NOT PUSH MYSELF...
WITHOUT PUSHING OURSELVES ...
WORKING HARD AT OUR OWN PACE... HUH?
Tch.

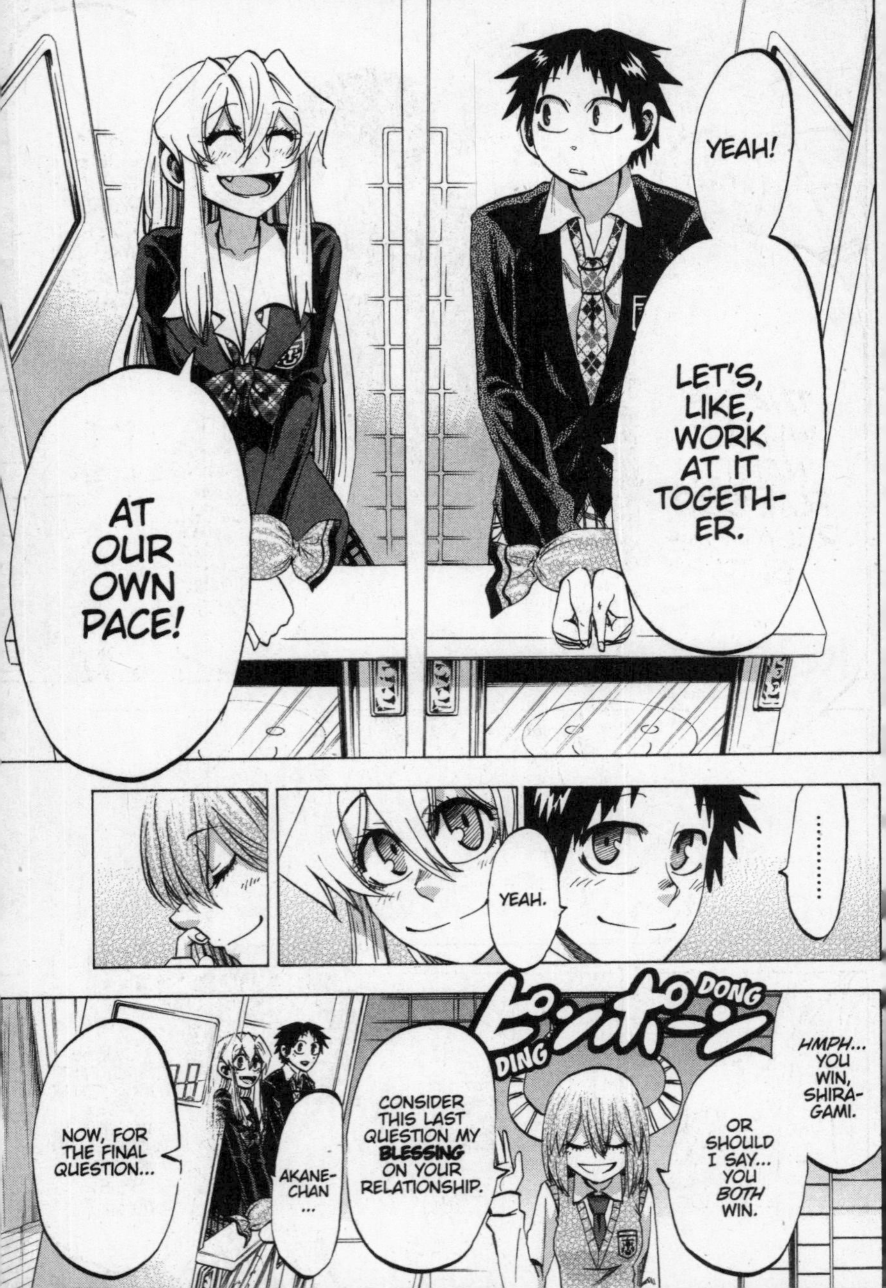
YEAH!
LET'S, LIKE, WORK AT IT TOGETHER.
AT OUR OWN PACE!
......
YEAH.
HMPH... YOU WIN, SHIRAGAMI.
OR SHOULD I SAY... YOU BOTH WIN.
DING DONG
CONSIDER THIS LAST QUESTION MY **BLESSING** ON YOUR RELATIONSHIP.
AKANE-CHAN...
NOW, FOR THE FINAL QUESTION...

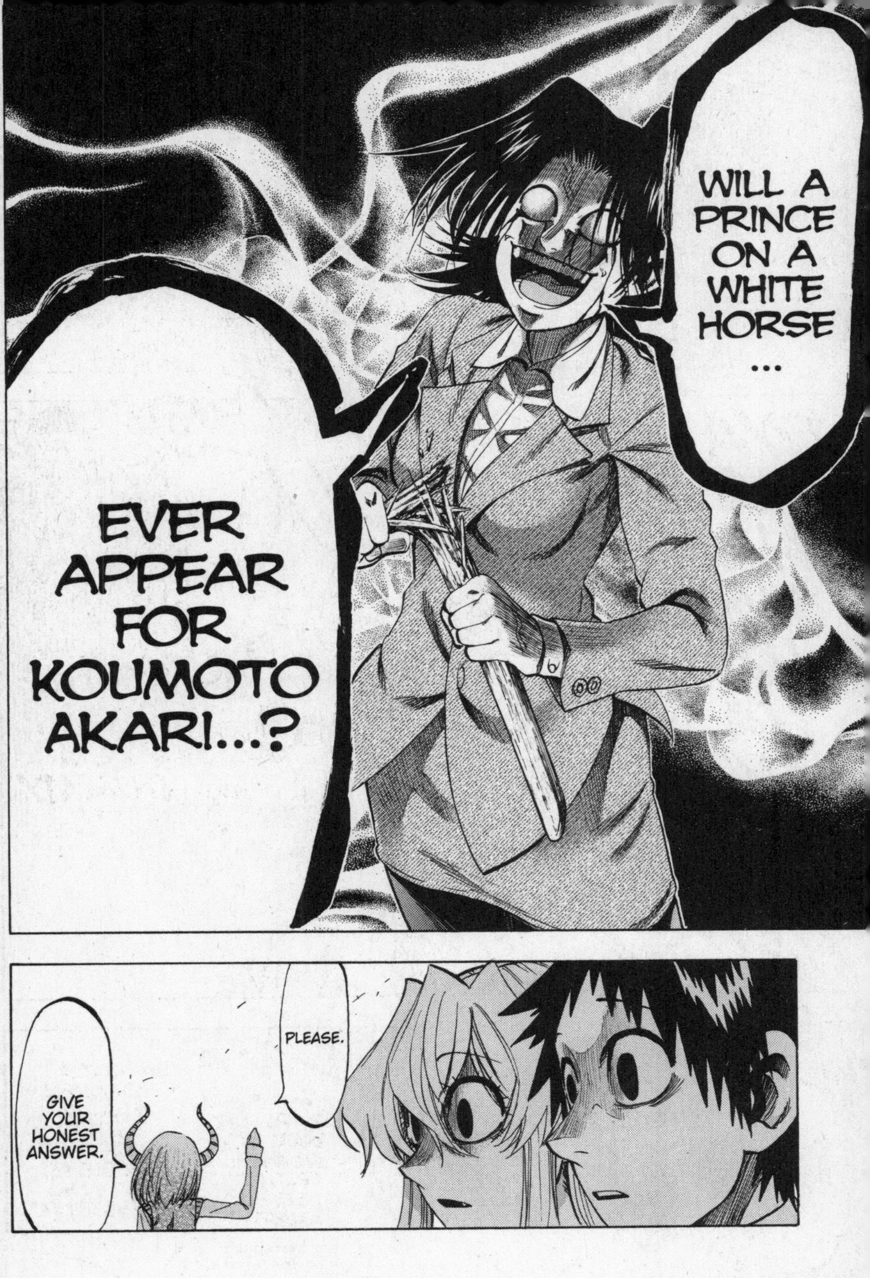
WILL A PRINCE ON A WHITE HORSE ...
EVER APPEAR FOR KOUMOTO AKARI...?
PLEASE.
GIVE YOUR HONEST ANSWER.

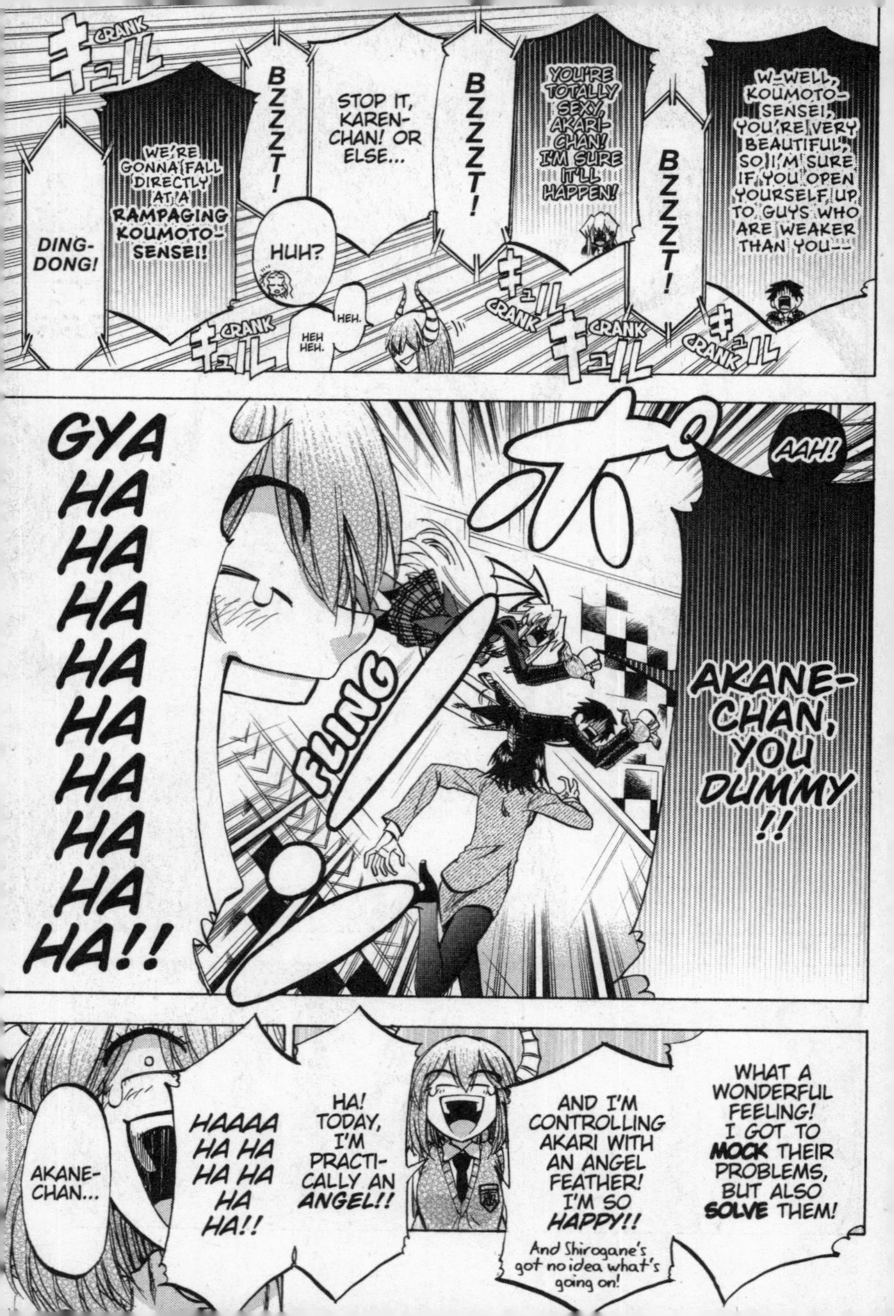
W-WELL, KOUMOTO-SENSEI, YOU'RE VERY BEAUTIFUL, SO I'M SURE IF YOU OPEN YOURSELF UP TO GUYS WHO ARE WEAKER THAN YOU--
キュル CRANK
BZZZT!
YOU'RE TOTALLY SEXY, AKARI-CHAN! I'M SURE IT'LL HAPPEN!
キュル CRANK
キュル CRANK
BZZZT!
STOP IT, KAREN-CHAN! OR ELSE...
HEH.
HEH HEH.
HUH?
BZZZT!
WE'RE GONNA FALL DIRECTLY AT A RAMPAGING KOUMOTO-SENSEI!
キュル CRANK
DING-DONG!
キュル CRANK
AAH!
AKANE-CHAN, YOU DUMMY!!
FLING
GYA HA HA HA HA HA HA HA HA HA HA HA!!
WHAT A WONDERFUL FEELING! I GOT TO MOCK THEIR PROBLEMS, BUT ALSO SOLVE THEM!
AND I'M CONTROLLING AKARI WITH AN ANGEL FEATHER! I'M SO HAPPY!!
And Shirogane's got no idea what's going on!
HA! TODAY, I'M PRACTICALLY AN ANGEL!!
HAAAA HA HA HA HA HA HA!!
AKANE-CHAN...

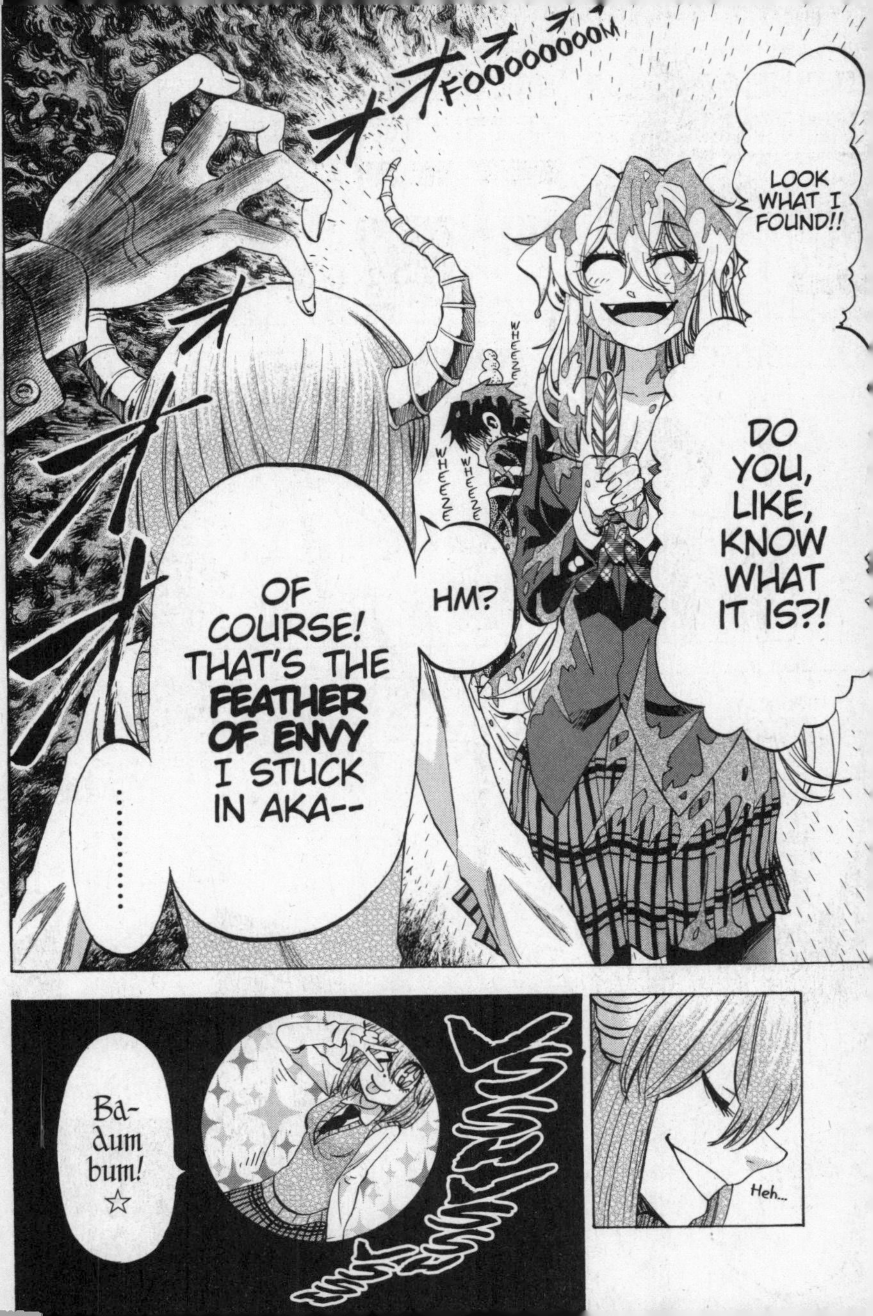
FOOOOOOOOM
LOOK WHAT I FOUND!!
DO YOU, LIKE, KNOW WHAT IT IS?!
WHEEZE
WHEEZE WHEEZE
HM?
OF COURSE! THAT'S THE **FEATHER OF ENVY** I STUCK IN AKA--
......
Heh...
Ba-dum bum! ☆

Chapter 88: "Let's Shadow the Student Body President!"

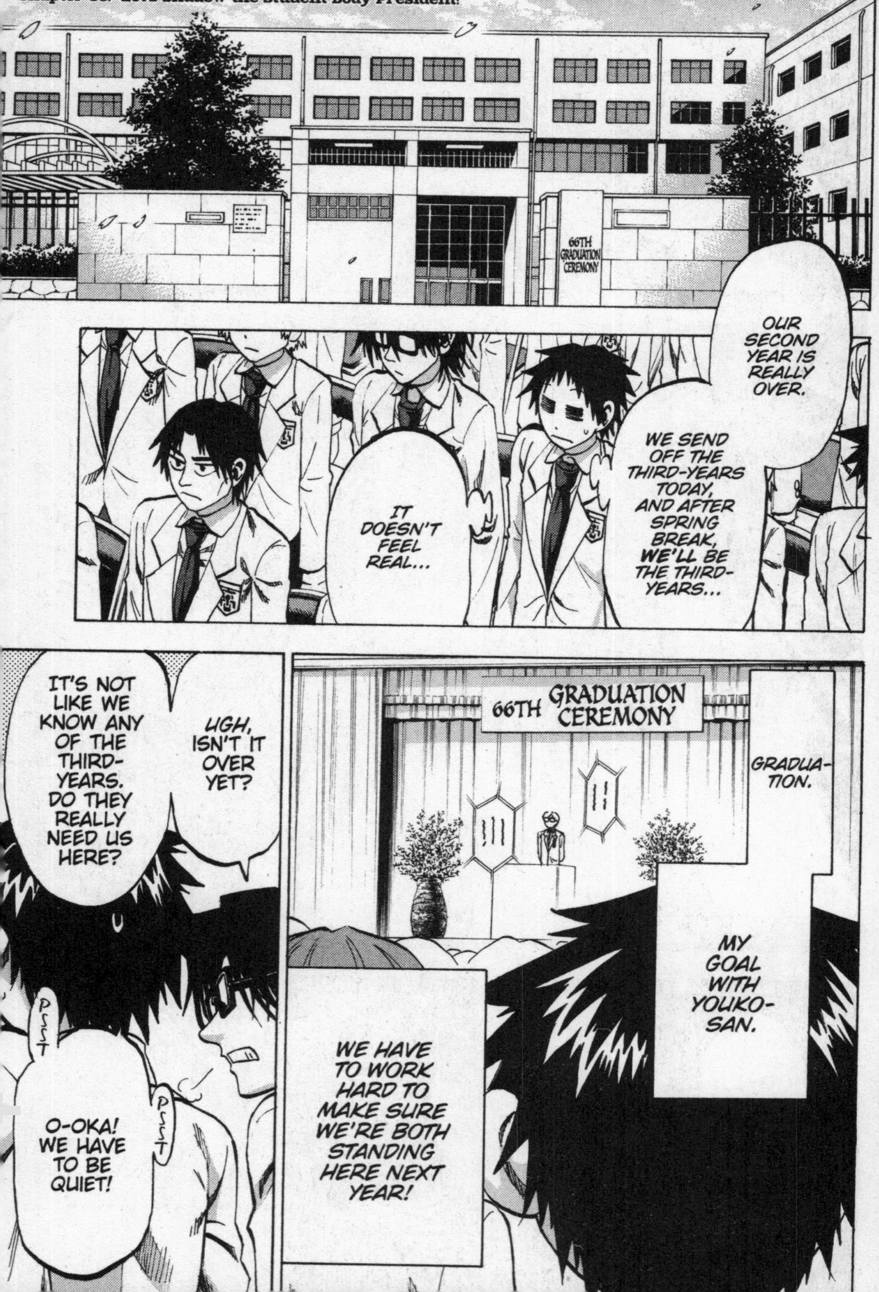
66TH GRADUATION CEREMONY
OUR SECOND YEAR IS REALLY OVER.
WE SEND OFF THE THIRD-YEARS TODAY, AND AFTER SPRING BREAK, WE'LL BE THE THIRD-YEARS...
IT DOESN'T FEEL REAL...
66TH GRADUATION CEREMONY
GRADUATION.
MY GOAL WITH YOUKO-SAN.
WE HAVE TO WORK HARD TO MAKE SURE WE'RE BOTH STANDING HERE NEXT YEAR!
UGH, ISN'T IT OVER YET?
IT'S NOT LIKE WE KNOW ANY OF THE THIRD-YEARS. DO THEY REALLY NEED US HERE?
PSST
PSST
O-OKA! WE HAVE TO BE QUIET!

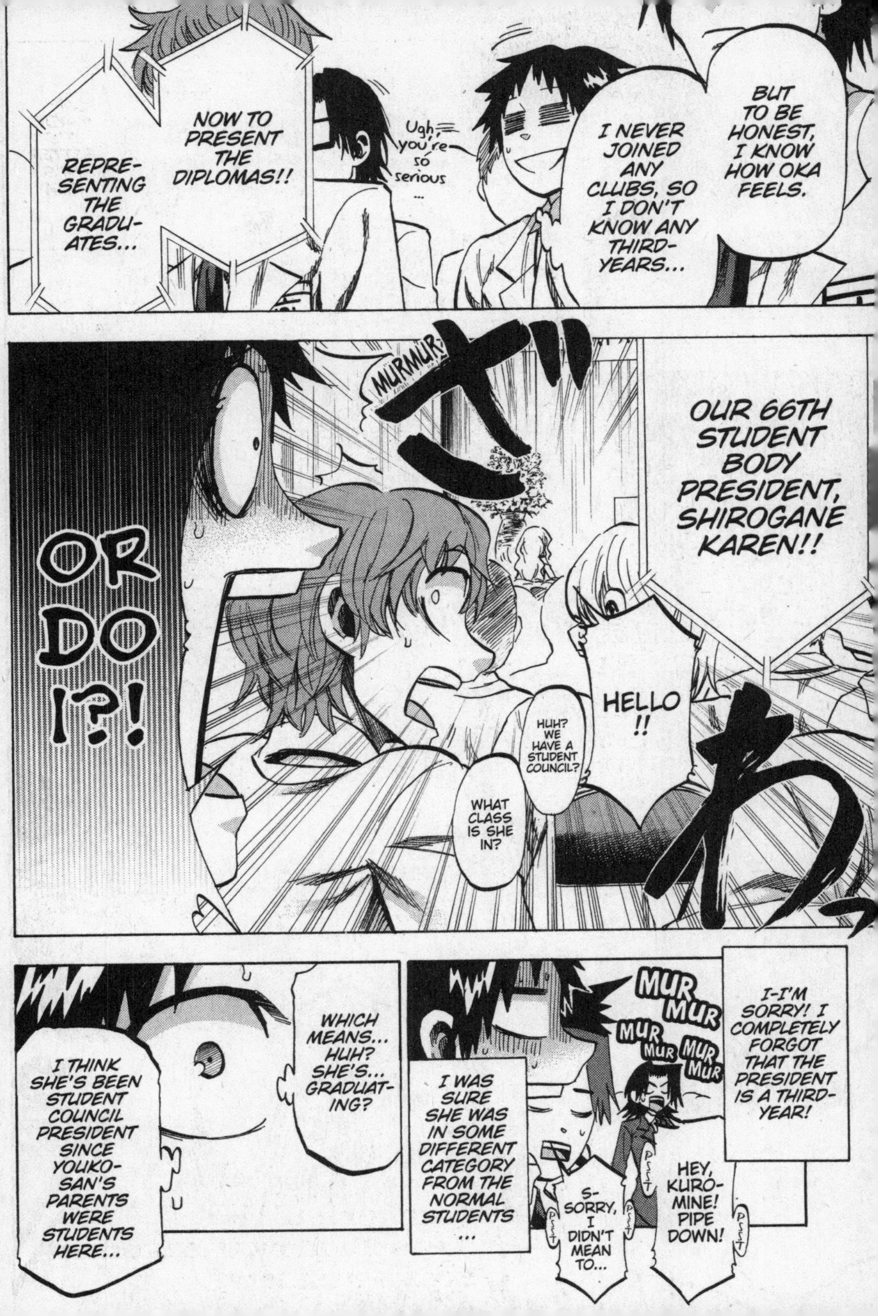
BUT TO BE HONEST, I KNOW HOW OKA FEELS.
I NEVER JOINED ANY CLUBS, SO I DON'T KNOW ANY THIRD-YEARS...
Ugh, you're so serious...
NOW TO PRESENT THE DIPLOMAS!!
REPRESENTING THE GRADUATES...
OUR 66TH STUDENT BODY PRESIDENT, SHIROGANE KAREN!!
HELLO!!
MURMUR
HUH? WE HAVE A STUDENT COUNCIL?
WHAT CLASS IS SHE IN?
OR DO I?!
I-I'M SORRY! I COMPLETELY FORGOT THAT THE PRESIDENT IS A THIRD-YEAR!
MUR MUR
MUR MUR MUR MUR
HEY, KURO-MINE! PIPE DOWN!
PSST
S-SORRY, I DIDN'T MEAN TO...
PSST
I WAS SURE SHE WAS IN SOME DIFFERENT CATEGORY FROM THE NORMAL STUDENTS...
WHICH MEANS... HUH? SHE'S... GRADUATING?
I THINK SHE'S BEEN STUDENT COUNCIL PRESIDENT SINCE YOUKO-SAN'S PARENTS WERE STUDENTS HERE...

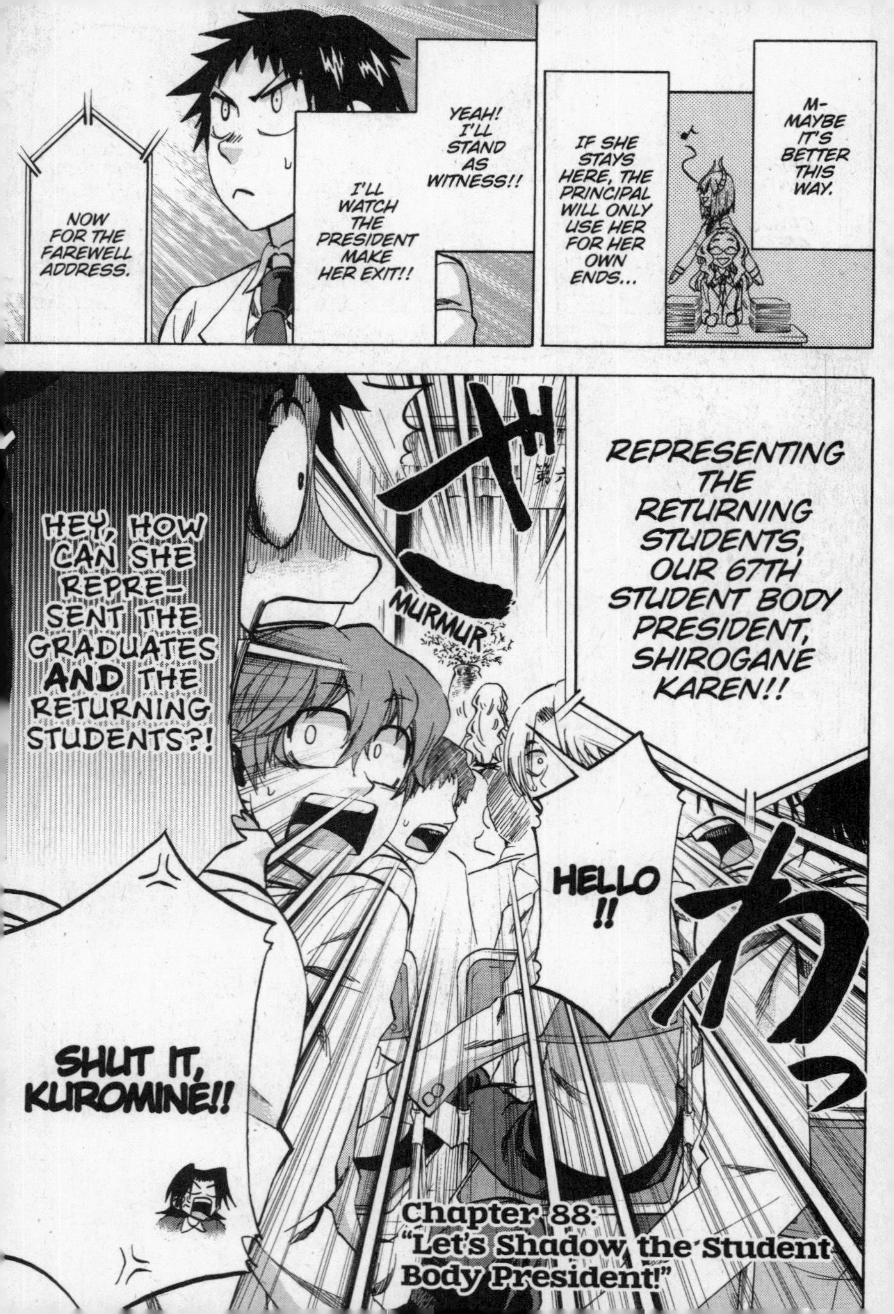
M-MAYBE IT'S BETTER THIS WAY.
IF SHE STAYS HERE, THE PRINCIPAL WILL ONLY USE HER FOR HER OWN ENDS...
YEAH! I'LL STAND AS WITNESS!!
I'LL WATCH THE PRESIDENT MAKE HER EXIT!!
NOW FOR THE FAREWELL ADDRESS.
REPRESENTING THE RETURNING STUDENTS, OUR 67TH STUDENT BODY PRESIDENT, SHIROGANE KAREN!!
MURMUR
HELLO !!
HEY, HOW CAN SHE REPRESENT THE GRADUATES **AND** THE RETURNING STUDENTS?!
SHUT IT, KUROMINE!!
Chapter 88: "Let's Shadow the Student Body President!"

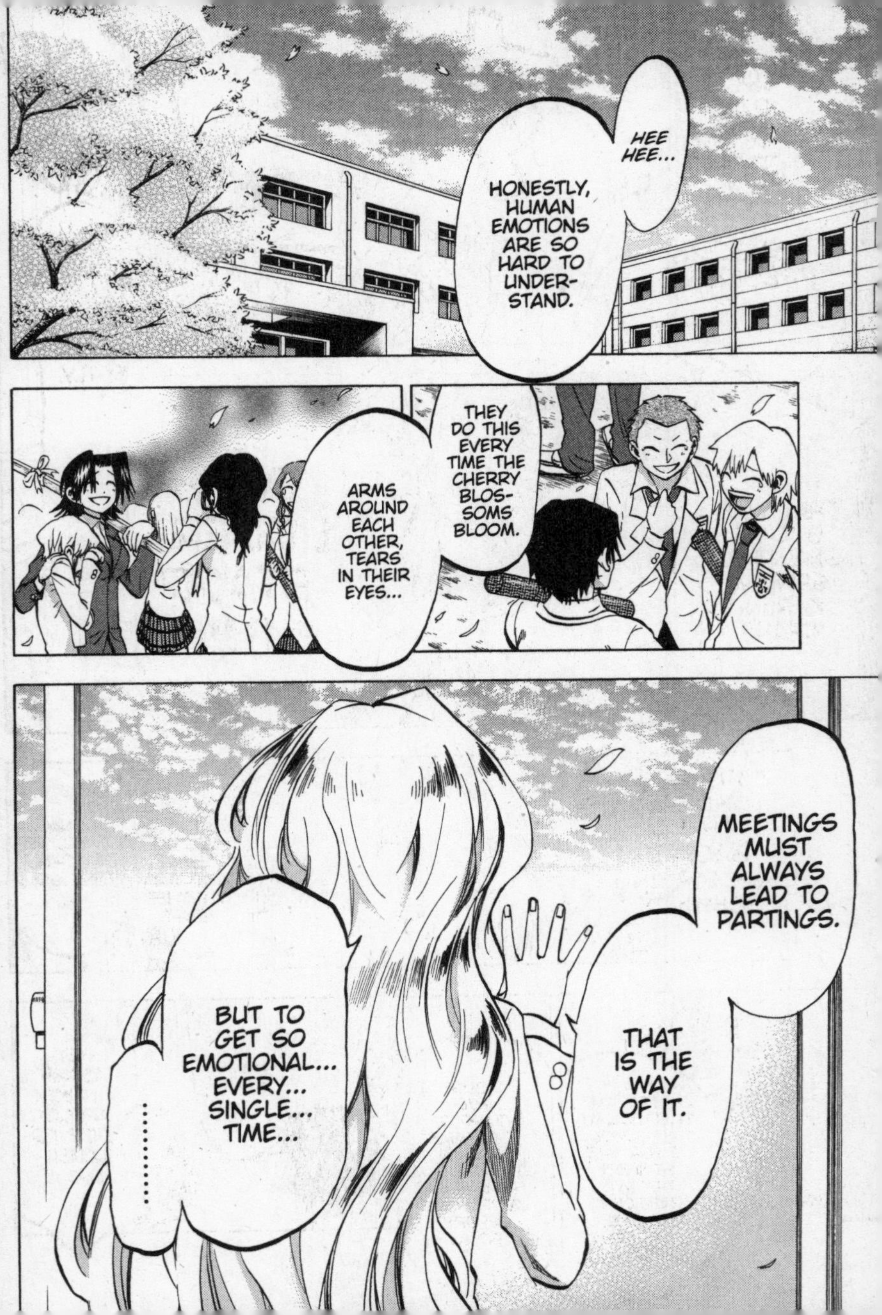
HEE HEE...
HONESTLY, HUMAN EMOTIONS ARE SO HARD TO UNDER-STAND.
THEY DO THIS EVERY TIME THE CHERRY BLOS-SOMS BLOOM.
ARMS AROUND EACH OTHER, TEARS IN THEIR EYES...
MEETINGS MUST ALWAYS LEAD TO PARTINGS.
THAT IS THE WAY OF IT.
BUT TO GET SO EMOTIONAL... EVERY... SINGLE... TIME...
......

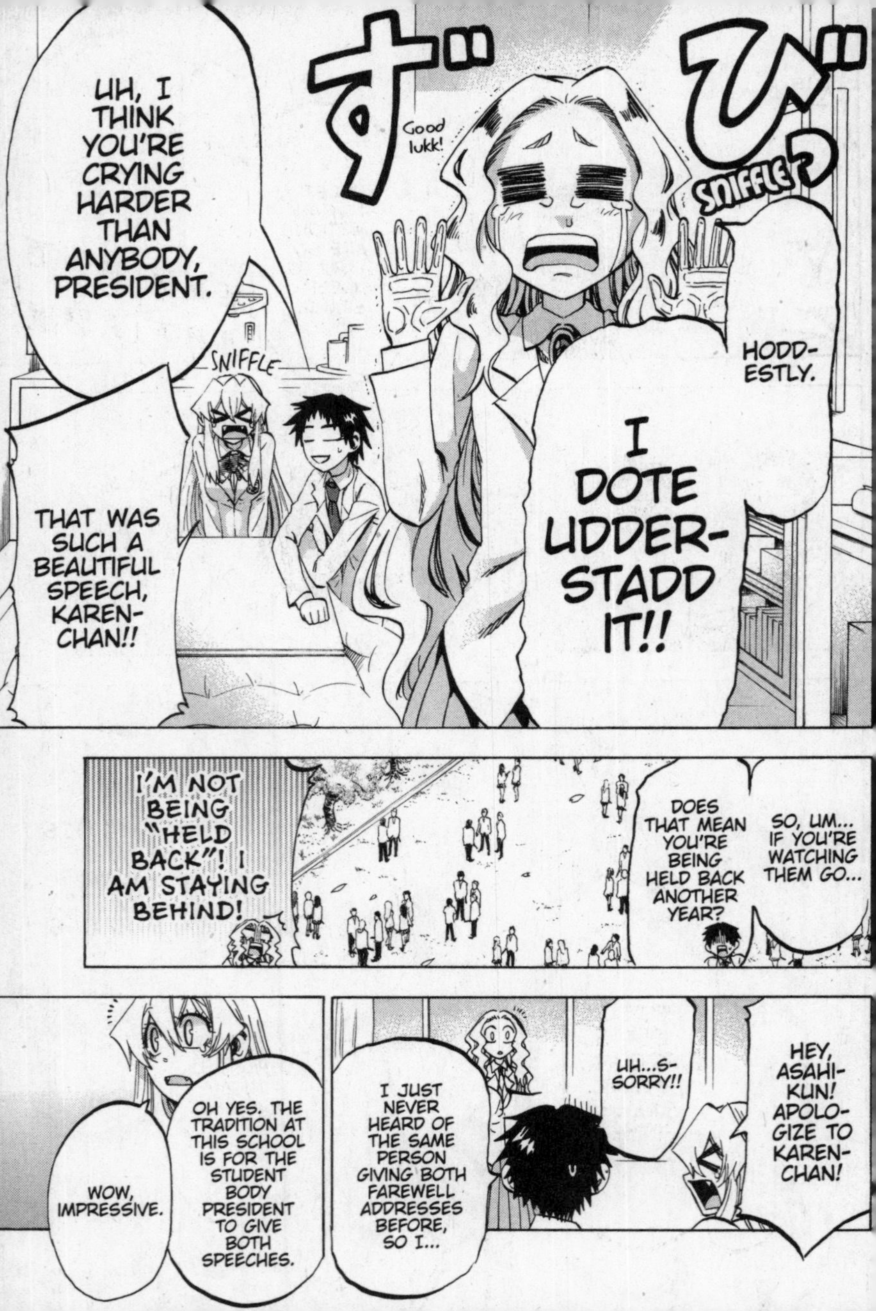

ずびっ
SNIFFLE
HODD-ESTLY.
I DOTE UDDER-STADD IT!!
Good lukk!
UH, I THINK YOU'RE CRYING HARDER THAN ANYBODY, PRESIDENT.
SNIFFLE
THAT WAS SUCH A BEAUTIFUL SPEECH, KAREN-CHAN!!
SO, UM... IF YOU'RE WATCHING THEM GO...
DOES THAT MEAN YOU'RE BEING HELD BACK ANOTHER YEAR?
I'M NOT BEING "HELD BACK"! I AM STAYING BEHIND!
HEY, ASAHI-KUN! APOLOGIZE TO KAREN-CHAN!
UH...S-SORRY!!
I JUST NEVER HEARD OF THE SAME PERSON GIVING BOTH FAREWELL ADDRESSES BEFORE, SO I...
OH YES. THE TRADITION AT THIS SCHOOL IS FOR THE STUDENT BODY PRESIDENT TO GIVE BOTH SPEECHES.
WOW, IMPRESSIVE.

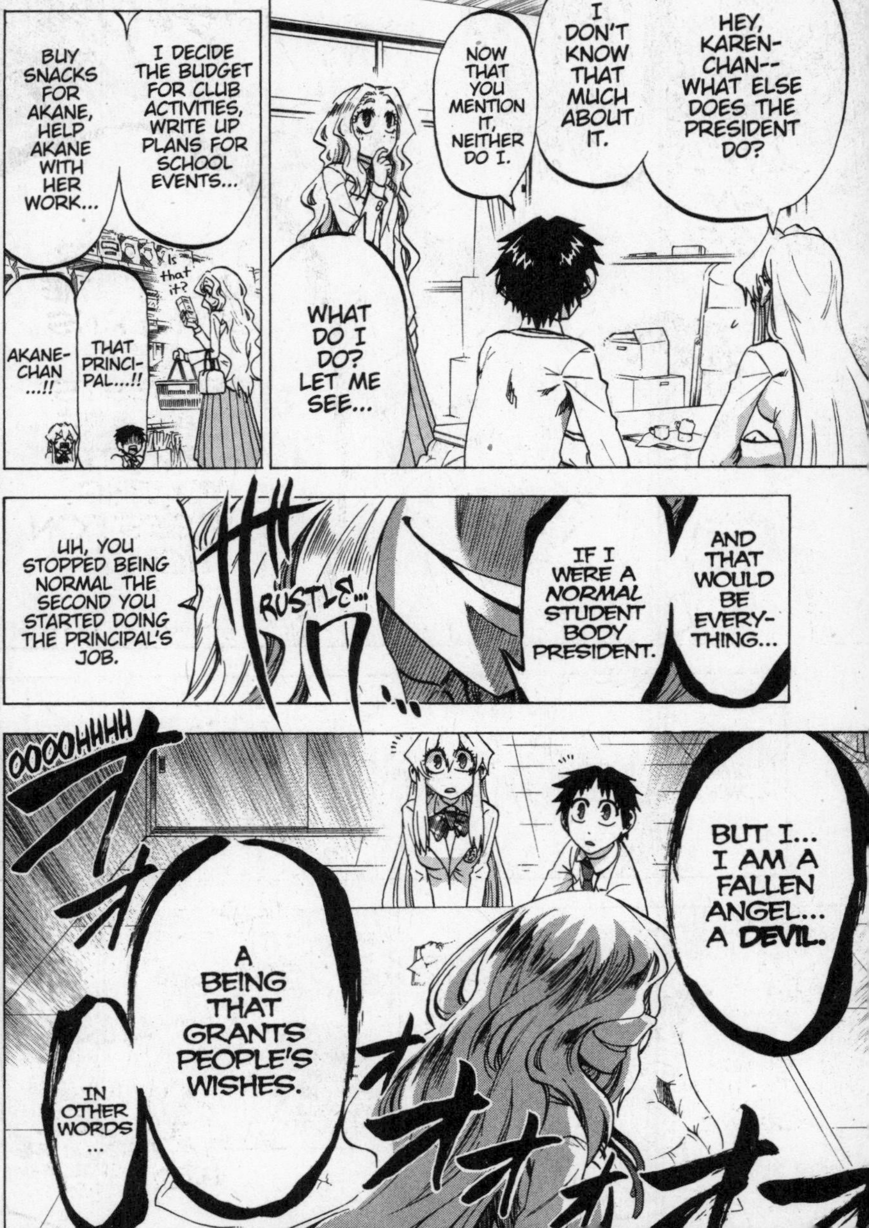

HEY, KAREN-CHAN-- WHAT ELSE DOES THE PRESIDENT DO?
I DON'T KNOW THAT MUCH ABOUT IT.
NOW THAT YOU MENTION IT, NEITHER DO I.
WHAT DO I DO? LET ME SEE...
I DECIDE THE BUDGET FOR CLUB ACTIVITIES, WRITE UP PLANS FOR SCHOOL EVENTS...
BUY SNACKS FOR AKANE, HELP AKANE WITH HER WORK...
Is that it?
THAT PRINCIPAL...!!
AKANE-CHAN ...!!
AND THAT WOULD BE EVERYTHING...
IF I WERE A NORMAL STUDENT BODY PRESIDENT.
RUSTLE...
UH, YOU STOPPED BEING NORMAL THE SECOND YOU STARTED DOING THE PRINCIPAL'S JOB.
BUT I... I AM A FALLEN ANGEL... A DEVIL.
A BEING THAT GRANTS PEOPLE'S WISHES.
IN OTHER WORDS...
OOOOHHHH

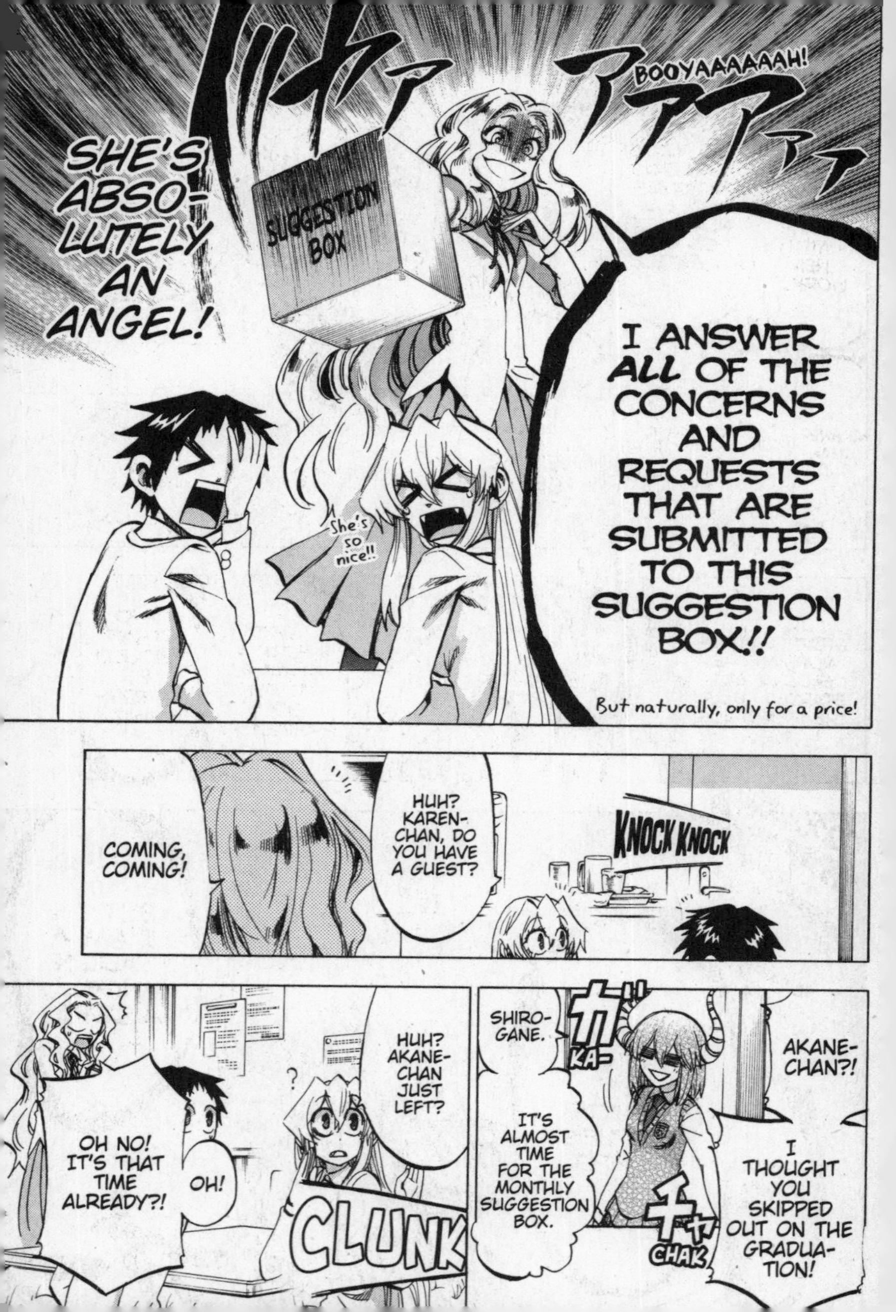
BOOYAAAAAAH!
SUGGESTION BOX
I ANSWER ALL OF THE CONCERNS AND REQUESTS THAT ARE SUBMITTED TO THIS SUGGESTION BOX!!
But naturally, only for a price!
SHE'S ABSOLUTELY AN ANGEL!
She's so nice!!
KNOCK KNOCK
HUH? KAREN-CHAN, DO YOU HAVE A GUEST?
COMING, COMING!
AKANE-CHAN?!
SHIRO-GANE.
KA-
I THOUGHT YOU SKIPPED OUT ON THE GRADUATION!
IT'S ALMOST TIME FOR THE MONTHLY SUGGESTION BOX.
CHAK
HUH? AKANE-CHAN JUST LEFT?
OH!
OH NO! IT'S THAT TIME ALREADY?!
CLUNK

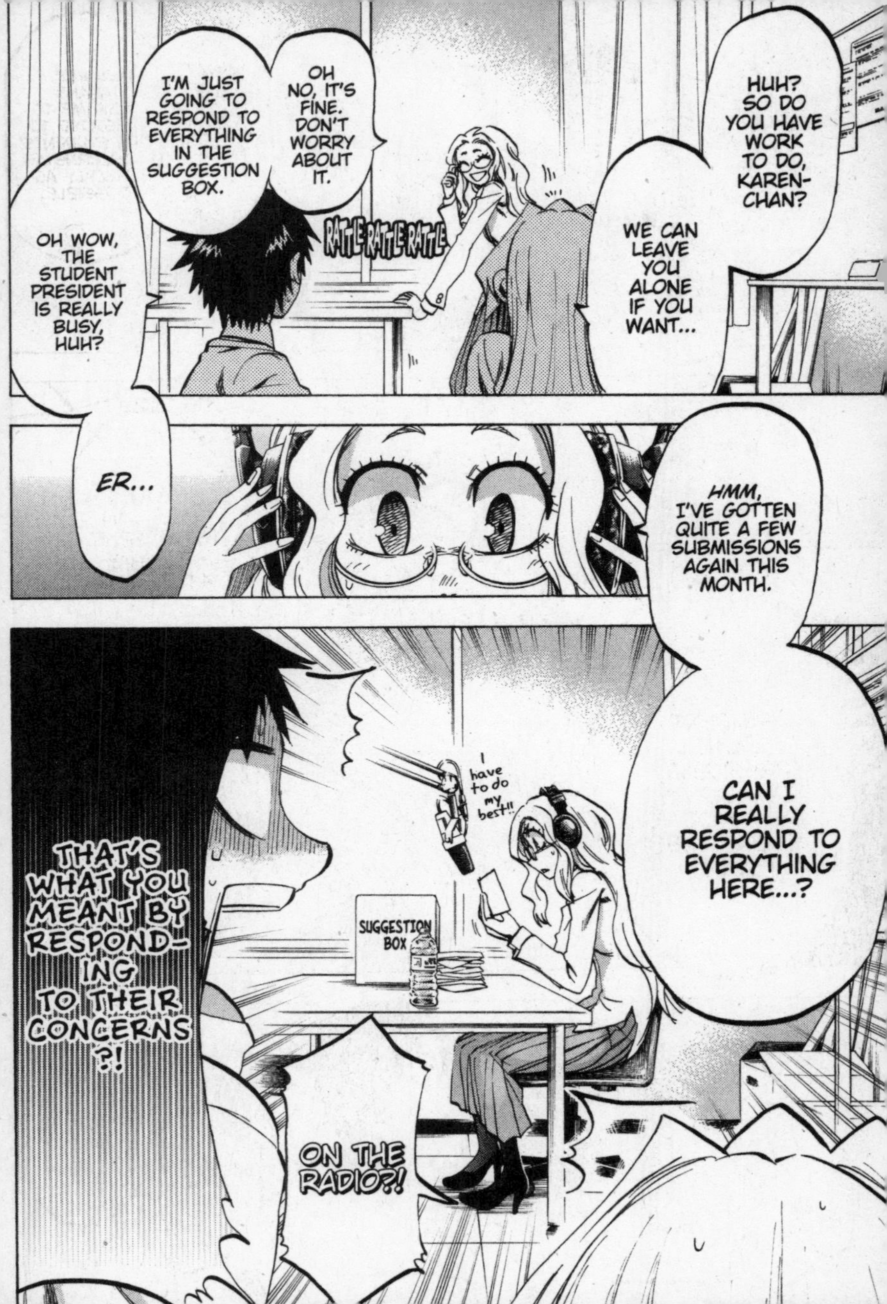
HUH? SO DO YOU HAVE WORK TO DO, KAREN-CHAN?
WE CAN LEAVE YOU ALONE IF YOU WANT...
OH NO, IT'S FINE. DON'T WORRY ABOUT IT.
I'M JUST GOING TO RESPOND TO EVERYTHING IN THE SUGGESTION BOX.
RATTLE RATTLE RATTLE
OH WOW, THE STUDENT PRESIDENT IS REALLY BUSY, HUH?
HMM, I'VE GOTTEN QUITE A FEW SUBMISSIONS AGAIN THIS MONTH.
ER...
CAN I REALLY RESPOND TO EVERYTHING HERE...?
I have to do my best!!
SUGGESTION BOX
THAT'S WHAT YOU MEANT BY RESPOND-ING TO THEIR CONCERNS?!
ON THE RADIO?!

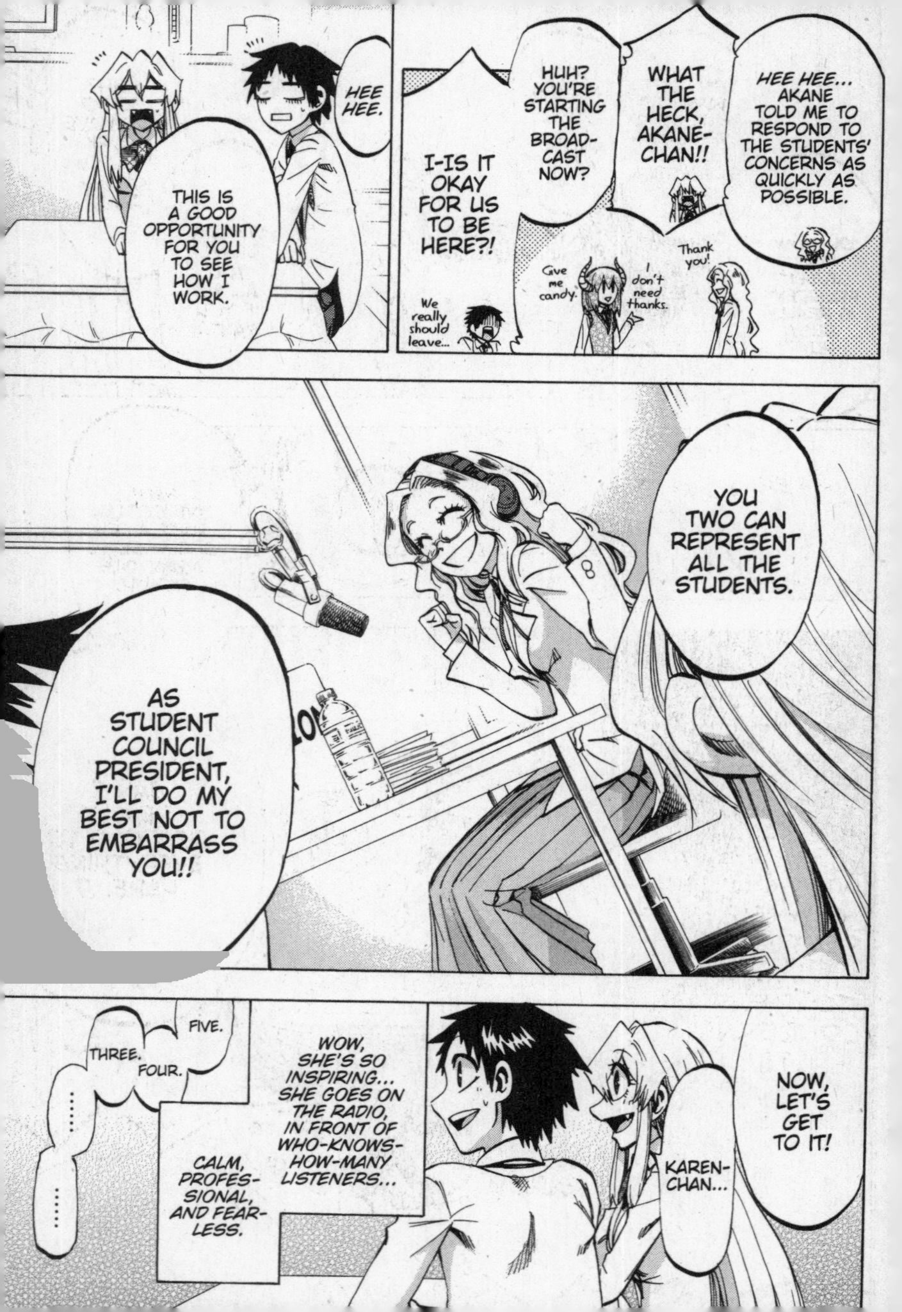
HEE HEE... AKANE TOLD ME TO RESPOND TO THE STUDENTS' CONCERNS AS QUICKLY AS POSSIBLE.
WHAT THE HECK, AKANE-CHAN!!
HUH? YOU'RE STARTING THE BROADCAST NOW?
I-IS IT OKAY FOR US TO BE HERE?!
Thank you!
I don't need thanks.
Give me candy.
We really should leave...
HEE HEE.
THIS IS A GOOD OPPORTUNITY FOR YOU TO SEE HOW I WORK.
YOU TWO CAN REPRESENT ALL THE STUDENTS.
AS STUDENT COUNCIL PRESIDENT, I'LL DO MY BEST NOT TO EMBARRASS YOU!!
NOW, LET'S GET TO IT!
KAREN-CHAN...
WOW, SHE'S SO INSPIRING... SHE GOES ON THE RADIO, IN FRONT OF WHO-KNOWS-HOW-MANY LISTENERS...
CALM, PROFESSIONAL, AND FEARLESS.
FIVE.
FOUR.
THREE.
......
......

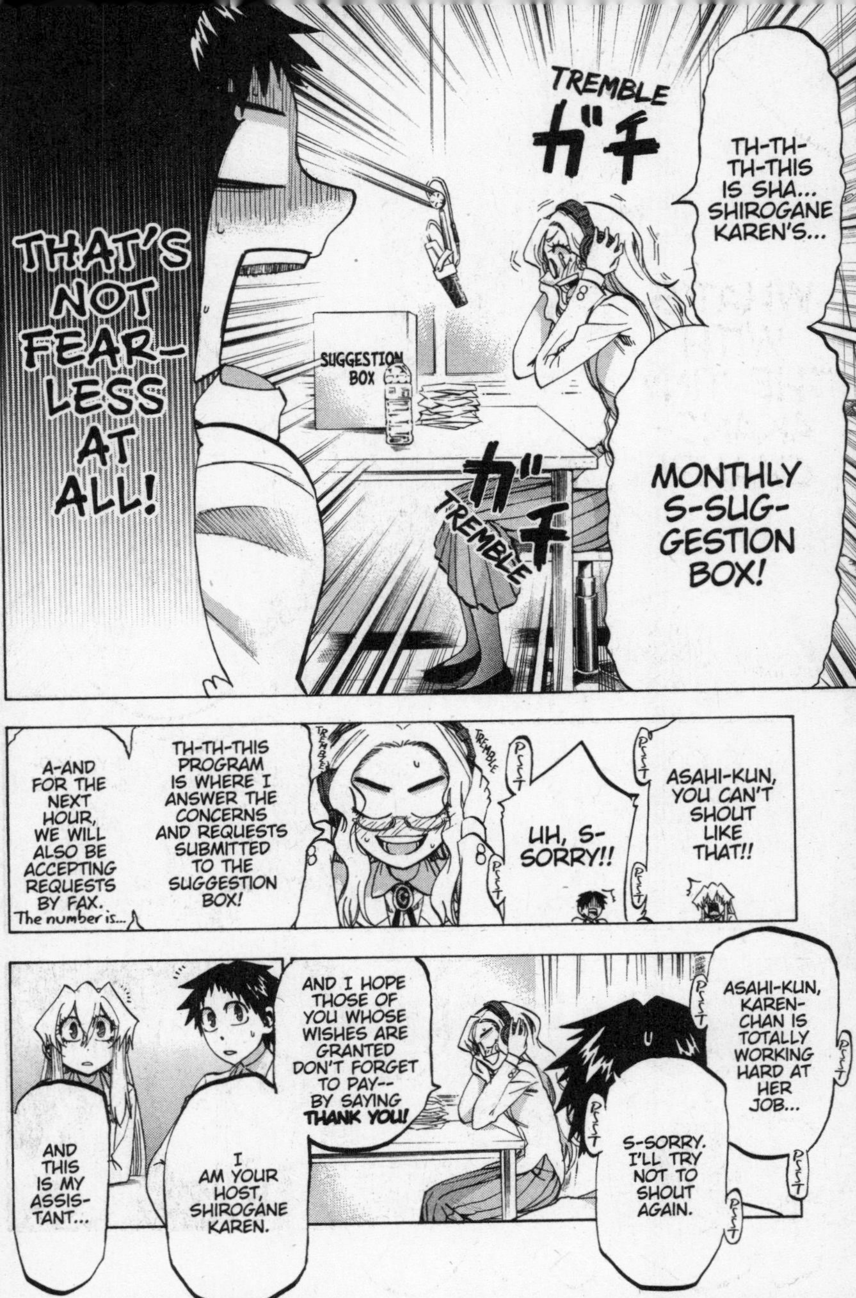
TREMBLE
ガチ
TH-TH-TH-THIS IS SHA... SHIROGANE KAREN'S...
MONTHLY S-SUG-GESTION BOX!
SUGGESTION BOX
ガチ
TREMBLE
THAT'S NOT FEAR-LESS AT ALL!
ASAHI-KUN, YOU CAN'T SHOUT LIKE THAT!!
PSST
UH, S-SORRY!!
TREMBLE
TREMBLE
TH-TH-THIS PROGRAM IS WHERE I ANSWER THE CONCERNS AND REQUESTS SUBMITTED TO THE SUGGESTION BOX!
A-AND FOR THE NEXT HOUR, WE WILL ALSO BE ACCEPTING REQUESTS BY FAX.
The number is...
ASAHI-KUN, KAREN-CHAN IS TOTALLY WORKING HARD AT HER JOB...
PSST
S-SORRY. I'LL TRY NOT TO SHOUT AGAIN.
AND I HOPE THOSE OF YOU WHOSE WISHES ARE GRANTED DON'T FORGET TO PAY-- BY SAYING THANK YOU!
I AM YOUR HOST, SHIROGANE KAREN.
AND THIS IS MY ASSISTANT...

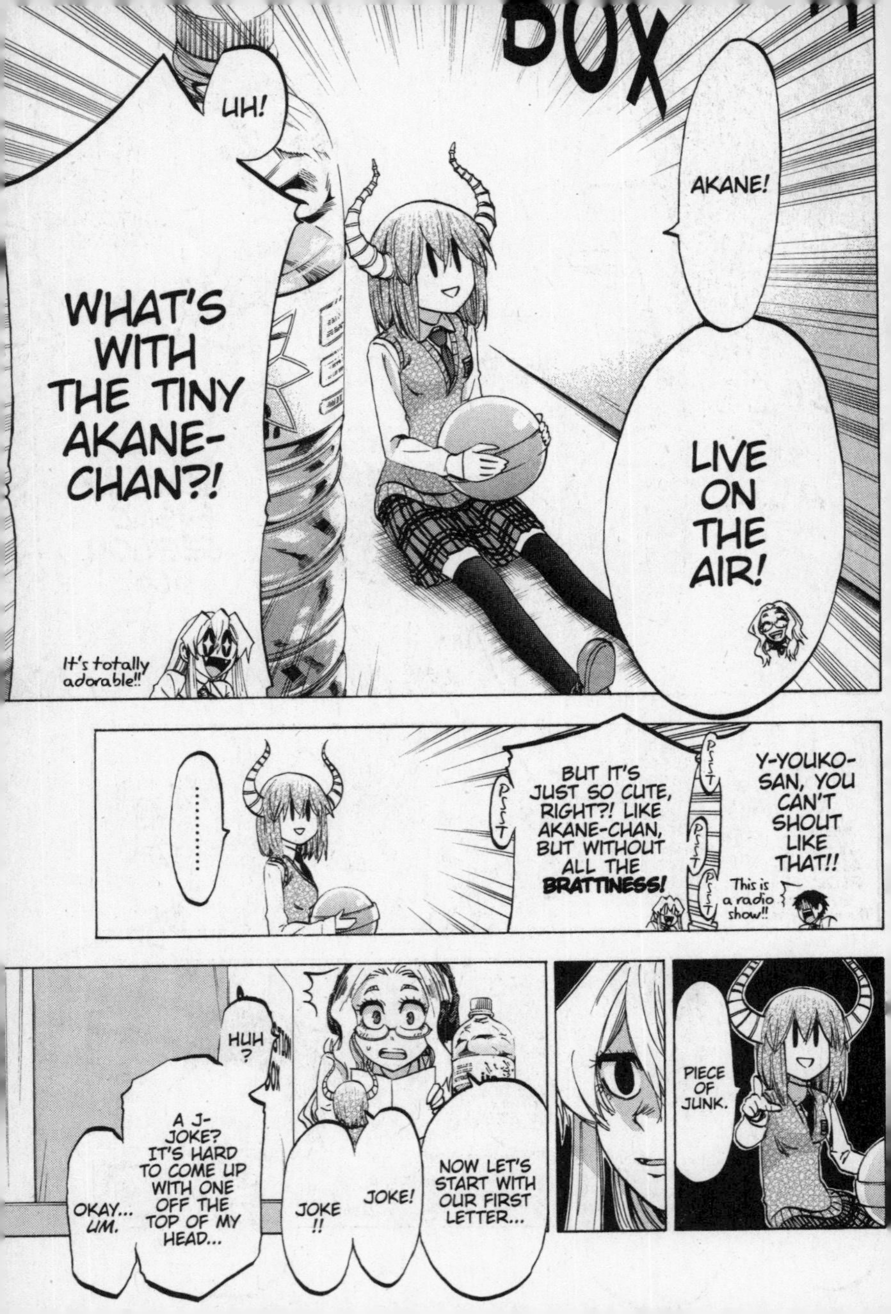
BOX
AKANE!
LIVE ON THE AIR!
UH!
WHAT'S WITH THE TINY AKANE-CHAN?!
It's totally adorable!!
Y-YOUKO-SAN, YOU CAN'T SHOUT LIKE THAT!!
This is a radio show!!
PSST
PSST
PSST
PSST
BUT IT'S JUST SO CUTE, RIGHT?! LIKE AKANE-CHAN, BUT WITHOUT ALL THE BRATTINESS!
......
PIECE OF JUNK.
NOW LET'S START WITH OUR FIRST LETTER...
JOKE!
JOKE !!
HUH ?
A J-JOKE? IT'S HARD TO COME UP WITH ONE OFF THE TOP OF MY HEAD...
OKAY... UM.

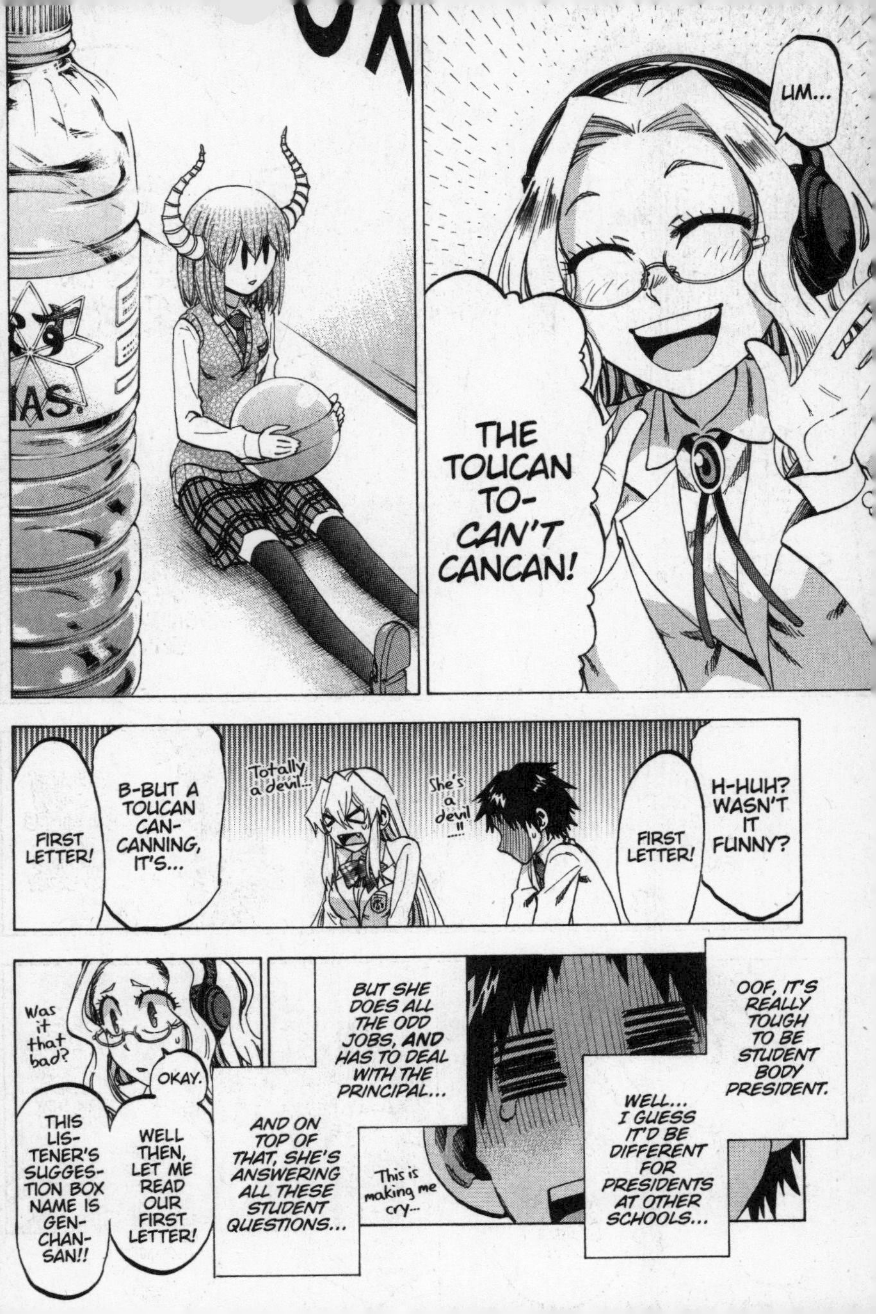
UM...
THE TOUCAN TO-CAN'T CANCAN!
H-HUH? WASN'T IT FUNNY?
FIRST LETTER!
She's a devil...!!
Totally a devil...
B-BUT A TOUCAN CAN-CANNING, IT'S...
FIRST LETTER!
OOF, IT'S REALLY TOUGH TO BE STUDENT BODY PRESIDENT.
WELL... I GUESS IT'D BE DIFFERENT FOR PRESIDENTS AT OTHER SCHOOLS...
BUT SHE DOES ALL THE ODD JOBS, AND HAS TO DEAL WITH THE PRINCIPAL...
AND ON TOP OF THAT, SHE'S ANSWERING ALL THESE STUDENT QUESTIONS...
This is making me cry...
Was it that bad?
OKAY.
WELL THEN, LET ME READ OUR FIRST LETTER!
THIS LISTENER'S SUGGESTION BOX NAME IS GEN-CHAN-SAN!!

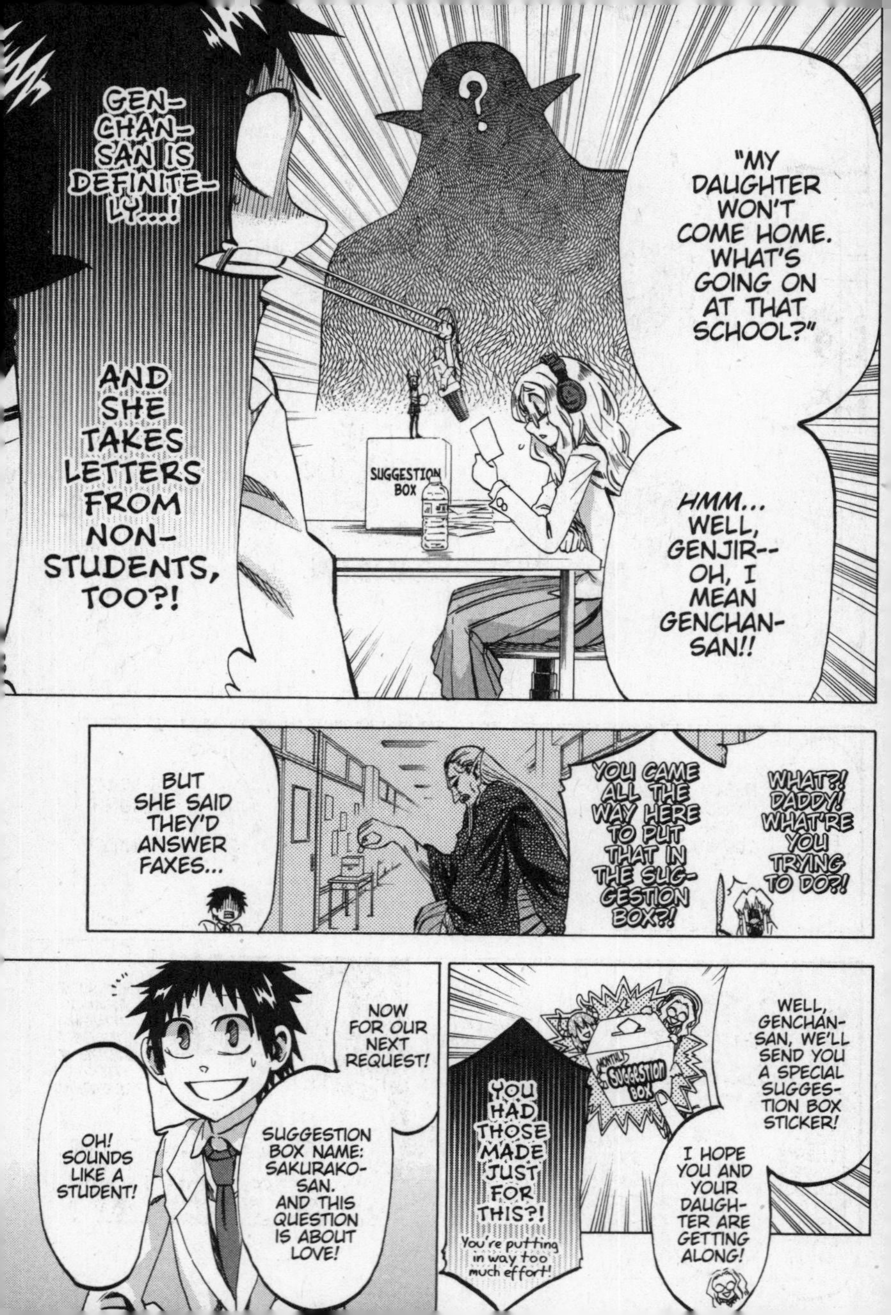

"MY DAUGHTER WON'T COME HOME. WHAT'S GOING ON AT THAT SCHOOL?"
HMM... WELL, GENJIR-- OH, I MEAN GENCHAN-SAN!!
SUGGESTION BOX
GEN-CHAN-SAN IS DEFINITE-LY...!
AND SHE TAKES LETTERS FROM NON-STUDENTS, TOO?!
WHAT?! DADDY! WHAT'RE YOU TRYING TO DO?!
YOU CAME ALL THE WAY HERE TO PUT THAT IN THE SUG-GESTION BOX?!
BUT SHE SAID THEY'D ANSWER FAXES...
WELL, GENCHAN-SAN, WE'LL SEND YOU A SPECIAL SUGGES-TION BOX STICKER!
I HOPE YOU AND YOUR DAUGH-TER ARE GETTING ALONG!
MONTHLY SUGGESTION BOX
YOU HAD THOSE MADE JUST FOR THIS?!
You're putting in way too much effort!
NOW FOR OUR NEXT REQUEST!
SUGGESTION BOX NAME: SAKURAKO-SAN. AND THIS QUESTION IS ABOUT LOVE!
OH! SOUNDS LIKE A STUDENT!

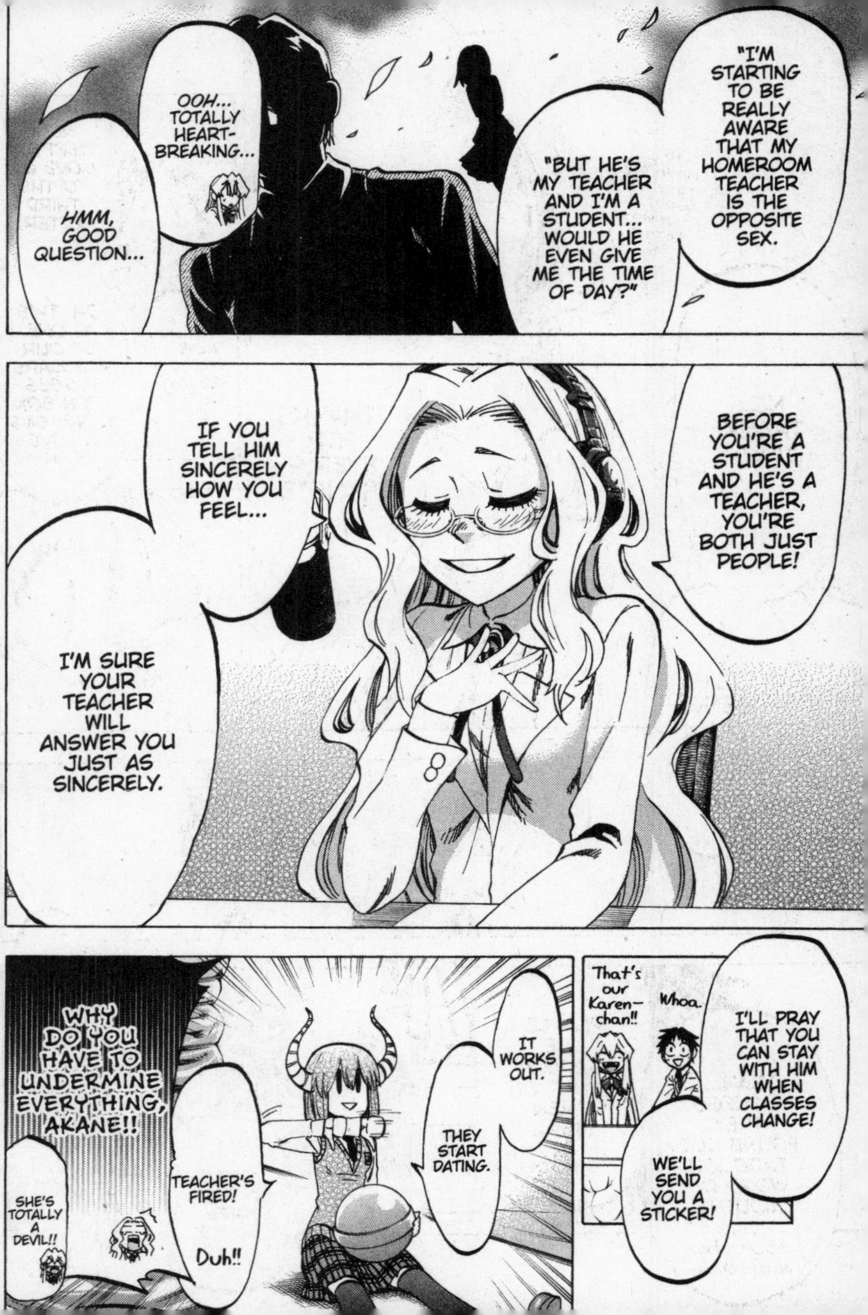
"I'M STARTING TO BE REALLY AWARE THAT MY HOMEROOM TEACHER IS THE OPPOSITE SEX.
"BUT HE'S MY TEACHER AND I'M A STUDENT... WOULD HE EVEN GIVE ME THE TIME OF DAY?"
OOH... TOTALLY HEART-BREAKING...
HMM, GOOD QUESTION...
BEFORE YOU'RE A STUDENT AND HE'S A TEACHER, YOU'RE BOTH JUST PEOPLE!
IF YOU TELL HIM SINCERELY HOW YOU FEEL...
I'M SURE YOUR TEACHER WILL ANSWER YOU JUST AS SINCERELY.
I'LL PRAY THAT YOU CAN STAY WITH HIM WHEN CLASSES CHANGE!
Whoa.
That's our Karen-chan!!
WE'LL SEND YOU A STICKER!
IT WORKS OUT.
THEY START DATING.
TEACHER'S FIRED!
Duh!!
WHY DO YOU HAVE TO UNDERMINE EVERYTHING, AKANE!!
SHE'S TOTALLY A DEVIL!!

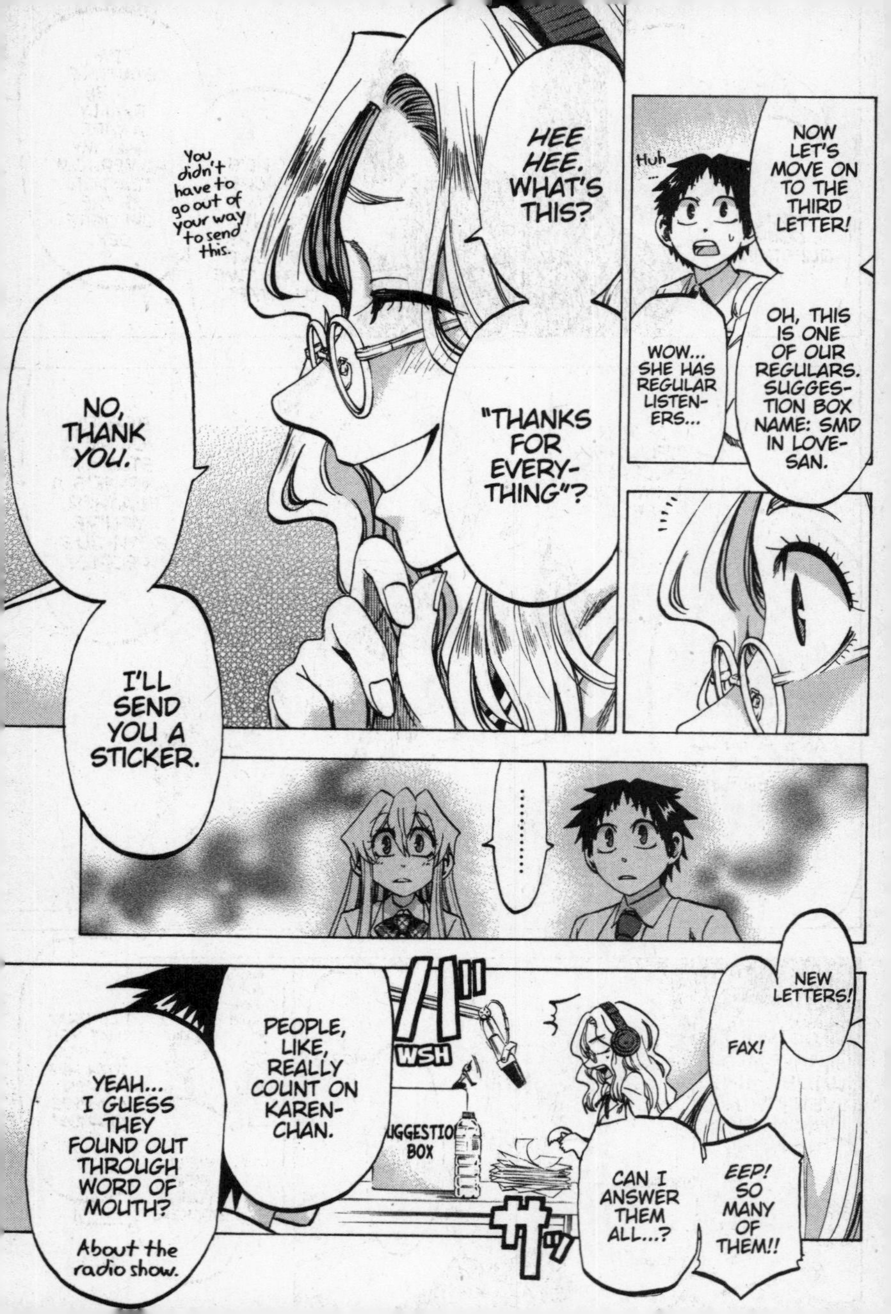
NOW LET'S MOVE ON TO THE THIRD LETTER!
Huh...
OH, THIS IS ONE OF OUR REGULARS. SUGGESTION BOX NAME: SMD IN LOVE-SAN.
WOW... SHE HAS REGULAR LISTENERS...
...
HEE HEE. WHAT'S THIS?
"THANKS FOR EVERYTHING"?
You didn't have to go out of your way to send this.
NO, THANK YOU.
I'LL SEND YOU A STICKER.
......
NEW LETTERS!
FAX!
EEP! SO MANY OF THEM!!
CAN I ANSWER THEM ALL...?
WSH
SUGGESTION BOX
PEOPLE, LIKE, REALLY COUNT ON KAREN-CHAN.
YEAH... I GUESS THEY FOUND OUT THROUGH WORD OF MOUTH?
About the radio show.

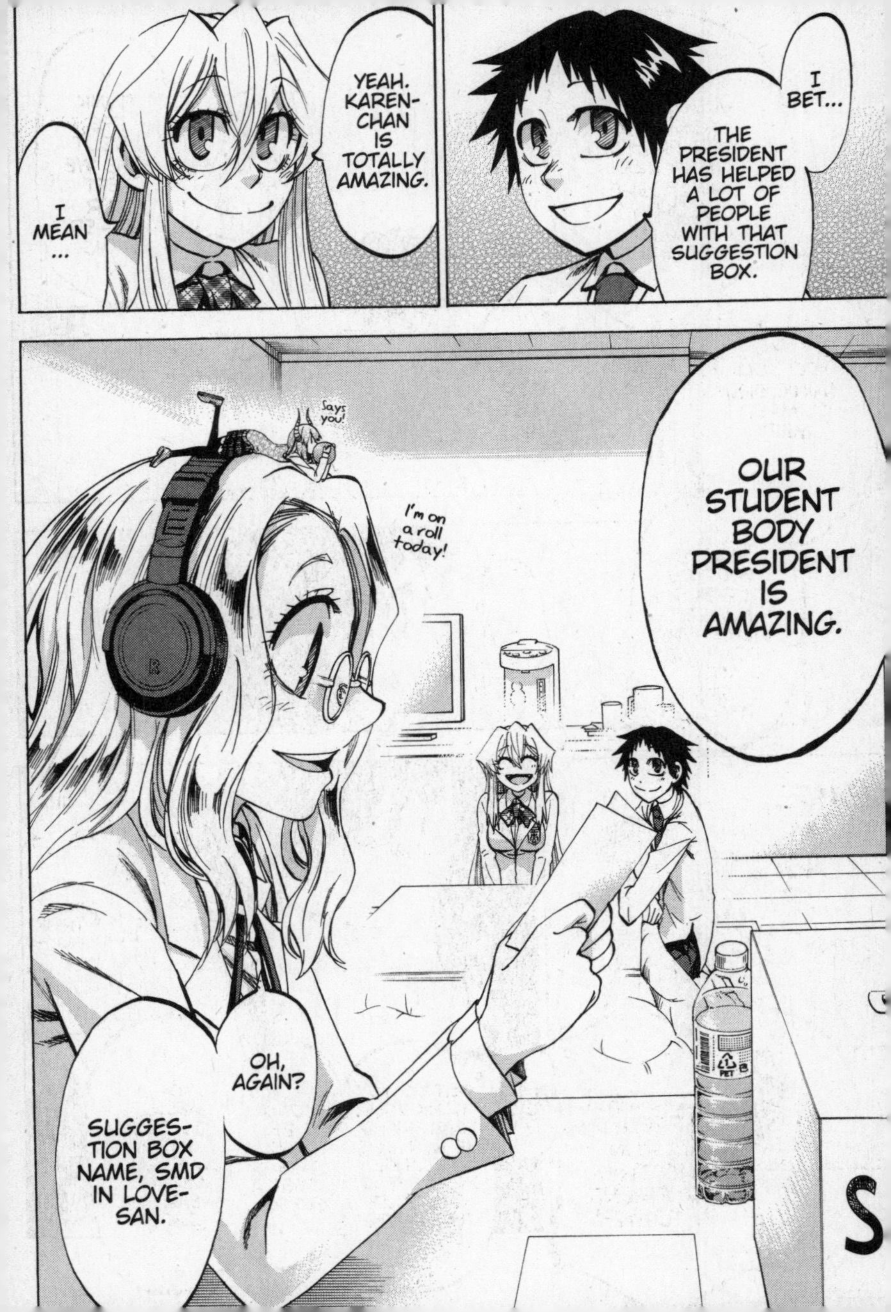
I BET...
THE PRESIDENT HAS HELPED A LOT OF PEOPLE WITH THAT SUGGESTION BOX.
YEAH. KAREN-CHAN IS TOTALLY AMAZING.
I MEAN...
OUR STUDENT BODY PRESIDENT IS AMAZING.
Says you!
I'm on a roll today!
OH, AGAIN?
SUGGES-TION BOX NAME, SMD IN LOVE-SAN.

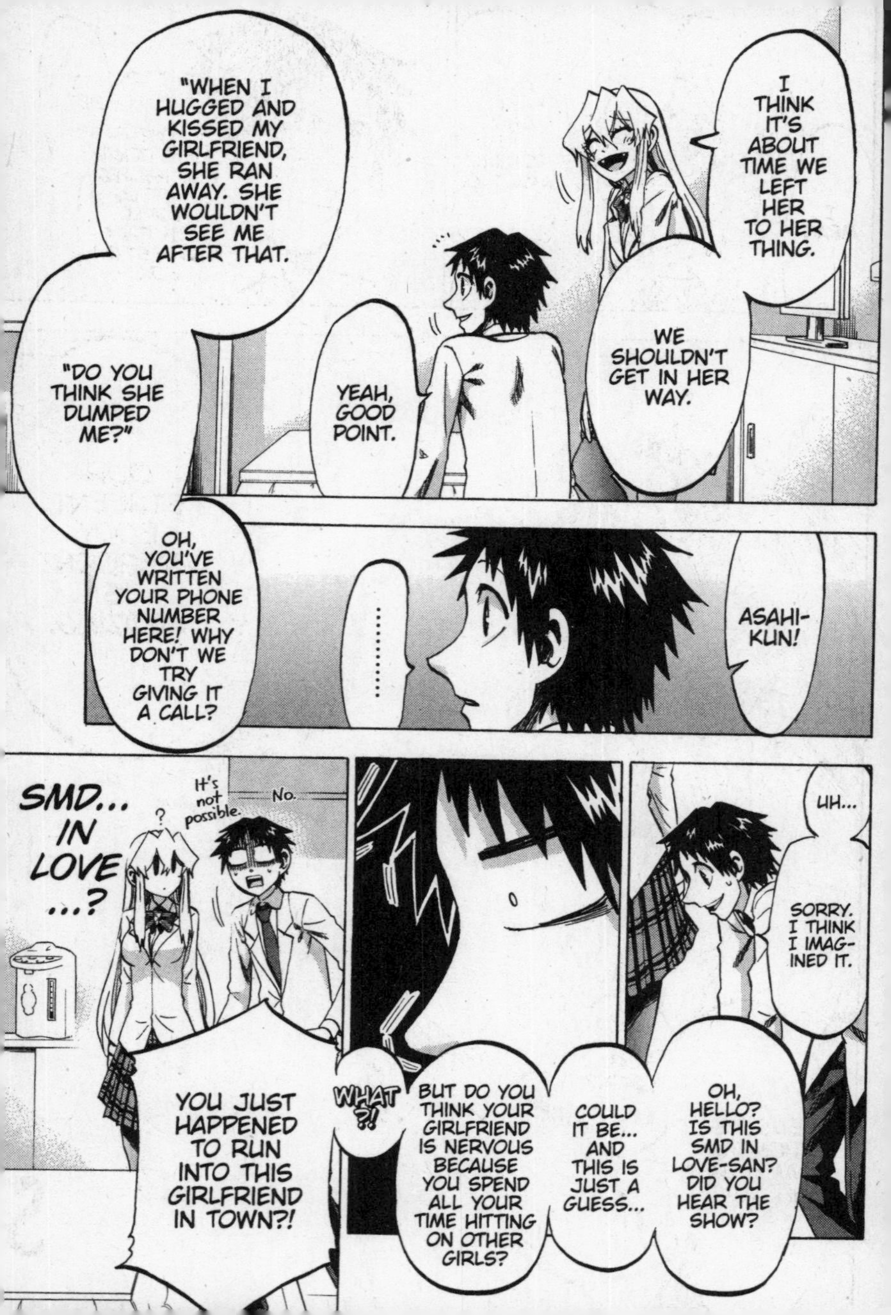
I THINK IT'S ABOUT TIME WE LEFT HER TO HER THING.
WE SHOULDN'T GET IN HER WAY.
YEAH, GOOD POINT.
"WHEN I HUGGED AND KISSED MY GIRLFRIEND, SHE RAN AWAY. SHE WOULDN'T SEE ME AFTER THAT.
"DO YOU THINK SHE DUMPED ME?"
ASAHI-KUN!
......
OH, YOU'VE WRITTEN YOUR PHONE NUMBER HERE! WHY DON'T WE TRY GIVING IT A CALL?
UH...
SORRY. I THINK I IMAG-INED IT.
SMD... IN LOVE ...?
No.
It's not possible.
OH, HELLO? IS THIS SMD IN LOVE-SAN? DID YOU HEAR THE SHOW?
COULD IT BE... AND THIS IS JUST A GUESS...
BUT DO YOU THINK YOUR GIRLFRIEND IS NERVOUS BECAUSE YOU SPEND ALL YOUR TIME HITTING ON OTHER GIRLS?
WHAT?!
YOU JUST HAPPENED TO RUN INTO THIS GIRLFRIEND IN TOWN?!

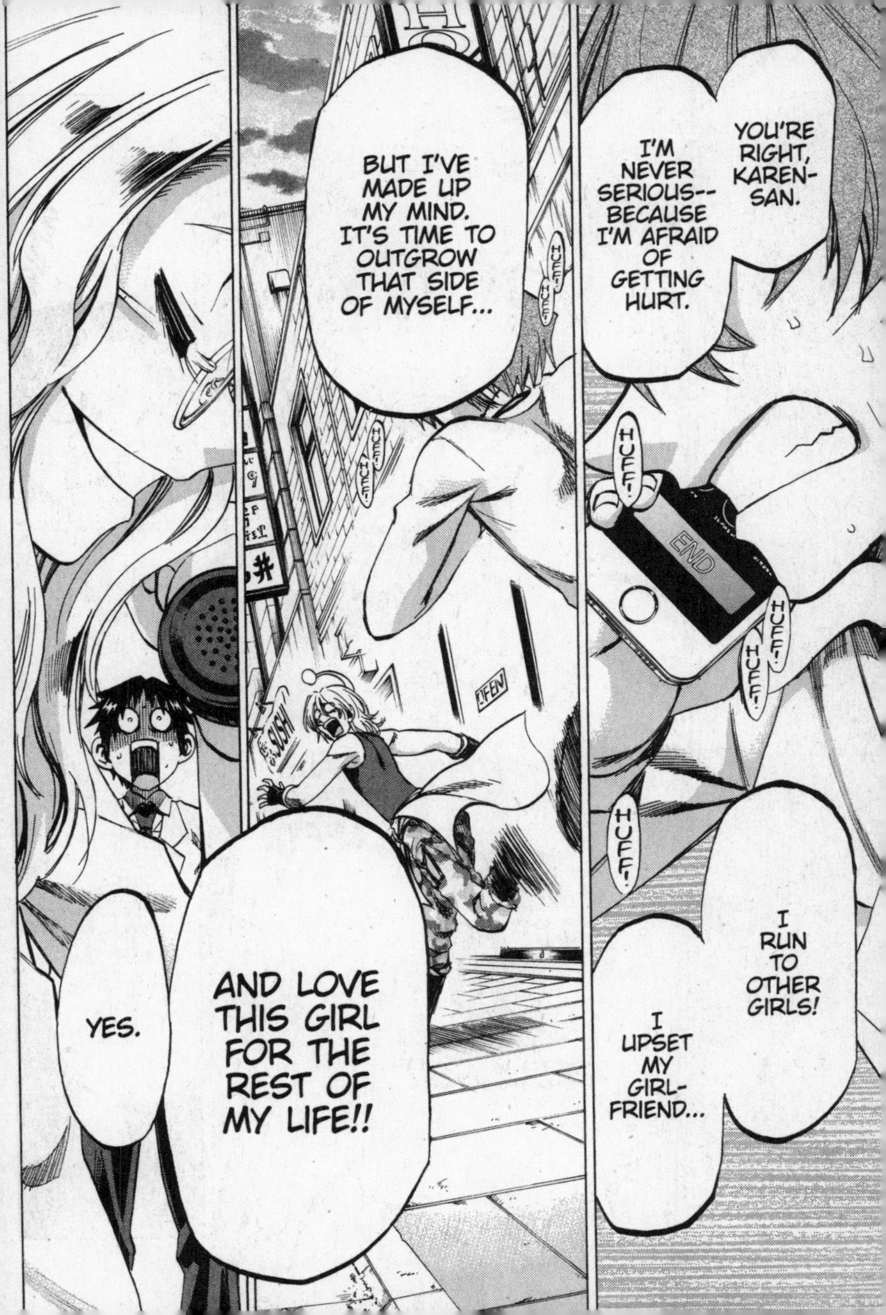
YOU'RE RIGHT, KAREN-SAN.
I'M NEVER SERIOUS-- BECAUSE I'M AFRAID OF GETTING HURT.
HUFF! HUFF!
END
HUFF! HUFF!
HUFF!
I RUN TO OTHER GIRLS!
I UPSET MY GIRL-FRIEND...
BUT I'VE MADE UP MY MIND. IT'S TIME TO OUTGROW THAT SIDE OF MYSELF...
HUFF! HUFF!
HUFF! HUFF!
AND LOVE THIS GIRL FOR THE REST OF MY LIFE!!
YES.

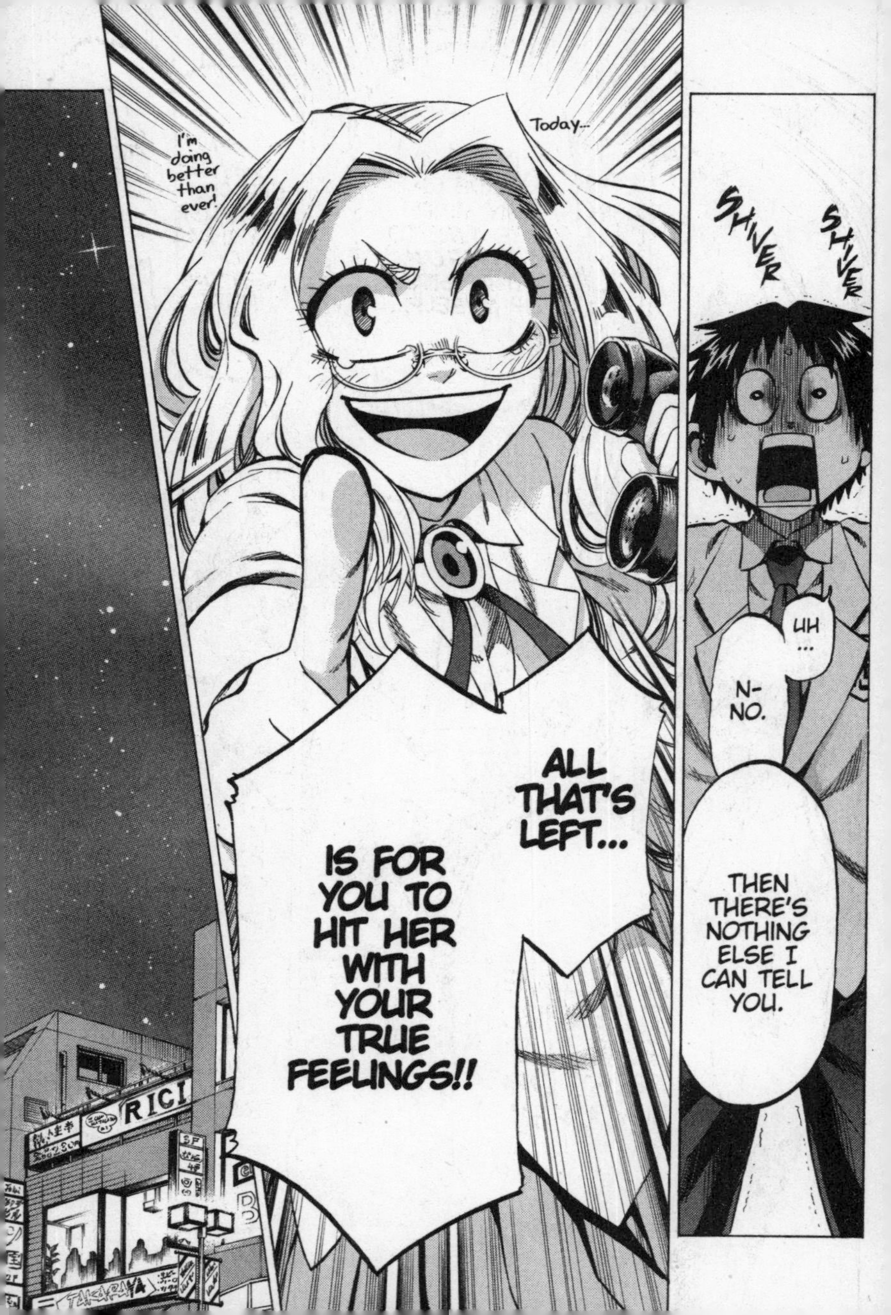
SHIVER
SHIVER
UH...
N-NO.
THEN THERE'S NOTHING ELSE I CAN TELL YOU.
Today...
I'm doing better than ever!
ALL THAT'S LEFT...
IS FOR YOU TO HIT HER WITH YOUR TRUE FEELINGS!!
RICI
TAKARAYA

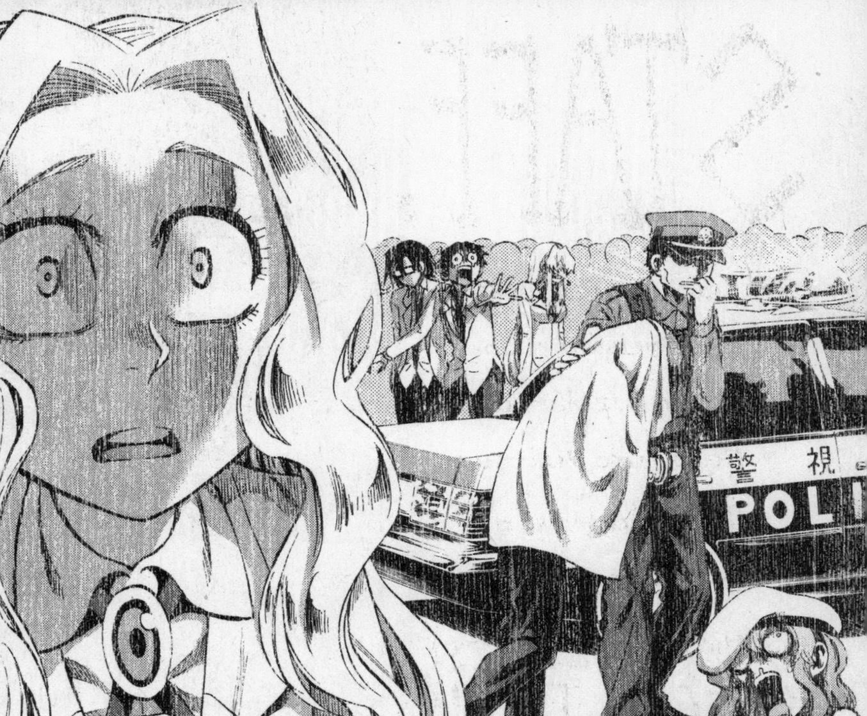
警
視
POLI

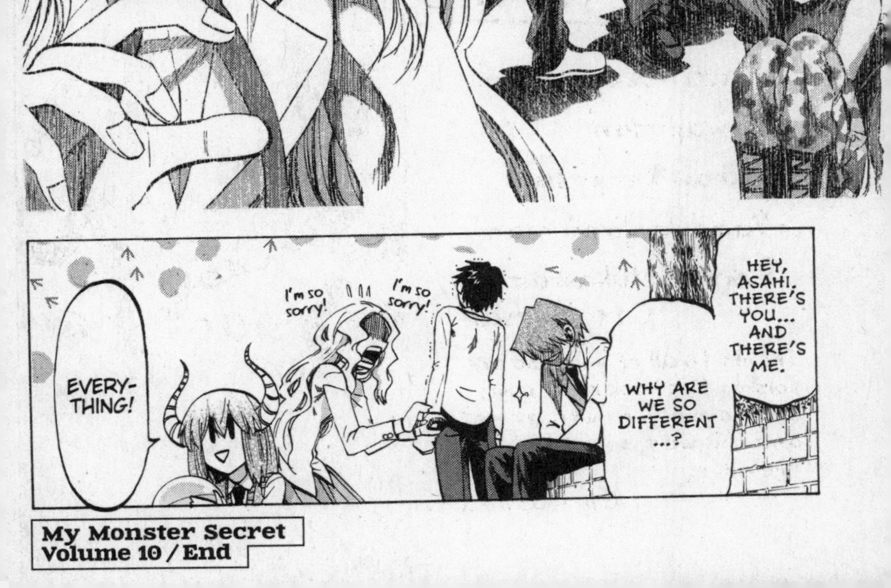
HEY, ASAHI. THERE'S YOU... AND THERE'S ME.
WHY ARE WE SO DIFFERENT ...?
I'm so sorry!
I'm so sorry!
EVERY-THING!

My Monster Secret Volume 10 / End

STAFF.

- Garage Okada-san
- Shuumeigiku-san
- Seijun Suzuki-san
- Nakamura Yuji-san
- Rie Hayashi-san
- Haruki Mana
- Hiroki Minemura-san

(in syllabary order)

SPECIAL THANKS.

- Araki Nozomu-san
- Kawaji-san
- Nakaie Kenji-san
- Yamada Jirou-san

Editor: Mukawa-san,
Otsuka-san

Thanks to all of you who are holding this book right now, and to everyone who let me and this work be part of their lives.

Eiji Masuda

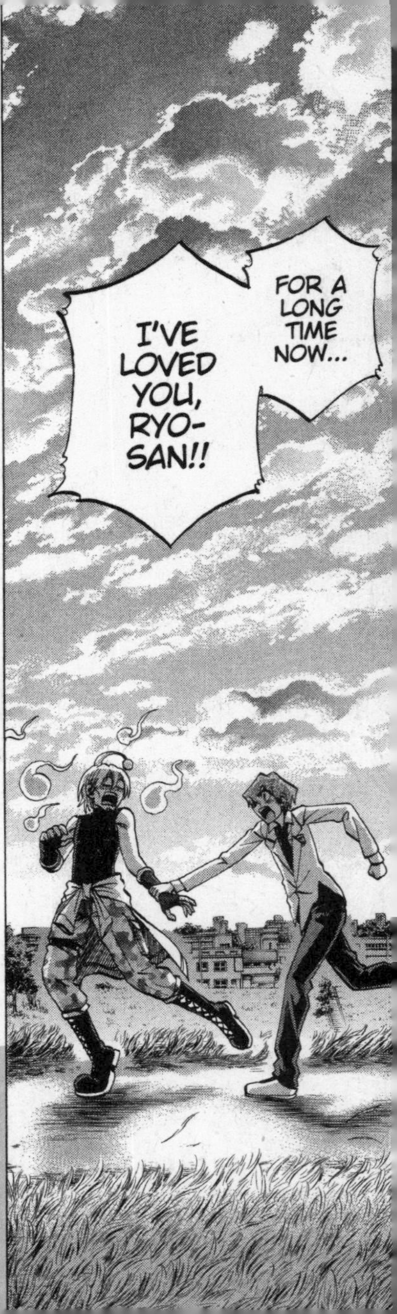
FOR A LONG TIME NOW...
I'VE LOVED YOU, RYO-SAN!!

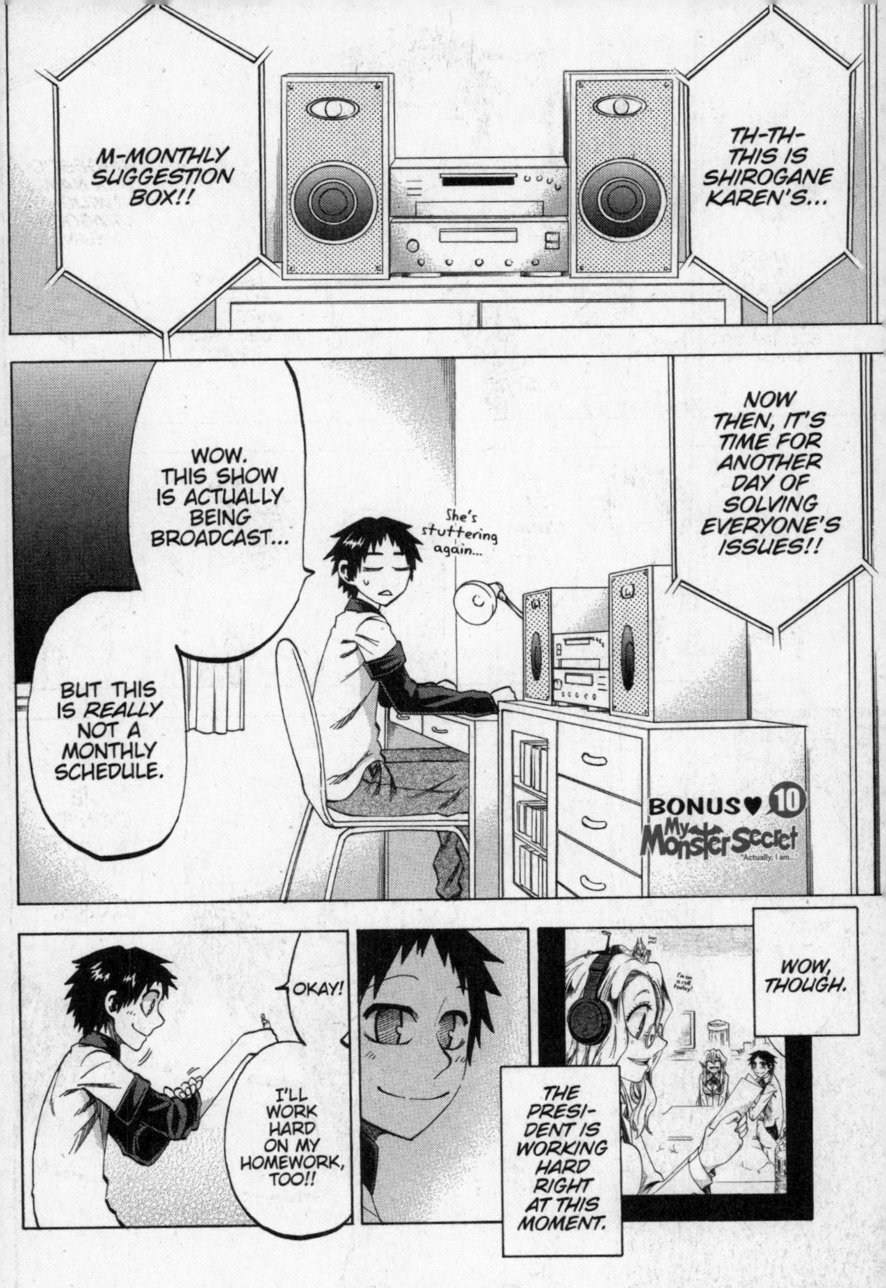
TH-TH-THIS IS SHIROGANE KAREN'S...
M-MONTHLY SUGGESTION BOX!!
NOW THEN, IT'S TIME FOR ANOTHER DAY OF SOLVING EVERYONE'S ISSUES!!
She's stuttering again...
WOW. THIS SHOW IS ACTUALLY BEING BROADCAST...
BUT THIS IS *REALLY* NOT A MONTHLY SCHEDULE.
BONUS♥10
My Monster Secret
"Actually, I am..."
WOW, THOUGH.
THE PRESIDENT IS WORKING HARD RIGHT AT THIS MOMENT.
OKAY!
I'LL WORK HARD ON MY HOMEWORK, TOO!!

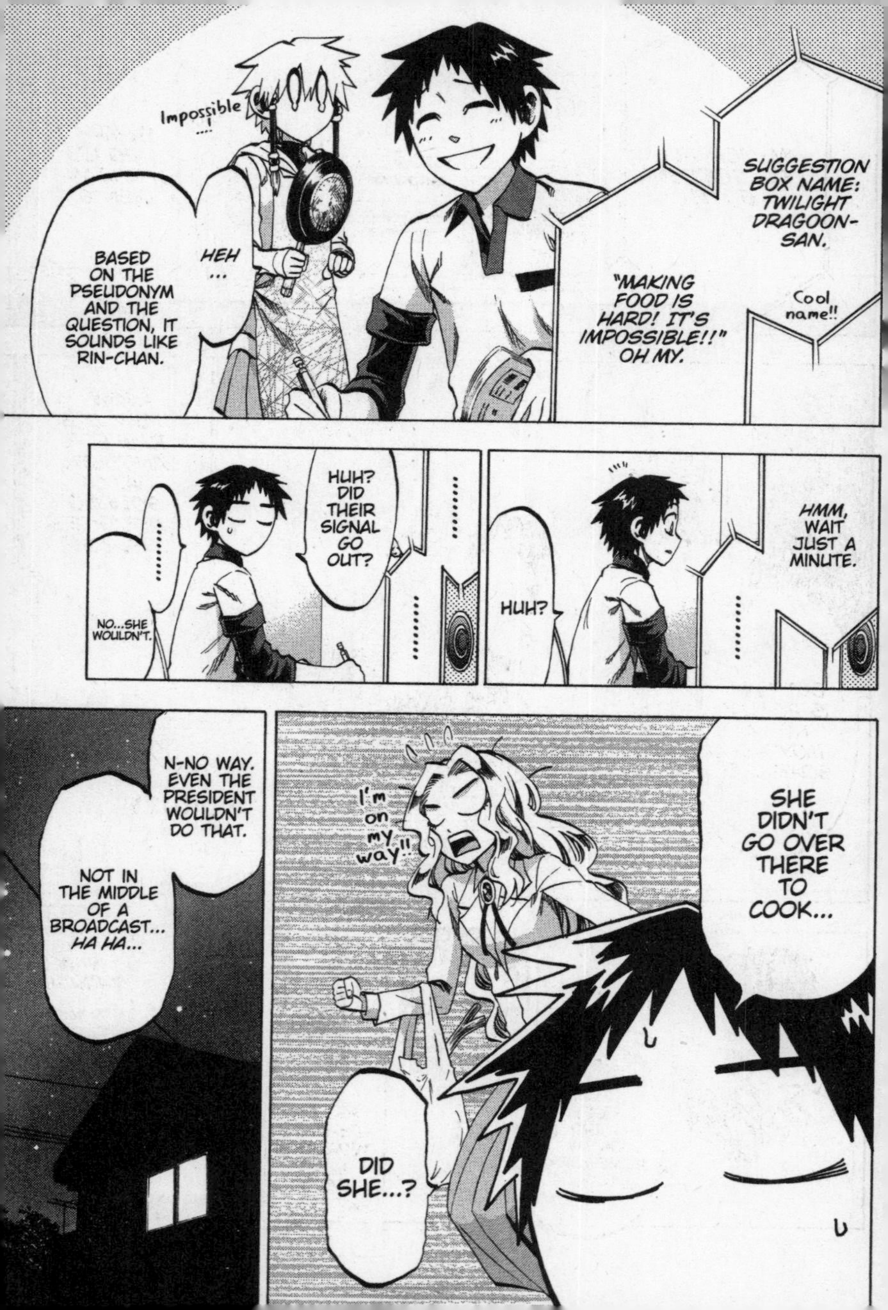
SUGGESTION BOX NAME: TWILIGHT DRAGOON-SAN.
Cool name!!
"MAKING FOOD IS HARD! IT'S IMPOSSIBLE!!" OH MY.
Impossible!....
HEH...
BASED ON THE PSEUDONYM AND THE QUESTION, IT SOUNDS LIKE RIN-CHAN.
HMM, WAIT JUST A MINUTE.
....
HUH?
....
HUH? DID THEIR SIGNAL GO OUT?
....
NO...SHE WOULDN'T.
SHE DIDN'T GO OVER THERE TO COOK...
I'm on my way!!
DID SHE...?
N-NO WAY. EVEN THE PRESIDENT WOULDN'T DO THAT.
NOT IN THE MIDDLE OF A BROADCAST... HA HA...

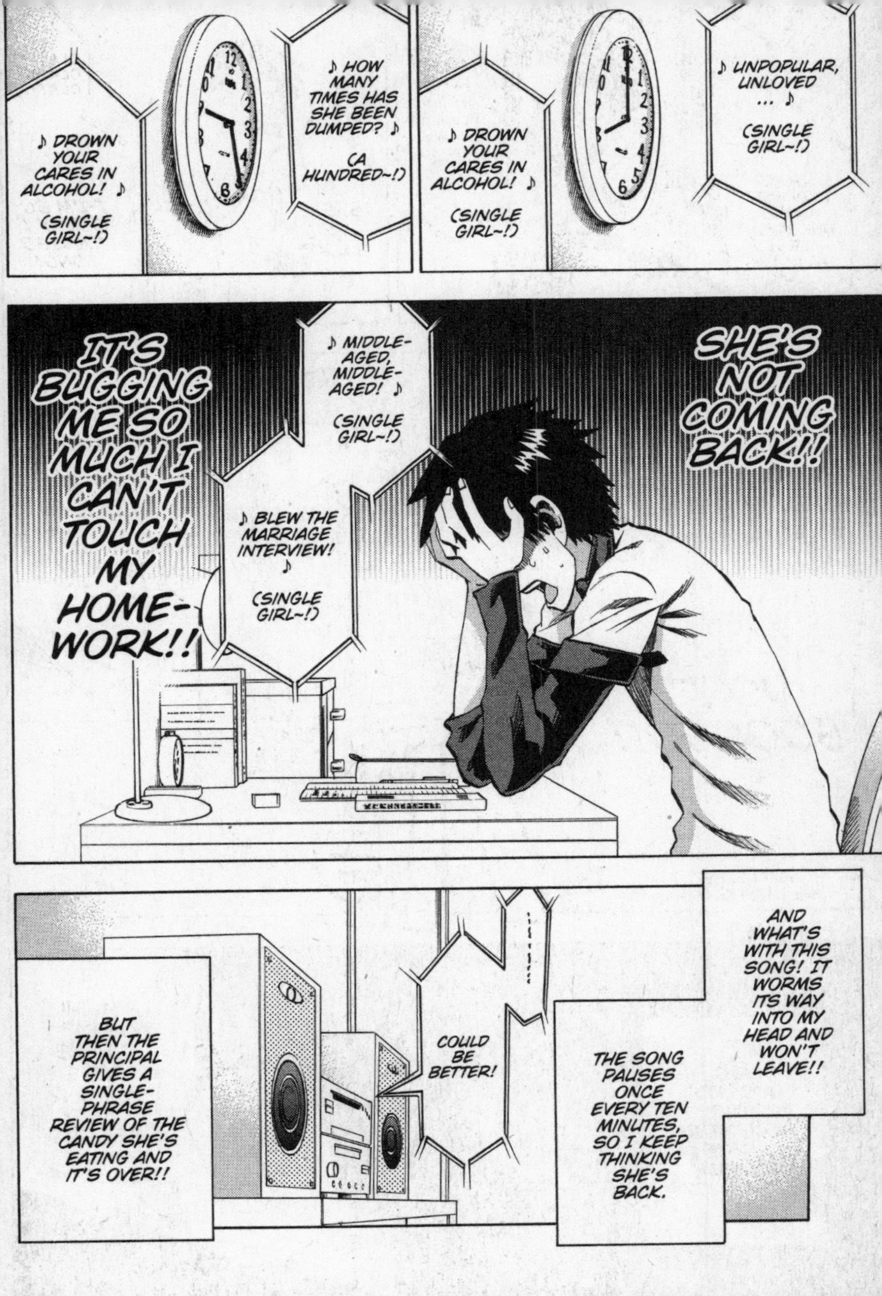
♪ UNPOPULAR, UNLOVED ... ♪
(SINGLE GIRL~!)
♪ DROWN YOUR CARES IN ALCOHOL! ♪
(SINGLE GIRL~!)
♪ HOW MANY TIMES HAS SHE BEEN DUMPED? ♪
(A HUNDRED~!)
♪ DROWN YOUR CARES IN ALCOHOL! ♪
(SINGLE GIRL~!)
SHE'S NOT COMING BACK!!
♪ MIDDLE-AGED, MIDDLE-AGED! ♪
(SINGLE GIRL~!)
♪ BLEW THE MARRIAGE INTERVIEW! ♪
(SINGLE GIRL~!)
IT'S BUGGING ME SO MUCH I CAN'T TOUCH MY HOME-WORK!!
AND WHAT'S WITH THIS SONG! IT WORMS ITS WAY INTO MY HEAD AND WON'T LEAVE!!
THE SONG PAUSES ONCE EVERY TEN MINUTES, SO I KEEP THINKING SHE'S BACK.
......
COULD BE BETTER!
BUT THEN THE PRINCIPAL GIVES A SINGLE-PHRASE REVIEW OF THE CANDY SHE'S EATING AND IT'S OVER!!

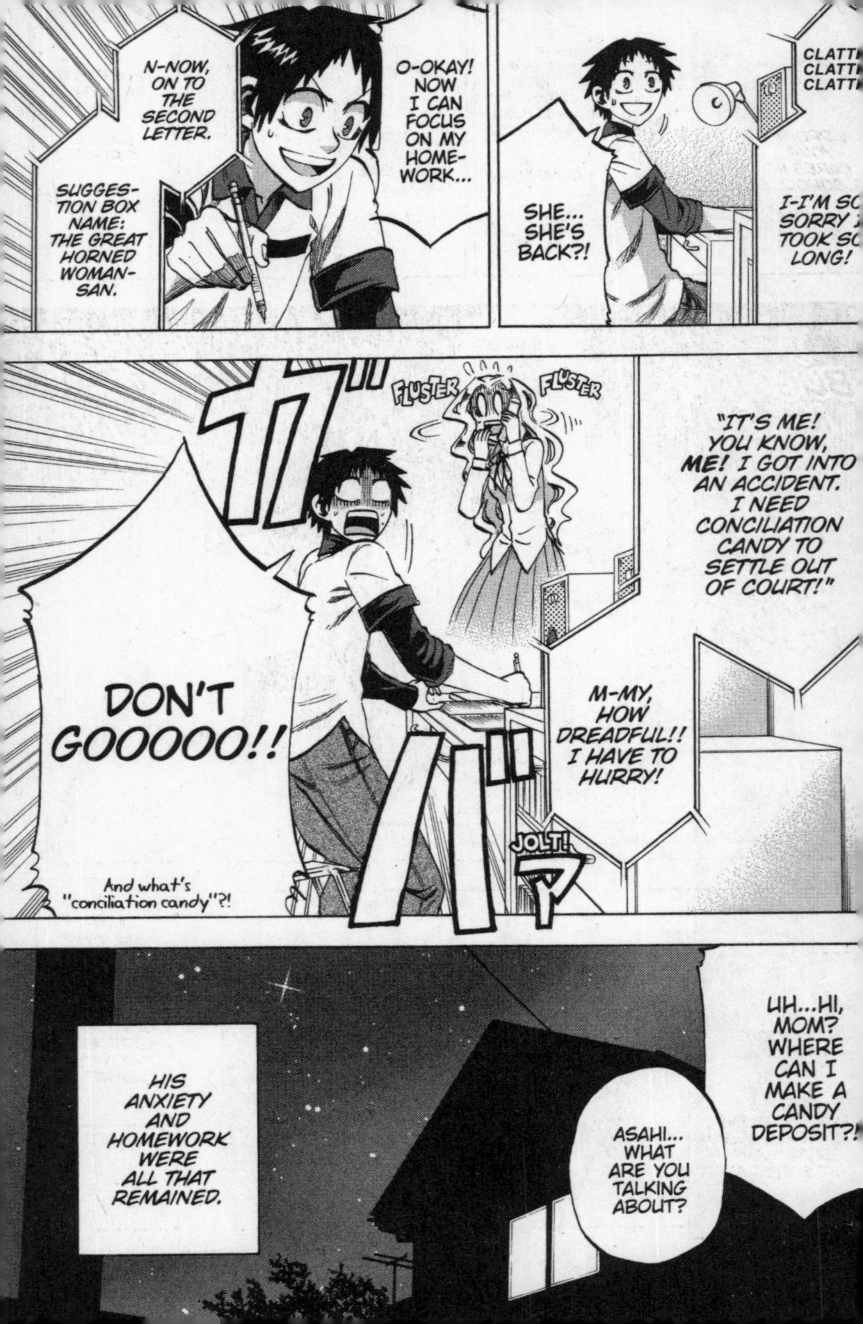
CLATT
CLATT
CLATT
I-I'M SO SORRY I TOOK SO LONG!
SHE... SHE'S BACK?!
O-OKAY! NOW I CAN FOCUS ON MY HOMEWORK...
N-NOW, ON TO THE SECOND LETTER.
SUGGESTION BOX NAME: THE GREAT HORNED WOMAN-SAN.
"IT'S ME! YOU KNOW, ME! I GOT INTO AN ACCIDENT. I NEED CONCILIATION CANDY TO SETTLE OUT OF COURT!"
FLUSTER
FLUSTER
M-MY, HOW DREADFUL!! I HAVE TO HURRY!
JOLT!
DON'T GOOOOO!!
And what's "conciliation candy"?!
UH...HI, MOM? WHERE CAN I MAKE A CANDY DEPOSIT?!
ASAHI... WHAT ARE YOU TALKING ABOUT?
HIS ANXIETY AND HOMEWORK WERE ALL THAT REMAINED.

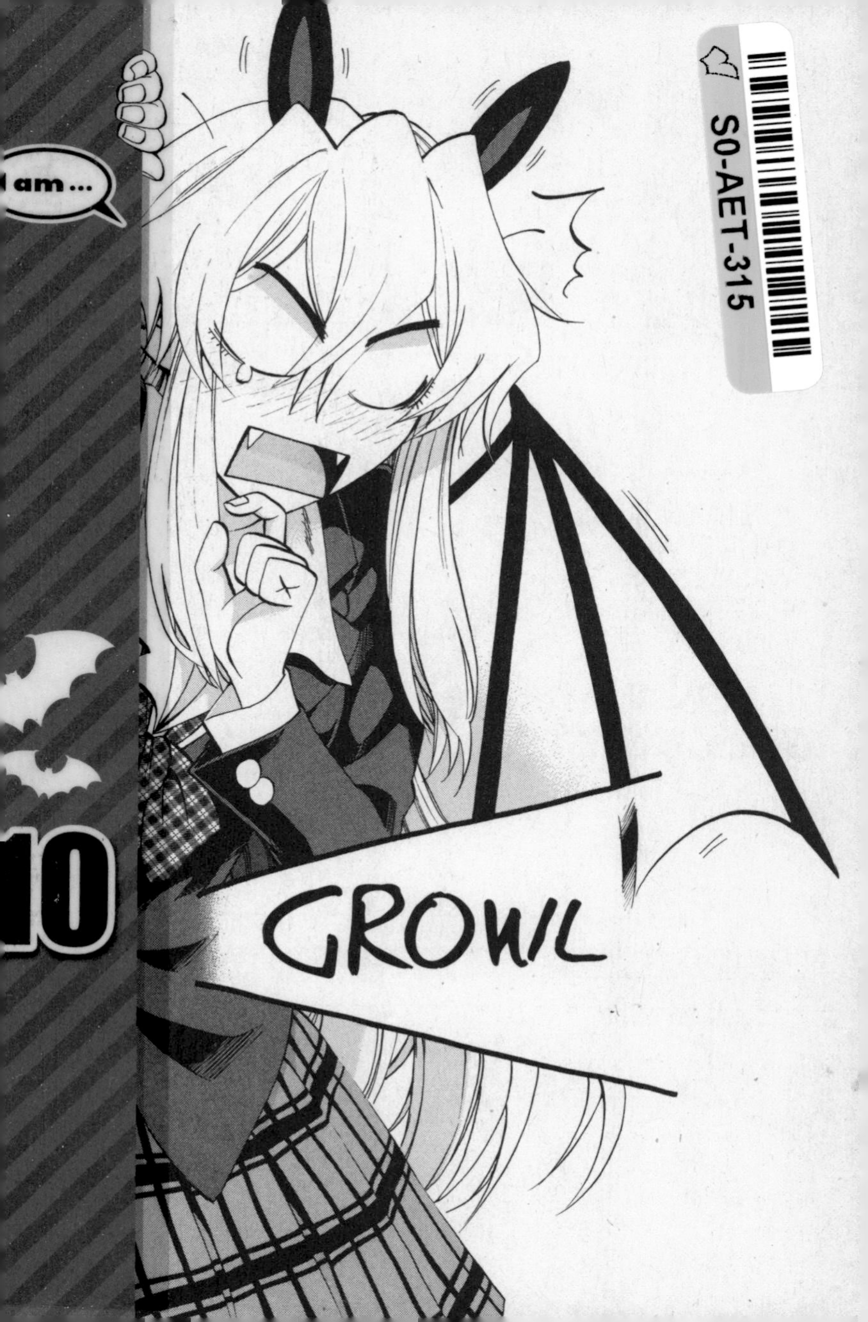
I am ...
10
GROWL